CW01643077

INTERSPIRITUALITY

Volume 2

The Future

INTERSPIRITUALITY

——— Volume 2 ———

The Future

of

Interspirituality: The Heritage

and

Interspirituality: The Future

Opening Message by His Holiness the 14th Dalai Lama

Foreword by Matthew Fox

Afterword by Ken Wilber

INTERSPIRITUALITY: THE FUTURE

with voices from over 120 global leaders and their organizations, initiatives, and events from 2015 to 2025

Light on Light press

Interspirituality: The Future
Volume 2

Editors
Rev. Shannon Marie Winters MS
Rev. Kurt Johnson PhD
Robert Atkinson PhD
Nomi Naeem MA
Chamatkara (aka Sandra Simon)
Karuna (aka Rev. Caroline Ashley)
Karen J. Gordon
Roger P. Briggs

Print ISBN: 978-1-958921-80-7
Ebook ISBN: 978-1-958921-85-2
Library of Congress Control Number: 2025946851

Published by Light on Light Press
An imprint of Sacred Stories Publishing, Fort Lauderdale, FL
Printed in the United States of America

DEDICATION

These Volumes are dedicated to the over one hundred twenty Featured Authors who have made the Volumes possible. Their articles, excerpts, abridgements, and twenty-five years of correspondence and attachments have enabled creation of a historical and thematic account of the interspiritual paradigm since the 1999 publication of Br. Wayne Teasdale's book, *The Mystic Heart: Discovering a Universal Spirituality in the World's Religions*, that named the paradigm. The Volumes mark the twenty-fifth anniversary of that publication and the tenth anniversary of *The Coming Interspiritual Age*, the book whose generative organization, The Interspiritual Dialogue, founded with Br. Teasdale in 2002, became the charity that is the parent of The Light on Light Press. We honor also the Featured Authors who have co-created the online resource *interspirituality.com*.

Introduction to the Volumes

We invite you to review the Introduction to the Volumes at the beginning of Volume 1. It will familiarize you with these important elements of the Volumes' format and structure, as subtitled therein: (i) Reference to "these Volumes"; (ii) Interval Notes; (iii) Features and Sections; (iv) History Sections; (v) Excerpts and Abridgments; (vi) Subsequent Fully Illustrated Volume; (vii) Titles; (viii) Endnotes; and (ix) Additional Notes.

Foreword by Matthew Fox

We also recommend you acquaint yourself with the Foreword to these two Volumes by Matthew Fox, along with the introductory sections, especially "History," located in Volume 1, and its Table of Contents. These will enhance your comprehension and enjoyment of the content in Volume 2: *Interspirituality: The Future.*

TABLE OF CONTENTS
VOLUME 2

THE DALAI LAMA

OPENING MESSAGE

HIS HOLINESS THE 14th DALAI LAMA

We humans are social animals; we are part of a community. All social animals have the sense of community. Without a community, one single individual cannot survive. So we must develop a reality where the entire world of human beings are one human community — we are brothers and sisters — one humanity!

As a social animal, human beings need those kinds of human emotions that bring together. Loving kindness brings together; compassion brings together. They minimize destructive emotions. Loving kindness brings together even anger and excess.

In the long run, compassion is much stronger than enmity. And compassion is our true nature. That is a given — human beings being one community, in loving each other. The worst thing is enmity in the name of different faiths — really unthinkable! All religions actually carry the message of *Love* — loving kindness, forgiveness, tolerance.

Biologically, we are all equipped with the seed of compassion. Young children? — no enemy. Young children? — they don't care about differences. They simply appreciate love, affection, a smile, and play together. They don't care about a different faith, different nationality, different color, or different country. In them, the sameness of human beings is very much alive.

Knowledge and education are key ingredients for the future. Step by step, we can make society a happier and more peaceful society. Nonviolence, compassion — with full confidence — these are key factors for the happier individual, happier community, and peaceful world. All religions carry this message of *Love* — kindness, forgiveness, tolerance, compassion.

In taking care of others, you get the fuller benefit. Respect others; love others. With that perspective, the whole atmosphere appears peaceful — for the individual level, family level, community level, and finally, the world level. Essentially, all religions carry this message.[i]

VOLUME TWO INTRODUCTION

> The real religion of humankind can be said to be spirituality itself, because mystical spirituality is the origin of all the world religions. If this is so, and I believe it is, we might also say that Interspirituality — the sharing of ultimate experiences across traditions — is the religion of the third millennium. Interspirituality is the foundation that can prepare the way for a planet-wide enlightened culture, and a continuing community among the religions that is substantial, vital, and creative [MH p. 26].

Br. Wayne Teasdale pointed to needed fundamental shifts in global awareness, some of which were already arising in his time and certainly are even more urgent today. Note that at least five of the "Eight Shifts" he noted as needed directly concern the role of science in relation to the world's religions.

- Appreciation of the interdependence of all realms of human life and the surrounding cosmos

- Growing ecological awareness, with recognition of the interdependence of humankind and the biosphere, including the rights of all biological species
- Dedication to nonviolence, with a commitment to transcend militancy and violence tied to national or religious identities
- Embracing of the shared wisdom in all the world's religious and spiritual traditions, past and present
- Growing friendship, and actual community, among the individual followers of the world's religious and spiritual paths
- Commitment to the depths of the contemplative pursuit and the mutual sharing of the fruits of this ongoing journey
- Creative cultivation of transnational, transcultural, transtraditional, and world-centric understanding
- Receptivity to a cosmic vision, realizing humanity is only one life form and part of a larger community, the universe

For Teasdale, these elements marked the threshold required for a healthy globalization and the participation of the world's religions through an unfolding "Interspiritual Age," which he defined as "The name for the age we are now entering where people are no longer isolated in their home tradition but are exploring other traditions, finding what is useful to their own growth." The elements from Teasdale above are even more urgent today than when he enumerated them twenty-five years ago.

Let's continue then with two recent clarion calls, beginning with a statement from the Friends of the Institute of Noetic Sciences whose Trustees have a number of contributions in these Volumes, along with the Chair of the Institute, Claudia Welss. It draws from the numinous awe that stems from what is known as "The Overview Effect" — the experience of viewing the Earth from space. It originated with the epiphany of our first astronauts as they viewed Earth from the far vantage point of the Moon. And, the experience has continued through generations of international space voyagers, many of whom were scientists. Its epiphany is a kind of "knowing" or gnosis that knits together the experience of reality through science *and* the "universal spirituality" inherent in our world's religions, as pointed to by Br. Teasdale.

> It was the view of the expanses of blue water that cover most of the Earth, the brown and green of the land masses, the swirling white of the clouds that inspired Edgar Mitchell on his return voyage from the Moon. It led him to have a profound experience; that the Earth was not simply a planetary orb floating in the emptiness of space but a living system encompassing the totality of experiences that included and went beyond our scientific understanding of the universe. It was the spiritual / mystical dimension in unison with the physical / material that led him to comprehend that all things were imbued with a universal consciousness. His experience mirrored that of the Renaissance philosopher and sage Giordano Bruno, who when he looked up into the sky comprehended the vastness and wonder of the universe. Giordano Bruno did not have, and did not need, the technology available to us today. His view of the universe came from a profound and deep wonder, from a "knowing" that went beyond the experiences of his bodily senses. Edgar Mitchell also experienced a knowing as he gazed upon the Earth. It was this spirit of wonder, the removal of the walls

> between the spiritual and the scientific that inspired Edgar Mitchell to found the Institute of Noetic Sciences (IONS). Noetic comes from the word "gnosis" which is a knowledge, an insight. It ignites emergent dedication to exploring the ways our manners of knowing can be one, and how we can discover and share that experience, that knowing. It is by exploring the deep connection between the spiritual and the scientific that we can further the awareness of consciousness, cultivating all the facets of the human experience, and sharing that important awareness with like-hearted people — as inspired by the insight of Edgar Mitchell's experience.[1]

There is a power in The Overview Effect to awaken our awareness to the urgency of experiential oneness. William Shatner, of *Star Trek* fame, said of his experience of The Overview Effect that it was:

> …the difference between intellectual knowledge and experiential knowledge.
>
> I saw more clearly than I have, with all the studying and reading I've done…. the Earth…It's a little tiny rock with an onion skin air around it. That's how fragile it all is. It's so fragile. We hang by a thread ... we're just dangling. Although we are just dangling, we're dangling together…We're entangled with each other…[2]

The statement from Friends of the Institute of Noetic Sciences concludes:

> ...reaffirming exploring the leading edges of science, creativity and spirituality to further the change of

> consciousness. Enhancing awareness, imbuing healing and balance through visionary technologies for creative, educational and scientific experiences; facilitating the growing awareness of a global movement in mind, heart and spirit.[3]

Note above, the primacy of the word "Consciousness." It is interesting, given the attention the word consciousness has had in recent decades, that Teasdale did not offer a definition of it in *The Mystic Heart.* The closest definition therein is the one he gave for "Interbeing" — "the…idea of the interconnectedness of everyone and everything" [MH p. 268]. The subject of consciousness was the one chosen by Dr. Deepak Chopra for his message to the 2018 Parliament of the World's Religions, through Light on Light's pre-event publication. The selection below is as originally published[4] and is endnoted to a longer version published subsequently.

Selected from

Science is Ready to Accept Consciousness

by Deepak Chopra

> Instead of conceiving reality from the bottom up, moving from tiny building blocks to larger and larger structures, one could do the reverse and create a top-down model. In other words, the starting point would be the whole, not the parts. So what do we know about reality as a whole?
>
> If reality "out there" is a construct dependent upon consciousness, explaining the universe entails explaining consciousness. Where physicalists are stymied by how atoms and molecules think, non-

physicalists are stymied by how mind creates matter. This impasse is broken by taking a concrete approach to mind; that is, by investigating the qualities of reality "out there."

The day-to-day work of scientists isn't dependent on explaining how mind arose in the cosmos — not yet. The relation between mind and matter has existed in philosophy for centuries and working scientists don't consider philosophy relevant to their research. Collecting data and doing experiments needs no help from metaphysics. But when you look at the unanswered questions in physics, biology, biochemistry, and neuroscience, it's more than a coincidence that all, without exception, impinge upon the same inability to know how consciousness actually works. By taking for granted the obvious fact that it takes a mind to do science, we've reached the point where science is leaving out the very component that might answer the questions that urgently need answering, not because philosophy demands it but because science does.

The sticking point is physicalism itself. If everything must be reduced to the smallest units of matter and energy, and yet there is zero evidence that mind follows that pattern, it is unscientific to cling to physicalism.

The real horizon is where the inconceivable source of mind meets the conceivable phenomena in nature. The problem of something coming out of nothing is exactly the same when the cosmos was born as when a thought is born. This is the level playing field where

> mind and matter can be investigated as two sides of the same process: consciousness interacting with itself.[5]

Fortunately, as further reported at the Toronto Parliament of the World's Religions and from which we share in multiple pieces by multiple authors below, there has been a recent historic recognition from *evolutionary* biology in mainstream science that Interspirituality is exactly the adaptive trait that would naturally arise within religion as the world moves toward inevitable globalization and multiculturalism. Recently, this recognition has been widely discussed by The Evolution Institute and in publications from Yale University and the John Templeton Foundation. It shows that Interspirituality is a natural, anticipated, adaptation by our species as it goes global and multicultural. Further, this is not only because that adaptive trait would be required of a globalizing civilization, but also because current evolutionary theory shows that natural selection at the level of groups and systems of groups chooses the best cooperators, not the best competitors. The "group selection revolution" in science has happened in just about the last ten years.

The good news is that both the religious and scientific understanding of what Interspirituality is, as a cultural phenomenon, includes the coexistence and synergy of the varieties (and integrities) of diverse religious expressions and narratives and the understanding of their underlying unity in our profoundly interconnected world. It should not surprise us then that the interspiritual community became a major place for the discussion of these new trends in mainstream science.

The publication by Yale / Templeton in their Series *The Foundational Questions of Science* invited immediate response from both the scientific and religious communities. The author of the first book in that series was Dr. David Sloan Wilson (then a distinguished professor at State University of New York, Binghamton, and a founder of The Evolution Institute).[6] In reading *The Coming Interspiritual Age*, Wilson recognized that the direction of Interspirituality — that of cooperation and partnership — was exactly the direction religions would take if, indeed, the direction of natural selection in more and more complex systems, like our ongoing world, was to define "fitness" (as in "survival of the fittest") as the best cooperator, not the best competitor. Knowing that among interspiritual leaders Kurt Johnson also held a doctorate in evolution and was on the staff of the American Museum of Natural History in New York City, Wilson invited him to State University of New York, Binghamton, to see what future cooperation might look like.

This was the beginning of three major conferences, with published results, laying out the emerging implication of what was happening in this transformation within mainstream evolutionary science. In retrospect, this should not surprise since the writing of both Wayne Teasdale and Bede Griffiths from the 20th century had explicitly stressed the significance to spirituality of what was happening in the New Physics and Neuroscience. These landscapes receive considerable note in discussions in many Features in the current Volumes. What followed in evolutionary science with the coming of the 21st century was somewhat of a surprise.

The contents from these three conferences and their publications could themselves worthily fill these current Volumes. Fortunately, the reports from all three are available in online publications, and new Features *in* the current Volumes also amplify their significance. Again, evidencing the "aging out" of materials online, the publication of the first conference by Evolution Institute, "Steering Toward the Omega Point," dated December 10, 2015, is no longer online from the

Institute but has been replaced by an archive with the same material hosted by David Sloan Wilson, author of the original Yale / Templeton publication noted above.[7]

You will recognize the names of many of the participants (in the order of their appearance in the publication), a number of whom also appear in these current Volumes: David Sloan Wilson, Kurt Johnson, Richard Clugston, Barbara Marx Hubbard, Marc Gafni, Zachary Stein, David Korten, Kevin Brabazon, Doug King, Mike Morrill, and Ken Wilber. The momentum and interest in these discussions was such that a second, much larger conference was convened in New York City at the Adler Library of the flagship humanist organization Ethical Culture on April 12, 2016. Entitled "Evolution, Consciousness and Altruism," it featured three panels of 7–9 participants each that were also videotaped. An audience of about one hundred joined the event. Videos are still extant at two websites and also were originally on the aforementioned Interspiritual Multiplex site.[8]

Contents from both events were published in the colorful initial e-publication of Light on Light Press's *Convergence Magazine* series as *Does Altruism Exist?* on October 26, 2017, and included an array of notable voices from the scientific and interfaith communities (in order of their appearance in that volume): Kurt Johnson, Yanni Maniates, David Sloan Wilson, Steve McIntosh, Herman F. Greene, Matthew Fox, Steve Farrell, Laura M. George, Catherine Bell, Tanja Andrejasic Wechsler, Ken Kitatani, Diane Berke, Elisabet Sahtouris, and Gaston Meskens. Six of these authors also have new Features in the current Volumes.[9]

Two months after the New York City event — to make wider participation possible — a follow-up conference was held on June 12, 2016, in Colorado at the Gold Hill Historical Site above Boulder.

It was also videotaped and included additional participation by Steve McIntosh, Steve Farrell, Kurt Johnson, Yanni Maniates, Marc Barasch and Woody Vaspra. And on July 16, Steve Farrell's Humanity's Team hosted an online discussion about the two events on its "Humanity's Stream." Ultimately, as noted in the colorful magazine and website portrayals of these conferences, the New York / Colorado connection — which traced back to earlier cultural activities of the United Nations NGO community across Colorado — led to the 2017 "Crestone Leadership Conference," the multiple international "Road to 2020" events from the combined constituencies of these activities, and even later, the meeting of members of these groups, led by David Sloan Wilson in dialogues with His Holiness the Dalai Lama in India, through the Mind and Life Institute. You will read much more about these as the Timelines and Features continue in this Volume and especially with its emphasis on the relation of Interspirituality, Ecospirituality, and current advances in science.[10]

Interspirituality and Movement Toward Inclusion and a Global Ethic

To jump ahead to 2019, when Kurt Johnson spoke about those developments between science and religion at the tribute event for Fr. Thomas Keating at the Aspen Chapel and St. Benedict's Abbey, Snowmass, he noted:

> Today, it is a general observation among many interfaith leaders that the day for us having to explain what the interspiritual experience or phenomenon is, is over. In today's world, where worldviews are now much more holistic in nature, there is the understanding of

> a universal spirituality underpinning all the world's religions.

In his summary of the history of Interspiritual to date (in 2016), he said the same thing. In his presentation to the *Mature Interspirituality* retreat of the Community of the Mystic Heart, later published in *Mature Interspirituality* (2017), the osmosis of the interspiritual experience out into the wider world of spirituality was already becoming apparent:

> In retrospect, it can be said that the modern day interspiritual experience was greatly advanced, implicitly, with the appearance of Br. Wayne's books (*The Mystic Heart*, *A Monk in the World*, and *Bede Griffiths, an Introduction to his Interspiritual Thought*) prior to his untimely passing in 2004. However, it has "morphed" in a manner to be "owned by everyone," as much of the interfaith world inevitably moved from an interfaith understanding to an interspiritual understanding — in effect "from head to heart" over the next decades. Today, Interspirituality is virtually synonymous with movements and narratives as wide-ranging as "spiritual but not religious," "unaffiliated," "nones," "universal, global, or world-centric spirituality," "multiple belonging," "evolutionary spirituality," and many many more. And today, large numbers of previously conventional academic and seminary institutions have broadly defined interfaith and interspiritual programs and curricula. Many of these are sometimes not even aware of the history above, which incubated modern Interspirituality from the original Foundationalist Discussion and the

> pioneer work of those like Merton, Teasdale, Griffiths, Panikkar and Keating.[11]

At the gathering of the Evolution Institute at State University of New York, Johnson continued:

> Further, a new frontier for Interspirituality is its synchronicity with the views of modern evolutionary biology that evolution is — at any higher level of complexity or for intelligent species — a matter of cooperation, not simply competition: the modern "co-operative view" of evolution.[12]

For those who know the history of the philosophy of science, you will know this traces back to the long-standing historical discussion of the separation of the world of science and the world of the arts or spirituality — what was historically dubbed "The Two Cultures." This was the prevailing worldview that the subjective realm of the humanities and the objective realm of science would remain separate, championed in C. P. Snow's famous 1959 lecture and subsequent book *The Two Cultures*. But, in the context of the discussion above, we see now that there has been an arising of a predicted third culture. In *The Third Culture*, John Brockman, scientific literature historian and founder of The Edge Foundation, further voiced rapid acceleration toward the global and holistic worldview we see in Interspirituality and the developmental view of history of the various integral philosophy communities. This development was further announced in the 1993 reprinting of Snow's own classic, in a new introduction by Cambridge University professor Stefan Collini.[13] The implications are serious. As David Sloan Wilson said at the recent conference "Steering Toward the Omega Point": "When it comes to evolution's relation to humankind and its cultures, someone has to be at the wheel. If not, we may find, in hindsight, that evolution took us somewhere we didn't want to go."[14]

Interestingly as well for these Volumes, the directions of the well-known Science and Nonduality Conferences [SAND] have been similar, and the interspiritual community was invited regularly. At their 2014 conference themed "Entanglement," Kurt Johnson's presentation was entitled "The Twin Pillars of Science and Spirituality." From that presentation:

> Just look around at the news today, and it is easy to see the predicament the world is in. Religion will either become part of the solution, or it will be doomed to remain part of the problem.... If we are to be able to create a healthy multicultural civilization, we are going to need to recognize the "twin pillars" of what that process will take.... The twin pillars comprise first, the deep inner spiritual work that we all know must be done worldwide, and to which we are committed as spiritual practitioners, teachers and leaders; and second, the necessarily complex work in the manifest world — intellectual and technological — that actually must be done to build such a world that will reflect the values and ideals to which we aspire.... As you know, the classic Heart Sutra is divided into two sections that echo these twin pillars. The first section is a statement about non-dual or awakened Truth, and the second is about the perfection of this Wisdom through Skillful Means.... In fact, our world is desperately trying to evolve to a juncture where these two aspects will be able to recognize each other and, historically, urgently

> just in the nick of time. What will be required is.... the merging of Spirit and Science, certainly the pinnacle of inclusion...[15]

Following on the same thematics, Shift Network's first Director of Peace, the late Philip Hellmich, echoed this emphasis on the joining of the sacred and secular in the unfolding age in his contributions to the World Mediation Organization's book *Strategies for Peace* entitled "Sacred and Secular Activists are Now Joining their Strategies for Peacebuilding."[16] Hellmich, as part of Search for Common Ground, had had extensive experience with peace mediation in Africa, from which came his well-known book *God and Conflict*.[17] He wrote:

> Conventional science itself has made strides in the last decade to join with a more holistic view of reality more prone to the foundations of peace. After more than a century of parroting the mantra of "survival of the fittest" and "the selfish gene," a new mainstream paradigm has emerged emphasizing altruism. In the first of Yale University and The Templeton Foundation's "Series in the Foundational Questions of Science," Dr. David Sloan Wilson (Wilson, 2015), summarizing work by himself and Dr. E. O. Wilson (the father of Sociobiology) in the "Quarterly Review of Biology," lay out proofs that "group" and "multi-level" selection in nature select not for processes and structures that serve self-interest groups but those that serve the well-being of the whole.
>
> This scientific revolution has spawned a surprising convergence between sacred and secular activists under a new rubric called "prosocial." Prosocial combines

> secular activism motivated by the new science with the sacred activism visioned by "Interspirituality" — or global, universal, world-centric, and "multiple belonging" spirituality — whose visioners (Teasdale, 1999; Johnson and Ord, 2012, 2013) proclaimed the following:
>
> "We are at the dawn of a new consciousness, a radically fresh approach to our life as the human family in a fragile world."

and continued:

> An ambitious and extensive document by the Canadian Research Institute currently influential in the United Nations community reports in detail on the varieties of interaction between complex elements of human culture, feedback loops re: human behavior, and resulting effects on the global environment both now and projected into the future. Interactions are highly nuanced, including innumerable interconnections of cultural narratives, religious beliefs, roles of science and technology in societies, changes and shifts in prevailing paradigms and worldviews (even social media), and the actual effects on multitudes of elements in the global environment itself and the relationship to biodiversity, environmental sustainability and so on. Across all these arenas, both the media, and fate, of humankind and the rest of the process of evolution are inextricably intertwined.[16]

Following on these developments between Interspirituality and science, in 2017, *The Interfaith Observer* solicited a summary of these developments in advance of the 2018 Parliament of the World's Religions in Toronto. For the 2018 event, the Parliament, following on its general theme "Toward a Global Ethic," aptly added the emphasis of The Promise of Inclusion, The Power of Love: Pursuing Global Understanding, Reconciliation, and Change.[18] The article appeared as "The Growing Edge of Interspirituality" as further adapted by TIO's editors. *The Interfaith Observer* (TIO) has served the global interfaith community for decades by regularly publishing articles and discussions on the roots, vision, and growth of the interfaith and interspiritual phenomena. Since it is an important resource for tracking the history and growth of Interspirituality, we take advantage of this opportunity and present an extensive Endnote herein that indexes all of the major articles published in TIO by the following important interfaith and interspiritual authors (along with the related books recommended): Edward Bastian, Diane Berke, Cynthia Brix, Cynthia Bourgeault, Adam Bucko, Kurt Johnson, Rory McEntee, Mirabai Starr, and Will Keepin.[19]

Let's move now to further sharing from the Toronto Parliament and the one-day pre-event on Interspirituality. We'll begin with the article solicited and published by *The Interfaith Observer*:[20]

The Growing Edge of Interspirituality

by Kurt Johnson

Br. Wayne Teasdale is famous for his interspiritual worldview embracing all the spiritual narratives of the world as one collective heritage, arising historically from the consciousness experience of our species, and seeks to draw from these resources the tools for altruistic behaviors that can actually build a world so envisioned. This is a beautiful sentiment, but how do we go about instituting it in our everyday lives, and what role do today's religions have in helping us do so?

These questions were the impetus behind my writing *The Coming Interspiritual Age* as a follow-up to Teasdale's now classic book *The Mystic Heart: Discovering a Universal Spirituality in the World's Religions* (1999) — in which he coined the word Interspirituality. After publishing this book, Teasdale founded the Interspiritual Association, which was incorporated in 2002 as Interspiritual Dialogue (ISD), and Interspiritual Dialogue n' Action (ISDnA) in 2005. Teasdale was critically ill during the last years of his life and devoted most of his time to finishing his two last books, *A Monk in the World* and *Bede Griffiths: An Introduction to His Interspiritual Thought* (both 2003). During this period, Teasdale's ongoing vision for Interspirituality was communicated mainly to those he worked closely with at the Interspiritual Association, known today as the Snowmass Interspiritual Dialogue.

Following Teasdale's death in 2004, Fr. Thomas Keating, whom Teasdale named as one of his mentors, continued to confer with Teasdale's interspiritual association through regular meetings. This helped him plan The Dawn of Interspirituality Conference held in 2013, which, in turn, spawned The Interspiritual Network which joins more than one hundred interspirituality-oriented associations and networks worldwide.

Later in 2004, Teasdale's association presented on the topic at the 2004 Barcelona Parliament of the World's Religions. Since then, Interspirituality has rapidly garnered popularity, going from just a few citations for Interspirituality at Google to nearly 100,000 today.

The Dawn of a New Consciousness

This rapid expansion reflects two major actualities, both of which hold long-term historical implications. First, what Teasdale termed Interspirituality was not new. Earlier, Raimon Panikkar had called it the intraspiritual experience, Matthew Fox deep ecumenism, and Thomas Merton the mystical communion. Eastern writers had added a number of expressions for it as well. The emerging paradigm actually reflected the vision of over fifty major historical religious figures who emphasized a "commonality of heart" across all the world's traditions. Thus, it is no surprise that today we see Interspirituality nearly everywhere, under a variety of names and with the brandings of diverse groups and leaders worldwide; not just as Interspirituality, but as global, ecumenical, universal, transtraditional, or world-centric spirituality, along with the spiritual but not religious, the nones, and the multiple belonging.

Second, evolutionary biology has come to recognize that Interspirituality is exactly the adaptive trait that would naturally arise within religion as the world moves toward inevitable globalization and multiculturalism, not only because that adaptive trait would be required of a globalizing civilization, but also because current evolutionary theory shows that natural selection at the level of groups and systems of groups chooses the best cooperators, not the best competitors. This recognition has been widely discussed by The Evolution Institute and in publications from Yale University and The Templeton Foundation.

The good news is that both the religious and scientific understanding of what Interspirituality is as a cultural phenomenon includes the coexistence and synergy of the variety and integrity of religious expressions and an understanding of their underlying unity in our profoundly interconnected world.

In *Mystic Heart – Discovering a Universal Spirituality in the World's Religions* (1999), his seminal work on Interspirituality, Wayne Teasdale heralded:

> *We are at the dawn of a new consciousness, a radically fresh approach to our life as the human family in a fragile world. This journey is what spirituality is really about. We are not meant to remain just where we are. We cannot depend on our culture either to guide and support us in our quest. We must do the hard work of clarification together ourselves. This revolution will be the task of the Interspiritual Age. The necessary shifts in consciousness require a new approach to spirituality that transcends past religious cultures of fragmentation and isolation. We need to understand, to really grasp at an elemental level that the definitive revolution is the spiritual awakening of humankind.*

This would manifest, he said, because of "a new set of historical circumstances," something that particularly rings true today.

Teasdale enumerated fundamental changes in global awareness necessary for a successful global shift toward the Interspiritual Age, some of which he noted as already happening. A number of these shared conclusions are now widely acknowledged and quoted worldwide. They are often referred to together as "The Interspiritual Declaration."

Interspiritual literature has gone through "three generations" of books. First came the primary seminal books of the paradigm, including both Teasdale's work and that of others who held similar views of Interspirituality. The second generation, elaborating these ideas and their implications in more detail. An example of this generation is

God of Love (2012) by Mirabai Starr. The third generation emerged when publishers then began saying "yes" to much more detail and elaboration on the implications of the interspiritual paradigm for specific traditions. It includes books such as *Interspiritual Meditation* and *The Interspiritual Mandala* (2014) by Edward Bastian (2015), *The New Monasticism* (2015) by Adam Bucko and Rory McEntee, *The Art of Community* (2016) by Charles Vogl, and *Mature Interspirituality* (2017) by Swami Shraddhananda.

Diversification and Global Hubs

As Interspirituality has become a household word, "ownership" of the paradigm has spread to myriad communities. There really is no core ownership of the paradigm now. There are people and groups using the word who have never heard of Br. Wayne Teasdale or the history elaborated above. The early propulsion of Interspirituality came from the contemplative community, the sacred activist community and the natural evolution of the interfaith experience.

The interspiritual paradigm has grown to become a dynamic global community echoing Br. Teasdale's question—what will humanity do now that the Wisdom Resources of the world's spiritual traditions are all available like a sumptuous banquet? Groups well-springing from Br. Teasdale's Interspiritual Dialogue are now joined in the dynamic Unity.earth platform (with elements ranging from education to scholarly writing, institutional and internet teaching, global festivals, online radio and TV series, spiritual tourism, indigenous partnerships and sacred site work, and concerted spiritual practice and social service). They too are a part of the wider Evolutionary Leaders.net array of over thirty circles of engagement, highlighted by media energies including the global *Ubuntu* outreach of Reggae legends Pato Banton and Antoinette "Rootsdawtah" Hall, a coterie of Artists in Service to Conscious Evolution, Global Peace Tribe's regular Awakening World programs and partnerings with, among others, Ubiquity University's Humanity Rising and State of the World.forum. From these roots have come, as well, the rapidly expanding Holomovement, based on the unitive vision of physicist David Bohn and, from progressive evolutionary scientists, the work of Prosocial.world and ProSocial Spirituality. Satyana Institute and the wider world of Interfaith & Interspiritual Seminaries continue their dynamic work in interspiritual education, as does The Spiritual Paths Foundation (originally founded with Fr. Keating) with its Interspiritual Meditation and Interspiritual Mandala programs. The Charis Foundation has taken up the mantle of the original Snowmass Dialogues. These join as well in a United Nations NGO Thematic Cluster with diverse annual activities including the 11 Days of Global Unity of We.net, World Unity Week, Peace Week, Interfaith Harmony Week, and International Yoga Day programs with the UN's Yoga Day committee and the NGO World Yoga Community.

These have been rich decades for Interspirituality and likely portents a positive world future if indeed Br. Teasdale's vision accurately assesses our human destiny:

> We are at the dawn of a new consciousness, a radically fresh approach to our life as the human family in a fragile world. This journey is what spirituality is really about. We are not meant to remain just where we are [MH pp. 4-12 sequence].

Endnotes and References for "Opening Message"[i]
and "Introduction to Volume 2"[ii]

HISTORY, continued

Diversification of Global Hubs

Let's turn now to the topic and history of "Diversification of Global Hubs" denoted in the above article published in *The Interfaith Observer*. As noted below, these Volumes are partitioned as of about 2015, considering both (i) the timeline sequences of activities, events, initiatives, publications etc., and (ii) the breadth of the content herein from all the Featured Authors. We resume Timelines and Benchmarks accordingly as below, grouped to parallel the timelines and content of this Volume.

TIMELINES, continued

Continuing from the Timelines in Volume 1 (**2001-2002; 2003-2006; 2007-2012**), we recommence for this Volume with:

2012-2016: **(11)** 1God.com founded by Ben Bowler in Australia [2015] (and later, see below, will join with the Interspiritual Dialogue Network, and others, to co-found UNITY EARTH) [2016]; **(12)** Interspiritual participation in the 2015 Parliament of the World's Religions (Salt Lake City) [2015]; **(13)** Founding of ContemplativeLife.org by Jeffrey Genung, Garden of Light.org by Rev. Deborah Moldow [2015]; **(14)** Members of Interspiritual Dialogue joined the Gaiafield Project subtle activism initiative [2015]; **(15)** Collaboration with

Evolution Institute and emerging Prosocial.world with events at State University of New York, Binghamton; New York City's Felix Adler Ethical Culture Library (April 12, 2016); and Gold Hill Historic Site, Boulder, Colorado (June 12, 2016) [2015-2016]; **(16)** Founding of the Charis Foundation for New Monasticism and Interspirituality by members of the Snowmass Dialogues to vision transition of the Snowmass Dialogues to today's Charis Snowmass Dialogues [2015-2016]; **(17)** Residential retreat of Community of the Mystic Heart with (i) presentation of the Sannyas robes of Br. Wayne Teasdale to Swami Shraddhananda's Sacred Feet Slate Branch Ashram (now Anugraha House, Kentucky, USA) and (ii) passing of the Acclimation re: the Universal Order of Sannyasa (see item 5 in 2007-2012 Timeline in Volume 1) of Br. Teasdale Sannyas lineage to the care of Swami Shraddhananda, Sacred Feet, and the full Sannyas program of Sacred Feet [2016]; **(18)** Founding of The Convergence Series on VoiceAmerica by 1God.com and Interspiritual Dialogue and one year of programs on The Interspiritual Age, and emergence of the UNITY EARTH network [2016]; **(19)** Interspiritual Event at United Nations Tillman Chapel in New York City by UNITY EARTH, Interspiritual Dialogue, and the UN NGO Committee for Spirituality, Values and Global Concerns (keynote [see our Vol. 3]: Dr. Andrew Vidich, co-author of *Let There Be Light: Experiencing Inner Light Across the World's Sacred Traditions*) [2016]; **(20)** Swami Shraddhananda closes Slate Branch Ashram and opens Anugraha House in 2017 (at jefifoundation.org). This has since been the headquarters address for Sacred Feet Yoga and The Jones Educational Foundation for the last eight years [2016-2017]; **(21)** Initial Charis Snowmass Dialogues (I and II [see charisinterspirituality.org (csd-past)]) [2016-2017]; **(22)** Interspiritual Dialogue joins Fr. Richard Rohr OFM, and Fr. Michael

Holleran (a Featured Author in these Volumes) in Interspiritual events in the New York City Roman Catholic community as part of the wider Contemplative Alliance noted by Featured Author Dena Merriam herein [2016].

2017-Covid Pandemic [3/2020]: **(1)** UNITY EARTH launches multifaceted "Road to 2020" series of interspiritual and cultural events enumerated further later in these Volumes [2016-2020]; **(2)** Crestone [Colorado] Leadership Conferences joining the interspiritual community further with United Nations NGO and Evolutionary Leaders communities [2017, aka "The Crestone Convergence"] and indigenous leaders [2018]; **(3)** Interspiritual leaders from Interspiritual Dialogue, UNITY EARTH and United Religions Initiative participate in International Urantia Conference, University of Denver (host Gard Jameson et al.) [2017]; **(4)** Founding of *The Convergence* and *Light on Light* e-magazines by initiating over twenty issues concerning Interspirituality and global issues [2017]; **(5)** *Convergence* magazine special issue on Altruism [2017]; **(6)** *Light on Light* magazine launches with issues on community, spiritual practice, and first special issue with the International Day of Yoga Committee at the United Nations ("UNIDY") and Guru Dileepji World Yoga Community [2018]; **(7)** *Convergence* magazine special issues on the "Road to 2020" and the 2018 Parliament of the World's Religions [2018]; **(8)** Dawn of Interspirituality Conference in Latin America convened by Satyana Institute et al. [2018]; **(9)** One-day Pre-Event at the Parliament of the World's Religions (Toronto) [2018]; **(10)** *Convergence* magazine special issues on Conscious Business and New York City and African Union events [2019]; **(11)** *Light on Light* magazine special issues on Sacred Sites, the International Day of Yoga with UNIDY, and Change-makers [2019]; **(12)** Interspirituality and science-related visit and discussion with the Dalai Lama in Dharamsala, India [2019]; **(13)** Tribute Event to Fr. Thomas Keating, Aspen Chapel and Snowmass Abbey [2019]; **(14)** Evolutionary Leaders' Gold Nautilus award-winning book *Our Moment of Choice*; subsequent *Our Moment of Choice* special issue of *Light on Light* magazine [2020]; **(15)** Humanity's Moment of Choice Radio Program on VoiceAmerica founded [2020]; and **(16)** Light on Light Press founded, dedicated to books on Interspirituality and the global paradigm shift [2020]; **(17)** Charis Snowmass Dialogues (II – VII) [see charisinterspirituality.org (csd-past)]) [2016-2020].

Covid Pandemic [3/2020] – Publication of these Volumes: **(1)** These global, online and in person Interspirituality events and media become annual: World Unity Week [June], the United Nations NGO and New York City Week of Spirituality [June], the International Day of Yoga [June], Peace Week [September], International Day of Peace [September 21], the 11 Days of Global Unity [September], the Global Oneness Summit [October], continuing annually [since their original foundings to present]; **(2)** Interspiritual Dialogue's Light on Light Press's annual special e-magazines issues with the International Day of Yoga Committee at the United Nations, special issues on *Sacred Sites and Spirituality in Nature*, and global *Change-Makers*; print books *True Light* [Sukyo Mahikari perspective], *Global Unitive Healing* [Baha'i perspective] and *May the Loveforce Be With You* [Divine Feminine Reiki Lineage] [2021- present]; **(3)** Light on Light e-publications with We.net's founder Rick Ulfik curate influential e-publication *Universal Principles and Action Steps*, gathering a century of statements and guidelines for transformation from diverse organizations around the world [2021]; **(4)** Satyana Institute hosts Women's Spiritual Leadership in the 21st Century Conference, March

4-6 [2022]; **(5)** Interspiritual Dialogue and Light on Light join "Igniting the Holomovement" event in Sedona, Arizona, with the Evolutionary Leaders and Holomovement founders [2023]; **(6)** growing from the Snowmass Dialogues' legacy, The Keating-Schachter Center for Interspirituality founded as a partnership between Naropa University in Boulder, Colorado, and Charis Foundation for New Monasticism and Interspirituality (Rory McEntee, Netanel Miles-Yépez, Adam Bucko, Alejandra Warden, et al.), Charis Foundation establishing its Charis Mandala Sanctuary in New Mexico, and Charis Snowmass Dialogues (VII-VIII) [2022-23]; **(7)** Interspiritual Dialogue and Light on Light become part of the Core Team of The Holomovement (at holomovement.net) and publish *The Holomovement* [2023] and *The Wave* e-publication [2024]; **(8)** Interspiritual Dialogues' Light on Light Press publishes with the Club of Budapest and the Laszlo Institute for New Paradigm Research print books *The Great Upshift*, *The Survival Imperative* and the e-publications *Our Sacred Mission* and *Humanity's Sacred Mission* [2024]; *The Awakening of Humanity* e-publication with cosmologist Jude Currivan, evolutionary biologist Kurt Johnson and integral theologian Doug King [2024], plan *The Power of Partnership* with Riane Eisler, Galia Benartzi and Roger Briggs [2026] and *The Experience of Group Consciousness* with the VISTAR Foundation and Featured Authors [2026]; **(9)** Interspiritual Dialogue's Light on Light becomes co-sponsor of the Illuminate Film Festival, the largest conscious film festival in the world [2024-25]; **(10)** The Evolutionary Leaders' large Sustainable Development Goals Thought Leaders Circle (sdgthoughtleaderscircle.org) host at St. John the Divine Cathedral, New York City, a day-long pre-event for the United Nations Summit of the Future, including the implications of Interspirituality in its deliberations; **(11)** After winning eight Nautilus

Awards, Light on Light Press is also awarded Nautilus's Best in Small Press [2024]; **(12)** Interspiritual communities continue activities with First Peoples (subsequent Feature section "A Sacred Convergence to Restore Balance — Mother Gaia and the Wisdom of Indigenous Peoples") culminating work from 2024-present [2025]; **(13)** Light on Light Press publishes books on the interspirituality of Yoga [*Light on Kundalini* by Karuna] with Introduction from the United Nations Yoga Day Committee and *The Way of Unity* by Dr. Robert Atkinson detailing the contributions of the Baha'i tradition to interfaith relations and world peace; and **(14)** Rory McEntee of Charis Foundation publishes *The Sacred/Secular Binary*; Ubiquity University, following on their ongoing global broadcasts of *Humanity Rising* convenes State of the World.forum; the Evolutionary Leaders, with multiple impact networks, cofound the Positive Media Alliance; Light on Light Press publishes *Interspirituality: The Heritage* and *Interspirituality: The Future*, a historical and thematic account of Interspirituality, on the 25th anniversary of Br. Wayne Teasdale's *The Mystic Heart: Discovering a Universal Spirituality in the World's Religions* [2025].

BENCHMARKS

Voices from Global Events: Interspiritual Dialogue, 1God.com and others form UNITY.EARTH

Features in these Volumes by Ben Bowler - Haji Syed Salman Chishty - Richard Clugston Geraldine Patrick Encina - Mussie Hailu - Kurt Johnson - Ken Kitatani - Chief Phil Lane Jr. Yanni Maniates - Deborah Moldow - Mindahi Bastida Muñoz - Chief Dwaine Perry

and voices from the 2018 Parliament of the World's Religions

[listed subsequently]

Below, in the context of "Diversification and Global Hubs," we elaborate in fuller detail the emergence of international activities, initiatives, events, and publications following the joining of Interspiritual Dialogue with the extensive Australian and Asian interfaith network 1God.com. 1God.com was founded by Australian interfaith leader Ben Bowler and colleagues and is today — including the Interspiritual Dialogue Network and numerous other organizations — an expansive network under the name UNITY EARTH (at unity.earth). As such, it is the home of diverse programs and events like World Unity Week, Peace Week, Purpose Earth, and annual far-flung international "Convergence" events.

The initial meeting of these two networks was arranged by the founder of Presence.tv — "A Global Conversation for New Earth; Toward an Integral Theology" — Doug King. King is the son of renowned theologian Max King, recognized as the founder of the school of thought known as *transmillennialism.*[1] This meeting, arranged for Atlanta, Georgia, in April 2016, led to what would soon become the UNITY EARTH transformational community working across the themes of Interspirituality, ecospirituality, and cultural transformation. This collaboration joining Ben Bowler, Derek Grimm, Irina Morrison, and iconic Reggae singers Pato Banton and Antoinette Hall of 1God.com with Kurt Johnson and Yanni Maniates of Interspiritual Dialogue and Evolutionary Leaders Circle leaders Deborah Moldow, Jeff Vander Klute, Ken Kitatani, and Mindahi Bastida Muñoz fostered what is now over a decade of collaborative initiatives and events which continue today. These had been spurred, as noted in Volume 1, by significant recognitions of the 2013 *The Coming Interspiritual Age* publication by such platforms at Namaste Publishing (with their e-magazines excerpted in Volume 1), Spirituality and Practice.com which had followed Br. Teasdale's vision for some time, and the Center for Action and Contemplation whose founder Fr. Richard Rohr OFM was a major visioneer of the emergence of Interspirituality from the wider interfaith experience.

As well, following immediately after this gathering in Atlanta, the Community of the Mystic Heart held its first residential retreat at the Sacred Feet Slate Branch Ashram (now Anugraha House), and home of the Jones Educational Foundation, of Swami Shraddhananda (aka Dr. Sonya Jones, comparative world religions professor, Honors Program, University of Kentucky), whose proceedings were published in 2017 as *Mature Interspirituality*.[2]

You have read about some of these activities already in the Timelines and Benchmarks of Volume 1, but we have moved the following more detailed accounts into Volume 2, breaking the Volumes at about the year 2015. A ready recollection of these important developments is bulleted below.

- 1God.com founded by Ben Bowler in Australia and later joins with the Interspiritual Dialogue Network, and others, to co-found UNITY EARTH [2014-2015].
- Founding of The Convergence Series on VoiceAmerica by 1God.com and Interspiritual Dialogue with one year of programs on The Interspiritual Age, and emergence of the UNITY EARTH network [2016]. As of 2025, there are over fifty archived programs from this VoiceAmerica series on Interspirituality, ecospirituality, and cultural transformation.[3]
- Interspiritual Event at United Nations Tillman Chapel in New York City by UNITY EARTH, Interspiritual Dialogue, and the UN NGO Committee for Spirituality, Values and Global Concerns [2016].

- Launch of UNITY EARTH's multifaceted "Road to 2020" series of Interspiritual and cultural events 2012- 2020: Chiang Mai, Thailand 2012; New York City and United Nations, USA, 2016; VoiceAmerica radio, 2016; multiple locations, India 2017; Rome-Assisi, Italy, 2017; Colorado, USA, 2017; Lake Mungo, Australia, 2017; Ethiopia and African Union, 2018; Colorado, USA, 2018; Toronto, Canada, 2018; Byron Bay, Australia, 2018; New York City, USA, 2019; multiple locations, India, 2019; Jerusalem, Israel, 2020; World Unity Week, online, 2020; coast to coast, USA, 2020; Peace Weekend, online, 2020.
- Crestone (Colorado) Leadership Conferences [aka Crestone Convergence(s)] joining the global interspiritual community further with United Nations NGO and Evolutionary Leaders communities [2017] and indigenous leaders [2018].
- Founding of *The Convergence* and *Light on Light* e-magazines culminating in over twenty issues concerning Interspirituality and global issues [2017].
- One-day Pre-Event at the Parliament of the World's Religions (Toronto) [2018].
- Post "Road to 2020" "Convergence" Events: World Unity Week, online, becomes annual [2021]; Peace Week, online, becomes annual [2022], Los Angeles, CA, USA "Convergence" Event [2023]; Dubai "Convergence" Event [2023]; "Awakening to Humanity's Sacred Mission" (with two-time Nobel Peace Prize nominee Ervin Laszlo) [2024]; "Meeting the Dreamer" event, Mildura, Australia [2025].

Selections from
Unity Earth Global "Convergence" Events
World Interfaith Harmony Week

International Interfaith Statements on the Occasion of World Interfaith Harmony Week

His Excellency Ambassador Mussie Hailu (2018):[4]

> One simple and yet profound practical action that helps to promote harmony among all people regardless of their faith traditions is the teaching of The Golden Rule which says, "Treat others the way you want to be treated." Practicing The Golden Rule helps to build trust, understanding, harmony, and respect among followers of different religions and will create the opportunity for them to come together to resist forces of division that spread misunderstanding and mistrust among peoples of different religions.
>
> We are living in a global village which is coming together more than ever, and our shrinking "Global Village" is evolving into a multiracial, multicultural and multireligious society. In this interconnected and globalized world, all nations are our close neighbors, and our well-being increasingly depends on how well we interact and live together with others based on the teaching of The Golden Rule.
>
> As you know, The Golden Rule has been around for a long time. But today it seems more relevant than ever

before. Living by The Golden Rule isn't always easy. To treat others like we want to be treated requires a constant, active consideration of how our words and actions affect others. By putting this time-honored principle into daily practice, and asking our friends, families, and leaders to do the same, we can work toward creating a greater understanding and respect for one another.

If we work together to address our common issues under the guiding principle of The Golden Rule, we can help to reverse the insane trends prevailing today in our world. If everyone does his or her part, together we can accomplish what is necessary.

The Golden Rule is the pathway for peaceful coexistence, human dignity, mutual respect, justice, and harmony to prevail on Earth among people and followers of different religions and cultures. World peace is only possible when we start to make peace within ourselves, our families, and in our respective communities.

May our hearts open more and our minds understand the depth of our calling as people who are living in the 21st century to serve humanity and Mother Earth.

Let us be in the presence of each other at deep levels of our thinking, feeling, and acting and be compassionate to each other. *Let us be instruments of peace and a living example of the teaching of The Golden Rule.*

His Excellency Haji Syed Salman Chishty (2018):[5]

We must try to understand that Human Beings occupy a unique position in this world and they are at the axis and centre of the cosmic milieu. By being taught the names of all things, we are given the keys to knowledge of all things, and thus, gain an understanding of all sacred and secret knowledge.

In fact, Human Beings are the channel of grace for nature; through our active participation in the spiritual world, we bring light into the world of nature. Because of our intimate connection with nature, our inner state is reflected in the external order. This explains why, when our inner being turns to darkness and chaos, nature is also turned from harmony and beauty to disequilibrium and disorder. Human Beings see in nature what we ourselves are and penetrate into the inner meaning of nature only by being able to delve into the inner depths of our own being. Those who live only on the surface of their being can study nature as something to be manipulated and dominated; only those who have turned toward the inward dimension of their existence can recognize nature as a symbol, and come to understand it in the real sense.

Peace indicates tranquility, mental calm, silence, serenity, reconciliation, amity, accord, concord, friendliness and harmony on the one hand, and the absence of or cessation of war, a state of reconciliation after strife and enmity, freedom from mental agitation or anxiety and freedom from civil disorder and strife as well.

There is a very close relationship between peace and harmony at the personal and societal levels.

Peace creates concord, balance, consistency, unanimity, compatibility, and stability at individual and collective levels and helps to affect accord in facts and viewpoints, and it acts and helps in making sympathetic relationships and mutual similarities the focal point of human concern. When peace and harmony are achieved in this real interrelated manner, the expectation for a trustful, promising, secure, and faithful existence of human beings becomes possible, which, in other words, can be called hope in harmony and peace.

2018 Parliament of the World's Religions Pre-Event

The Toronto Parliament took place from November 1–7, 2018. The one-day Pre-Event was held on October 31, 2018, at The St. James Cathedral Conference Center. It was co-sponsored by UNITY EARTH, the Interspiritual Dialogue Network, the United Religions Initiative, and the United Nations NGO Spirituality and Values networks. The gathering was called "The Toronto Convergence" in the context of five other previous Convergence events sponsored by these groups and whose proceedings had been published by the Light on Light Press in their free e-magazines under "The Convergence" banner.[6] The event assembled nearly one hundred leaders, with another seventy joining virtually. Since the event produced a series of publications under the titles *Waking Up, Growing Up, Cleaning Up, Showing Up, Linking Up and Lifting Up* — six monikers summarizing the elements needed for real world change — the Toronto Convergence was also subtitled: "Unifying the Unifiers."

Shared here for perpetuity, and for their significance to the current Volumes, are selections from the offerings of the following authors, as published in the original e-publication by Light on Light.[7] We also note where various of these Features were subsequently published online in full.[8]

Michael Bernard Beckwith - Patrick Carolan - Deepak Chopra - Duane Elgin
Ashok Gangadean - Jonathan Granoff - Grove Harris - Victor H. Kazanjian Jr.
Brian McLaren - Dena Merriam - Terry Patten - Llewellyn Vaughan-Lee
Monica Willard - Ken Wilber

After Deepak Chopra's offering, which has already been shared above, Ken Wilber (whose vital book, *The Religion of Tomorrow: A Vision of the Future of the Great Traditions — More Inclusive, More Comprehensive, More Complete*, had appeared in 2017) followed with his introduction of the themes *Waking Up*, *Growing Up*, *Cleaning Up*, *Showing Up*, and *Opening Up.* Since these themes are fully included in his Afterword to the current Volumes, we do not repeat them again here, but we endnote the locations where both articles by Chopra and by Wilber were published, in full, online in 2018, and are still available, at least for now.[9] Thus, we follow here with important selections from the presentations at the Toronto Convergence (in their original published form) reflecting Wilber's themes, after an Introduction to them by the late Terry Patten.[10] The series concludes with two Reflections from The Convergence events by Victor H. Kazanjian Jr., then executive director of the United Religions Initiative, and the well-known author, speaker, activist, and public theologian Brian McLaren.

THE FUTURE

by Terry Patten

No one can say with certainty how our civilizational crisis will play out. We don't know how much suffering and destruction — human and nonhuman — might lie ahead, or how soon. But we do know, with increasing certainty, that the actions of human beings have created an existential predicament; and we can also know that the actions of human beings — for good or for ill — will determine the future of our great grandchildren and most other living beings.

The stakes could scarcely be higher. We cannot wait to "see what happens" before we act on this awareness. Rather, we are obliged right now to do whatever we can to help prevent or mitigate the horrific scenarios that we may have set in motion. What could be a greater moral imperative?

Only human beings can protect and defend the future of life on Earth from human beings. It will take conscious individuals making deliberate choices based on the best information available — people presuming responsibility to make a difference. Nothing could be more honorable and worthwhile.

The word activist conjures images of sit-ins, people circulating petitions and raising money and marching and organizing and meeting, and getting people to the polls. But it also means doing research, starting businesses, making loans, and changing one's diet. When people creatively act on their moral intuition, all kinds of things happen. The world of activism is very big, diverse, and dynamic. And it requires — and helps us along in — transcending the collective trance.

Gratitude, Grief, and Spiritual Activism

Spiritual life involves growing into a wise and healthy relationship to reality. The word spiritual points to the deepest level of being — essential and existential. Spiritual growth and development enable us to glimpse the bountiful grace in which we live — the beauty of the world, and the privilege of conscious embodied existence. Gratitude is universal spiritual wisdom, and it is sufficient.

Such gratitude is awake. It is realistically in touch with loss and death and threat — not in denial. Saints are grateful even while resonating empathically with suffering. Everything we love is mortal, even the living Earth. Everything regenerates, and yet it is also wounded and under threat. The heart breaks to see the destruction of vulnerable people, living creatures, and wild places. We want to protect them. We want to help. As Joanna Macy so sagely puts it, "If everyone I love is in danger, I want to be here, so I can do what I can." Activism is simply acting on the impulse to "be of benefit" to something greater than yourself, in a whole variety of ways. Not all of them look like overt activism, but many do. All are natural expressions of human maturity.

But exactly how can we effectively address the totality of this crisis? If addressing it requires knowing exactly how the crisis will unfold and exactly what it will take to prevent it, then we can't. As we have seen, no one, not even the best of scientists, has that degree of omniscience, especially with the kind of wicked predicament we are facing. There is no way that we can address the whole tangle of causes and consequences — everything is connected to everything else.

Our predicament requires a revolutionary transformation of every aspect of human life — a "Great Transition" or "Great Turning." It will ultimately require revolutionary changes in human consciousness, behavior, culture, and the physical, economic, and political infrastructure of our whole civilization. It is so vast and intricate, it easily seems impossible.

We might be tempted to despair, but despair easily becomes a self-fulfilling prophecy. And yet, because this huge transformation has so many aspects, every one of us can readily find ways to magnify love and sanity and beauty and truth and human connection. Every one of us can find many things we can actually *do*.

Paradoxically, the many little things we can do — each of which may seem in itself woefully insufficient to our total predicament — may well be a good start. We will continue to see the endings of life all around us, and we will grieve for all of the losses we witness. Our spirit and consciousness will go through a transformative ordeal as we take in new terrible truths about our predicament. But many actions on many levels, when collectively engaged (and perhaps further catalyzed by positive black swan breakthroughs), may ultimately add up into a single great action. At our micro level, there are many things we *can* do, and *are doing*, to address even our mega crisis.

To be an effective agent of change does not mean we have to know everything. But it does require opening to another level of transformation and creativity. Our predicament presents us with a vast demand and limitless opportunity for growth. Our crisis seems overwhelming, and yet we live in a universe of awe-inspiring creative potential — in nature, in our fellow humans, in the evolutionary process, and certainly in ourselves. The story of evolution is a story of miracle after miracle. We must simultaneously take in the magnitude of the problem — grieve for much inevitable suffering — and do what we can on behalf of creative solutions, on every scale. To do both requires great openness on our part — openness to growth and to creative responses that we didn't know were possible. We give ourselves over to something that feels true. We magnify health and wholeness, even in the face of fragmentation — and in our trust of the larger process, we also become more effective. Our souls are positively stirred, and conscripted. This process of growth is clearly never-ending.

From Growing Up to Waking Up to Linking Up — Personal and Collective Practice

What exactly does that look like for each of us personally? We can live a whole life of practice. And that expresses itself through a whole spectrum of *Integral* practices, both personal and collective.

In *Integral Life Practice,* I and my co-authors introduced the phrases "Waking Up" (to higher states of consciousness that intuit our divine nature) and "Growing Up" to higher developmental structures of consciousness. Others, including Ken Wilber and Dustin Diperna, have expanded on this sequence to include "Cleaning Up" (shadow work, healing, and forgiveness), and (following my writings on integral activism) "Showing Up" (committed courageous action in the world). Others, including Kurt Johnson, Jude Currivan and myself, have added "Linking Up" (practice in community that builds a social movement).

Here I would like to add an additional phrase, still aspirational, and yet, I think, now an evolutionary imperative: Syncing Up. Deep and profound practice *in* and *among* communities of practice can liberate ever deepening alignment to what is most fundamental and universal about what all practitioners are participating in. Each of us is a fractal expression of Wholeness as it reasserts itself, like an immune response, in the face of an urgent global crisis of fragmentation. As we become more and more deeply surrendered to the heart of wholeness, we will cease to live in our superficial and divided ways. We will learn to notice *and presume* the greater divine wholeness that we are all serving.

Let's look at the following in the context of "Waking Up," "Growing Up," "Cleaning Up," "Showing Up," "Linking Up," "Lifting Up," and "Opening Up."

The "Ups" — Some Quick Definitions

Adapted from the Editors' "Welcome" in the publication for the 2018 Toronto Parliament of the World's Religions pre-event on Interspirituality: "Over seventy of you have contributed to this publication for the Toronto Parliament. We've grouped the thematics highlighted below in phrases that we know you understand, following on the work of integral philosopher Ken Wilber — Waking Up (to our Divine Nature, our full moral capacity), Growing Up (building a world that reflects those Heart values), Cleaning Up (healing, reconciliation, and shadow work), and Showing Up (activism and speaking Truth to power). To these the Evolutionary Leaders Circle has added in recent years, Linking Up (creating cooperative and synergized work together), and Lifting Up (co-energizing and co-inspiring)."

Subsequent to this, in publications since 2020 (including two with our Light on Light Press), Wilber has stressed "Opening Up" (opening to the multifaceted full potential of our Consciousness), a phrase he first introduced in 1977 in his iconic book *The Spectrum of Consciousness.* He included "Opening Up" as one of five key dimensions of human wholeness (or transformation) in his recent book, *Finding Radical Wholeness: The Integral Path to Unity, Growth, and Delight* (June 2024).[11]

about WAKING UP

Selected from

Overcoming the Illusion of separateness

by Dena Merriam

The mindset that kept the religions apart is based on what some call the "domination gene," the need to dominate over and feel superior to the "other," and this other can be the religious other, the ethnic or racial other, the other defined by class or economics, or other species. Before we as a human community can overcome this domination mindset, we must recognize the many subtle ways in which it permeates our thinking and controls our personal and collective behavior. It controls the way we interact with other species and life forms, with our Mother Earth, and our fellow humans. If we could as a collective overcome this outdated mindset, many of the injustices that cause harm today would be set aright, and Mother Earth's life systems would not be under threat. It would eradicate the hierarchies that structure our societies and help us reclaim the unity with the natural world that is our birthright.

In reality, there is no separation, there is no other. More and more people seem to be waking up to this realization at the conceptual level, but how does this translate into human behavior? It may be easier to see how this applies to our view and treatment of fellow humans, but it has far greater implications.

We are here to care for not compete with one another. Our Mother Earth is giving us an opportunity to understand this, for only by coming together as a community of life will we be able to repair the damage we have done; only by overcoming the domination instinct will we be able to truly progress. And by erasing our sense of separateness we will come closer to knowing our unity with the Divine.

In order to seize the opportunities before us for true human growth, we must do our own internal work to move beyond the illusion of separateness and take responsibility for the results of past actions. In this way, we can help foster the upward movement of humanity.

about GROWING UP

Selected from

St. Francis's Ecological Paradigm

by Patrick Carolan

Throughout most of Christianity, the dominant social paradigm reflects the theory of human domination over nature. St. Francis of Assisi proposed a completely different paradigm, one that seeks total ecological integrity. He did not separate the spiritual world from the material world. He viewed the Earth and all nature as God's creation, a place of continual incarnation. St. Francis taught that we had to live in relational solidarity with all creation. His spirituality is beautifully expressed in the poem "Cantle of Creatures."

His idea of caring for all creation was not a paternalistic concept of having dominion over creation. So how did we get from this beautiful theology of oneness with God and all of God's creation that St Francis lived to a world of separation and individualism?

St. Thomas Aquinas taught that non-rational creatures do not have moral value. He believed that the world was created by God as an ordered and unique whole displaying its beauty as well as the beauty of the Creator, and which was bequeathed to man that he may have dominion over it. Bonaventure developed a different theology of creation. For Bonaventure, creation is relationship.

Richard Rohr, OFM states: "Without some form of incarnation, God remains essentially separate from us and from all of creation. God, who is Infinite Love, incarnates that love as the universe itself." Thomas Merton was quoted as saying: "We will not save what we do not love. It is also true that we will neither love nor save that which we do not experience as sacred." Thomas Berry, a Catholic priest, in his book *The Sacred Universe,* describes religious experiences as "emerging as a sense of the awesome aspects of the natural world."

Today, almost fifty years after Lynn White, Pope Francis calls us to move forward in a bold cultural revolution. He calls for us to rise up, not in a revolution of guns but a revolution of Spirit. To stop living in a world where we are all separate and come together in a world of interbeing, a world where we are part of God's creation not separate from creation.

about CLEANING UP

Selected from

Seven Stages of Great Transition
A Pathway to a Sustainable and Surpassing Future

by Duane Elgin

The human family has entered a time of unprecedented change and profound choice. Powerful forces of our own making are accelerating and converging. The collective impact of escalating climate disruption, rising population, unsustainable consumption, and species extinction could be catastrophic. It is vital that we envision the future being shaped by these powerful trends.

It is important to recognize how challenging it is to look at the new world emerging in this century. Collectively, we have never gone through the kind of fiery rite of passage that lies just ahead. Engaging with our collective future takes emotional courage as it brings up existential fears and deep-seated wounds. However, there finally comes a point when we cannot turn away — when we must look squarely at critical trends or surrender our world to ruin....

Humanity is growing up. Just as a teenager makes many missteps in their maturation, so too can the human family be expected to struggle in finding our way to early adulthood. It is unrealistic to expect billions of humans to make the transition from collective adolescence to early adulthood in a single step. Instead, I envision a series of stages that seem likely in making this great transition — Seven Stages of Great Transition 2018–2100.

These seven stages describe a process of great transition for the human family — a time of collective initiation and collective awakening that takes us into a more mature species-civilization.

The world has broken apart in countless ways and is now reassembling itself in new ways that include: 1) an "eco-ethic" that prioritizes the well-being of the Earth system; 2) a new economic paradigm that views aliveness as our true wealth, encouraging people to move toward where they feel most alive — in nurturing relationships, caring communities, time in nature, creative expressions, and service to others; 3) a new democracy is emerging as Earth citizenship takes hold from the local to the global level; 4) a new understanding of the universe as a single, living system of which we are an integral part; and 5) a new view of humanity's journey as bio-cosmic beings learning to live in a living universe.

about SHOWING UP

Selected from

The Perennial Quest for Peace on Earth

by Michael Bernard Beckwith

Today's news and social media make it impossible to avoid the blunt reality that we are living in a post-truth society wherein breaches of trust, respect, compassion, and dishonoring of the rights and dignity of our global family have become the new normal. Alternative facts fill the airwaves, attempting to convince us that we are not interconnected and interdependent, that only a proliferation of nuclear weapons can protect one nation from the encroachment of another.

Like no other time in history, the technological revolution has accelerated our ability to reshape our world. Visionary solutions to challenges including global warming, world hunger, healthcare, and education have been put in motion. As the paleontologist and Jesuit priest Pierre Teilhard de Chardin coined, the next label for *Homo sapiens* may be "Homo progressivus," while visionary architect and inventor Buckminster Fuller suggested we will evolve into "hetero-techno sapiens." What they are both telling us is that we human beings are the essential vehicles for fulfilling our perennial quest for peace on Earth. It is through our individual inner work and spiritual practices that we embody that mandate and put it into action as the beneficial presence on the planet that each of us is.

The truth is, we can no longer afford not to recognize how the actions of our global family impact the entire planet.

In order to move in the direction of peace, we must make a choice to live in love rather than fear, to practice wisdom rather than ignorance, value nonviolence over aggression. The question I ask myself is, "Am I willing to do the inner work required to cultivate unconditional love, compassion and forgiveness — qualities that dissolve a sense of separation from the wholeness of life, that hold together the fabric of the created world?" Each of us is a choice-point in the center of the universe. What will be your choice?

As the acknowledgment that we are members of one global village finds its home in more and more hearts, it announces that now is the season to become a spiritual evolutionary who realizes that the solution to the world's challenges is a spiritual one, that only through love, compassion, and peace can we create international well-being. Such a response to Spirit's clarion call, to recognize and honor our interconnectivity as one world family, acknowledges that we are aware of the verdant, beautiful inner landscape of goodness that is inherent within all beings. It is through such an awakened state of consciousness that we can move forward united as one global heart, together beaming a cosmic smile across the universe.

about LINKING UP

Selected from

The United Nations — A Catalyst for Interfaith Actions

by Monica Willard

The Parliament of the World's Religions brings people together from all over the world who represent diverse religions, spiritual and indigenous traditions. We gather with hope and deep convictions that we can make a difference in our personal lives and in the world. Our specific traditions may differ and yet we share many common values.

The United Nations' (UN) has worked for over seventy years to bring nations together to address global issues. Amid all the political strife, violence and injustice in the world, the Member States of the United Nations work together to create priorities and programs that are designed to make a better world for everyone. Peace, human rights, the environment, climate change, and the economic condition and well-being of people everywhere are just some of the many UN agenda issues.

I would like to share some specific ways that the United Nations documents and programs offer a catalyst for Interfaith Actions that can transform the world.

How different would our world be if governments, businesses, religious and spiritual traditions and each person really knew and practiced the thirty principles in the Universal Declaration of Human Rights?

The opportunities for Interfaith impact on global issues and local communities by engaging with the United Nations has grown substantially since 1946. Member States increased from the initial 56 to the current 193, plus the two observer members of the Holy See and Palestine. During that same time, the interfaith movement has expanded.

A very special UN Resolution for the interfaith community is World Interfaith Harmony Week, the first week of February. This resolution was first observed in 2011 with participation increasing annually.

There are so many additional areas where the UN can be a catalyst for interfaith action. One issue that threatens the fate of our planet is nuclear weapons. …Interfaith action is needed on this critically important issue. There are many political steps that we can take. Many religions have institutional policies calling for the end of nuclear weapons….

Awareness, political action and prayers are needed. May the UN be a catalyst in your work. May Peace be in your heart, your home, community, nation and in the universe. May Peace Prevail on Earth!

Selected from

The United Nations — Understanding Interfaith Leadership Vision

by Grove Harris

Standing up, linking up, speaking up, and acting up. We have to do it all. We work in coalitions at the United Nations, using the human rights frame towards social and environmental justice…. We can be peaceful warriors; we were born for this.

The SDGs offer an interconnected framework for change, but have not gone far enough in redirecting us away from the unsustainable growth model. All solutions depend on stopping the explosion of our over consumption; it is a prerequisite for changing course. Everything needs to be respected for its contribution to the full cycle of life, and evaluated for the damage it does. Cradle to cradle thinking is required of us at this time, as is change in our consumption patterns.

We listen to learn, in particular from women.

The interfaith movement has the opportunity to acknowledge its limitations and to look forward to an increased relevance [to] the world.

The spirit of love may indeed provide the key to the transformation we so urgently need at this historical moment. We can shift from the golden rule to the platinum rule, where we listen to others speaking with their own authority and autonomy, about how they are impacted....

We must rise up in this creative moment, to address the deeper systemic concerns, and seize the opportunity of the interfaith movement as an umbrella for the collective influence of the many religions, which are among the largest multinational organizations in the world. Our challenges cannot be solved on the level on which they were created and there is never enough to satisfy greed. We can focus on the primal needs that peace requires: clean water, women's rights, food sovereignty, and health. We can trust that love and spirit will augment our efforts beyond our limited vision.

about LIFTING UP

Selected from

Call to Love in Action

by Jonathan Granoff

This is a call to all who love the planet and all its inhabitants. Let us together bring love into action.

This is a call to bring that love that has no borders, that emerges from the heart and soul, into personal, local, national and global action.

Love is a power and source, easily understood yet forever deep and mysterious. Its profound ability to open meaning, heal, awaken insight, and gift life with grace is beyond any measurements. It is priceless and cannot be bought or sold.

Love is real, essential, powerful, and supreme. When awakened it can change everything.

Whether we effectively address crushing poverty, adequately organize ourselves to protect the global commons such as the oceans, the climate, and the rainforest — living systems upon which civilization depends — and eliminate nuclear weapons before they eliminate us, defines not only what our destiny will be. These issues determine whether we even have a destiny.

Globalization reminds us that we are in fact one human family and the living ecosystem of the planet is our shared home. We cannot find security by attempting to dominate each other, nor by trying to dominate nature. Learning to live in harmony with each other and nature is not an ideal; it is both a moral and practical imperative.

We can change the entire way nations act by demanding that every person running for office answer these questions. How they are answered will impact every life, every family, every nation, and every community.

If several billion people demand answers to these questions, the political actions of the nations of the world will change.

What are your plans to address crushing poverty and ensure sustainable livelihoods and productive, just employment?

What are your plans to protect the global commons such as the oceans, the climate, and the rainforests — the living systems upon which all civilization depends?

What are your plans to eliminate nuclear weapons?

If we answer these questions correctly, our responsibilities to generations to come will be fulfilled. This is an authentic expression of love in action. We ask you to share this Call to Bring Love Into Action!

about OPENING UP

Selected from

The Power of Love

by Llewellyn Vaughan-Lee

UNITY EARTH holds the essential vision that we are one living, interconnected ecosystem, a living Earth that supports and nourishes all of its inhabitants. If we acknowledge and honor this simple reality, we can begin to participate in the vital work of healing our fractured and divisive world, and embrace a consciousness of oneness that is part of our spiritual heritage. Whether we speak of the *unio mystica* of the Christian mystics, the *unity of being* of the Sufis, or *the unity of existence* of the Upanishads, we are recognizing a primal truth that is at the foundation of all of life: spiritually and physically we are One Being.

Oneness is not a metaphysical idea but something essential and ordinary. It is in every breath, in the wing-beat of every butterfly, in every piece of garbage left on city streets. This oneness is life, life no longer experienced solely through the fragmented vision of the ego, though the distortions of our culture, but known within the heart, felt in the soul. This oneness is the heartbeat of life. It is for each of us to live and celebrate this oneness, to participate in its beauty and wonder. And through our awareness, and actions born of this awareness, we can help to reconnect our world with its original nature.

Love will remind us that we are a part of life, that we belong to each other and to this living, suffering planet. Love will reconnect us to the sacred ways known to our ancestors, as well as awaken us to new ways to be with each other and the Earth. We just need to say "yes" to this mystery within our own hearts, to open to the link of love that unites us all, that is woven into the web of life. And then we will uncover the love affair that is life itself, and hear the song of unity as it comes alive in our hearts and in the heart of the world.

REFLECTIONS

The Role of Imagination in Global Transformation

by Victor H. Kazanjian Jr.

When I was a boy, I used to love to lie on the ground, close my eyes, feel the earth beneath me, and imagine — imagine what was below me, imagine who or what walked in that very place before me, imagine the round ball floating in space upon which I was lying. Then I would look up at the sky, into the blue, and imagine — imagine all that was happening above me, that collage of birds, clouds, the sun, the stars, the vast expanse of interstellar space. Often my imagining was met with messages that I needed to stop wasting my time with such frivolous thoughts, that I needed to grow up, put aside all this daydreaming and focus on more serious things, more practical things. And so I did, sort of, well not really. I pretended to focus on more serious things, but actually I never stopped lying on the ground, looking up at the sky and imagining.

As I grew up, I heard others talk about using their imaginations as a source of transformation. I heard Dr. King talk about having a dream and imagining a world of peace with justice from his vantage point on the mountaintop. I heard Rigoberta Menchu Tum of Guatemala speak about using the imagination to break the mental bonds of colonialism and oppression and reclaim one's own indigenous power. I remembered Albert Einstein's words that "the true sign of intelligence was not knowledge but imagination." I read Black Elk's vision that he had as a child of standing on the highest mountain of them all, and round about beneath him was the whole hoop of the world where all lived together like one being. I thought about Nelson Mandela, in that cold prison cell night after night, imagining a new South Africa, and the pathways to get there. I listened to Elise Boulding, grandmother of Peace Studies, who promoted imagination as the most powerful tool we have to envision the peaceful future that we desire. And I continue to hear my sister, Valarie Kaur, tell us that revolutionary love requires imagination so that we can envision the struggles of our present reality not as the darkness of the tomb, but as the darkness of the womb ready to birth new consciousness and new actions into our broken world.

The wisdom offered to us from indigenous, religious, spiritual and humanistic traditions calls us to use our imaginations to envision a healed, whole humanity and planet. We are invited to use our imaginations to remove ourselves from that which constrains our minds, our bodies and our souls — to be free from the chains that others have placed on us and to free ourselves from the chains that we have placed on ourselves, chains that limit and distort our imagination and its ability to transform our world.

There is a picture on the wall of my office sent to me by a friend who was an astronaut. It is a picture that she took from the space shuttle, which she was piloting — a picture of the Earth from deep in space. Perhaps you have seen something similar; the blue, green

Earth, a perfectly round ball floating in an infinite sea of black. It is a magnificent image, so beautiful, so peaceful, so serene.

Gazing upon that image, it seems unfathomable that upon that beautiful sphere moving through the universe, its inhabitants are locked in a life and death struggle with each other. From thousands of miles up in space one is free from the sounds and stench of war and violence, injustice and oppression that plague the peoples of this planet. Reading the daily news, rife with stories of violence, death and destruction, one perhaps yearns for such distance from the suffering below.

But if this was our only view of humanity, as an observer from so far away, we would be unaware that on this same planet, amidst the violence and suffering, there is life and love, beauty and possibility. In India and Pakistan, in Iran and the United States, in Uganda and Nigeria, in Argentina and Chile, in the Philippines and Indonesia, in Australia and New Zealand, between Palestinian and Israeli families, people of different backgrounds and identities are engaging in acts of compassion and kindness. In each of these places, people are falling in love and forming friendships. And in each of these places, people of different beliefs are gathering to deepen their understanding of each other, to forge bonds of relationship and to work together to create cultures of peace, justice and healing in their communities. In my work with the United Religions Initiative, I witness this on a daily basis. I see firsthand the vast numbers of people participating in global transformation by making their imagined reality come to life.

I am not a pollyannic person. I am a descendent of genocide, the Armenian Genocide. I grew up aware of the horrors that human beings can inflict upon each other by learning about other genocides including slavery, the Holocaust, Cambodia, Rwanda and the systematic oppression and attempted extermination of Indigenous Peoples and their cultures throughout the world. I was also awakened to the systematic and ongoing injustices and oppressions that continue to devastate the lives of people of color, women, religious minorities and the LGBTQ community. And I weep that too often religion is used to justify these atrocities or obscure their existence. This is the ground in which my imagination is rooted, ground that has also been watered by rivers of tears, tears of both sadness and joy.

My Armenian grandfather used to tell me that sadness and joy were sisters. One is never without the other, and together they offer a life worth living. Here was a man who had experienced the depths of human cruelty and emerged with a belief that the possibility for the healing of humankind lay in the potential of the imagination to inscribe on the hearts and in the minds of human beings a vision of a transformed world and to equip them with the tools to attain it.

Every day, I am inspired by those around me whose imagination, vision and actions are transforming our world in a positive way. I see this transformation as connecting us to "the wholeness that is at the heart of humanity" (as Dr. Howard Thurman so beautifully taught), a wholeness which honors the diversity of human experience and the natural world as it also points to that which we share in common. It is the awakening of this desire for wholeness, within one's self, in one's relationships, among human communities and in all of creation that is the essential task of all who seek global transformation.

"We all flow from one fountain Soul," the great naturalist John Muir wrote. "All are expressions of one love… flowing… in grand undivided currents, shoreless and boundless over all creeds and forms and all kinds of civilizations, peoples and creatures, saturating all..." In his wanderings through the wilderness in the United States and

Canada, Muir discovered a diversity of land and life inconceivable to those whose perspective was limited by place and circumstance. And as he gazed upon that world, he saw both the beauty of the particularity of things, and also a wholeness connecting one thing to another, and he proclaimed, "The power of our imagination makes us infinite." Now that is a powerful invitation for our work of global transformation.

Selected from

The Unity Earth Convergence at the Toronto Parliament

by Brian McLaren

It feels like humanity is at an adolescent stage these days. In the US, we elect a Barack Obama and then a Donald Trump. Europeans create the EU and open borders, and then Brexit happens and there's talk of the whole thing crashing down.

I work in the world of religion, and I think you can take the adolescent formula and multiply it by ten or twenty. Members of a religion can act like they're living in 2120 or 2220 one day, and the next, other members of the same religion act like they're living in 1820 or 1920.

I believe religion at its best works as a culture's moral imagination. It asks, "What kind of world is possible next? What are our next steps to grow toward that better world?" This is a progressive, prophetic, or evolutionary way of understanding religion.

Something is happening among us in this progressive multi-faith movement. We are like a vanguard within each faith community, and we are hearing the same message and "singing the same song."

Visionary, creative, progressive leaders across traditions are coming together as never before. We are discovering a common vision of a future defined by the common good and undergirded by common values. We envision each of our traditions transitioning to a new phase of maturity in which we are neither enemies nor competitors to one another, but neighbors, colleagues, and friends. We each bring unique treasures to the table, treasures our counterparts need, just as we need the treasures they bring. We are finding ways of being genuinely ourselves while at the same time welcoming and appreciating one another.

It is time for us to unite our collective wisdom to determine what the progressive multi-faith movement needs at this urgent moment. Human civilization is going through a turbulent adolescence. People like you and me, as creative and forward-leaning leaders rooted deeply in many faith traditions, can embody maturity, wisdom, and generosity. This is our calling. This is our privilege — at this turning point in history.

Endnotes and References for "History" Section[iii]

TOWARDS A GLOBAL ETHIC

extending the theme of the 2018 Parliament of the World's Religions

Dr. Ashok Gangadean of the World Commission on Global Consciousness and Spirituality and Margaret Gest Professor of Global Philosophy at Haverford College, Pennsylvania, USA — noted throughout the above commentaries on the Parliament and its interspiritual discussions with Br. Teasdale and other interspiritual pioneers — writes below on the theme of the 2018 Parliament: Towards a Global Ethic. The Feature below is written with Dr. Gangadean's noted "Dimensional Markers," as in /Monologue/ to ((Dialogue)), etc. These enhance deeper nuances and meanings within the text. The "single strokes" (also called "single brackets")- /X/ mark when thought, language, script, mentation, rationality are lodged in /monocentric/ "I===It" space; and, the "double brackets"- ((X)) mark when one makes the crossing into the more evolved ((Integral, Holistic, Dialogic: I===Thou Literacy)). The difference and relation between these two contrasting "dimensions" of literacy and mental processing add an extra dimension of profundity to the narrative if the reader can read with that depth of attention.

((Evolutionary Emergence)) of ((Global Ethics))

by Ashok Gangadean

The Emergence of ((Global Ethics)) inaugurates a ((dimensional)) shift to an unprecedented access to the long sought for ((Source Code)) governing all forms of life. As we shall now see this evolutionary breakthrough of the ((Primal Foundation)) of ((Moral Life)) beyond all /borders/ and localized "ethical" narratives is just one ((co-expression)) of astounding disclosures of ((Global First Philosophy)). Please note at the outset that I use this "((…))" Source Code Technology ((Notation)) as a constant re-minder in our current ((Meditation of Global Ethics)). As our Meditative Narrative unfolds it will become increasingly clear why our Inter-dimensional ((shift)) to the mental processing of ((Source Life)) is the technology of ((Global Ethics)).

The Missing Code of ((Global Ethics))

The 2,500 + years of innovative explorations of diverse First Philosophies (First Narratives) on a Planetary scale, East, West and Other converge on a frontier quest for the long missing yet ever emerging and presiding "Code" of What is ((First)). Our revered First Narratives (including Scriptures), now seen in a ((Global Light)), have arrived at an ((inflection point)) of a Primal ((Source Science)) which governs all aspects of our Human Condition. Our deepest ((meditation)) on ((What is First)), by whatever ((Name)), reveals that Primal Being (the Field of Reality) is Boundless and ((Infinite)) hence the ((Source)) of all. Nothing can "be" outside of ((Infinite Being)), ((Infinite Presence)), and all possible forms of life are thus ever sustained and funded by ((Infinite Source)). This is the foundation of the Presiding ((Moral Law)), of ((Global Ethics)), and all Humans exist and live under the Jurisdiction of this ((Source Science)).

((Global Wisdom)) Emerges with Our Dimensional Shift to ((Source Code))

Crossing into the ((Space)) of ((Global Ethics)) becomes accessible only when the ((Mind operating Technology)) of the ((Source Code)) is activated. For millennia, the perennial call of ((What is First)) and our great First Narratives responded relentlessly with brilliant innovations as our First Responders gravitated to our ((Infinite Source)). However, when we stand back in a ((Global Light)) it becomes clear that our best efforts were hitting an "invisible barrier" as they converged towards the threshold of ((Source Life)). What was missing was the ((Source Technology)), the ((Source Code)), the mind-operating access code that dilates the ((portal)) to ((Infinite Presence)). This is the ((Ethos)) of ((Global Ethics))…The ((Ethics)) of ((Source Life Minding)).

In the context of ((Global First Philosophy)), it becomes clear that the supreme ((technology)) is the technology of how we Humans conduct our minds, the mind-operating or "mentation process" in metabolizing Reality. It makes all the difference in the World (and a World of Difference) how we process Reality and co-create our lives, our experience, our life worlds, our technology of life-making (world-making). It becomes clear in the space of ((Global Reason)) that our mind-operating processing is where the Ethics of Being Human originates. And if and when our all-important mind-operating code is impaired, derivative and severs us from ((Source Life)), our lives suffer deep dysfunctions and existential pathologies individually and collectively.

Our Historic Breakthrough to ((Source Code)): ((Portal to Presence))

What, then, is the ((Source Code))? What is the relevance of the conduct of our minds to ((Global Ethics))? What is the alleged "invisible barrier" in gaining intimate ((access)) ((Being)), to What-is-First, to ((Source Life))? And why ((speak)) of ((Source Science))? Why is the perennial ((quest)) of diverse "First Philosophies" a quest for the missing ((First Science)) of all "sciences"?

These ((queries)) have been explored in great depth over recent decades in a range of ((public performances)). But on this occasion, given a compressed ((space and time)) let's remain ((focused)) on this unprecedented ((birthing)) of ((Global Ethics)), the vital ((foundation)) of diverse "ethical narratives."

End of the Age of Code Chaos and Code Conflation: Ethics as Right Mentation

When we stand back and dilate our ((Global Lens)) to ((review)) the range of our diverse narratives of "Ethics" on a planetary scale through the ages it becomes strikingly clear that the heart of "ethics" turns on how we are using (conducting) our minds, our consciousness, our rational intelligence, our processing of Reality. **Let's call this the process of "mentation**." In this context, it becomes clear that our deepest form of "conduct" or life "practice" is our conduct of mentation. We humans as "rational beings" are gifted with the power to use our wills in co-processing our lives, our experience, our life-worlds, our living realities. This is why how we conduct our mentation is all-important in the meaning and significance of the content of our lives. We ARE as we mind. And if our mentation code eclipses, represses, or severs us from a healthful intimacy with ((Source Life)), we suffer wide ranging existential dysfunctions and human pathologies individually and collectively.

Mentation Code Is All-important in Moral Value

The historic introduction of a **missing ((code notation))** to end the "code chaos," to end the pernicious and chronic "code conflation" syndrome is of supreme value in our journey to ((Source Ethics)), our journey to the existential maturation of ((Being Human)), our journey to ((Global Ethics)).

To bring this code breakthrough to ((light)), let's pause for a moment and sample a few highly revered classical Narratives of Ethics through the ages.

Some Samples of Pre-Code Narratives of Ethics

Socrates and Plato: Ethics of Logos (Source of Life and Rational Light)

Looking back to classical Greek origins of the discourse of Ethics in the formative teachings of Socrates and Plato, we find Socrates (through Plato) calling on humans to exit the caves of ignorance of everyday culture and make the crossing out of the "cave" in to the Light of Logos in the urgent call to "Know Thy Self." And Plato (in the character of Socrates), in his historic *Republic* dialogue, pioneers the path to Wisdom in quest of "Justice" to the Primal Logos, the universal Light of Reason, the Form of all "forms." The light of rational enlightenment which is the foundation of truth and knowledge, and Goodness Itself. Logos is the ultimate First Principle, the source of all Being, Truth, Wisdom deeper than "knowledge." And Plato famously declared that until such Wisdom presides in the society there will be no Justice in the Polis. So, what is this profound "shift" from our everyday caves of ignorance into the Source Light of Logos at the heart of Ethics?

Buddha's Meditative Ethics: Call for Detachment from "Self"

Let's look Eastward to the historic breakthrough of Buddha's Enlightenment Ethics. Buddha was trained in Vedic Yoga Science but was moved by the existential suffering of the people to probe deeply into the existential cause of widespread existential suffering. His world shifting breakthrough in his Enlightenment was meditatively ((seeing)) into the medical depths of human suffering. In effect, his breakthrough in the articulation of the Four Noble Truths turned on the malpractice in mentation. His meditative ethics called upon all humans to become "mindful," to "mind our minding" and make the profound shift to the Primal Space of Being which was beyond the customary mentation habits and addictions and attachment to beings, things, separately existing units.

When we shift our "mentation" to Buddha Dharma (Right Minding) we humans rise to a higher form of Life in the Buddha Dharma (Infinite Moral Law) which is the human space of Wellbeing and Personal Flourishing. When we "let go" of Ego, Self, and entities, and rise meditatively into the Unified Field of ((Emptiness)). But what is this "shift?" What is "meditative mentation?" Is letting go of "Ego life" the key?

Aristotle's Virtue Ethics: Cultivation of Right Reason and Practical Wisdom (Phronesis)

Let's turn now to Aristotle and Kant. Aristotle, the protege of Plato, articulated a profoundly important Narrative of Ethics where he picks up from his teacher in declaring that "All things aim at The Good," the

Light of Reason. And Ethics, Practical Wisdom for humans (rational beings) turns on cultivating a moral life of "virtue" which performs practical actions with "practical wisdom" according to principles of Right Reason, Phronesis, which is the key to Moral Virtue (Moral Excellence). Here, too, the moral value (meaning) of an act turns upon the principle or moral standard or motive that "produces" the conduct. The moral significance of an action is not found in the external "behavior" (severed from the mentation) but traces to the moral motive of the agent, the virtue of "mentation" according to Practical Wisdom. So here, too, Moral Value turns upon the "mentation" or rational code that governs any conduct in consideration.

Kant's Quest for the Foundation of Ethics: The Moral Person

As we now focus on Kant's historic advances to the "Fundamental Principle of the Metaphysics of Morals," we see even more clearly that the essence of Moral Worth, flowing from Good Will, turns upon the sole motive of Reverence for the Moral Law, the motive of acting from Duty moved by a Good Will. Kant sought (in the rational space of First Philosophy) to uncover the ultimate foundation of Moral Law and Good Will. Briefly, Kant saw that the "Moral Person," acting from "Good Will," is not the "self" of the everyday ego-based human, is not the subjective "will" of the empirical self.

Kant saw that the "Free Will," Moral Agency, flows from the higher "Self" beyond everyday empirical life and culture and psychological interests and motives. Human psychological desires and quest for happiness are irrelevant to Ethical performance, Good Will and Moral Worth. The moral value of an ethical "act" lies solely in the mentation of Duty, reverence for the ultimate moral law. So, again, we find the source of moral worth and legitimacy of ethical performance traces to the performance of a Good Will acting from a higher Moral Self ever honoring the motive of reverence for the Law. The Moral Being (First Person) is NOT the everyday "self" but a primary legislative participant in a Moral Community where each Person embodies Intrinsic Value, a Sacred Polis, wherein a Moral Rational Being is never to be "objectified" and treated as a means to subjective ends. So here, too, we find a profound "shift" from everyday empirical culture and life to a deeper Moral Dimension where Autonomous Agents form a Sacred Polis.

Lord Krishna: Vedic Science and the Meditative Ethics of Yoga

The Yogic Ethics introduced in the *Bhagavad Gita* provide still another powerful exemplar of how deep meditative First Philosophy (Vedic Science) calls for a radical detachment from everyday life and personal (ego-based) identity and objectified "action." Vedic First Philosophy, grounded in meditative technology of mentation, reveals that Reality (Infinite Being) is the Primal Unified Field (Brahman, AUM), the living foundation of Mindful Yogic Action. Lord Krishna, the Voice of Infinite Presence, AUM, coaches the existentially paralyzed warrior Arjuna, the everyday human facing an inevitable mora life crisis on detaching from mentation addictions and practices that alienate the everyday person from direct intimate access to Source Life in communion (Yogic Mentation) with Infinite Presence.

This meditative ethics insists on a profound shift from the mentation of everyday alienated life to the liberated and healthful meditative mentation of awakened Yogic Performance. Yogic Action is profoundly flowing with the Unified (non-dual) Field of Infinite Brahman which medically ends the existential alienation and suffering that emanates from the fragmenting mention of pre-Yogic Moral

Action. Again, this radical shift from everyday pre-critical life to a Mindful Mentation of Integral Yogic Moral Performance turns upon a radical upgrade in the technology of mentation. This mentation shift echoes the kind of mentation shift called for in Buddha's Dharma Ethics wherein everyone encodes the Buddha Self. But how are we to process and understand the nature of this all-important mentation shift? This is the threshold of ((Global Ethics)).

Christ Ethics: Logos in the Flesh

Finally, still another exemplar of a Moral Teaching in the Judeo-Christian Biblical tradition is the emergence of Christ Ethics in the context of the perennial quest for intimacy with What-is-First, with our Infinite Life Source. Interestingly, in the opening of *John's Gospel*, he makes still another vital step towards the birthing of Global Ethics. He moved from the Judaic First Name, Yahweh, to the Greek "Logos" announcing that "In the Beginning is the Word (Logos)," the Word was with "God." The Word was God...and the Word becomes Flesh in the Christ.

In this Narrative of the Life of Jesus as Christ, it becomes clear that something profound emerges in the Living embodiment of our Infinite Source. Jesus models and teaches a Living Principle of Christ Ethics. When Jesus (as Christ) "speaks" "I am the Way, the Truth and the Life" this is a higher form of Christ Speech in Communion with Infinite Source. Everyday humans are lodged in "sin," existential alienation and separation from Infinite Source, in this case the Logos. The "path" to Christ Being, the embodiment of Source Love, liberates fallen humans into Risen Beings in communion with Logos. In Living the Ethics Law of Christ Love, sinners are transformed from existential "death" to Risen Life. In some sense, we must "die" to be Born Again.

So entering into Christ Ethics calls for a radical shift from everyday "alienated life" (and mentation) to a higher Life in communion with Infinite Source. How, again, are we to "understand" this radical shift to Living the Christ Principle, the Logos Moral Law?

From Code Chaos to the Missing ((Source Code)): Historic Clarification of ((.../.../...)) Codes

These selected diverse classical Ethical Narratives are each magnificent, and there are so many more we might have included. Great as they are, is it clear what they may have in "common"? They are so diverse and held apart in relative /silos/ so it is not readily ((apparent)) whether they all spring from a fundamental ((Global Moral Law)). Yes, they all call for a certain profound "transformation" in how we use our minds or conduct our actions. But it is not at all clear that they are all calling for a "switch" or "upgrade" in our mind operating "code" called for by a Fundamental or Ultimate Global ((Source Code)).

The Meditative Ethics of Buddha and Yoga Vedic Ethics call for a mindful meditative life. It is not clear that the diverse narratives of Plato, Aristotle, Kant or Christ Ethics flow from a shared fundamental ((Source Law)). Indeed, the diverse First Narratives through the ages have their own signature (so to speak) and have been taught and received within a pervasive "code chaos" and Code Conflation which renders them in /silos/ that eclipses access to the ((possibility)) of a deeper ((Source Science)) and common Foundational ((Moral Code)).

And the historical evidence in a ((Global Context)) shows that there were no explicit "code markers" to make explicit the fundamental ((transformation)) from a derivative /Code of Life/ to a fundamental ((Source Code Technology)) in mentation. Instead, the enterprise of First Philosophy itself remained stalled facing diverse /silos/ and multiplicity lodged in deep "code chaos" and the chronic "Code Conflation" syndrome. Thus, the "Age of Code Conflation."

In my ((journey)) as a Global First Philosopher over decades living in and through our widely diverse First Narratives and Scriptures of What-is-First, I was guided to introduce innovative "Code Markers" (Explicit Onto-Logical Notation) to bring into the open as never before Alternative Code Mentation Technology markers to move beyond the inhibiting /silos/ that artificially kept our diverse First Narratives apart.

The ((breakthrough)) came with the simple, almost obvious recognition that ((Infinite Source)) by whatever "name" MUST be Infinitely ((One)) and thus the ((Ultimate Fundamental Generative Source)) of all possible Words, Worlds, Scripts, Cultures, Religions, Ideologies, Forms of Life and First Narratives. Indeed, it is an obvious ((Axiom)) of First Philosophy that ((What-is-Frist)) Being Infinite, Source of All, Infinitely Unifying, beyond any and all /fragmentation/, /divisions/, /silos/…had to ((be)) of a deeper ((dimension)) of any and all /derivative/ forms of life.

This, of course, is not the occasion to go in depth into this Inter-Code breakthrough. This exploration has been presented in various publications over the past decades. Suffice it to say in this highly compressed narrative space that this ((breakthrough)) to the long missing yet ever emerging ((Source Code)) came with the recognition that diverse First Narratives could not be lodged in /silos/ but HAD to be generative expressions from the ((Infinite Source Code)). Let this ((opening)) be a ((Prelogue)) to the forthcoming ((Sequel: Part II)) that answers the above ((queries)) in greater depth. So, let's part for now with the following consideration: Can you find any ((consensus call)) amongst the above "samples of ethics" in our journey to ((Global Ethics))?

Please join us in the forthcoming ((Sequel)) in this series' Volume 3.

Continuing our commentary, the Science and Nonduality Conference (SAND) at this same time echoed the same landscape of "inclusion" in the context of the spiritual traditions and science. And its content helps us make the turn to Ecospirituality. Whether it is in the nexus of the interspiritual work of Br. Wayne Teasdale, Fr. Thomas Keating and their global colleagues, and that of Teasdale's colleague at Fordham University, eco-theologian Fr. Thomas Berry — or the iconic explanations of Joseph Campbell on the archetypal understanding of Earth as "Mother" — we see this turn toward "Gaia" both in science and within the World's Religions.

The theme for SAND was "Living Transformation," and Kurt Johnson, a regular speaker at SAND, spoke on "Recent Major Shifts in Science and Religion Change the Basic Underpinnings of 'Living Transformation.'"[1] From his presentation:

> The global context of "living transformation" took several historic, albeit *hopeful*, turns in 2015. These promise to develop pivotally from that year on. In 2015, Pope Francis addressed the United Nations and the US Congress. He joined more heads of state at the UN than had ever attended, just as the UN adopted a revised millennial development agenda.
>
> Francis's Papal Encyclical "On the Care of Our Common Home" [*Laudato Si'*] was a direct response to conclusions by mainstream science that climate change

is both real and threatening. Further, the encyclical poignantly addressed its myriad social implications. Soon after, global institutions moved down "the road to Paris" for 2015 World Climate Summit.

This coincides with a huge turnabout in science — the emergence of a new dominant paradigm in evolutionary biology heralded by a January 13, 2015, book from Yale University Press: Templeton's "Foundational Questions in Science" series. In *Does Altruism Exist? Culture, Genes and the Welfare of Others* ("DAE"), David Sloan Wilson elaborates science's conclusion that "group-" and "multi-level-" natural selection are real, and that they select for structures and processes that serve the well-being of the whole and not self-interest groups.

The new science states, in the words of Wilson and his colleague E. O. Wilson (Harvard University's father of modern sociobiology), "Selfishness beats altruism within groups. Altruistic groups beat selfish groups. Everything else is commentary." The implications are huge.

If, when it comes to groups, nature prefers structures and processes that serve the whole, there is — as Wilson further explains — no mystery why our world is sinking in a load of dysfunctional organizational principles. Further, if in fact nature is not only friendly to altruism, but prefers it, perhaps social idealists of all kinds, perhaps sacred and secular activists have *not*

> been swimming upstream against an uncaring or cruel evolutionary process as the decades-long mantras of the selfish gene and Social Darwinism would have had us believe.[2]

Following soon was the September 8–10, 2018, second Crestone Leadership Conference. It was subsequent to the larger 2017 Crestone gathering detailed hitherto. These conferences, also billed as "Convergences" of the UNITY EARTH community, followed on two years of UN Forum 21 Institute and partners' sponsoring a series of conferences on "Spirituality and Sustainability" in Rome and Assisi, Italy.[3]

Diversity and the Global Ethic

Movement towards a global ethic has diverse elements. And, they occur across both space and time. Revelations and epiphanies in current time elicit echoes from the same movements of the heart ages ago — what is in the *perennial heart* of our species. This is a part of "living transformation" — looking both ways. The sense of "care for our common home" elicits new senses of justice, new actions toward "putting things right" — the task of truly transcending *and* including. The very entreaty of *Laudato Si'* brings with it reminders of the heinous injustices of the Doctrine of Discovery. Basking in promises of new energy for a flourishing human future educes the echoes of Hiroshima and Nagasaki. Thus the harkening of our world's most forward wisdom with reverberations of the deepest wisdoms from our past. Today's welcome, and long overdue, attention to the wisdom of First Peoples and foundational cultures — our collective "original instructions" — is part of that. We have a tremendous opportunity to join them, here and now. We close our ears at our own peril.

The region around Crestone, Colorado, is a renowned "Peace Site" and sacred shared land and shared aquifer for Western American Indigenous Peoples. Joining to lead the second Crestone Conference were indigenous leaders Mindahi Bastida Muñoz, Tiokasin Ghosthorse, and others from Bio-Cultural Sacred Site initiatives featured by Light on Light's e-publication *Sacred Sites and Spirituality in Nature* following soon after the Toronto Parliament, in early 2019. It also became the base location for Sacred Sites ceremonies carried out for the historic "Four Corners" area of the Southwest United States.[4]

Reflecting interspiritual underpinning for this of Sacred Sites and First Peoples, activities were widely supported by foundations representing emerging new movements in Eastern traditions, like Sukyo Mahikari and its United Nations NGO under Evolutionary Leaders Circle member Ken Kitatani — another Contribution Author in these Volumes. Here we can set the stage for further linking the thematics of Ecospirituality and Gaia-related science with our many contributions in these Volumes from First Peoples.

Let's begin by sharing the meeting of Mindahi Bastida Muñoz with Pope Francis in 2018, facilitated through the previously cited Rome-Assisi conferences.[5]

The Annual **Rome-Assisi Conferences on Spirituality and Sustainability** and meeting of Mindahi Bastida Muñoz with Pope Francis, 2018

Mindahi Bastida Muñoz - Ken Kitatani - Richard Clugston

The purpose of these annual conferences is to bring together visionary people from a range of ecological-spiritual perspectives, centers, and movements. Participants dialogue about transformative global change based on spirituality and sustainability. They also identify key recommendations for creating a spiritual and sustainable global future.

The Conference draws inspiration from eight previous Assisi conferences in the 1990s featuring Thomas Berry. It also draws inspiration from St. Francis and St. Clare, from the papal encyclical on ecology *Laudato Si'*, from the Earth Charter, and from the work of leaders in spirituality and sustainability.

Mindahi Bastida Muñoz traveled by invitation to the Vatican to attend a conference organized by Cardinal Turkson titled "Saving Our Common Home and the Future of Life on Earth." The conference brought together indigenous and young activists, scientific experts, religious leaders, and Vatican officials to assess the impact of Francis' 2015 encyclical "Laudato Si' on Care for Our Common Home." While there, Mindahi was able to meet Pope Francis and hand deliver a letter to him.[6]

The letter requested the following:

1. To announce your support for our initiative to protect and restore sacred sites in the world
2. To give back to Indigenous Peoples the sacred objects and artifacts that are in possession of the Vatican and to support our demand to Nation States in this regard
3. To rescind the historical Papal Bulls, affecting Indigenous Peoples' lives and territories

You can read the full letter below:

The Spirit is love

Protection of Sacred Sites in the World

Indigenous Peoples around the World are the caretakers of Mother Earth. It is the time of the New Dawn, it is time for the acknowledgement of their biocultural wisdom to protect life, and we need to pay respect to their spiritual and material sustainable practices.

Biocultural diversity and biocultural heritage are related concepts that intertwine culture and biodiversity. In Indigenous Peoples' thoughts and philosophies, culture and biodiversity are interrelated and seen as unity. To be precise, thinking and feeling about the web of life as an interconnection allows us to think and act in a biocultural way of being.

Given the continuous deterioration of life systems of our Mother Earth, it is urgent to restore the most affected places in the world. The Ancestral Sacred Sites play a key role in the restoration of those affected places because Ancestral Sacred Sites are energetic points that elevate the capacity of Mother Earth to restore systemic balance.

Worldwide, Ancestral Sacred Sites are interconnected. This means that they work together energetically and potentiate the capacity of a single Place to restore the balance of a nearby affected area or region. It is through reciprocity and specifically through ancestral rituals (by offerings and payments) that we as Ancestral Spiritual Leaders can accelerate and assure the healing process.

The proposal of biocultural sacred sites for humanity (Spiritual Reserves of Humanity) before UNESCO is crucial when we understand the connection between conservation and spiritual and cultural practices of Indigenous Peoples. We are presenting this initiative in order to strengthen and protect our territories and sacred sites and to mitigate the effects of Climate Change worldwide with emphasis in Indigenous Peoples' Territories.

We kindly request Your Holiness and the Vatican:

1. To announce your support for our initiative to protect and restore sacred sites in the world
2. To give back to Indigenous Peoples the sacred objects and artifacts that are in possession of the Vatican and to support our demand to Nation States in this regard
3. To rescind the historical Papal Bulls, affecting Indigenous Peoples' lives and territories

In gratitude and deep respect,

Indigenous Peoples Representative in the Vatican City, July 4, 2018.
Mindahi Bastida Muñoz (Otomí-Toltec, Mexico)

Continuing our commentary, here we must also note the emergence of the Subtle Activism movement (with its Gaiafield projects and others) which emerged simultaneously with the ecospiritual and First Peoples' initiatives introduced above and previously. Accordingly, we join names of contributors in this short section into the contributors names "word cloud" of the Section on the Wisdom of Indigenous Peoples just below.

In 2014, members of the Interspiritual Dialogue Network — Oscar Miro-Quesada, Kurt Johnson, Roger La Borde, and Diane Berke — hosted a tele-summit call on "The Emerging Inter-Shamanism Inherent in the Emerging Interspiritual Age."[7] An emerging dialogue, cooperation, synergy and co-working, they suggested, would be expected to inevitably arise across persons from the world's shamanic practices (indigenous and other), the varied landscape of "energy work," and the contemplative practitioners that connect with ancestral wisdom keepers of their (and others') traditions.

Br. Teasdale was himself an active part of this conversation, reflected in his comments in *The Mystic Heart.* In fact, nearly fifty members of this Interspiritual Dialogue Network, including many authors and spiritual constituency leaders, had been corresponding, or speaking personally, about this for some time — actually for nearly a half-decade or more — and many had met in person at the Dawn of Interspirituality Conference in 2013. Grand Father White Morning Owl, an associate of Fr. Thomas Keating's First Peoples' colleague Grand Father Gerald Red Elk, described the purpose of this Circle this way:

Grand Father White Morning Owl

> The intention of our circle gatherings is to open ourselves to the understanding and respect of the spiritual journey, the variety of revelations and the transformational powers of each. All evolved souls share a common Compassion. Having awakened Compassion, we are motivated to act Altruistically.
>
> We are all spiritual beings having human experiences. Many of us have been here many times, through millennia. We are actually divine beings, with our feet on the ground and our spirits in eternity. We are also the instruments through which the ultimate reality perceives creation. We actually stand halfway between the microcosm and the macrocosm.

> We are co-creators of this dream as well. At this time in human history, the technology of communication is allowing us to bring together individuals who have experienced higher dimensions and perspectives, through different doorways.
>
> In accessing the people who have come through, or passed through, different doorways — shamans, awakened souls, from a myriad of religions, as well as seekers who were simply "awakened" spontaneously and have no explanation — we discover that none of us has an explanation. It is simply a phenomenon.
>
> Trying to grasp the magnitude and diversity of universal creation with the organizing computers we call our brains is comparable to measuring the ocean with a measuring cup.

In 2015, these groups were afforded the opportunity to share their discussions — some directly, some anonymously — with members of a similar circle formed around the Gaiafield Project founded by Dr. David T. Nicol.[8] Dr. Nicol's book, *Subtle Activism: The Inner Dimension of Social and Planetary Transformation*, in the State University of New York series in Transpersonal and Humanistic Psychology appeared in 2015. The groups were linked together by a rather serendipitous meeting of Sufi Leader Llewellyn Vaughan-Lee, SHIFT Network's Director of Peace, Philip Hellmich, and Kurt Johnson who began discussing this at a 2015 meeting of the Contemplative Alliance at Half Moon Bay, California. Vaughan-Lee suggested these conversations within the Contemplative Alliance be connected with Dr. Nicol's work and his emerging Gaiafield Project. Soon after, at Kurt Johnson's invitation, Nicol and his colleague

David Sun Todd published, in the Sacred Sites issue of *Light on Light Magazine*, "Subtle Activism: Harnessing the Power of Earth's Sacred Sites for Planetary Healing." They summarized:

> David Nicol has called his work "subtle activism," a modern term for an ancient approach. Subtle activism expands the reach of consciousness-based approaches like meditation, ritual and prayer beyond the narrow modern focus on personal growth to the realm of collective planetary healing, realigning spiritual work with ageless wisdom traditions whose intent has always been to serve the whole of life. This approach tends to lead naturally to a recognition in harmony with shamanic knowledge.... and that ceremonial practices conducted in association with these sacred sites have a special power.... In our times, new expressions of subtle and sacred activism are emerging that seek to apply this ancient knowledge of sacred sites to help humanity through its current initiatory crisis.[9]

Additionally, there was much more to emerge from this joining. For two years, every Friday, David Nicol hosted an intimate conference call on subtle activism with Philip Hellmich, Avon Mattison (co-founder of Pathways To Peace), Claudia Welss (now Chair at the Institute of Noetic Sciences), Cynthia Jurs (of the Earth Treasure Vase initiative) and Dr. Leslie Meehan (author of *Our Birth as Holo Sapiens*), along with Kurt Johnson. Collaborations that grew from this included many by Welss and Johnson, who became President of the Friends of the Institute of Noetic Sciences, and, especially between Avon Mattison and the many peace-related projects and international events — like PeaceWeek.org — that were emerging from UNITY EARTH and its constituencies. This circle on subtle activism also produced broadcasts on subtle activism on "The Convergence" VoiceAmerica series hosted by the Interspiritual Dialogue and UNITY EARTH.[10]

Endnotes and References for "Global Ethic" Section[iv]

Let's now take up this discussion — from First Peoples and foundational cultures — to a newly concerted level with this Subtitle:

A Sacred Convergence to Restore Balance
Mother Gaia and the Wisdom of Indigenous Peoples

Featured Authors in these Volumes - DeShannon Barnes-Bowens - Constance Buffalo
Geraldine Patrick Encina - Patricia Anne Davis - Grand Father White Morning Owl
Chief Phil Lane Jr. - Oscar Miro-Quesada - Mindahi Bastida Muñoz - David T. Nicol
Chief Dwaine Perry - Jon Ramer - Brian Russo - David Sun Todd

Our Featured Authors in this section are, respectively, Toltec and Mayan Elders Mindahi Bastida Muñoz and Geraldine Patrick Encina; Choctaw and Dine' / Navajo Elder Patricia Anne Davis; Yankton Sioux Hereditary Chief Phil Lane Jr., Ramapough Lenape Chief Dwaine Perry; Curandero Oscar Miro-Quesada; Ifá-Òrìṣà Iya Rev. DeShannon Barnes-Bowens; and Chippewa Elder Constance Buffalo; with Jon Ramer, co-visioneer of "Solstice Unites" and Brian Russo, the creator of "HALOS." Their Features follow on these Volumes' discussions of global Earth and Gaia issues with a *Roundtable* on the Interspirituality of Original Peoples and Nations in the context of the world's original spiritual and religious traditions. Since this section is structured as a Roundtable, with the contributors speaking to each other, we omit the word "by" in their attributions.

Introduction

Patricia Anne Davis, Jon Ramer, Chief Dwaine Perry[1]

We live in a time of profound chaos and awakening. The fragmentation of truth and a deepening crisis of disconnection threaten our ability to unite around a common purpose. Yet beneath these differences, a deeper, unifying truth calls us home: the sacred relationship with Mother Earth and the elemental forces that sustain life.

You are not separate from nature — you are nature.
Earth is your body.
Water is your blood.
Fire is your energy.
Air is your breath.
The elements are not outside you.
They are you.

Indigenous wisdom teaches that to restore balance, we must honor these forces — not as resources to be exploited, but as living relatives to be respected. This is our common ground: a shared foundation from which we rise.

Awakening Sacred Alignment: Knowing, Speaking & Acting with Purpose

The greatest challenge of our time is not just climate collapse, systemic injustice, or war — it is the widespread sense of *powerlessness* that convinces us change is beyond reach. As Otto Scharmer describes, *the future is not shaped by old patterns, but by our capacity to sense and co-create what is yet to come.*

Five Shifts for Sacred Alignment

A call to reorient how we know, see, and act — grounded in wisdom, wholeness, and responsibility across generations.

1. Know through ourselves, not just about ourselves – Access wisdom that moves through us, guided by the interconnected field of life.
2. See through the eyes of the whole – Move beyond personal perspective to perceive through our shared humanity and planetary kinship.
3. Unlock new pathways – Discover possibilities that arise when we release habitual thinking and open to emergence.
4. Embody our role in Earth's evolution – Recognize ourselves as stewards and co-creators of a regenerative future.
5. Commit to intergenerational regeneration – Act with the awareness that our choices ripple through time, shaping life for future generations.

A Call to Co-Create the Future

To embody this wisdom and activate as a movement of renewal, we commit to:

- Weaving Collective Wisdom – Creating spaces where shared insight transcends individual viewpoints.
- Expanding Perception – Designing experiences that dissolve separation and reveal our deep interconnection.

- Activating Evolving Potential – Cultivating the conditions for bold, regenerative solutions to take root.
- Empowering Sacred Agency – Awakening a shared sense of purpose and responsibility in all who gather.
- Focusing on Intergenerational Impact – Ensuring our work honors and benefits the next seven generations.

Through this work we step into a *Sacred Convergence*, where purpose and possibility align. In ceremony and solidarity, we reclaim our role as caretakers of the Earth, protectors of the elements, and co-creators of a just and regenerative future.

Together, we rise.
Together, we awaken.
Together, we restore.

ROUNDTABLE

Spirituality of Original Peoples and Nations In the context of the world's spiritual traditions and religions

Mindahi Bastida Muñoz

The spirituality of Original Nations and Peoples is based on the sacred relationship with nature and the cosmos. The spiritual practices acknowledge the movement of celestial bodies, seasons and also the ecosystems.

The acknowledgement of the Great Spirit in every manifestation of Life is key to the practices of these Peoples and cultures.

In general, the four sacred elements: the fire, the air, the water and the earth, are meaningful in the tangible and intangible realms. The reverence to these sacred elements is always key in the spiritual practices. Another aspect is the notion of time and space as a unit, manifested in diversity. Time is very relevant because in the cycles of the manifestation of life through the seasons, different rituals are carried out on specific dates, as for the calling of the rain and for the celebration of harvest and other rituals, such as the fires ceremonies.

Regarding space, the spiritual practices acknowledge the sacred landscape, the sacred sites such as volcanoes, springs, tops of mountains, caves, and where the river meets another river or the river meets wetlands, lagoons, caverns, or the sea. The spiritual practices of Original Nations and Peoples are always inclusive to other beings. In this respect, the entities, deities, and spirit guardians are called and acknowledged through prayers, invocations, dances, and songs, but also through offerings and payments. These practices elevate not just the consciousness but the interconnection between the material and the spiritual world. When there are other spiritual manifestations coming from a religious practice, it is very likely that it is acknowledged if the protocol is met.

The spiritual practices of Original Peoples are rooted in principles, the Law of Origin, and ancestral wisdom. When carrying out rituals and ceremonies, the protocol is to acknowledge the ancestors, supernatural entities, and life manifestations that have existed since time immemorial. It's important to ask permission to carry out rituals and ceremonies to the guardians, caretakers, or caregivers of the land, all of which is sacred. Today, the spiritual practices of Original Nations and Peoples are very relevant. Based in ancestral wisdom, they can support life systems and remember who we are as human beings. In other words, we have the chance to practice this spirituality so we can thrive and transcend and come back home.

Today there is a high need for religions and spiritual groups in the world to acknowledge the spiritual authority and the spiritual practices of Original Nations and Peoples, so they can carry out interspiritual and interfaith gatherings, but mostly to acknowledge the sacred relation between humans and nature and the cosmos, where anthropocentric thought is not as important as the relationship directly with the Great Spirit and the manifestations of all beings in the material world. For that, we need to go from the me to the we, where the ego vanishes and we behave, assuming our collective responsibility. We must act responsibly in the web of life, in reciprocity, deep respect, relationship, and responsibility about the care of life. The spiritual practices kept for millennia by Original Nations and Peoples is the key to protect and regenerate life systems. In doing that, we can recover a collective dignity as humans.

We need to serve not just the spiritual, but the material energy. In that way we can celebrate life, with our responsibilities, carrying out ceremonies and rituals to acknowledge and ask for guidance to carry out actions that help recover balance and harmony with nature and the cosmos. The time for unification has come, so we collectively face and address the systemic crisis. This is the time to come in synch with life cycles and acknowledge that we are one in the diversity.[2]

How Original Peoples Live in Their Ecosystems

Geraldine Patrick Encina[3,4]

From a very young age, I was keen on learning more and more about how original peoples in different ecosystems lived in such a way that they would try to do the least harm to their place, where they chose to spend a few years, if necessary. It was so interesting to me to know that people were not needing to force nature to have abundance, and to change the perspective of what it is to be rich, as a person or as a community.

When I was eighteen years old, I met who would become my husband, Mindahi. We met in a gathering that was held in Ecuador. It was held in 1993, a year after the Earth Summit in Rio de Janeiro. What I learned from his words was that this way of living was still possible today — still in the midst of a changing world where modernity and so much of the speed of delivery of things is what keeps people moving. I came to visit him in Mexico soon after.... That stayed in my mind for several years, and that's when I was beginning my PhD studies in a career that I had to create myself at the time — which is very well known today — that is Ethnoecology. As such in Mexico, there was no such career when I started my studies.

So, in this opportunity, I began to make a deep dive into the ancient Mesoamerican calendars and started to unveil what was happening in terms of the calendar.... The list is long, but the studies are going to be able to help people reconnect with their ancestral time-keeping systems and understand what it was that their ancestors were observing in nature and where those ceremonies were meant to happen throughout the year — ceremonies that today, some are still being carried out.... So, there is that aspect. But there's also just the beauty of knowing that when you, as a community, dedicate this time, in ceremony, to honor what nature provides when everything else is enabling.... It's beautiful to understand what your role is and how, when you have done your work.... nature will respond.... There is all of this we can understand from this kind of study, and that is why I've dedicated twenty years of my life to this study.

There is an opportunity today, despite what we might feel in terms of climate change, that we can live according to the cycles of nature

— like, really, really know so much about what is going on with our garden backyard, with our farm, with our pond or lake, in terms of the cycles of nature. And that is why people who are into permaculture.... are definitely one, two, three steps more advanced than other people who opted out of those opportunities back in the day. And it's never too late to actually begin to learn how to read nature in ways that will benefit the way you flow within those cycles. That is basic sense. But, in the same way, we should check in with Mother Nature every single day, every single week, every single month, to get a feeling of whether you are going along with her flow or against her flow.[3]

Visit our work at earthtimekeepers.org to learn much more about the details of this important work. The productions we make are not about religions or gods.... Our project is about the rescue and dissemination of the wisdom of great cultures, about their philosophy of seeing the world, the Universe, of integrating the human being as part of something much bigger. It's about their philosophy and cosmovision of the world, where human beings assume their sacred roles and responsibilities in ensuring the natural unfolding of lifecycles, large and small. The immersive experiences help audiences of all ages connect to their ancestors and remember our original purpose as earthlings....

Our work embraces important sacred sites, located in different parts of the planet, which symbolize the message of the original instructions and the philosophy of good living from the conception of various ancestral cultures. The sacred sites are selected based on their regional and historical importance, accessibility, similarity of paradigms and, above all, on the principles and ways of living of their stewards. They are an inspiration to the rest of humanity that must participate actively in the regeneration of biocultural territories around the world. Join us at earthtimekeepers.org to learn more and be inspired by this work.[4]

The Dawning of a New Global Civilization: The Vision and Understanding of Indigenous Peoples[5]

Hereditary Chief Phil Lane, Jr.

The vision of all ancient prophecies is that a New Global Civilization is inevitable.

A New Global Civilization will be manifested when there is a shared commitment to placing the common good ahead of any national, ethnic, religious, or selfish interests. The full consciousness and acceptance of the Oneness of the Human Family is the fundamental prerequisite for the reorganization and administration of the world as One and to establish peace on earth.

The concept and understanding of the Oneness of Humankind, deeply anchored in all First Nations Teachings, is a spiritual truth that all the human sciences including anthropology, physiology, and psychology now confirm.

This New Global Civilization, in the process of emerging, is only possible when the voices, the wisdom, and the vision of Indigenous Peoples are justly and respectfully represented and whose ancient wisdom is truly heard, understood, and acted upon by all members of the Human Family.

The Vision and Understanding of Indigenous Peoples

The full recognition of this fundamental truth of the Prior Unity and Oneness of our Human Family and All Life, requires the abandonment of prejudice of every kind — race, class, sexual orientation, color, creed, nationality, gender, degrees of material wealth, anything that causes our Human Family to consider themselves superior or inferior to others. Abandoning all prejudice is a great spiritual challenge and requirement for all of us at this critical time of transformation.

The full consciousness and acceptance of the Oneness of the Human Family is the fundamental prerequisite for the reorganization and administration of the world as One, the Home of Humankind. Universal acceptance and realization of this spiritual principle are essential to any successful attempt to establish Peace on Earth.

Prophecies, like Black Elk's, were given when our Indigenous ancestors still rode free on the High Plains of Turtle Island. They plainly trace the advent of a "Hoop of Many Hoops," a "Global Commons" in which all nations, races, creeds, and classes are closely and permanently united in recognizing the Oneness of our Human Family.

The advent of this New Global Civilization was foretold not only by our Indigenous Peoples of the Americas, but, as well, by the Ancient of Days, and many other Faith Traditions Globally.

These prophecies of the Americas include the 2012 Mayan Prophecies, The Reunion of the Condor and the Eagle, the Eighth Counsel Fire, the Return of the White Buffalo, the Prophecies of Black Elk, The Peacemaker, Quetzalcoatl, Sweet Medicine, Handsome Lake, the Hopi, and many others.

The Spiritual Reality of Oneness

The spiritual reality of the Oneness of the Human Family should, therefore, be universally proclaimed, taught in every school, and affirmed in every nation as preparation for fundamental changes in how nation-states function and the systemic structures of our unfolding global society. World peace will only be fully achieved when this spiritual reality of the Oneness of All Life is realized.

These prophecies are firmly and unshakably rooted in the spiritual understanding and consciousness of the Oneness of the Human Family and all Life. From this spiritual understanding and consciousness naturally unfolds the realization of:

The Equality of Men and Women,
The Balancing of the Extremes of Wealth and Poverty,
The Elimination of All Prejudices,
The essential Unity of Science and Spirituality,
Universal Education,
The Independent Investigation of Truth, and
Unity in Diversity.

Keeping the Sacred Fire Burning[6]

Chief Dwaine Perry

It has become a practice for some folks while in public communications, zoom calls, etc., when asked where they are from, to say, "on the land of …" and then the name of the tribal people who inhabited that land prior to the arrival of Europeans and the forced removal or genocide of that people. It seems like a respectful thing to do.

When I was growing up in the fifties, we played "cowboys and indians" and watched western movies where the indians were savages and the really evil villain was the medicine man. As time went on, we began to see Native Americans portrayed with more nuance and then respect and even a kind of idealization. The medicine man we learned is a shaman with access to great wisdom and healing powers. Movies have changed. Lots of attitudes have changed. But the reality of many Native tribes is still quite dire.

The Ramapough are still here in New York and New Jersey, and I live on what was their land. They are struggling to keep their language and customs alive and to preserve the sacredness of what remains of their land, much of which continues to be gobbled up by suburbia and mega-mansions. In recent years, the tribe has fought numerous legal battles just to have the freedom to hold public ceremonies on the small patches of Mother Earth they can still call theirs. These ceremonies have been attended by Native people from all over the world and hundreds of non-Native people in the area (myself included).

The tribe was recognized by the State of New Jersey as the Ramapough Indians in 1980. Their effort to achieve federal recognition was thwarted largely by intense lobbying from, yes, Donald Trump. Trump claimed the Ramapough were not legitimate and would bring waves of crime. Of course, he also feared they would establish a casino that would compete with his own just miles away in Atlantic City. The story of this struggle is told in the film *American Native* (2013).[7]

Over the years, they have dealt with the classic definition of environmental racism. Portions of a toxic waste dump of the Ford Motor Company became the site for affordable housing for many of the Ramapough people. The contamination has been linked to nosebleeds, leukemia, and other ailments. They also have been at the forefront of the battle to stop the Pilgrim Pipeline from carrying gasoline, diesel, kerosene, aviation fluid, and heating oil through their land.

My community and I have a long history of fighting for human rights, today focusing primarily on issues of concern to the Ramapough Munsee nation, decolonization, and the indigenous community at large. I have sat with Elders and indigenous leaders in the Himalayas, the Andes, and throughout North America. My journey to Standing Rock was instrumental in establishing the Split Rock Sweetwater Prayer

Camp in northern New Jersey. I and my community are currently working to establish the first Embassy of Sovereign Indigenous Nations of the Western Hemisphere.

While I sometimes speak sardonically, I am a serious man who, against all odds, seeks to unify people and bring together native and non-native peoples to work together for a kinder humanity, honoring the living Earth and all creatures as sacred. Please visit my various media assets which are endnoted again here.[6]

Taripaypacha: The Prophesied Era of Re-Encounter and our Global Interspiritual Future[8]

Oscar Miro-Quesada

The Essence of Taripaypacha

The Taripaypacha, or Era of Re-Encounter, represents a period of spiritual renaissance and profound reconnection with spiritual truth and ancestral wisdom ways. *Taripay* translates to "to find" or "to encounter," and *Pacha* again signifies "earth, time, space, world, place, realm of consciousness...essentially, a shared experience of Being." Thus, *Taripaypacha* can be understood as the temporal interlude when humanity rediscovers its spiritual roots and chooses to align with inviolate behavioral cosmic principles. This reconnection is not just a historical or cultural event, but a profoundly personal and spiritual journey for each individual.

The Taripaypacha is a time of heightened earth-honoring vision, spiritual awareness, and species-wide communal harmony. During this era, individuals and communities reverently connect with their mythic and genealogical ancestors, mother nature, and our cosmic pleroma. This period is characterized by a resurgence of traditional healing rituals, ceremonial artistry, and general revitalization of indigenous wisdom and cultural values. In pre-Columbian mystical traditions and Andean cosmology, the Taripaypacha is not simply a temporal phase but a multidimensional embodiment of Being and universal consciousness. It involves a profound internal and external transformation, where individuals reconnect with their core luminous essence as cosmically sovereign immortal souls within the collective consciousness of their planetary community.

The Taripaypacha also has significant cultural and societal implications. It is a period when traditional practices and knowledge systems regain prominence, influencing social structures, governance, and family life. The values of sacred reciprocity (*ayni*), respect for nature (*hayñinqaypara sallqa mamapacha*), and communal well-being (*sumaq kawsay*) are re-emphasized, fostering a cohesive and resilient interdependent society.

In contemporary times, the concept of Taripaypacha has gained renewed interest, especially among indigenous movements and scholars advocating for the recognition and preservation of Andean cultural heritage. It resonates with global discourses on sustainability, environmental conservation, and the need for a holistic approach to development.

The resurgence of interest in Taripaypacha also aligns with broader trends of decolonization and the reclamation of indigenous identities. It offers a framework for understanding and addressing modern challenges by drawing on ancient wisdom and practices emphasizing harmony, balance, and interconnectedness.

Taripaypacha and our Global Interspiritual Future

Shamanism's timeless exploration of the imaginal and noetic dimensions of consciousness resonates with eminent expanding human capabilities vitally emerging in our time. Tremendous hope emerges in the expanding capabilities in consciousness afforded by new emerging potentials in scientific technology.

Although shamanism, humanity's oldest spiritual tradition, and generative AI, a leading-edge technological innovation of our time, may seem worlds apart in origin and methodology, both systems are extraordinary tools for accessing vast reservoirs of knowledge, transcending conventional epistemological boundaries, and finding solutions to complex problems. Shamanism employs altered states of consciousness to navigate the imaginal pleroma — a realm where archetypal and noetic dimensions of reality converge. Similarly, generative AI utilizes computational networks capable of exploring and synthesizing information across vast datasets, effectively constructing novel pathways within an algorithmic multiverse. Both mechanisms enable us to access the unknown and bridge the finite human perspective with infinite creative intelligence.

Shamanism's strength lies in its ability to access realms beyond ordinary perception. Shamans engage with archetypal patterns, spirits, and multidimensional consciousness through trance, ritual, and visionary techniques. Research in neurophenomenology suggests that altered states induced by shamanic practices synchronize neural activity, fostering integration across the brain's networks. These states allow profound immersion in the imaginal pleroma, a Jungian concept of the symbolic and archetypal substratum underpinning reality.

Just as shamans catalyze personal and collective transformation through healing rituals, generative AI can advance fields like climate science, where predictive modeling is crucial for mitigating environmental degradation. The transformative potential of these systems is not just theoretical, but a reality that can inspire us to tackle the challenges of our time with renewed vigor.

The Promise of Our Time

The notion of Taripaypacha encapsulates the essence of Andean mystical traditions, offering profound insights into the cyclical nature of time, the importance of spiritual renewal, and the re-encounter with ancestral wisdom. As the world faces unprecedented challenges, the Taripaypacha provides a valuable paradigm for fostering resilience, sustainability, and earth-regenerative harmony. By honoring and revitalizing these ancient traditions, contemporary societies can find pathways to a more balanced and spiritually enriched future.

The Pluralistic & Interspiritual Nature in African Traditions

[selected for the Roundtable here from the Feature on Ifá-Òrìṣà Traditions published in full in Volume 3, and also, in part in our Interspiritual Community Section of Volume 2]

DeShannon Barnes-Bowens

...Harvard Divinity School professor, Dr. Tracey E. Hucks, highlights African American Ifá-Òrìṣà devotees with Interspiritual beliefs and pluralist practices in her groundbreaking book, *Yoruba Traditions & African American Religious Nationalism*. An Òrìṣà priestess who Dr. Hucks interviewed said,

> I have no trouble going to Christian church. They singing to Jesus, I'm singing to Esu (*an Òrìṣà*). I know in my mind we singing to the same person. I can go to

> the mosque and have no difficulty because I know in my mind Allah and Olodumare (*a name of God or the Divine in Ifá-Òrìṣà tradition*), are one and the same.[9:1]

Chief Aina Olomo, now an ancestor, was an honored Ifá-Òrìṣà priestess and Interfaith minister. She was committed to the spiritual advancement of Yoruba theological concepts. When Dr. Hucks interviewed Chief Olomo about her practice of Christianity and Islam before she came into the Ifá-Òrìṣà tradition she said,

> I did not have to throw away or completely ignore the religious tenets that had given my family spiritual solace for generations. Because of ancestral veneration I could integrate them into my African spirituality.... It does nothing for the already damaged self-esteem to belittle or dismiss the religious beliefs of our immediate fore-parents.[9:2]

These devotees never used the word interspiritual to describe their beliefs and practice, yet it is what they embody and live. This conscious way of being in the world is not surprising because similar sentiments are expressed in the Ifá divination system.

Howard University professor and Yoruba Ifá priest, Dr. Kọ́lá Abímbọ́lá, emphasizes how Ifá-Òrìṣà traditions, which he refers to as Yoruba Religion, offers practical guidelines on how people can connect across difference throughout the world.[9:3] In his book, *Yoruba Culture: A Philosophical Account* ....My spiritual godfather in Ifá-Òrìṣà tradition would often share the adage, "*S/he who knows one book, knows none*," emphasizing the importance of becoming familiar with the views of other religious traditions to combat ignorance and realize our connection to each other. It is evident in the above story,

Ọrúnmìlà determined it was beneficial for his children to gain wisdom from another religion.

I am moved when I witness the expansive nature and fluidity Ifá-Òrìṣà practitioners display in the world. Many devotees embody a deep sense of pride. We know despite a concerted effort to destroy the sacred teachings of indigenous African spiritual systems like Ifá-Òrìṣà traditions, they survived due to the cultural memory that lives in our ancestors.

Endnotes for this Feature[v:9]

Final Unitive Comments

Uniting Through the Beauty Way: Reprising the Words of Mindahi Bastida Muñoz

Brian Russo

The dawn of the Unitive Age is the emergent period in our human and planetary evolution that recognizes the fundamental unity of all life and catalyzes the power and potential of global collaboration for the creation of a flourishing future. The Unitive Age marks a pivotal shift in human consciousness — where the power of our unity rises above the conflicts that once divided us. We enter this new time by embodying the wisdom of our ancestors through the Beauty Way which reveals that this "conflict" is itself an illusion. As Venerable Dhyani Ywahoo says,[10] "All is vibration, and what has the appearance of conflict is better understood as dissonance and discord, or energies seeking resolution in harmony." From this higher-octave perspective, we have a greater capacity to resolve the discordant, unhealthy aspects of ourselves with the love and understanding necessary to bring us back to a state of health and harmony. In this way, we transcend the "us and them" mentality that has caused us to mistake our diversity for irreconcilable differences. This shift allows us to embrace diversity as our greatest strength, uniting our unique gifts to heal separation and create the harmony of the New Earth.

The power of our unity in diversity is beautifully expressed through the convergence of the Judeo-Christian New Earth Prophecy, Hopi Rainbow Prophecy, Eighth Fire Prophecy, Eagle and Condor Prophecy, and so many more. Such diverse prophecies foretell how our alignment with the divine will orchestrate the healing of our planet. They call us to gather beneath the sacred Tree of Life and remember that we are united through our shared roots in the one Source. It is here that we affirm kinship and embrace the *ubuntu* way of living based on the fact that "I am" only because "we are." In this spirit of interbeing, we care for one another and the Earth, recognizing that our destinies are woven together in the great web of life.

To conclude with the words of Mindahi Bastida, "The time for unification has come." We advance this Unification Process by following the Original Instructions for walking the Beauty Way. These instructions hold the key to protecting and regenerating Mother Earth as they guide us to live in balance, respect, and reciprocity with all creation. Original Peoples honor the spiritual authority of these instructions through their spiritual practices and call us to do the same. By acknowledging this spiritual authority and our sacred responsibility to heal Mother Earth, we recognize how we have damaged the web of life and choose to transform our harm into harmony. As Mindahi says, the Original Instructions "direct us and tell us what, how, where, and when to carry out activities" so that we may "reaffirm who we are and evaluate how we are behaving with Mother Earth." In following these instructions, we embody the spiritual practices — prayers, dances, and songs — that restore our alignment with the sacred rhythms of life. Walking the Beauty Way allows us to integrate ancestral wisdom with modern innovation to usher in the Unitive Age and be the stewards our ancestors prayed we would become. United, we are the prophecy of a more beautiful world coming into being.[11]

The Prophets Spoke. Now It's Our Turn to Listen

Constance Buffalo

Long ago, visionaries came to the Anishinaabe — also known as the Ojibwa — with powerful prophecies. They spoke of the arrival of the "light-skinned ones," and every word they offered has come to pass. Now, the final prophecy — the seventh — calls to us. It urges us to remember who we are, and to rise to what this moment demands.

This is not a message for Native peoples alone. It is a wake-up call for all who seek a better way — who feel the urgency, the responsibility, and the longing to create a future that sustains life.

Two roads lie before us.

The Black Road brings destruction, disconnection, and the erasure of what matters most.

The Red Road leads toward healing, justice, and renewal — a sacred path that can ignite the long-awaited Eighth Fire: a time of peace, balance, and well-being for all peoples, and for the Earth herself, who has birthed and nourishes us all.

This is not about politics. It's about possibility.

It will take courage to change, vision to imagine what's next, and bold action to become who we're meant to be.

In 2026, walk further with us.

The upcoming release of *another volume in this series, especially devoted to Community and Spiritual Modalities adds a promise* not only of greater clarity — but a deeper call.

To walk the Red Road.

To live it.

To become it.

Endnotes and References for "Indigenous Peoples" Section[v]

DIMENSIONS OF SACRED ACTIVISM

It is often said that Br. Teasdale's books *The Mystic Heart: Discovering a Universal Spirituality in the World's Religions* and *A Monk in the World: Cultivating a Spiritual Life* represent the perennial, inherent, "two sides of the coin," "complementary elements," "yin and yang" of the world of the heart — being and doing. It is tantalizing to note Teasdale's choice of a subtitle for *A Monk in the World — Cultivating* [doing something with] *a Spiritual Life*. It is reminiscent of Fr. Thomas Keating oft-noting to us that "meditation is really initial inquiry; but, when something answers, *that* is contemplation — dialogue." It's thought-provoking also that Br. Teasdale invited Ken Wilber to write the Foreword to *A Monk in the World*. Chronologically, this was soon after Br. Teasdale's well-known dialogues with Ken Wilber that are now on YouTube (search under "Brother Wayne Teasdale and Ken Wilber" at YouTube) — one of the last public dialogues Br. Teasdale conducted, and against the advice of his doctors. As previously noted, this was also when Br. Teasdale had sent a note to his "Association" in New York City and Chicago that because of his need to finish that book he might be out of touch for some time.

Undoubtedly, Br. Teasdale chose Ken Wilber for that Foreword because of Wilber's emphasis on *the Ups*, which comprise an entire section in our Volume 2 under "Voices from the Parliament of the World's Religions." Fundamental to that view is that *Waking Up* is not enough. Unless it also involves *Growing Up*, *Showing Up*, *Cleaning Up*, *Opening Up*, and the other *Ups*, actual transformation in the three-dimensional landscape will never be realized. This understanding was foundational to both Teasdale and Wilber, as it should be to all of us.

The Dimensions of Sacred Activism are, of course, huge. Thus, we devote two sections to it: "Toward Holism and Transformative Change" and "Educating for Direction," initiating the first subtitle with a most appropriate topic — intersectionality.

TOWARD HOLISM AND TRANSFORMATIVE CHANGE

Features by Jeanette Banashak - Ramesh Bijlani - Cynthia Brix - Patrick Carolan
Emily A. DeMoor - Aditi Kaul - Alejandra Warden

Interspirituality, Intersectionality, and the Natural World

by Jeanette Banashak

> Remember the plants, trees, animal life who all have their
> tribes, their families, their histories, too. Talk to them,
> listen to them. They are alive poems.
> Remember the wind. Remember her voice. She knows the
> origin of this universe.
> Remember you are all people

> and all people are you.
> Remember you are this universe
> and this universe is you.
> Remember all is in motion, is growing, is you.
> —Joy Harjo

> The very fact that all the traditions are trusting and sharing with one another is a powerful sign of the unity they all teach and honor. This oneness — freedom from alienation and insecurity — is the sure foundation for a better world. It means that we will try to help each other rather than hurt each other.
> —Beatrice Bruteau

What are the interrelationships among nature, Interspirituality, and intersectionality? How do we uplift and build upon Br. Wayne Teasdale's interspiritual framework and his devotion to what he called *natural mysticism*? These intriguing questions prompted the following thoughts and reflections. For Teasdale (1999), the "realization and tangible experience of unity" (p. 174), known to many as the Divine, Source, Spirit, or Ultimate Reality, is revealed through nature. Teasdale maintained that without nature, Interspirituality is not complete. Thus, nature is a critical component in our spiritual and human development. Without experiences in and with nature, humans miss out on understanding themselves, their reciprocal relationships with the natural world, and the possibility of embracing their ecological identity *as* nature.

Natural Mysticism

In *The Mystic Heart* (1999), Teasdale begins a chapter on *natural mysticism* by sharing an example from his childhood. He recalls being in his backyard at night when he was five years old. As Teasdale gazed at the stars, he also noticed the smells and sounds of the spring evening. This moment brought him to a state of wonder and astonishment. Teasdale's amazement led to questions about the origins of the stars. He describes an "inner, intuitive connection" (p. 273) that proclaimed he would ultimately understand what he was seeking. Br. Wayne's "cosmic awakening" led him to become a priest and pursue a spiritual vocation. He suggests that many of us have the capacity to remember significant moments in our lives when nature reveals herself to us. These encounters encourage our engagement with the Interspiritual Age.

In describing natural mysticism, Teasdale (1999) explained, "[S]spirituality — indeed, Interspirituality — would be incomplete without the inclusion of the mystical wisdom that comes to us through the natural world and the cosmos" (p. 174). He maintains that human development and opening to consciousness happen in conjunction with our relationship to the mystic heart of nature. "Everything in [nature's] domain is an occasion for the revelation of the divine" (p. 174). We encounter ultimate reality ever intimately when we access the sights, sounds, feels, tastes, smells, and intuitions of the natural environment. Furthermore, natural mysticism upholds the unity of and interrelationship with every being and everything that has existed, exists, and will exist. Teasdale describes the bond that becomes secured as we tap into our intrinsic connection with the natural environment. The harmonious relationships are uplifted when we open ourselves to awe and wonder and leave behind control and expertise. As conservationist and author, Rachel Carson (2017) asked, "What if I had never seen this before? What if I never see it again?"

(p. 52). We already belong to nature, and our increased awareness supports deepened appreciation of divine reality.

Intersectionality

In the Interspiritual Age, we focus on what we have in common with one another while not dismissing our differences. However, in addition to understanding each other, we work to strengthen everyone through our responsiveness to strengthening equity in the workplace and in society. Perhaps it is in the space of commonality that the intersectional work of considering age, ability, race, ethnicity, gender, sexual and affectional orientation, socioeconomic status, religion, educational status, national origin, and work experience can be accomplished. Although Br. Wayne Teasdale (1999) did not use the word intersectionality, I believe that this term has much in common with Interspirituality. For example, they both inform one another. Intersectionality, coined by legal scholar, civil rights advocate, and critical race theory scholar Kimberlé Crenshaw (1989), is defined as "a prism for seeing the way in which various forms of inequality often operate together and exacerbate each other." In the 1940s and for several decades afterward, activist, legal scholar, and Episcopal priest Pauli Murray connected race, sex, and gender discrimination by challenging segregation laws as unconstitutional. Additionally, in the 1930s and beyond, social movements leader Bayard Rustin advocated for human rights and against discrimination. These two Black, queer leaders were some of the first to describe and fight against the intersections of exploitation, marginalization, powerlessness, cultural imperialism, and violence. Overlapping identities of race, class, gender, sexual/affectional orientation, ethnicity, and ability need to be considered when engaging in interspiritual practices, behaviors, and attitudes. These practices must support the pursuit of equity for all, including the natural environment.

Practitioners within the interspiritual movement are poised to promote and advocate for intersectional work. At its core, Interspirituality encourages collaboration, inclusivity, justice, and harmony among seekers of varied religious, spiritual, and ethical traditions.

Environmental Intersectionality

Environmental intersectionality exposes how disadvantaged populations such as Indigenous Peoples, people of color, and low-income families are more apt to live in geographic locations with higher exposure to toxic and hazardous wastes, air and water pollution, and other environmental hazards (Bullard et al., 2007). It is not usually possible for these disadvantaged populations to advocate for fair wages, affordable housing, or safe living conditions such as clean air and water. How does someone who is already fighting for the right to exist equitably have time, energy, resources, and power to also fight for climate justice?

Women have fewer opportunities to take climate advocacy action when they are deprived of political power, education, and economic independence. Indigenous women are especially vulnerable to living within proximity to such hazards as pesticides, chemicals (e.g., produced by coal, oil, tar sands), military instillations, weapons testing, and uranium (Bullard et al., 2007). Furthermore, individuals with diverse abilities do not always have access to safe places during climate emergencies, let alone occupy a seat at the decision-making table. Interspiritual nature-centered spaces become hospitable and inclusive where all voices and communication styles matter, and all bodies and beings are welcome. Nature and humans coexist together and interrelate as one entity.

One example of interspiritual and intersectional work took place during the Dakota Pipeline Protest in 2016. Indigenous communities and youth from Standing Rock initiated and organized the protest in order to advocate for their rights to the region's water, ancient burial grounds, and cultural places. Non-indigenous allies as well as an intersectional group of religious and spiritual leaders, farmers, celebrities, and politicians showed up to add their support (2018). This is an example of community resilience, which may be cultivated by respecting, revering, and appreciating nature (Davidson, 2023) and building relationships and reciprocity with nature (Kimmerer, 2015). Wayne Teasdale (1999) encouraged a several step process he called natural meditation as a practice of connection with "all of nature, the earth, and the cosmos" (p. 205).

A Practice: Natural Meditation

Teasdale's (1999) natural meditation begins by walking or sitting and lovingly gazing on an object in nature, such as a tree, flower, or mountain. With a heightened awareness of the aliveness of the more-than-human-world, Robin Wall Kimmerer (2021), scientist and member of the Potawatomi nation, calls these aspects of nature "beings" rather than objects because they are *"respected as unique, sovereign beings equal to or exceeding the power of humans."* According to Teasdale, receiving and luxuriating in the sights and sounds of the natural environment enables connection with all beings. The next step of Teasdale's natural meditation is to gaze at the sky, contemplate the unity of all of creation, and "activate [our] awareness that [our] consciousness is as vast as the sky" (p. 206). Lastly,

Teasdale encourages meditators to deeply feel the joy that emerges from their direct experience with nature and to offer gratitude for the interrelationships nourished.

A Practice: Forest Bathing

Another mindful, slow, and gentle nature immersion practice, akin to Teasdale's (1999) natural meditation, is a *shinrin yoku* (forest bathing) walk. This practice was initiated in 1982 by Tomohide Akiyama of the Japanese Ministry of Agriculture as a way to protect Japanese forests and to reduce stress for overworked professionals (Li, 2018). Research has shown that there are many positive healing effects of forest bathing experiences, including decreased stress, improved mood, decreased blood pressure, increased natural killer cells that fight cancer, improved immune function, and more.

Along with the many physiological and psychological benefits of our intentional immersion into the natural environment, social and emotional bonds are fostered as we build and nurture relationships and reciprocity with our more-than-human world. A series of invitations frame the hours or days of immersion in natural settings. These invitations include appreciating and loving the individually unique characteristics of the beings present and past as well as recognizing the commonalities among different species. Indigenous Peoples have been supporting reciprocal relationships among humans and nature for millennia. Furthermore, since the dawn of human existence, 99% of humans have been intimately engaged with nature. In addition, since the human genome has been stable for approximately 250,000 years, we have evolved on a cellular level to connect with nature. The Interspiritual Age invites humans to center mutual relationships with nature over the consumption of nature to benefit all of us — humanity as well as the more-than-human world.

Often excluded in definitions of intersectionality is the more-than-human world. In her preface of *The Mystic Heart* (1999), Beatrice Bruteau suggested that in the Interspiritual Age, we will choose nonviolence in support of each other, rather than harm (p. xvii). It is my experience and belief that through an understanding of intersectionality, and by participating in practices such as natural meditation and forest bathing, our appreciation, care, and love of nature will increase, as well as our activity in eco / environmental justice. Let us include our more-than-human kin, the trees, birds, insects, flowers, and every being that ever was, is, and will be into our appreciation of what it means to be human beings who live on this planet we call Earth.

References for this Feature[vi:1]

The Return of Sacred Feminine and Interspirituality

by Alejandra Warden

> *Humankind has not woven the web of life. We are but one thread within it.*
> *Whatever we do to the web, we do to ourselves. All things are bound together. All things connect.* ~ Chief Seattle[1]

As if Chief Seattle's wise words had heralded the dawn of a new worldwide awareness of the web of life of which we are all a part, the last century has revealed a great shift in our vision of reality, one that increasingly perceives the unity and interconnection of all things. The emergence of a global environmental movement to protect the natural world and address climate change, the establishment of international mutual aid organizations to alleviate world poverty and hunger, and the creation of the World Wide Web and the Internet are but a few notable examples of the increase and diffusion of this great change that has become part of our daily experience.

In the world of spirituality and religion, this profound shift has led to the emergence of Interspirituality, a perspective based upon the recognition of the common fabric and unity of shared experience behind all Wisdom Traditions. Every day more people explore religions, spiritual paths, and philosophies beyond their own and integrate from them elements they need or are drawn to.

What is not always known about this evolution is that it is a reflection of the return of the Sacred Feminine to our lives. The Sacred Feminine, worshiped for thousands of years as the goddess, the great mother, the feminine side of the divine, and the feminine principle, manifests throughout the cosmos in many ways. She is the container of creation, the web that connects the whole of life together, and she is found in each of us through her many attributes, shapes, and graces.

Our sense of unity, as well as our ability to listen, our openness, and our sensitivity, are feminine qualities that belong to all of humanity. So are the "deep, lived knowledge of the feminine nature of the soul's relationship with God, the soul's true state of receptivity to the divine."[2] And although in some spiritual contexts these qualities (often not recognized as feminine) have been developed and encouraged on a collective level, especially in the West, for hundreds if not thousands of years, everything related to the feminine was generally and increasingly devalued up to the point of forgetting and burying the worth of the feminine in our lives. Now the Sacred Feminine has returned to remind us of what has been suppressed, degraded, and pushed aside.

The call toward interconnectedness and a union beyond separation and distance that resounds within us is one of the ways the Sacred Feminine has returned to the world. She has come to show us how all life is completely interrelated, to reawaken and remind us of our original knowing of union, a memory that lives in the depth of ourselves — the experience of unity with our mother in her womb and our environment in our first years of our lives — and to give birth to a new consciousness capable of recognizing this interrelatedness. The Sacred Feminine as the divine weaver has returned to re-weave and re-link what had been severed — Heaven from Earth, spirit from matter, root from branches — and to reveal the one source that nourishes all paths, the common heart that beats and animates all things. Above all, she has returned to remind us that as the feminine face of the divine — its body, its vessel, its shape — she is the binding force of love, and thus that love is the body and soul of all things. And that it is through her, within the labyrinth of her appearances, the veils of her creations, and the web of all reality, that we come to know the essence beyond all form.

The Sacred Feminine manifests in many ways. One of the most direct encounters with her is found in an experience of mystic Hildegard Von Bingen:

> *I heard a voice speaking to me: 'The young woman whom you see is Love. She has her tent in eternity... It was Love which was the source of this creation in the beginning when God said: 'Let it be!' And it was. As though in the blinking of an eye, the whole creation was formed through Love. The young woman... holds*

> *the sun and moon in her right hand and embraces them dearly... The whole of creation calls this maiden 'Lady.' For it was from her that all creation proceeded, since Love was the first. She made everything... Love was in eternity and brought forth, in the beginning all holiness, all creatures without any admixture of evil. Adam and Eve, as well were produced by love from the pure nature of the Earth.*[3]

As the mother of creation, the feminine knows the unity and interrelatedness of the created. This relational feminine knowing, which today has become a call toward union on a worldwide level, "is crucial for a realized Interspirituality."[4]

For Brother Wayne Teasdale, Interspirituality included the many paths that lead to the divine and all the names by which the nameless one is called. He realized that although different Wisdom Traditions have their own stories, beliefs, and practices, they share certain universal principles — "the shared heritage of humankind's spiritual wisdom,"[5] which are the foundation of all of them — and that Interspirituality is this "common ground"[6] where all of them meet. It is from this common ground that it has been possible to initiate and eventually achieve real dialog and engagement that leads to "a deep appreciation of, respect for, and openness to the treasures"[7] of the different traditions. As a result, little by little the walls that have separated them for so many years have begun to fall, and the hope for a real peace and an understanding capable of putting an end to religious wars and discrimination is growing.

Interspirituality is slowly becoming a household name. Interspiritual dialog and practice are re-envisioning the world of religion and spirituality. Today, interspiritual gatherings of various kinds bring together people from all Wisdom Traditions. Strong links are being established among many of them, and everyone is invited to participate in these meetings. The Sacred Feminine herself and her spiritual practices have been incorporated into interspiritual circles through the presence of certain traditions, such as ancient shamanic paths that for millennia have celebrated Earth as the great mother, as well as new ecological lines of spirituality that have renewed the appreciation, care, and value of our planet, often referred to by them again by the name of the ancient Greek goddess Gaia.

Underlying this movement is a profound change in human consciousness being brought about by the Sacred Feminine. Over hundreds and hundreds of years, humanity developed more and more acutely a consciousness that focuses on what differentiates and separates us rather than what unites us. One of the characteristics of this consciousness of differentiation is that it sees life as if through a magnifying glass, seeing and observing mainly its parts. This consciousness in humanity has brought major scientific and technological advancements and great cultural and social progress, and it has allowed for the process of individuation of the human being to take place.

In contrast, the feminine intrinsic knowing that is unfolding and growing today notices and appreciates what makes us similar and brings us closer. Brother Wayne Teasdale saw the emergence and significance of this change in human awareness. He stated, "We are at the dawn of a new consciousness, a radically fresh approach to our life as the human family in a fragile world," and he understood that this shift in consciousness required "a new approach to spirituality that transcends past religious cultures of fragmentation and isolation."[8]

Transcending this culture of fragmentation and isolation is a calling of the Sacred Feminine and a reason for her return to birth a new dimension of consciousness, a relational understanding of existence. This relational consciousness represents a marriage of the awareness of differentiation with the intrinsic, innate feminine knowing of unity. And it is reached through our feminine qualities with vulnerability, receptivity, and sensitivity leading the way. For it is only when we soften the harsh walls of distinction, peel away the armor that keeps us apart, and open our hearts and minds to the sacredness in other ways and other paths and other thoughts that this new consciousness can live within us. This major contribution of the Sacred Feminine is often unacknowledged. She is the source of our ability to integrate not only aspects of ourselves to become whole, but also to build bridges of connection and understanding with others and other points of view, to value others and learn from them, and to restore value to the feminine in all of us and to the Earth.

Interspirituality responds to the influence and invitation of the Sacred Feminine to an expansion of ties among spiritual paths by reflecting the common underlying foundation that unites the Wisdom Traditions — the cause of the influence that they have exerted on each other throughout history — and "the essential spiritual interdependence"[9] that exists between them. Her influence is also felt in the call of Interspirituality for an interaction of people from different traditions, for an openness to learn from them and their beliefs, and for a recognition that through the wide variety of "spiritual experience and insight"[10] we can achieve greater understanding and perspective. As the world opens more and more to Interspirituality, we can hear the voice of Sacred Feminine as our guide and our muse.

Endnotes and References for this Feature[vi:2]

From Interfaith to Interspirituality

Looking for Similarities Leads to Discovery of Oneness

by Aditi Kaul & Ramesh Bijlani

Whether religions originated in a human necessity or in the way humans are wired is debatable; probably both played a role in the birth of some ideas and practices which may be termed religious. While current views of the beginnings of primitive religions are a mental construct based primarily on deductive logic and speculation, a little more substantive evidence supports our knowledge of the origin of religions that took root during the last 5,000 years. These religions originated in the East, and may be classified into two major streams. One stream is the insight-based tradition that includes Hinduism and its sister religions such as Buddhism, Jainism, and Sikhism; the other is the revelation-based tradition that includes Judaism, Christianity, and Islam. The overall impact of all religions on human life has been positive. Sri Aurobindo has said, "Each religion has helped mankind. Paganism increased in man the light of beauty, the largeness and height of his life, his aim at a many-sided perfection; Christianity gave him some vision of divine love and charity; Buddhism has shown him a noble way to be wiser, gentler, purer; Judaism and Islam how to be religiously faithful in action and zealously devoted to God; Hinduism has opened to him the largest and profoundest spiritual possibilities ..."[1]

However, man is a mental creature, and the intellect is quick to categorize and classify. Hence, all religions have got further divided and subdivided into multiple sects and cults. Further, the collective ego, more than anything else, has led to conflicts between the followers of different religions, and between groups within the same religion. The fundamental ideas of all religions being geared for love and oneness, conflicts between religions are surprising. As a Buddhist monk said at an interfaith event, "Conflicts between religions are like water catching fire." But all the same, religious conflicts are facts of history, which cannot be wished away. According to the *Encyclopedia of Wars* by Charles Phillips and Alan Axelrod, out of all known historical conflicts, almost 7% had religion as their primary cause.[2] However, quoting the same source, Lurie says that while religious conflicts account for about 7% of all wars, they have been responsible for less than 2% of all the people killed in warfare.[3] However, this dispassionate view of religious conflicts is no justification for complacency.

Fortunately, while the ego, including the collective ego, has a tendency to divide, its antidote, which is love, has also been planted in us. While religious conflicts continue, the overall trend has been for religious conflicts to decline in their ferocity. Sri Aurobindo remarked as long ago as 1916, "Mankind seems now indeed inclined to grow a little modester and wiser; we no longer slay our fellows in the name of God's truth … … we are beginning to look at other religions and philosophies for the truth and help they contain and no longer merely in order to damn them as false or criticise what we conceive to be their errors."[4] The first World's Parliament of Religions held in Chicago in 1893 was a landmark that brought global leaders of religious and spiritual traditions to a common platform in a spirit of unity. And, the historic address at the Parliament by Swami Vivekananda was a milestone in the ensuing popular engagement of the West with ancient Indian wisdom as a potential solution to the problems of human existence. The 20th century perhaps saw more interfaith dialogues than conflicts.

The Past as a Process of Progressive Unfolding

The taming of the collective ego during the 20th century created an opportunity for universal love to manifest. One of the tangible results of this process was interfaith dialogues. Interfaith dialogues are permeated by two basic ideas. First, the acceptance of diversity of faiths not as a necessary evil, but as an expression of the cultural variation that breaks the monotony of uniformity. Second, the willingness to acknowledge and appreciate the similarities between religions, which far outnumber and outweigh the differences. The similarities are at the level of the spiritual philosophies underlying different religions rather than their rituals and ceremonies. There are three fundamental principles on which the spiritual philosophies underlying all religions are unanimous. First, that the creation of the material universe, including our world, was not an accident; it was the result of the Intelligent Design worked out by a Conscious Being that has always been there and will always be there. "This world was not built with random bricks of Chance."[5] Secondly, the Conscious Being has an all-pervasive presence in Its creation; the presence is called the Spirit. "In a body obscuring the immortal Spirit / A nameless Resident vesting unseen powers … He sits, unfelt by the form in which he lives / And veils his knowledge by the groping mind."[6] Thirdly, the Conscious Being has a design, a plan, for Its creation, which It knows how to implement. "It is an architecture high and grand / By many named and nameless masons built / In which unseeing hands obey the Unseen…"[7] Since the fundamental features of the spiritual philosophies underlying all religions are the same, and the differences that are there are not irreconcilable, the transition from interfaith to Interspirituality was a natural corollary. Moving from religious conflicts through interfaith to Interspirituality within the span of a century has been an amazing unfolding at an unprecedented pace in the history of mankind.

A Retrospective Analysis

Sri Aurobindo has looked at the history of societies as a cyclic process.[8] In terms of that cycle, the dark ages of Europe (c. the 6th to the 16th century) were the age of convention. As a rebellion against the age of convention was born the European Renaissance, which ushered in the age of reason. In the early stages of the age of reason, the proponents of rationality came in conflict with religion. In the conflict, eventually rationality triumphed because after a long spell of stagnation, Europe was yearning for liberation from the dominance of authority and testimony. Rationality was the way to that liberation, and that in turn created fertile ground for the spirit of enquiry and freedom of thought to flourish. The result was phenomenal developments in science and technology, which so revolutionized human life within three hundred years that science came to be looked upon as the new religion. "The Renascence gave back to Europe on one hand the free curiosity of the Greek mind, its eager search for first principles and rational laws, its delighted intellectual scrutiny of the facts of life by the force of direct observation and individual reasoning, on the other the Roman's large practicality and his sense for the ordering of life in harmony with a robust utility and the just principles of things."[9] However, science could not for long fill the space religion was forced by the society to vacate because science did not eradicate the problems of human existence, such as inequality, injustice, cruelty, misery and suffering — problems for which religion offered at least some solace if not a solution. But that did not lead to the return of religion. The tool that had led to the growth of science, namely rationality, was pressed into service for solving the problems of human existence. Among the results were two contrasting systems of government — democracy and communism — both rational and both well-intentioned, but both failed. The finest product of rationality that was designed to create a better world was humanism. "The mind of man is to be released from all bonds, allowed freedom and range and opportunity, given all its means of self-training and self-development and organised in the play of its powers for the service of humanity. And all this too is not to be held as an abstract or pious sentiment, but given full and practical recognition in the persons of men and nations and mankind. This, speaking largely, is the idea and spirit of the intellectual religion of humanity."[10] Humanism, which Sri Aurobindo has called the "religion of humanity," was also doomed for failure. Not only did sorrow and suffering persist in spite of science and other rational approaches, but the tempting energy-intensive lifestyle enabled by technological developments also brought with it environmental depletion and pollution on a scale that threatened the very existence of life on planet Earth, called Mother Earth in the Indian tradition. Before man arrived on the planet, "Primal peace was there and in its [of the Earth] bosom / Held undisturbed the strife of bird and beast. … The Mighty Mother [Earth] lay outstretched at ease."[11] Thus, science and technology have added a new dimension to the problems of human existence and have created a sense of urgency with which something needs to be done.

The reason why neither religion nor rationality could eradicate sorrow and suffering was that neither went to the root of the problem, which is the rather low level at which human consciousness has stayed for thousands of years. Thus, the stage was set for the next stage in the cyclic process — the suprarational age. "Man proceeds by various stages out of these beginnings towards a rational age …

Finally, the human evolution must move through a subjective towards a suprarational or spiritual age in which we will develop progressively a greater spiritual, supra-intellectual and intuitive, perhaps in the end a more than intuitive, a gnostic consciousness. He will be able to perceive a higher divine end, a divine sanction, a divine light of guidance for all he seeks to be, think, feel and do, and able, too, more and more to obey and live in this larger light and power. That will not be done by any rule of infra-rational religious impulse and ecstasy, … but by a higher spiritual living for which the clarities of the reason are a necessary preparation and into which they too will be taken up, transformed, brought to their invisible source."[12] When the Western world started looking at something higher than reason for solving the problems of human existence, it turned to spirituality. And, it discovered in ancient Indian wisdom the spirituality that suited its secular mind the most.

Our Hypothesis

In light of above, we hypothesize that at least three interrelated factors have contributed to the progressive movement from religious tolerance to interfaith dialogue, and from interfaith dialogue to Interspirituality. First, neither science nor other rational approaches were able to solve the problems of human existence. Therefore, although rapid and spectacular developments in science successfully banished religion, science failed to fill the vacuum that it had created. Secondly, the environmental impact of technological developments ended up aggravating the problems of human existence. Thirdly, as a result of developments in theoretical physics, science started stretching its boundaries. As a result of its arrogance tamed by its failures and follies, and its restricted framework challenged by its own advances, science matured and mellowed down. Science stepped aside to let something higher than reason and better than religion occupy the space which science itself had made religion to vacate. Religious tolerance, science-religion dialogue, and interfaith dialogue were the offsprings that came to occupy that space, and Interspirituality followed.

The Contributions of Science

Science banished religion from life, and science unwittingly brought forth something better than conventional religion. Science is primarily based on rationality, and science itself cleared the path for the suprarational. "… science has already enlarged for good the intellectual horizons of the [human] race and raised, sharpened and intensified powerfully the general intellectual capacity of mankind."[13]

The Divine has a design for the world, and Sri Aurobindo has emphasized that evolution of consciousness is the key process for executing the design. Evolution from matter to living creatures has essentially been a step-by-step manifestation of the consciousness hidden in matter. Man is the latest, but not the final product of evolution. But man is unique in having an urge to evolve, and the capacity to do so. Thus, man can collaborate with nature, and accelerate further evolution. And, Sri Aurobindo has also visualized that the next leap in evolution beyond man is not too far. Modern science may be seen as a divine intervention that has used man as an instrument for accelerating the process of evolution. In its early days (the 16th through the 19th century), modern science facilitated the transition from religion to spirituality by interposing a period of "secular refrigeration," to use one of the pithy expressions of Sri Aurobindo. In the 20th century, science has contributed to the unification of the world through spectacular advances in transport and communication. Unification of the world is likely to promote a sense of Oneness, which is the key practical implication of the spiritual worldview too.

The Contrast Between the East and the West

During the last 500 years, the theater for the successive phenomena of science-religion conflict, science ousting religion from life, and the return of refined religiosity was primarily Europe to start with, but soon engulfed other countries with a primarily Graeco-Roman heritage, most prominently North America. The East, particularly India, never had any conflict between science and religion. The Hindu tradition, based on Vedanta, looks upon Truth to be Infinite, of which many finite truths can be a part. Scientific truths are a part of the whole Truth. Scientific developments merely added details to certain aspects of Truth. As Sri Aurobindo said in his Uttarpara Speech in 1909, "This [Hinduism] is the one religion that can triumph over materialism by including and anticipating the discoveries of science and the speculations of philosophy."[14]

Toward the Future

The Mother had an eye on the future when she said, "Instead of taking these religions in their outward forms which are precisely dogmas and intellectual conceptions, if we take them in their spirit, in the principle they represent, there is no difficulty in unifying them. … And even this unification which already demands a return to the Spirit behind things, is not enough; there must be added to it a vision of the future, the goal towards which humanity is moving, the future realisation of the world, that last 'spiritual revolution' Sri Aurobindo speaks about, which will open a new age, that is, the supramental evolution."[15]

Keen on reconciliation rather than confrontation, interfaith dialogues look for and highlight similarities between religions on one hand, and on the other tend to ignore, minimize, and gloss over differences. Interspirituality goes one step further. It acknowledges commonalities between religious traditions, and promotes spiritual practices common to them. The next step would be the recognition and awareness of Oneness of all creation. The world would leave behind all religions as sacred relics of the past, and embrace spirituality. Such a world would result not from evolution of concepts, but from evolution of consciousness. Therefore, in this world of the future, the average level of human consciousness would be significantly higher than it has been for several millennia. The level of consciousness translates into human nature. The higher level of consciousness would mean a shift from an ego-driven consciousness to a love-driven consciousness. That shift goes to the very root of the problems of human existence. The movement from religions to spirituality is likely to be a global wave that will transform the world. When Sri Aurobindo talked of the world moving away from all religions towards spirituality about a hundred years ago, his was perhaps a lone voice. But now many thinkers and spiritual teachers are speaking the same language. Many of them have perhaps never read Sri Aurobindo, which makes it even more significant. What it means is that a new consciousness has established itself in the Earth atmosphere, which in turn has started making more and more persons see the future of the world the way Sri Aurobindo saw it. Just to cite two examples, Gary Zukav says that evolution so far has favored the selfish species that could control the environment better. Future evolution would favor the species that loves all life. The five-sensory mean and selfish man is going to give way to the multi-sensory magnanimous and altruistic man.[16] David

Hawkins, a psychiatrist, has quantified consciousness. On Hawkins' scale, 200 is an important cut-off point. At a level below 200, man is arrogant because separative ego dominates his psyche. At a level above 200, people "put back into the world as much energy as they take." David Hawkins says, "The collective level of consciousness of mankind remained at 190 for many centuries and, curiously, only jumped to its current level of 204 within the last decade."[17] The decade Hawkins is referring to is roughly 1980-1990.

Religions could not eradicate the problems of human existence because they existed when mankind was not ready for spirituality. Religions, while being founded in spirituality, also laid the foundations of spirituality one day taking over from them. Spirituality will be able to transform the world because the evolution of consciousness would then be at a stage when it would be natural for the average man to express love inspired by Oneness.

Our greater self of knowledge waits for us,
A supreme light in the truth-conscious Vast:
It sees from summits beyond thinking mind,
It moves in a splendid air transcending life.
It shall descend and make earth's life divine.[18]

Endnotes and References for this Feature[vi:3]

Dancing Within the Mother: Intersubjectivity and Unitive Consciousness

by Emily A. DeMoor

What do dancing frogs have to do with the cosmic whole? "There is only one consciousness, and it is cosmic," writes Diogo Ponte and Lothar Schäfer in *Carl Gustav Jung, Quantum Physics and the Spiritual Mind.*[1] The authors use the metaphor of an ocean, which Jung connects to the Mother archetype, to describe how elementary thoughts, things, or entities exist in an invisible massless wave state of potentiality, which is one of indivisible wholeness. They explain that we are able to understand the world because the forms within our minds and those of our world come from the same cosmic source. "For each one of us the birth of a conscious self is out of a realm of nonempirical forms, in the same way in which the birth of an empirical world is out of a realm of virtual states."[2]

The birthing of the empirical world from an indivisible wholeness points to a unity that is both seen and unseen. Viewed from an interspiritual perspective, we might think of it in terms of a "cosmotheandric experience," a term coined by Spanish-Indian theologian Raimon Panikkar to describe a union in which the cosmos, the divine, and humans participate in the substance and activity of one another in an intersubjective relationship.[3] This trinity, so to speak, is "the ultimate triadic structure of reality"; it is everywhere and pervades everything — the very rhythm of being.[4]

Literature provides a way to envision such abstract notions. In *The Dance of the Frogs,* by nature writer Loren Eiseley, a young, unnamed scientist encounters Albert Dreyer — an esteemed and mysterious elder scientist — in a tavern. In a rare candid moment, the usually private Dreyer divulges his experience of being caught up in the Spring rite of frogs returning to the water for mating and laying eggs. Dreyer recollects, "The water was pulling them — not water as we know it, but the mother, the ancient life force, the thing that made us in the days of creation, and that lurks around us still, unnoticed in our sterile cities."[5] Dreyer was being pulled as well, and spontaneously participated in the dance: "Even as I leaped, I was changing. It was this, I think, that stirred the last remnants of human fear and human caution that I still possessed. My will was in abeyance; I could not stop. Furthermore, certain sensations, hypnotic or otherwise, suggested to me that my own physical shape was modifying, or about to change. I was leaping with a growing ease."[6]

Dreyer recalls, "It was just then that the wharf lights began to show. We were approaching the end of the road, and the road… ended in the river. It was this, I suppose, that startled me back into some semblance of human terror. Man is a land animal. He does not willingly plunge off wharfs at midnight in the monstrous company of amphibious shadows."[7] Dreyer explains, "Nevertheless their power held me. We pounded madly toward the wharf, and under the light that hung above it, and the beam that made a cross. Part of me struggled to stop, and part of me hurtled on. But in that final frenzy of terror before the water below engulfed me I shrieked, *Help! In the name of God, help me! In the name of Jesus, stop*!"[8]

Since this event, Dreyer was no longer able to handle research with frogs. Earlier in the story, we learn that Dreyer wears a black glove on one hand. The narrator recalls the moment when the mystery of the glove is revealed: "He paused and drank, and then, seeing perhaps some lingering doubt and confusion in my eyes, held up his black-gloved hand and deliberately pinched off the glove. A man should not do that to another man without warning, but I suppose he felt I demanded some proof. I turned my eyes away. One does not like a webbed batrachian hand on a human being."[9]

Eiseley's fiction points to a cosmic drive towards unity, wholeness, and ongoing life. Returning to Panikkar's cosmotheandrism, we might think of the ancient life force in Eiseley's story as the evolutionary energy of love, referred to as "Omega" by Teilhard de Chardin. On a cosmic level, it is the divine allurement that continues to draw all of creation into unitive relationships; the cosmic Mother who draws her children back into the maternal womb of potentiality.

While Eiseley uses chimerism[10] as a literary device, scientists have discovered that fetal-maternal microchimerism occurs within humans during pregnancy when cells are exchanged between a fetus and the mother. The fetal cells can remain in the mother for decades. And, though their effect has not been definitively established, recent data indicate "the promising role of microchimeric cells in the maternal response to tissue injuries by differentiating into many lineages."[11] As a result of Dreyer's empathic fusion[12] with the frogs, he becomes more compassionate and can no longer do research with them. Having joined them returning to the Mother, he is now one with them and the cosmic drive towards wholeness.

In another part of the world, the Kalapalo tribe of central Brazil, which was uncontacted until the late 19th century, organize their society at the level of kin groups during the Fall, Winter and Spring, but during the summer they come together in rituals that give birth to the powerful beings from the beginning of time. Evolutionary cosmologist Brian Thomas Swimme explains that the ritual "sings them into existence." He continues, "As the singing and dancing go on for weeks, even months, there is a consequent merging of the singers with the beings they are singing about. In the joy of this collective experience, they transcend their smaller familial identities. In the deep experiences of the ritual, they can say, "I am the Kalapalo people…" In doing so, they awaken to a larger dimension of self."[13] Swimme invites us to invent processes that move us toward the realization that we are, first and foremost, Earth and universe.

How might we create these processes? What would they look like? In a time when global climate change, white nationalism, and other "isms" threaten to tear us apart, understanding ourselves as part of a cosmotheandric whole in which entities pass from the implicate order to the explicate order and back again in an ongoing dance of creation is foundational to transitioning to a new way of being. Experiences of intersubjectivity heighten an awareness of wholeness and engender a vision of how to move forward together. By becoming one another, in the company of the angels and spirit guides, we may joyfully join in the sacred dance of potentiality.

Endnotes and References for this Feature[vi:4]

The Alchemy of Gender Equity and Reconciliation as a Pathway for Interspiritual Harmony

by Cynthia Brix

The principle of "love thy neighbor as thyself" — or its equivalent — can be found *within* every religious tradition, but it also applies equally *across* the major world religions. Indeed, the different world religions *are* each other's closest neighbors! As Fr. Thomas Keating has said:

> The spirit of interspiritual dialogue is so important for the peace of this world. … It is not enough to simply respect and listen patiently to others' presentations of their religious beliefs. What needs to be added to the interreligious dialogue is to *love* other religions; to see in them the presence of Ultimate Reality. This

> is the oneness of all creation that all the religions are seeking."[1]

As Desmond Tutu expressed this same inspiration,

> "God is not a Christian." God cannot be confined to any one tradition, because all traditions are contained *in* God.

When sincere, open-minded, open-hearted people of diverse faith traditions come together, and speak from the depths of their hearts, they often discover that they are all engaged in a common quest and are seeking to realize a shared Absolute, which goes by many different names across their diverse traditions. This was one of the great discoveries of the Snowmass Conference, convened by Fr. Thomas Keating over a period of 32 years. In short, these religious leaders from diverse traditions discovered that although religious difference has long been a source of tremendous conflict in the world, it can also provide a source of mutual enrichment, elevated insight, and serve as a profound unifying force for humanity. As Desmond Tutu put it, "Instead of separation and division, all distinctions make for a rich diversity to be celebrated for the sake of the unity that underlies them. We are different so that we can know our need of one another." In the Qur'an (5:4), this teaching is made explicit that God created human diversity for a divine purpose, so that we can learn from our differences, and thereby grow in love for one another, and for God. As the Buddha said, "Hatred never ceases by hatred, but by love alone" (Dhammapada).

"Love one another, as I have loved you" (John 13:34) is the new (and final) commandment Christ gave to his disciples. This *same* principle can be expanded to apply to the diverse religious communities of the world. Just as God loved every human community, and gifted each with a unique revelation and religion, so this "new" commandment is given to *all* the religions and their respective faithful communities, sanghas, tariquas, etc.: Love one another, just as *God* has loved all religions, and their respective adherents.[2]

How to achieve this in practice? One promising pathway is to apply gender equity and reconciliation work to foster interreligious healing and reconciliation — both *within* each religious tradition, and also *across* the major world religions. By tapping the systemic gender injustice that is common to all religions, gender reconciliation work in interspiritual and interfaith religious contexts can provide a vast — yet still untapped — leverage for systemic healing and transformation *across* the major religions, so as to eventually become a global beloved community.

There is a curious irony that the religions of the world seem to meet in both the highest and the lowest levels — at the mystical heart of the soul's communion with God or the Absolute, and at the most tragic subjugation and oppression of fully half of the human family. As one spiritual leader wryly remarked, "The religions seem to meet in God and gutter." Indeed, and yet because the gutter of gender oppression is a deplorable place where the religions meet, it is also a place of profound potential for systemic alchemy of transmutation, reconciliation, and restoration of the traditions to their wholeness and harmony.

For this to be done properly, we must hold the traditions at once accountable to their highest spiritual standards and exalted teachings, *and* at the same time to full accountability for where they have fallen short. To do one without the other would leave something still incomplete, but to do both together holds the potential for true healing within each tradition, and also for unifying the traditions through mutual purification, liberation, and shared reverence and revelation of the Divine.

Gender entails multiple dimensions, and every human being has a legitimate voice in the gender conversation. Women across the world religions share a very similar experience, particularly in terms of their unique challenges in spiritual and religious life. Similarly, the LGBTQ+ community also experience common afflictions across the religious traditions. Cultivating skillful nonjudgmental awareness of these imbalances is crucial for gender reconciliation work.

"Who wrote the books?" asks Jetsunma Tenzin Palmo. "The books from all the religions were written from the male perspective," she replies, "and in that perspective women are always a bit of a danger, and therefore the thing to do is to keep them down so that they don't have a voice. For millennia now, most of the major religions have been busy in suppressing the feminine voice, even while they worship the feminine — like the Virgin Mary, Quan Yen, or Lakshmi, and Saraswati.

"In Buddhism, for example, wisdom is a female — a feminine force. The perfection of wisdom is Prajñāpāramitā, who is female. She is the mother of all the Buddhas. The buddhas are born of wisdom, like Sophia. It's always been understood that the feminine has this kind of special intuitive understanding, but it wasn't nurtured, because women remained uneducated and often the deeper practices were not allowed or given to them. Yet, things are changing. Many of the senior teachers in the Buddhist world now are women — not only in the West, but also in Asia. And in places like Vietnam, Taiwan, and Korea, where nuns are much better educated than in the Tibetan system, there's also a lot of social outreach, as in Catholicism. Nuns run schools, hospitals, orphanages, retreat centers, colleges, and universities.

"Any choir, to be balanced, needs female as well as male voices — that's what brings the harmony. So it's not like if women get one bigger slice of the cake, the guys get a lesser slice of the cake. The Dharma is not a cake! It brings harmony. Everybody wins. It's a win-win situation for the whole world."

Once recognized, these awakenings serve to bond women *and* men across the religions, in a new shared quest. As women discover deep and striking parallels in their challenging experiences, they begin to bond over their common affliction, which strengthens their resolve, increases their mutual compassion, and diminishes or dissolves altogether their concerns about the differences across their respective faith traditions. As men become aware of the systematic oppression and are awakened more fully to the plight of women in religion, irrespective of their faith tradition, the vast majority of men are shocked and dismayed by this, and are genuinely inspired to take substantive action toward fostering authentic healing and transformative change. Thus, the gender dysfunction is universal across all the major religions, and for this very reason, skillful healing work across the gender divisions naturally leads to systemic healing and bonding *across the entire spectrum* of world religions.

We have been fortunate to witness this kind of mutually beneficial healing in our interreligious applications of the Gender Equity and Reconciliation International (GERI) program, and also in the interspiritual conferences organized in Satyana Institute's project called Dawn of Interspirituality. In 2009, we convened a women's spiritual leadership conference in Turin, Italy, with 75 women from 15 countries spanning primarily Christian, Buddhist, and Hindu traditions. As the women shared in depth about their spiritual lives, they discovered significant parallels in their experiences, including lack of voice and influence, marginalization within their respective religious institutions, and in some cases exploitation and sexual abuse. These common experiences led to a recognition of systemic oppression of women that was universal across their religions. In another interspiritual conference we organized in Costa Rica in 2018, we conducted a "silent witnessing" exercise in a mixed-gender group of over 100 religious leaders and practitioners from nine different major religions. The result was profound, as women and men of diverse faith traditions realized together the vast and systemic injustices of gender oppression that are common to all their traditions, as well as the ways that all religions are called to transform this injustice, rather than continue to perpetuate it.

Garrett Evans, a panelist on the young adult session, shared his wisdom and earnest plea, addressed especially to the elders and prominent religious leaders at the conference:

> In almost every major world religion, there has been this profound betrayal of the genuine spiritual impulse, particularly in relation to gender and sexuality. The heart of these traditions is about guiding and protecting and inspiring us on our journey home. So, to hold that, and at the same time to acknowledge the betrayal creates the space where new life can be breathed into the traditions; so they don't have to — I mean in one form they *do* have to die — but they get to rise again.

As men witness systemic parallels in women's treatment across the religious traditions, they are inspired and motivated to take action to do something about it. For example, as described by Craig Parker, a leading member of the clergy in Boston who attended a GERI retreat for religious leaders:

> Rarely have I experienced such vulnerability, rawness, empathy, and grace as I did on this retreat. I will treasure the stories I heard, and I plan to implement the lessons learned as I engage with students, young professionals, prisoners, and fellow ministers. I especially appreciated the honoring and blessing ceremonies we created for each other. I was surprised at how much they moved me to tears.

Another example comes from Rev. Philbert Kalisa, an Episcopal priest from Rwanda who is the Founder and CEO of REACH in Rwanda, which has done remarkable healing and reconciliation work for over 20 years between Hutus and Tutsis following the horrendous Rwandan genocide. He reflected:

> The sharing from women to men touched my heart deeply, and pushed me to repent for not speaking out some of the injustices I see often in our churches and societies connected with our culture that doesn't consider women as equal to men. I made my decision not to keep quiet anymore. I will advocate for women created in the image of God as our mothers, wives, daughters, sisters and nieces.

Reflecting on her experience in a GERI workshop, author and spiritual teacher Mirabai Starr said:

> It's all about Oneness, and so this gender work is not different than the Interspiritual. They both have exactly the same goal: to bring us to that place of Oneness, and of unity. All spiritual paths are about that, and this work is absolutely about that. I didn't feel any kind

> of "sociopolitical psychobabble" going on, ever. There was a very graceful way of continually bringing it back to the heart, where it all is. I was deeply moved by all this, and am eager to see how these two modalities of the Interspiritual and the gender equity and reconciliation come together.

In the United States today and many other countries, refusal to accept LGBTQ+ equality is still creating major divisions in many churches and spiritual communities. Responding to this dilemma, a new initiative is being developed that applies the GERI methodology with a specific focus on diversity of gender identities, human sexuality, and intersectionalities. The purpose is to bring healing and mutual understanding between "straight" and "queer" people in spiritual communities, and to skillfully embrace the challenges in contemporary society that contribute to LGBTQ+ shame and hiding, and finally to foster webs of relationality and bonding in a united sense of Oneness that supersedes "us and them." These workshops offer a new "third" dimension to LGBTQ+ programming that otherwise often focuses either on workshops for LGBTQ+ people, or on diversity and anti-bias training for straight people. As one participant reflected, "sometimes we can feel so different [as queer people], but if we have more sessions like these, the enlightenment is that we, as [all] people, are so similar and we have the same struggles, which should connect us rather than drive us further apart." An older gay man noted with surprise in relation to straight stories shared that "We are actually more alike than different." Meanwhile, straight people became more aware of their privilege when asked to listen to the stories of others.

Five key themes are emerging from these workshops: the importance of safe spaces, enabling courageous conversations, embracing taboo topics, healing and ritual experiences to re-connect sexuality and spirituality, and deep connection across multiple differences, which together offer a glimpse of what the church could be in its worship spaces. The ultimate goal is to create a gender-inclusive "Kin-dom of God" as a form of Beloved Community.

GERI at the Parliament of World Religions

GERI leaders have maintained a long-standing commitment to introducing their work at interspiritual conferences, especially the Parliament of the World's Religions (PoWR). At the three most recent PoWR conferences (in 2015, 2018, and 2023), we presented a session titled *Transforming Patriarchy in Religion: The Promise of Gender Equity and Reconciliation*, which included a panel of leaders in our work, plus an interactive experiential engagement with the transformative GERI process. Over 300 religious leaders from diverse spiritual and religious backgrounds attended these sessions, and many reported an important awakening experience, and a deeper resolve to embrace gender healing in their lives, and in their spiritual communities.

Conclusion

Because gender oppression in various forms is universal across the religions, applying the work of gender healing and reconciliation can serve as a powerful catalyst for leveraging systemic healing and unity across the religious traditions. As Rev. Ray Hammond put it, "Radical love and community is not just what we preach and teach, but who we are and what we do."

Endnotes and References for this Feature[vi:5]

Interspirituality and Activism

by Patrick Carolan

Br. Wayne Teasdale was a mystical visionary. A Catholic Monk, he was a leading proponent of mutual understanding between the world's religions and believed in coming together in dialogue. He was very active and a strong supporter of the Parliament of World Religions, working tirelessly to help create an interfaith dialogue which he described as "Interspirituality." His vision of Interspirituality was not so much from the perspective of the rites, rituals and rules but rather as a sharing of the mystical experience. He believed that our spirituality should promote and lead to unity of all creation not separation.

Like the early 20th century Jesuit priest Teilhard de Chardin, Teasdale believed that humanity's religious experience and spiritual paths were part of our existential evolutionary process. He did not accept that religion was static and unchanging. Rather, he understood that evolution was not just about our physicality but more our spirituality. Interspirituality was part of the ongoing process of spiritual evolution. Teasdale felt that churches and religion had to evolve from a model centered around individual salvation and towards the creation of what our potential could be in both consciousness and heart. As Teasdale wrote in *A Monk in the World*, "The Church is now required to radiate Christ's radical love and not simply insist on his unique salvific role."

For Br. Teasdale, the concept of Interspirituality was built on the idea of the interconnectedness of all creation bringing with it a purpose to build community leading to the creation of a new Earth where we all share responsibility to one another and the planet as a whole — a belief that is shared by many visionary thinkers. As Diarmuid O'Murchu wrote in *Quantum Theology: Spiritual Implications of the*

New Physics, "We need to rediscover our role as co-creators with God, participants in the transformation of the world into the "new heaven and the new earth." He went on to say, "We are confronted with what seems to be a fundamental truth about all life: connectedness and interrelatedness are interwoven throughout the entire fabric of creation."

The late 20th century Catholic priest and visionary thinker Thomas Berry wrote, "We will go into the future as a single sacred community, or we will all perish in the desert." Teasdale, Berry and others were not talking about how we practice religion. They weren't suggesting that we all have to become Catholic or Muslim or convert to some other religious practice. They were talking about a spirituality of oneness with all creation. They followed a long line of visionary spiritual thinkers from all religions who taught and lived a spirituality, not of separation, but of connection. Folks like St. Francis of Assisi and the early 13th century Muslim / Sufi visionary thinker Shams-i Tabrīzī. Teasdale and Berry are part of the group of mystical visionary thinkers throughout our entire history in every religious tradition who promote this same concept.

Teasdale was a strong proponent and actively engaged in issues of social justice. He wrote: "We are at the threshold of a new age, a Second Axial Age, a decisive period that will be characterized by a deep sense of community among the religions — of interspiritual wisdom — and a profound commitment to environmental justice. The Second Axial Age will thus also be the Interspiritual Age and the Ecological Age." He would often talk about what he described as "the emergence of interspiritual wisdom." As Bob O'Hearn, writing about Teasdale in *Western Mystics*, described it: "We now know that each one of us inhabits, rather than possesses, what can be called local awareness. It makes our life tangible by filtering it through parameters of knowing and being that allow for this local type of consciousness, this knowing person here and now who is self-aware. When someone has a mystical experience, he or she is propelled into a cosmic kind of perception. The enlightened are those who have broken out of their local and regional, or individual and species awareness and have discovered other realms of consciousness beyond this sphere."

Today, when you think about Interspirituality and activism most people focus on the idea of religious traditions coming together, maybe organizing a joint prayer vigil or protest around an issue of justice. Maybe working together trying to get a specific piece of legislation passed or raising awareness around issues like hunger. All very important things, however, it is based on two faulty concepts. The first is the idea central in the teachings of most faiths, particularly the Abrahamic traditions, that says we are here so we can get to there. Everything we do is important only insofar as it helps us get to Heaven. As theologian John Haught suggested, faith / theology is based on the belief that "our personal salvation can be assured if we concentrate on what lies above while being both grateful for and detached from the seductive goodness and beauty of the material world."

The second concept, which a great deal of faith activism is based on, is the idea of stewardship. We develop programs centered around the idea of "caring for." About sixty years ago, a man named Lynn White wrote an article "The Historical Roots of Our Ecological Crisis." In it he suggested that the environmental crisis was partially a result of the teachings from the Abrahamic faiths around the concept of dominionism, the idea that we have dominion over all creation. After White's article was published, we began to see a change in our theology and our activism. We began to evolve into a stewardship model. We evolved from dominion over to caring for. We talked about being good stewards of creation and caring for the poor. All very important and worthwhile but not transformative. The Catholic theologian Elizabeth Johnson suggests that stewardship is one of the main causes of the -isms: racism, sexism, homophobia, etc. The stewardship model of activism is still hierarchical and anthropic. It is based on a system where "we" are responsible for caring "for." Then we get to define who is the "we." In western culture, "we" is defined as white males. The stewardship model of activism is nothing more than a dominionist with a conscience.

Br. Teasdale believed that our activism should be transformative. He felt that our religions needed to evolve beyond a model of acceptance of each other while we wait for salvation. Rather, we need to come together in a new understanding, a new consciousness of oneness. Sr. Ilia Delio, in her article "The Death of God and the Rebirth of God," writes: "Jesus' integral consciousness of wholeness evoked a genuine revolution in cosmic and social relations, a new creativity, a new structure of existence based on community and shared values. He saw all human beings (and indeed the whole creation) as part of himself and called his disciples to a new future, to create a transformed earth, where all could live together in justice, mercy, and peace." Teasdale understood that to create this new Earth, religions would have to come together and re-imagine who we are. They would have to rediscover community and our relationship to all creation. In her book *The Not-Yet God: Carl Jung, Teilhard de Chardin, and the Relational Whole*, Ilia Delio tells us, "The new spiritual awakening must begin in the depths of our own minds as we journey into the Christ Self, the psyche, and conquer all that prevents us from embracing our divine reality." For Teasdale, justice and spirituality were deeply connected.

You could not have justice without Interspirituality. There had to be a coming together or as we say in Christianity, a "come to Jesus moment." But this coming together has to move beyond tolerance and even acceptance. Our faith communities and religions have to reimagine and refocus our efforts and energies towards the inner mystical transcendence. We have to stop waiting for the sky God to rescue us and find that place where the divine begins and ends — that place where all creation is one.

Endnotes and References for "Sacred Activism, Holism" Section[vi]

EDUCATING FOR DIRECTION

Features by Diane Berke - Julie Krull

Becoming Creatures of Boundless Love

A Vision for Interspiritual Education

by Diane Berke

We have been given the gift of life
in this perplexing world
to become who we ultimately are –
creatures of boundless love,
caring, compassion, and wisdom.
—Wayne Teasdale, *The Mystic Heart,* p. 3

Tolstoy once wrote, "Grow spiritually, and help others to do so. It is the meaning of life." For many of us, the nature of that growth is captured clearly and succinctly in the beautiful words of *The Mystic*

Heart cited above. Twenty-five years since they were first released into this world, these words continue to be a powerful beacon for our own lives and our work in the world.

In August 2002, together with a group of dedicated colleagues, I founded One Spirit Learning Alliance, an interspiritual educational nonprofit dedicated to preparing spiritual care providers to serve the evolving spiritual needs of an increasingly complex and interconnected world. Since our founding, we have trained and ordained more than 1,200 interspiritual ministers and spiritual companions / counselors.

For four years prior to starting One Spirit, I had served as director of an interfaith seminary that was the oldest of its kind in the world. Two events in 2001 led me to the decision to leave that institution and create a new vehicle to take the work we'd been doing to a deeper level of understanding and expression. One was what occurred on September 11, 2001, which heightened the urgency of building bridges of respect and understanding between faiths and recognizing and honoring our shared humanity. The other was my encountering Brother Wayne Teasdale's book, *The Mystic Heart: Discovering a Universal Spirituality in the World's Religions*, in which he coined the term Interspirituality.

I immediately felt a deep resonance with Wayne's vision of Interspirituality, with its emphasis on direct experience of awakening to the underlying unity of being and on the sharing of resources across Wisdom Traditions for accessing and stabilizing that experience. The 20th-century non-dual spiritual text *A Course in Miracles* teaches, "A universal theology is impossible, but a universal experience is not only possible but necessary." While much of traditional interfaith dialogue focused on discussing and comparing theology, the work we had been called to was much more about creating space in which we could meet in the heart of that shared experience.

At the Parliament of the World's Religions held in Barcelona in 2004, One Spirit's beloved founding Associate Director Rev. Dr. Joyce Liechenstein met Dr. Kurt Johnson, who was there as part of a group presenting Wayne's vision of Interspirituality to the Parliament for the first time. After returning to New York, Joyce introduced Kurt to One Spirit, and he quickly became a treasured friend and colleague. Serving as a board member, spiritual advisor, and faculty member for many years, Kurt played an invaluable role in helping One Spirit deeply ground itself in the vision of Interspirituality and become one of the pioneers of developing interspiritual education.

A Vision of Interspiritual Education

In his book *The Coming Interspiritual Age,* Kurt points out two overarching aims of interspiritual education. The first and most important is the cultivation of *experiential unity consciousness.* It is very easy to talk about unity and Oneness, but the awakening and rooting of that as a lived reality in the heart comes only through a depth of ongoing contemplative practice, a commitment to the inner work of transformation, a willingness to engage in the personal and collective healing and growth that are catalyzed by the crucible of creating authentic community, and an outward expression of the implications of unity through engagement in loving service. Each of these are thus essential dimensions of interspiritual education.

Another priority for interspiritual education, which Wayne referred to as the second activity required by Interspirituality itself, is the study and dialogue necessary to heal the historical and ongoing wounds and divisions among the religions of the world. This study and dialogue must honor and appreciate the rich diversity and differences in beliefs and worldviews of our many traditions but also focus on and emphasize the foundational ethical standards and values they all hold in common. Every tradition contains a universalist thread of teaching pointing to the "family-hood," or interconnected nature, of the whole of reality or creation, yet these shared values and ethical principles can easily get lost in the details of the particularistic threads of theology and praxis. Interspirituality lifts up and shines a light on those aspects of spiritual wisdom that are the shared heritage of all humanity.

Hazrat Inayat Khan, founder of the Sufi Order of the West, wrote in *The Unity of Religious Ideals* that if we look at the level of the intellect (concept and belief), we will always find what divides us and makes us different, but if we look at the level of the heart, we will always find what joins us and makes us the same. Interspirituality has been described as "spirituality through the lens of the heart." Interspiritual education must cultivate and nurture the wisdom of the heart as well as the knowledge of the mind.

A Framework for Mature Interspirituality

In his extensive work with mature practitioners from diverse cultural and religious backgrounds over many, many years, Wayne realized that such practitioners — despite clear and rich differences in language, cultural frameworks and expressions, theological foundations and beliefs, and individual personalities — tended to share certain qualities or characteristics that were recognizable beyond these differences. He saw these shared characteristics as fruits of a fully realized inner life, and thus as elements of a mature Interspirituality. They can also serve as *aspirations* for what we seek to cultivate in ourselves, our relationships with others, and our way of being in the world.[1] The nine elements Wayne elaborated in *The Mystic Heart* are:

1. Fully actualized moral / ethical capacity
2. Solidarity with all living beings
3. Deep non-violence
4. Humility
5. Regular spiritual practice
6. Mature self-knowledge
7. Simplicity
8. Selfless service / compassionate action
9. Prophetic voice

In thinking about and working with these elements, it becomes clear that they are not independent of each other. Rather, they interrelate, overlap, and inform each other as we cultivate them in ourselves and express them in our lives. Together they help us weave a beautiful tapestry for living the highest and deepest qualities of the human spirit.

In personally exploring and sharing these elements with others, I have found it helpful to think of them as falling naturally into three clusters: honoring our interconnectedness with all of life; embracing the deep inner work of transformation; and engaging the social concerns of our world.

Honoring Our Interconnectedness with All of Life

(Elements 1, 2, & 3)

Element 1 – Fully actualizing our moral / ethical capacity

All religious and spiritual traditions contain an ethical dimension which is universal and unvarying in its essentials, based on the principle of *non-harm.* Wayne points out that a fully actualized moral and ethical capacity "is based in a transformed inner nature. The moral dimension of the spiritual journey has nothing to do with external rules and regulations but with a fundamental, radical reorientation of the person's inner commitment to be established permanently and concretely in love and compassion" (TMH, p. 113).

Through the inner work of transformation that is the heart of the spiritual journey, we can become so firmly established in love and the reality of our Oneness with all life that we will *naturally* live in a way that does not cause harm to others or ourselves. But this inner transformation takes a very long time, and along the way we need guidance in how to live harmoniously in community with others. Wayne says that the moral and ethical codes found in every religion and spiritual path can be thought of like training wheels on a bicycle. As we are learning to ride, to stay upright and balanced — as we are engaging in the work of becoming fully grounded in love and compassion — we need and use these moral and ethical guidelines to keep us from falling over and hurting ourselves and others.

Element 2 – Living in solidarity with the cosmos and all living beings

Since ancient times, mystical experience and wisdom have confirmed "the unity of all aspects of reality ... The experience of the interconnectedness of everything is part of the perennial tradition, a primordial vision gained from the insight of countless mystics across the millennia ... all were keenly aware of the unity and interrelationship of everything" (TMH, p. 113, 114).

Wayne points out that "science is catching up to [this ancient mystical and spiritual wisdom] in its understanding of this fundamental unity. … quantum physics indicates that the universe is a 'complicated web of interdependent relationships.' Each relationship is intrinsically connected with every other, and all of them are part of the totality" (TMH, pp. 115-116).

When we experience and live with a realization of the profound interconnectedness of all being, we recognize every part of creation as precious and worthy of being treated with dignity, care, and respect.

Element 3 – Cultivating deep non-violence

Once we begin to recognize the interconnectedness of all life, there is a natural and organic movement toward living a life of deep non-violence, which is the expression of the attitude and practice of non-harming (TMH, p. 116).

While many of us may associate the term "non-violence" with social justice movements like the Civil Rights movement, anti-war efforts, or other resistance to systemic oppression, we can recognize that the meaning of non-violence is broader and deeper than simply refraining from physical violence. Quaker educator and author Parker Palmer defines non-violence as "the commitment to act in every situation in ways that honor the soul" (Parker Palmer, *A Hidden Wholeness*).

Richard Rohr describes soul as "anything's ultimate meaning which is held within. Soul is the blueprint inside of every created thing telling it what it is and what it can become. When we meet anything at that level, we will respect, protect, and love it" (Center for Action and Contemplation, Daily Meditations).

Embracing the Inner Work of Transformation
(Elements 4, 5, & 6)

Element 4 – Cultivating and living in humility

Wayne points out that humility — a quality that all religions and spiritual traditions agree is essential to the spiritual life — is often very misunderstood, especially in western culture where it is "confused with weakness, with bowing and scraping before others" (TMH, p. 127).

Genuine humility is looking truthfully at ourselves, without ego-inflation, defensiveness, or self-diminishment. It is an honest self-assessment of both our current shortcomings and limitations *and also* the strengths and gifts we have to contribute to life.

True humility in the spiritual life asks us to recognize both our highest spiritual potential to live as kind, loving, wise, and compassionate human beings *and* the fact that we are "works in progress" who fall short of that potential again and again. We learn to accept and live within the reality of that gap, allowing it to motivate us to keep growing in our capacity to love.

Element 5 - Embracing a regular spiritual practice

Wayne writes that regular spiritual practice is the *means* by which inner transformation occurs. He calls daily spiritual practice the "technology" of inner change (TMH, p. 126), without which such change is impossible. Moreover, he says, the spiritual practice(s) we engage in must be *contemplative.*

Contemplative practice opens us to unitive experience with what is beyond our sense of small, separate self. Contemplative practices can include any practices or activities that draw us into a state of full presence, undivided attention, receptivity and availability to life as it is in this present moment. In addition to the rich body of practices available to us through the shared heritage of our Wisdom Traditions, everyday activities can become contemplative practices when we engage them with the intention of being fully present in the moment, awake, and lovingly attentive to whatever is unfolding within and around us.

Element 6 - Cultivating mature self-knowledge

Mature self-knowledge rests on the foundation of humility. "Humility," Wayne writes, "is the basis of an honest, mature self-awareness that accepts ourselves as we are, without covering up, making excuses, or blaming others. … Mature self-knowledge happens when we move beyond denial — denial of our faults and limitations, our buried motives or hidden agendas — and beyond judgment of others, beyond projection on others of our own need for inner work" (TMH, pp. 141, 142).

We can cultivate mature self-knowledge through honest self-reflection and through feedback from others we trust to be lovingly direct and honest with us. Yet truly moving beyond denial and projection, uncovering and looking honestly at our buried motives and hidden agendas, involves deep and often difficult inner work. In psychological terms, this may be described as "shadow work," which has been called by Integral theorist Ken Wilber "western psychology's greatest contribution to spirituality."

Our shadow consists of the "dark" side of our personality — "dark" as in hidden from the light of our conscious awareness, like the dark side of the moon which is perennially hidden from our view. It consists of those qualities, traits, and behavioral expressions we have learned, through socialization, to judge as unacceptable in ourselves. We deny them as a part of ourselves, and further distance ourselves from them by projecting them out onto others, onto the world. Through shadow work, we reclaim the energy that has been trapped in these projections so it can be reintegrated and expressed in healthier and more creative ways. As Swiss psychologist Carl Jung said, "We do not become enlightened by imagining figures of light, but by making the darkness conscious."

Engaging the Social Concerns of Our World
(Elements 7, 8, & 9)

It has always been the case, but is especially so in the 21st century, that the spiritual life cannot be lived truly cut off from the life of the larger world we share. The fruits of our inner development through contemplative practice must, and inevitably do, express themselves in our engagement with the world around us, with the social dimension of life. Wayne writes, "A viable spirituality today is socially engaged; it does not turn its back on the sufferings of the world, but squarely faces them and contributes to their mitigation and alleviation. … the more outward expressions of the inner journey, the social dimension that is found in all traditions of spirituality … apply to fruits of the mystical life to the sphere of social concerns, and the demands of compassion and love in active society" (TMH, pp. 147-148).

Element 7 – Living a life of simplicity

With startling directness, Wayne writes, "A person who does not understand and practice the virtue of simplicity is only playing around on the spiritual journey" (TMH, p. 152). In a society driven by consumerism, materialistic values, and busyness as a symbol of importance and success, living simply is intensely countercultural and involves simplifying our lives both outwardly and inwardly.

On the outer level, living simply means being mindful and intentional in our choices around what and how much we consume. We respect that the earth's resources are finite, and that the choices we make concerning our lifestyle and consumption concretely impact the lives of countless people and other living beings all over the world. Wayne points out, "When we voluntarily embrace a simpler lifestyle that does not require squandering … precious resources, degrading the environment, oppressing other species, and depriving the poor, simplicity of life reveals itself concretely as a great generosity of spirit. … In our social realm, the adage 'live simply so that others may simply live' wisely demonstrates the practical efficacy of true spirituality" (TMH, p. 149-150).

Living simply inwardly involves discerning what is essential from what is not; centering our lives on what truly matters; and removing the clutter and distractions of what is not really important from our lives and focus of attention. Author and psychologist Lee Jampolsky encourages us, "At least three times a day, stop and ask yourself what is really important. Have the wisdom and courage to build your life around the answer."

Element 8 - Engaging in selfless service and compassionate action

Seva, the Sanskrit word for selfless service, refers to service performed without any expectation of result or reward for the person performing it. Yet, people who offer this quality of service share that, almost always, they *receive* as much or more than they *give*. *Behaviorally,* the giving may seem to be one-way, but *experientially*, a reciprocity of giving and receiving happens organically.

This element is closely related to Element 2, living in solidarity with all living beings. The more deeply rooted we become in an understanding and experience of our interconnectedness with all life, the more responding to suffering wherever we encounter it becomes both a moral imperative and a natural, automatic response — just as the body naturally mobilizes and directs a healing response to a point of injury.

Research in neuroscience tells us that we are literally hard-wired for empathy. It is a natural quality of the human heart to be moved by suffering. Yet, true compassion must be more than simply feeling care and concern for others' well-being. That feeling must be translated into action to realize its full transformative potential, both on the world around us and on ourselves. As Thích Nhất Hạnh expressed it, "Compassion is a verb."

Element 9 - Embodying & empowering the prophetic voice

With this element, our focus shifts from the personal to the systemic. The prophetic voice is the dimension and expression of compassion that seeks not only to alleviate existing suffering but also to address and transform the systemic causes of suffering. Archbishop Desmond Tutu described this difference this way: "There comes a point where we need to stop just pulling people out of the river. We need to go upstream and find out why they're falling in."

The prophetic voice is willing to speak truth to power — to call out social and cultural structures, institutions, and systems that create and perpetuate suffering through injustice and oppression. It calls us to name and bear witness to unjust and oppressive systems and institutions, and to engage in the struggle to change them wherever they exist.

Because we are profoundly interconnected, "injustice anywhere is a threat to justice everywhere," as Rev. Dr. Martin Luther King, Jr., pointed out. And so we are called by conscience and compelled by our vision of the inherent unity of life to work for justice not only for all human beings but also, increasingly, all living beings, including animals, living ecosystems, and the earth itself.

Conclusion

In *The Mystic Heart,* Wayne wrote, "We need to understand, to really grasp at an elemental level, that the definitive revolution is the spiritual awakening of humankind" (TMH, p. 12). The world is crying out for this awakening, this revolution, and it is this cry to which interspiritual education must respond.

Endnotes and References for this Feature[vii]

The Feature above is one of a number in these Volumes centering on the history, and interfaith and interspiritual contributions, of the One Spirit Interfaith Seminary in New York City — that second oldest, and the largest, interfaith and interspiritual seminary in the world. It has consistently formed its curricula around elements of Br. Teasdale's, and other Interspiritual Pioneers' vision and work. One Spirit has transitioned now, due to earlier Covid era realities, from its decades long physical location in New York City to a fully online platform (1spirit.org) and continues its major contributions to the global interfaith and interspiritual communities. See "The Growing Edge of Interspirituality" (by Kurt Johnson) herein and Features in

Volumes 1 and 2 by One Spirit leadership, past and present, including Featured Authors Diane Berke, Kurt Johnson, DeShannon Barnes-Bowens, Leslie Reambeault, and Melissa Stewart (along with visiting faculty like Andrew Harvey and nearly a dozen graduates who have gone on to significant leadership roles in the world's interfaith and interspiritual communities). You can find the named Featured Authors above in the Tables of Contents of both Volumes.

Millennials as R/Evolutionary Interspiritual Architects

by Julie Krull

A defining trait of the Millennial generation is their departure from conventional religious practices and institutions. This trend, often misinterpreted as a decline in spirituality, reflects a deeper yearning for authenticity and relevance in spiritual engagement. Studies have shown that while Millennials may be leaving churches, temples, and mosques, their spiritual curiosity and hunger for meaningful life remain undiminished. This disillusionment with traditional religious forms stems from various factors, including perceived rigidity, lack of alignment with progressive social values, and scandals that have undermined the credibility of religious institutions. Instead of signifying a loss of faith, this exodus represents a search for a more personal, direct experience of the sacred, one that transcends dogmatic boundaries and resonates with the complexities of modern life.

Social Values and the Call for an Inclusive Spirituality

Millennials are a values-driven generation, with a strong emphasis on inclusivity, diversity, social justice, and environmental stewardship. Their spirituality is inherently intertwined with these values, reflecting a holistic understanding of their place in the world. This generation seeks a spiritual path that not only fosters personal growth and transformation but also compels action toward a more just, compassionate, and sustainable world. The interspiritual movement, with its focus on the interconnectedness of all life and the wisdom that flows from multiple spiritual traditions, resonates deeply with these aspirations. It offers a framework where spirituality becomes a bridge rather than a barrier, encouraging dialogue, mutual respect, and shared action for the common good.

Technology as a Catalyst for Spiritual Exploration and Community

Another distinctive aspect of Millennials is their fluency with digital technology. This proficiency has transformed their spiritual journey, enabling them to explore diverse traditions, philosophies, and practices with unprecedented ease. The internet, digital platforms, and social media have become fertile grounds for spiritual discovery and community building, allowing Millennials to connect with like-minded individuals across the globe, share insights, and cocreate spaces for interspiritual dialogue and practice. This digital dimension of the interspiritual movement amplifies its reach and impact, making spirituality more accessible and adaptable to the needs of a generation that values flexibility, diversity, and collaboration.

Leadership in the Workplace and Conscious Parenting

As Millennials step into leadership roles within organizations and as parents raising the next generation, their influence on the cultural and spiritual zeitgeist becomes even more pronounced. In the workplace, they champion values such as authenticity, purpose, and work-life balance, reshaping corporate cultures to be more humane, inclusive, and aligned with broader social and environmental goals. This leadership style, rooted in their interspiritual orientation, emphasizes empathy, collaboration, and a sense of shared purpose, offering a model for how diverse perspectives and strengths can be harnessed toward collective goals.

As parents, Millennials are keenly aware of the importance of raising conscious, compassionate children who are attuned to the interconnectedness of all beings and the planet. Their approach to parenting is often characterized by an openness to exploring a variety of spiritual perspectives, fostering in their children a sense of wonder, curiosity, and respect for different paths. This commitment to nurturing a spiritually aware and socially engaged generation is perhaps one of the most significant contributions of Millennials to the evolution of the interspiritual movement.

Conclusion

The interspiritual movement, with its vision of a world where the boundaries between spiritual traditions are transcended in favor of a more unified, compassionate approach to the sacred, finds in Millennials a generation uniquely equipped to bring this vision into fruition. Through their departure from traditional religious institutions, commitment to social values, adept use of technology, and emerging roles as leaders and parents, Millennials are not only participants in the interspiritual movement but also its architects. Their journey toward a more inclusive, holistic spirituality reflects a broader evolutionary shift in human consciousness, one that holds the promise of a future where spirituality serves as a unifying force for healing, transformation, and the betterment of the world. As this generation continues to evolve and realize the potential of Interspirituality, their legacy will likely be seen in the emergence of a more compassionate, interconnected global community, grounded in the wisdom of the heart and the spirit of collaboration for the good of the whole.

Endnotes and References for "Sacred Activism, Education" Section[vii]

INTERSPIRITUALITY, SCIENCE, AND THE FUTURE

Features by Robert Atkinson - Diane Berke - Roger P. Briggs
Calvin Chatlos - Jude Currivan - Jeff Genung - Kabir Helminski - Robert Hesse
J. J. and Desiree Hurtak - Ervin Laszlo - Thomas Legrand
David Lorimer - Kate Sheehan Roach - Susan Soleil - David Sloan Wilson

How fitting now to move from the entire flow of content of these Volumes 1 and 2, and the sections just above on the vision of First Peoples, foundational cultures, and Sacred Activism to contributions by some of the most creative and impactful leaders in today's global scientific and futurist communities and their views of Interspirituality, science, and — crucially — the future.

The section begins with Roger Briggs, author of *Emerging World* offering "A Meta-Framework for Human Evolution," drawing heavily from the work of Jean Gebser, Merlin Donald, and Riane Eisler. Next is noted UK cosmologist Dr. Jude Currivan, recent author of *The Cosmic Hologram* and *The Story of Gaia*; then Dr. Robert Atkinson, an understudy of Joseph Campbell, and well-known for his book *The Story of Our Time* (and most recently, *The Way of Unity*). Then follows Features by Drs. J. J. and Desiree Hurtak, authors of multiple books on futurism and founders of the Academy for Future Science. The next Feature is from five key voices from current mainstream evolutionary science who have been pioneers in the game-changing shift in mainstream evolutionary science (from recent publications by Yale / Templeton and Prosocial.world) on understanding cooperation in evolution and how altruism (goodness) actually evolves. We follow with the 2024 Nautilus Grand Prize Winner, Dr. Thomas Legrand, and his message in *Politics of Being*, David Lorimer, Chair of the Galileo Commission, and then Sufi thought leader, Kabir Helminski. The Section concludes with two-time Nobel Peace Prize nominee and systems science pioneer Dr. Ervin Lazslo whose two books on global upshift were also Gold Nautilus Award winners in 2024. Along with these, see two contributions elsewhere in these volumes by Claudia Welss, Chairperson of the renowned Institute of Noetic Sciences.

A Meta-Framework for Human Evolution

by Roger P. Briggs

We now understand the evolution of life on Earth within the larger context of an evolving universe that produced a star with a planet where life could begin. However, we are still lacking a coherent story and evidence-based framework for the very recent evolutionary development we call *humanity,* and our signature achievement, *culture.* Well-known frameworks such as Spiral Dynamics provide insight and meaning for the more recent stages of human development, but do not address the deeper time-scape going back to the first toolmakers millions of years ago, which is where the story of humanity begins. Although *cultural evolution* is now widely recognized by academic scientists,[1] its underlying driver, the *evolution of consciousness,* remains largely outside mainstream science. Here we unify the evolution of culture and consciousness by bringing together the work of Jean Gebser, Merlin Donald, and Riane Eisler with the most current fossil and genomic evidence from paleoanthropology, to construct a meta-framework for *psychocultural* evolution. This meta-framework is the deep story of humanity that helps make sense of today's civilizational meta-crisis, and points the way to a positive future for humans and all life on our planet.

Part One – Jean Gebser (1905 – 1973): Structures of Consciousness

While witnessing firsthand the rise of Hitler, Jean Gebser had the vision in 1932 of humanity evolving a new structure of consciousness. In his early writings, he named it the *integral consciousness*. Over the next twenty-five years, Gebser developed the first framework for the evolution of culture and consciousness — psychocultural evolution — which he laid out in detail in his two-volume work, *The Ever-Present Origin* (1956). This was a remarkable achievement given how little was known at that time about human evolution.

Gebser called our current psychocultural stage the *mental structure of consciousness*, reaching its climax with modernity and the scientific revolution. Like many scholars, he dated the origin of the "modern mind" to roughly 2,500 years ago in the Axial Age societies such as Classical Greece. He also recognized the ending, or collapse, of the mental consciousness in the 20th century, with horrific world wars and nuclear weapons, necessitating a new way of seeing and being in the world — the integral consciousness.

To build his framework for human evolution, Gebser worked backward in time from the mental stage. Using the Greek mythologies and older texts such as the Epic of Gilgamesh and the Torah, he proposed the *mythical stage* preceding the mental, and coinciding with the emergence of spoken language. Oral storytelling was the primary source of meaning within the tribes of the mythical cultures, who also made beautiful cave paintings in Europe and elsewhere 20,000 years ago.

Reaching even deeper in time, asking what came before the mythical stage, Gebser turned to the ethnographic studies of the still-pristine cultures of Samoa and New Guinea by Margaret Mead and other cultural anthropologists. From this he surmised a pre-linguistic stage in which communal ritual was the primary source of meaning and social cohesion. He called this the *magical stage*.

But Gebser could go no further back in time — because in those days virtually nothing was known about the deep origins of humanity. He called the pre-magical stage the *archaic* and likened it to the consciousness of the new-born infant, but beyond that could say very little. Even so, Gebser had created the first psychocultural framework for human evolution:

Archaic – Magical – Mythical – Mental – Integral (emerging today)

He described these as both *stages* of culture and *structures* of consciousness that evolved over time, with each one *transcending and including* the previous, in holonic fashion. Today, although we are governed mainly by the mental consciousness (all that thinking and rationality), our mythical consciousness is alive and well, which is why stories are still so meaningful and important for us. Gebser also correlated his stages and structures of consciousness with human developmental stages from birth, aligning remarkably well with Piaget's developmental stages.[2]

Part Two – Merlin Donald (1939 –): Memory Systems and Mimesis

Merlin Donald, the Canadian neuroscientist turned cognitive paleoanthropologist, knew nothing about Gebser's work[3] when he began to investigate psychocultural evolution in the late 1980s. In his book, *A Mind So Rare: The Evolution of Human Consciousness* (2001), Donald proposed and described a strikingly similar progression of stages in the evolution of culture and consciousness:

Episodic – Mimetic – Mythic – Theoretic

Here the *episodic* refers to the "pre-human" consciousness of mammals and birds, while the *mythic* and *theoretic* map exactly onto Gebser's *mythical* and *mental*. However, Donald's seminal contribution was identifying and describing the *mimetic* stage and the unprecedented capability he called *mimesis*. Mimesis gets right to the heart of the question: what was it our early ancestors had that allowed our lineage to "veer off" from the rest of life on this planet, and into a new realm of domination and power we still maintain today? This watershed moment is evidenced by the appearance of manufactured stone tools, beginning about 3 million years ago in Africa, signaling a quantum leap in cognitive capacity, and a new regime of evolution on our planet, *cultural evolution*.

Not only did the first toolmakers have grasping hands with opposable thumbs but also, according to Merlin Donald, they evolved a new memory system, known as *semantic memory*, that interacted with existing memory systems, taking them beyond the *episodic* consciousness of other mammals and birds. This new cognitive capacity, known as *mimesis*, is what made toolmaking and the transmission of culture possible.[4]

Manufacturing a stone tool requires not only manual dexterity but also sourcing of the right materials, and then using highly refined skills and sequential procedures to shape the material into a useful tool. It wasn't simply that one individual was suddenly able to do all this, but that the knowledge and skillsets were *transmitted* to others through imitation — mimesis — over many generations. The art of toolmaking spread far and wide, throughout Africa, and then Central Asia, and eventually everywhere. It went viral, and new innovations continually advanced the technology. Toolmaking was the birth of true culture, where a knowledge base is passed along beyond lifetimes, and continually added to. We know of no other life forms that can build knowledge and innovate technology over many generations, and millions of years.

Donald's work on mimesis illuminated Gebser's archaic stage, yet he did not recognize Gebser's magical stage. However, by putting these together we arrive at the Gebser-Donald synthesis:

1. **Mimetic Stage** – early tools, family groups, transmission of knowledge, birth of culture
2. **Magical Stage** – communal ritual, clans, cooperative hunting
3. **Mythical Stage** – spoken language and story-telling, tribes, self-aware consciousness
4. **Mental/Theoretic Stage** – written language, cities and nations, causality and science

Part Three – Paleoanthropology and the Fossil Record

Paleoanthropology provides the physical evidence for human evolution, in the form of stone tools and skeletal remains, and it provides a timeline based on its ever-improving dating methods. Before 1960, most paleoanthropologists were looking unsuccessfully in Asia for human origins. But when Louis and Mary Leakey discovered *Homo habilis* in East Africa, attention turned to that continent, and the field exploded with new discoveries. Today, by some counts, we have identified some twenty-one different species comprising our lineage, with only one survivor, *Homo sapiens*. We know that cranial volume (brain size) *tripled* as the *Homo* lineage evolved, and this didn't happen to our closest relatives the chimpanzees and bonobos. No one knows why. And who were the Neanderthals, and why did they disappear? Or did they? Fascinating questions, but for the purposes of anchoring the Gebser-Donald synthesis into real time, the archeological record now shows four "major transitions" as our lineage evolved:

First Transition: 3.5 – 3.3 Million Years Ago

Toolmaking began, signifying the birth of true culture. The earliest known stone tools, found in North Africa, date to 3.3 million years ago and are attributed to Australopiths.[5] By about two million years ago, *Homo erectus* was innovating new tool designs and spreading into Central and Southeast Asia. The First Transition is when our lineage diverged from all other life forms, taking an entirely new direction. We propose this transition as the beginning of the **MIMETIC STAGE** of culture and consciousness.

Second Transition: 900,000 – 800,000 Years Ago

A gap in the fossil record and recent genomic evidence[6] suggest that a near-extinction event occurred for our ancestors between 900,000 and 800,000 years ago, likely caused by climate change.

Out of this crisis came a new species in Africa, now called *Homo heidelbergensis.* Some members of this species migrated to Europe and became the Neanderthals, while others stayed in Africa to evolve into *Homo sapiens* by about 300,000 years ago. With a large brain and many sophisticated behaviors, *heidelbergensis* was the first of our ancestors we might call "human"[7] and was the last common ancestor of both Neanderthals and modern humans. This transition signals the emergence of the **MAGICAL STAGE** of culture and consciousness.

Third Transition: 73,000 – 60,000 Years Ago

Another near-extinction event occurred around this time, reducing the *Homo sapiens* population on Earth to perhaps only a few thousand in Africa. The mega-eruption of Mt. Toba in Sumatra 73,000 years ago triggered a 1,000-year global winter that pushed our ancestors to the brink of extinction. By about 60,000 years ago, the surviving humans had achieved a *Great Leap*[8] in cognitive capacity that has been called *the Big Bang of consciousness*.[9] This is clearly evidenced in the fossil record by a whole new generation of advanced tools like fish hooks, sewing needles, and musical instruments. Spoken language was mastered around this time, giving birth to the storytelling cultures. These now-fully modern humans left Africa and spread rapidly over all the habitable continents, to become the near-geologic force we remain today. This major transition, the Great Leap, launched the **MYTHICAL STAGE** of culture and consciousness.

Fourth Transition: 10,000 – 5,000 Years Ago

After millions of years living close to nature as nomadic gatherer-hunters, our ancestors began living in large, permanent settlements.

By about 9,000 years ago, people were living in large *proto-cities* like Çatalhöyük (in present-day Turkey). These were largely egalitarian, peaceful, cooperative societies without gender ranking. The archeological record shows no signs of social stratification at this time — dwellings and nutritional levels were similar across entire populations. The art shows that women and men lived in partnership, without patriarchy or matriarchy. Then, between about 6,000 and 5,000 years ago, this changed radically when true cities with hierarchical societies and patriarchal power structures emerged in several locations throughout the Middle East. Cities became city-states and then empires. War and conquest became the norm, and the rest is history.

Indoor living in crowded cities, along with the domestication of animals and plants, contributed to an increasing *separation* from the natural world. Written language was invented, as was poverty and wealth, and war and empire. This is our current stage, the era we call history, the era of civilization. To understand the nature of this fourth major transition and why it has led to our planetary meta-crisis today, we must turn to the work of Riane Eisler.

Part Four – Riane Eisler (1931 -): Hierarchies of Domination

Most scholars, including Gebser and Donald, consider the Axial Age to mark the origin of the "modern mind." The Axial Age, some 2,500 years ago, was a spectacular cultural flowering that produced the likes of Socrates, Pythagoras, and Plato, Lao Tze and Confucius, the Buddha, Isaiah, and later, Jesus. The Greeks were so advanced in their knowledge and methods they correctly determined the circumference of our planet and the distance to the moon. Considering such capabilities, it makes sense to date the origins of our present mental/theoretic stage to Classical Greece.

However, there is something more foundational and ubiquitous that predates the Axial Age by thousands of years and underpins our present psychocultural paradigm. It was Riane Eisler, in her book *The Chalice and the Blade* (1987), who so clearly identified the deeper cultural substrate of the last 5,000 years: *social stratification* and *hierarchies of domination*.

Between about 6,000 and 5,000 years ago, monumental architecture appeared for the first time on Earth in Sumeria (modern day Iraq). To build massive temples, palaces, and pyramids required armies of slaves and someone to be in charge of them. This was a new social order with rigid social hierarchy maintained by top-down patriarchal power structures. We call this social model *civilization*, and it later appeared in widely separate locations including Egypt, India, China, Meso-America, and South America.

In early civilizations, all-powerful emperors occupied the top of the hierarchy and, with armed forces, could impose their wishes on large populations. Walled cities and evidence of organized armies appear in the archeological record for the first time, as war and empire-building became the recurring theme of history for the next 5,000 years. Poverty and wealth were born together, for they can only exist together, and men were now ranked above women, as they have been ever since. Large-scale agriculture, the domestication of animals, and indoor living in cubicles fueled a growing sense of "man over nature."

Riane Eisler recognized this new social order and named it *domination-oriented culture*, and it has been our primary operating system up until today. Only the names, faces, and weapons have changed over the course of what we call "history." For 5,000 years, the paradigm of domination has produced war and violence against our brothers and sisters, and the desecration of the natural world. Indeed, nearly all our problems today are the result of the domination of people and Nature.

The domination orientation is rooted in a *material* view of the world — a world made of inert objects separated in space. This *material consciousness* must have evolved synergistically along with hierarchies of domination. It presents us the world we know so well, what we call "reality," with object and subject separated in Cartesian duality. The material consciousness *objectifies* the world. Women are owned by men as objects, and all people are objects, as are other animals, trees, rivers, and Mother Earth herself, all there for us to exploit for personal gain. At the center of our material view of the world is *ME* and *my* subjective experience, *my* needs and wants, and *my* importance. A new form of selfhood — the fully-individuated egoic self — emerged with the material consciousness and manifested powerfully in the emperor archetype.

The domination-oriented culture and the material consciousness synergistically support each other and emerged together, comprising the fourth major psychocultural stage of human evolution, the *material-dominator stage*. We can squarely place its origin to 5,000 years ago, when hierarchies of domination first appeared. The consequences of this evolutionary development have been profound.

The Gebser-Donald-Eisler Meta-framework

We can now integrate these four major parts into a meta-framework for human evolution, shown below in two forms, including the emerging fifth stage envisioned by Gebser in 1932 (all dates are approximate and rounded for simplicity):

1. 3 Million years ago **Mimetic** Stage emerges Toolmaking begins
2. 900,000 years ago **Magical** Stage emerges *Homo heidelbergensis*
3. 60,000 years ago **Mythical** Stage emerges Speech, the Great Leap
4. 5,000 years ago **Material-Dominator** Stage emerges Civilization 1.0
5. Emerging Today **Integral/Planetary/Unitive** Stage Ecological Civilization

The Great Transition

For the last 5,000 years, the material structure of consciousness and the domination-oriented culture have governed human affairs and determined the course of history. But today, as civilization is unraveling and our ecosystems are collapsing, we know we can't continue on the same path. Is there an alternative to the domination-oriented model of civilization and a path to a positive future for humans? The answer is yes, if we can achieve the *fifth* major transition, the *Great Transition*, to a new culture and consciousness.

For Jean Gebser nearly a century ago, this was the transition from the *mental rational* consciousness to the *integral* consciousness. For Riane Eisler, it's the transition from hierarchies of *domination* and *power over* to hierarchies of *actualization* and *empowerment*, that is, to *partnership* culture and consciousness. Today, many people are writing and speaking and dreaming about a new world based in partnership and calling it by many names: the New Earth,[10] the Age of Interspirituality, the ecological civilization, the ecozoic era, the symbiotic culture, the unitive consciousness, the planetary consciousness, civilization 2.0, Game B, and more. All these names express the same vision of a world that works for everyone in harmony with Nature, born from an emerging new psychocultural regime, the fifth major stage of evolution in the human story. The Gebser-Donald-Eisler meta-framework for human evolution points to the possibility of a new era of partnership, peace, and prosperity for humanity and all life on Earth.

Endnotes and References for this Feature[viii:1]

An Emergent Interspiritual Cosmology

by Jude Currivan

Writing in his seminal work of 1999, *The Mystic Heart: Discovering a Universal Spirituality in the World's Religions*, Brother Wayne Teasdale declared that "we are at the dawn of a new consciousness" and invited a collective awareness to "understand, to really grasp at an elemental level that the definitive revolution is the spiritual awakening of humankind."

Dr. Kurt Johnson and David Robert Ord subsequently wrote in their book *The Coming Interspiritual Age* (2013) of Interspirituality being "the common heritage of humankind's spiritual wisdom and the sharing of wisdom resources across traditions" in a movement "toward the experience of profound interconnectedness, unity consciousness, and oneness" and "so based on the heart and unconditional love that it would be impossible to feel separate from anything."

While they and many other spiritual leaders have appreciated the evolution of human consciousness needed to manifest such an awakening, all three authors concurred that it would emerge due to "a new set of historical circumstances."

In the ensuing years, the urgency for such emergence has only increased, and with it the necessity for new circumstances to support its awakening. Now, as I write in the early days of 2024, and when I and many others are wishing for a truly hope-full New Y-era, I sense that rather than despite, it is instead *because* of the existential threats we face, the scale of turbulence and polarization, and collective exhaustion at the unsustainability of the status quo, that have the evolutionary potential, as has been the case historically, to offer such new circumstances to usher in an epoch of Interspirituality.

When the term Interspirituality was coined twenty-five years ago, while its founding was on a commonality of spiritual wisdom, one key 'tradition' was exempt from its remit — the secular science of a reductionist and materialist paradigm. Yet it is this paradigm, harking back to its late 19th century heyday, that has pervaded our collective worldview and societal organizations ever since. Inclusive of economics, corporate and governance structures, education and much more, the entirety of its hierarchical-based and siloed perspectives and resultant policies and practices have continued to drive separation-based choices and behaviors and, accordingly, maintained conflicts, exploitations, inequities and injustices with regard to people and our planetary home, Gaia.

Although the early 20th century scientific revolution of quantum and relativistic physics offered substantial clues that this mechanistic paradigm of separation was at best incomplete, discoveries since have tended to focus on technologies enabled by such insights rather than deeper consideration of their cosmological and societal implications.

Now, however, and somewhat similar to a century ago, it is scientific breakthroughs unable to be understood in terms of the prevailing reductionist paradigm that are revealing a radically new and scientifically-evidenced perception of the more fundamental nature of reality and convergent with the wholistic precepts of Interspirituality.

Its 21st century scientific revolution is compellingly underway, and its recent breakthroughs are rapidly expanding across all scales of existence. Increasingly, its discoveries and evidence across numerous fields of research from cosmology to biology, planetary sciences, neuroscience and studies of collective human behaviors including supernormal and noetic phenomena, will transform our view of the universe. Not only at its smallest and largest scales, as with the scientific revolution of the 20th century, but also its revelations at every level in between and vitally that of our everyday lives, are profoundly relevant to each and all of us. In doing so, far more than a scientific revolution, it offers to underpin and serve a (r)evolution in human consciousness. Crucially, its most essential findings are showing that instead of being something we have and experience at different levels of self-awareness, as an empirical and existential reality, mind and consciousness are what we and the whole world truly are. As wisdom teachings have maintained, universal mind literally and meaningfully in-forms the appearance of our universe, as its semblance and not its fundamental nature. As Interspirituality declares, it is its unity, expressed in manifold complexity and diversity, rather than separation or uniformity, that is indeed the authentic nature of its unitive reality and that we ourselves are its microcosmic co-creators.

The unity consciousness espoused by Interspirituality incorporates both this emergent scientifically-based understanding and the experiential perspective of indigenous Wisdom Traditions which communally perceive no separation between material and spiritual realms, only differentiation of wholeness.

Its cosmology is of an innately living, evolutionary and unified universe existing and evolving as a unitive entity; a finite thought form in the eternal and infinite mind of the Cosmos. The evidence is showing that its manifest appearance arises from deeper non-physical realms of causation, as digitized and vitally meaningful in-formation, which is pixelated at the most minute scale of existence. And with its in-formed reality manifesting holographically, its entirety is expressed in nested and relational complexity of its differentiated and diverse parts at all scales within its inherent wholeness.[1, 2, 3] Beginning 13.8 billion years ago, not in the implied chaos of a Big Bang but as an incredibly ordered and fine-tuned first moment of an ongoing Big Breath, the new story of its unitive narrative tells how, as space has since expanded from its miniscule birth and time flowed forward, our entire universe meaningfully and purposefully exists TO evolve.

Its universal sentience embodies a profound evolutionary impulse driven from the innately relational circumstances of its birth and ever since, not by random occurrences and mutations, but through resonant and harmonic interplays of forces and influences that are meaningfully and coherently in-formed and guided. In doing so, over its vast arc of emergence, it has and continues to journey from simplicity to complexity and diversity, with ever greater levels of individuated and collective self-expression, self-awareness, and interdependence.

In 2017, analysis of tiny temperature fluctuations in relic radiation from its earliest era and filling the whole of space, were seen to display on a cosmological scale the characteristic so-named fractal patterns of a holographic and unitive universe that have also been discovered at all smaller levels of existence, from vast galactic clusters, to planets, plants, people, and down to atomic scales.

Furthermore, the 2022 Nobel Prize for Physics, widely considered only to be given for non-contentious and "settled science," was awarded to three researchers for their investigations over many decades. Showing that for quantum phenomena to manifest at all, our entire universe must be nonlocally unified, they helped confirm what had been theoretically predicted half a century before.

While their work had experimentally probed this at laboratory and planetary scales, in 2018, a multi-affiliated team led by MIT researchers did so at a cosmological level. In nonlocally entangling photons of light in a laboratory with stellar photons from 600 light years away and testing of the entangled measurements triggered by light from two quasars, the most distant being 12.2 billion light years away, they succeeded in verifying the cosmological nature of nonlocality. Crucially, demonstrating that such universal wholeness is fundamental rather than a result of specific choices of measurement, has proven that apparently "localized" phenomena are actually intrinsic aspects of our whole universe's nonlocally unified nature.

A Unitive Narrative

A unitive narrative that integrates this emergent evidence-based cosmology and the tenets of Interspirituality was recently drafted by members of the SDG Thought Leaders synergy circle of the Evolutionary Leaders to serve the healing of our collective worldview from separation to a perspective of unity in diversity and empower the conscious evolution of humanity.[4,5]

In realizing the unitive nature of reality, it naturally calls for a collective celebration of our inner lives as a doorway that further supports an inclusive Interspirituality which provides essential principles, values, and practices for awakening to, experiencing, and embodying unitive consciousness.

As Dr Robert Atkinson, author of *A New Story of Wholeness* (2022), proposes: "This empowers us to envision and cocreate a love-based rather than separation-based future in which regenerative and sustainable development leads to peace as a natural outcome of a world that works for all beings and our planetary home."

Dawning of a New Earth and Unitive Age

Transcending its manifest appearance and unifying the earthly and the divine in a living, evolutionary, and unitive universe is a realization that its and our interbeing is all-pervaded by love.

At its heart, the spiritual awakening of humanity is a collective remembering of this truth and birthing of authentic hope within the depths of our emergent psyche.

With the rising of our Sun each morning, I give thanks for my experience of materiality as essential for the exploration of my soul. And I am reminded, re-hearted, and echo the words of poet Mary Oliver: "When it's over, I want to say: all my life I was a bride married to amazement. I was the bridegroom, taking the world into my arms. When it is over, I don't want to wonder if I have made of my life something particular, and real. I don't want to find myself sighing and frightened, or full of argument. I don't want to end up simply having visited this world."

As embraced by Interspirituality, this is the emergent call, it seems to me, of a universe that is inviting us to consciously experience, explore, and evolve in alignment with its inherent evolutionary impulse and, with regard to our planetary home, as shared in the unitive narrative: "Gaia's continuing emergence is embodied in collaborative and synergistic relationships and dynamic co-evolutionary partnerships on a planetary scale, where, now, the conscious evolution of humanity may be realized as an integral part of our planet's own evolutionary progress and purpose."

For, if there were ever "a new set of historical circumstances" to celebrate Interspirituality and herald the dawning of a New Earth and Unitive Age, surely it is here and now.

Endnotes and References for this Feature[viii:2]

Science Futures and Future Spirituality as a New Consciousness Cosmology

by J.J. Hurtak and Desiree Hurtak

The James Webb Space Telescope (JWST) was sent on a mission to look at the early beginnings of the universe. What they expected to find was hydrogen and other basic elements and maybe a few primitive star systems. Specifically, many scientists today were contemplating that if we looked back in time, 13.5 billion years ago, just short of the 14 billion years that is considered to be the origin of the universe, it would look quite simple and primitive. To the astronomer's surprise, instead what they found were nicely formed, although sometimes more flat, large and luminous galactic clusters and nothing that looked like the beginnings of the Big Bang.[1]

There are several possibilities to explain why the "early" stars appeared so ordered and advanced. One, the Telescope was not really seeing as far back in time as they thought or two, the beginnings of the universe were earlier than had previously been calculated or three, the early gas clouds burst with one another creating advanced structures. However, the fourth possibility is: the universe was not designed from "nothing," but from the beginning there was a "divine design." That is, there was a Grand Design behind the universe that had specifically been created for the birth of life forms, which is also what the ancient texts of the East and West have said.

Many cosmologists of the 20th century debated how exactly our universe began. American astronomer Edwin Hubble advanced the "Big Bang" model which precluded its present energy uniformity until it underwent a period of inflationary expansion.[2] Of course, there were also many other theories, such as from the Russian astronomer Alexander Friedmann[3] who first considered the expanding universe, which included the possibilities that the universe was either flat, a sphere, or "hyperbolic." However, we are proposing a model that shows this was not the first universe, but a mere offshoot of an already existing universe. Other astronomers are also starting to consider this model that proposes the existence of a multiverse; that is, our universe is one of many universes and may be a mere offshoot from the previous universe.[4]

Consequently, if there is not just one universe but many different universes, as detailed in a multiverse reality that is being discussed at present, this could be consistent with the possible role of a spiritual or higher Consciousness Design. Even in biblical terminology, a pluralistic universe of new "heavens" is contemplated (*Isaiah, chapter 66:22*), with a Universal Mind as Source. So, it is remarkable that the most recent findings of NASA's James Webb Space Telescope in 2023[5] have shown precisely the advanced existence of massive geometric-sized astrophysical realms existing very close to the time line of the so-called "Big Bang event," at the near beginnings of physical existence.

Looking at Eastern philosophy, we see the possible notion of how the universe is another petal of a vast lotus flower that was birthed, not from nothing, but from something. Similarly, we have proposed that this is an "open-ended universe," which to us means that there is always ongoing unfoldment. Not that universes don't die out, but that they spawn in their process other universes. This would further explain how many universes could have arisen from a variety of different initial states or configurations without the rate of expansion and excluding most of the physical constants having to be very carefully specified as organizing principles of a mechanistic substructure. Each individual universe construction and mental configuration contains an indefinite number of other coexisting universes, with all variations and all possibilities.

Moreover, in all of this, the beginnings of the universe would not need to be initially physical, but as we read in the Bible, there was the Thoughts and Logos of God behind the formation of the sun, moons, and stars that were formed.

But what would that mean? It would mean, as other philosophers have said, there was the emergence of a Consciousness Universe, and we still exist in a universe of "consciousness management," which directly relates to a quantum nonlocal field that could be prevalent throughout our realm. This also may be the source behind not only the formation of the universe, but also the ongoing physical evolution of human life that is becoming very difficult to explain in terms of the short time that life has evolved on planet Earth.

The Consciousness Universe can be "reached" by the human mind as shown by the transcendental abilities of saints, sages, and yogis throughout the ages. They have demonstrated their ability to influence the matter field by their Consciousness. Scientists have now accepted this, knowing that we as Observers can influence such things as atomic particles, as seen in the "Double Slit" Experiment.

So, not only is there a greater Consciousness many call "The Creator" or God behind our universe, but also, at the same time, we have some of those qualities as well that can influence our world. This is clearly different from what many are calling a "simulated universe." Instead of putting us as puppets being influenced by a higher reality, we are also influencers in what we are creating here on Earth. The ancient African cultures understood that we are being given the ability to affect our own reality, and when their world environment went awry, they looked deeper within themselves to try to change their consciousness, knowing that they, too, were influencing their reality.

We live at a time of unique discovery where empirical observation and evidence suggests a greater scale of evolutionary development capable of crossing both physical and mental boundaries. Thus, with the James Webb Space Telescope, we may also be on the verge of discovering the numerous exoplanets and the possibilities for life in the universe. We also may be on the verge of understanding that there is a consciousness field, which the ancients have written about for thousands of years, which is behind the formation of our universe.

All this moves us closer to the understanding that Artificial Intelligence (AI) may not have the consciousness abilities to tap into a greater understanding of the universe that is beyond the logic of their functioning mechanisms, but comes from the soul-spirit that we have within us.

According to *The Keys of Enoch*®[6] by J.J. Hurtak, we are part of a greater cosmology of consciousness whereby we can acquire evidence through "experiences" with greater realms that are spoken of in both Eastern and Western theology. If we read the ancient texts of both the Vedas and the Bible, it should leave no doubt that we live in a dynamic universe that is not happenstance or slowly learning how to develop, but a universe designed for consciousness and soul evolution.

We propose that as we grow in our understanding of science, involving everything from our DNA codes to stellar formations, we are coming closer to realizing that there is a "process of soul evolution" that is built into all aspects of the world around us. In the Bible, the Source of Consciousness had many names. One was called "the *Elohim*" (*Genesis 1:1*), and the Buddhists and Hindus say that there was created not one world but a plethora of "cosmic worlds."

We believe that we are now being prepared to understand this larger, ancient roadmap as our science advances to show that behind all life exists a higher "Divine Consciousness." Yet, we are not saying that we created the universe, but we are part of a greater Mind, and the greater Mind(s) is behind the detailed workings of the universe.

In conclusion, Life can be "limitless and infinite." Humanity and Mind are not to be confined to the evolutionary process of this planet. "Heaven" is the privilege of finding peace within greater ecumenical spirituality and service to life, even life in new frontiers. We believe we are conscious beings able to flow from dimension to dimension of the Universal Mind and cocreate within ourselves a consciousness cosmology. Indeed, a new science and a new spirituality working together can meet the challenges of a vast and awesome universe!

Endnotes and References for this Feature[viii:3]

ProSocial Spirituality: Evolutionary Science Meets Interspirituality

by Diane Berke, Jeff Genung, Kate Sheehan Roach and Susan Soleil

Wayne Teasdale's prescient clarity — brilliantly displayed in *The Mystic Heart* — made his 1999 seminal work not only a harbinger of things to come on the eve of the millennium, but also a forward pass into the very future Wayne's battle with cancer threatened to deny him. As those involved with the interspiritual movement's many outcroppings know firsthand, Br. Wayne's work is very much alive in the present day through the ongoing nature of his legacy. ProSocial Spirituality is one of many projects that might be considered a posthumous collaboration with Dr. Wayne Teasdale, inspired by *The Mystic Heart*.

ProSocial Spirituality began in 2019 as an evolutionary research, training, and technology partnership between two nonprofit organizations, the Evolution Institute and Contemplative Life, made possible by a grant jointly sponsored by the Templeton Religion Trust and the Issachar Fund. Contemplative Life's Director of Content, Kate Sheehan Roach, and One Spirit Learning Alliance Founder and Spiritual Director, Rev. Diane Berke, took the lead in co-developing a program inspired by a question asked independently and almost simultaneously by two interspiritual trailblazers who were close friends and colleagues of Wayne Teasdale in the final years of his life, Dr. Kurt Johnson and Jeff Genung: "What would happen if we formed a new group framework by combining Wayne Teasdale's Nine Elements of Interspirituality with Elinor Ostrom's Core Design Principles?" In January of 2019, Kurt Johnson had published in *Kosmos Journal* the extensive article "Evolving Toward Cooperation: David Sloan Wilson's New Evolutionary Biology," which was a full review of interspiritual principles in the context of the emergent new paradigms in evolutionary science.[1]

And so, within Prosocial, a field study was born. A team of educators and researchers, led by Prosocial.world founder and evolutionary biologist Dr. David Sloan Wilson, built an experimental framework and methodology designed to explore how variation in understanding and implementation of core spiritual principles and social design principles impacts group function and adaptability. Diane Berke and Kate Sheehan Roach worked together to develop and deliver a curriculum that introduced Wayne Teasdale's interspiritual elements as the "vertical dimension" whereby group members cultivate spiritual grounding and transcendence, alongside Nobel Prize-winning cultural design principles by which the "horizontal dimension" of social cohesion is strengthened.

In his proposal to the Templeton Religion Trust, Wilson wrote: "Our major hypothesis is that nearly all groups need a strong vertical and a strong horizontal dimension to function at their best. The vertical dimension sanctifies the purpose of the group and cultivates a state of mind of being part of something larger than oneself. The horizontal dimension channels this psychic energy into effective social action. As long as a meaning system results in a strong vertical and horizontal dimension, it shouldn't matter whether it is religious or secular."

The Origins of ProSocial World: Biological Sciences Meet Social Science

In 2009, political scientist Dr. Elinor "Lin" Ostrom was awarded the Nobel Prize in Economics for a research program that rocked the field by dismantling the long-held theory known as the tragedy of the commons. This theory had long held that people sharing common pool resources would compete to exploit those resources for their own maximum advantage if left to their own devices, leading to the overuse and depletion of those resources. This old school of economic theory argued that private ownership or government control was necessary to prevent this otherwise inevitable "tragedy." Lin and her husband Vincent, also a political scientist, disproved this theory through extensive field research.

The Ostroms encountered groups all over the world that were sharing common pool resources effectively without overexploitation. They compiled a vast global database that showed, across cultures, that when certain voluntary systems and practices are present, groups can self-govern in a way that resources are not overexploited. Significantly,

Lin Ostrom noted that these successful groups exhibited eight basic operating principles in common. With these guiding principles in place, people in these groups were able to put their shared interests ahead of their competing individual interests. And so, Lin Ostrom demonstrated that while the tragedy of the commons is a very real potential, it is not inevitable.

This groundbreaking work came to the attention of evolutionary biologist David Sloan Wilson, whose research interests include the study of altruism and unselfish behavior from the perspective of evolutionary theory. He posits that while the evolutionary selection principle commonly called "survival of the fittest" does indeed decide the competitive victors among individuals within a group, this no longer holds true in studies of evolutionary selection between or among groups. At the level of group selection (also called multilevel selection), the groups most likely to survive and thrive are those made up of the most cooperative individuals in what has been termed "survival of the kindest."

Wilson summarizes his theory with a nod to Rabbi Hillel's famous saying: "Selfishness beats altruism within groups. Altruistic groups beat selfish groups. Everything else is commentary."

From 2009 to 2012, Wilson and Ostrom worked together to explore how the principles she had discovered in common pool groups that successfully cooperated related to his work with multilevel evolutionary theory. Could these principles be generalized to groups working toward other types of goals? Could they be taught and intentionally put into practice by any kind of group to enhance cooperation and group effectiveness?

The result of this collaboration was the development of the original ProSocial change methodology, built on the foundation of these eight

Core Design Principles (CDPs), adapted from Ostrom's original "rules for the commons":

- Clear group identity and shared sense of purpose
- Fair distribution of costs and benefits
- Inclusive decision making
- Monitoring progress toward goals
- Timely and appropriate feedback for helpful and unhelpful behavior
- Fast and fair conflict resolution
- Recognition of group and member autonomy
- Appropriate relationships with other groups

Subsequently, Wilson collaborated with contextual behavioral psychologists Dr. Paul Atkins and Dr. Steven Hayes to incorporate practices and tools for increasing psychological flexibility into the ProSocial methodology in order to support people's willingness and ability to embrace change. Their 2019 book, *Prosocial: Using Evolutionary Science to Build Productive, Equitable, and Collaborative Groups*, has served as the textbook for hundreds of people and groups that have been trained in ProSocial principles and practices, and the training continues to evolve.

ProSocial Meets Spirituality

Shortly after the publication of *The Coming Interspiritual Age*, co-authored by Kurt Johnson and David Robert Ord, Wilson reached out to Johnson, a fellow evolutionary biologist as well as a former Episcopal monk and longtime contemplative practitioner. If modern evolutionary theory, including multilevel selection, is true, Wilson said, we would expect to see a movement like Interspirituality — the discovery of, and emphasis on, a universal spirituality within the rich diversity of religious beliefs and expressions — arise within the world's religions.

The friendship that developed between Wilson and Johnson, and their common interest in bringing the insights of science and spirituality together, catalyzed many fascinating conversations with major thought leaders, including a one-to-one conversation between Wilson and His Holiness the Dalai Lama in Dharamsala. In this meeting, organized by the Mind and Life Institute, Wilson proposed that current evolutionary science — no longer restricted to genetic evolution or framed exclusively in terms of selfishness and competition — can explain the clear necessity of compassion and altruism to any viable future, shed light on personal and cultural transformation, and be consciously directed for the good of all people and the planet. This, he points out, "is nothing less than a merging of science and the kind of universal spirituality… His Holiness stands for when he calls for an ethics for the whole world."[2]

> Over time, the ProSocial methodology has proven very effective in helping groups learn to function more cooperatively and effectively. Yet something more was needed. As Wilson wrote, "Evolutionary theory distinctively identifies the small group as a fundamental unit of human social organization, required for both individual well-being and effective action on a larger scale. … Yet, small groups don't automatically work well, and even when they do, they can become part of the problem higher up the scale, such as a street gang, a terrorist cell, a predatory corporation, or a rogue nation.

> We must consciously seek to create small groups that benefit individuals as well as society as a whole."
> —David Sloan Wilson, *This View of Life*

The question naturally arose whether incorporating training in universal spiritual values into ProSocial World's curriculum might further support creating groups that benefit society (and the planet) as a whole. In considering how best to do this, Jeff Genung recalled how he and Kurt Johnson had been struck by the possibility that Lin Ostrom's work and Wayne Teasdale's work might dovetail with one another. And so, Jeff introduced Teasdale's Nine Elements of Mature Universal Spirituality as a complement to Prosocial's Eight Core Design Principles.

Teasdale's Nine Elements[3] naturally fall into three clusters that span the breadth of a well-rounded, mature spiritual life. They are:

Honoring Our Interconnectedness with All of Life

- Fully actualizing our moral/ethical capacity
- Living in solidarity with all living beings and the cosmos
- Cultivating deep nonviolence

Embracing the Inner Work of Transformation

- Cultivating and living in humility
- Embracing a regular spiritual / contemplative practice
- Cultivating mature self-knowledge

Engaging with Social Concerns of Our Shared Public Life

- Living a life of simplicity
- Engaging in selfless service and compassionate action
- Empowering and embodying the prophetic voice for justice, compassion, and world transformation

ProSocial Spirituality Meets Creating Trustworthy Space

When Susan Soleil, formerly on staff with the Charter for Compassion, took the lead at ProSocial Spirituality in 2024, she worked closely with Diane Berke to add the dimension of creating trustworthy, contemplative space where the inner work of transformation can be done in a context of community. To create such a space in largely virtual programs, they incorporated principles and practices from Parker J. Palmer and the Center for Courage and Renewal's "circles of trust" methodology.[4]

The following elements of the Center's work have been incorporated into the ProSocial Spirituality trainings:

Guidelines for Creating Trustworthy Space — The "Touchstones"[5]

In *The Courage Way*, Shelley Frances writes:

> Touchstones are our operating guidelines for holding the meaningful conversations of inner work and trust building. … The magic and mystery of this collection of practices comes from the chemistry of how they combine to catalyze trust. Together, these touchstones create a hospitable "container," one that enables people to show up with integrity and authenticity so that they can engage in honest conversation. (*The Courage Way*, p. 42).

The Touchstones for creating trustworthy space are:

- Give and receive welcome.
- Be present as fully as possible.
- Extend invitation, not demand.

- Speak your truth in ways that respect other people's truth.
- No fixing, saving, advising, or correcting each other.
- When the going gets rough, turn to wonder.
- Practice asking open, honest questions.
- Attend to your own inner teacher.
- Trust and learn from the silence.
- Commit to and maintain confidentiality.
- Know that it's possible for the seeds planted here to keep growing.

These simple but powerful guidelines encourage participants to cultivate skills of deep listening with full presence both to others and to one's own inner knowing and intuition; respecting what Parker Palmer calls the "hidden wholeness" and inner wisdom within everyone, and letting go of the tendency to see others as needing to be "fixed"; recognizing one's own reactivity and, in its place, cultivating curiosity and openness to inquiry; a capacity to frame questions that invite deeper listening to one's own inner wisdom; openness to the creativity, inspiration, and insight available in a space of receptive silence; and patience and trust in the natural unfolding of the inner transformative process.

The Use of "Third Things"

Another important element of creating trustworthy space for transformative inner work is the use of what Parker Palmer calls "third things." In *A Hidden Wholeness,* he writes:

> Every practice that creates a circle of trust must keep the space between us open and free and yet focused on things of the soul. We must be intentional about exploring the real issues of our lives … But our

> explorations must be invitational, giving everyone the freedom to engage those issues in his or her own way. When our intentionality becomes heavy-handed or our openness becomes aimless, the soul will not show up.
>
> In Western culture, we often seek truth through confrontation. But our headstrong ways of charging at truth scare the shy soul away. … We must invite, not command, the soul to speak."[6]

Third things allow us to explore a topic metaphorically, through a poem, a story, a piece of music, or a work of art that opens a lived experience of that topic. The use of third things invites us to recognize the intersection of our personal story with a larger collective (even, perhaps, a universal) story through touching us on a level beneath our cognitive, conceptual, rational ways of knowing.

The Ongoing Evolution of ProSocial Spirituality

Funded by a three-year grant from the John Templeton Foundation, ProSocial World continues to develop research and training initiatives exploring the impact of integrating modern evolutionary science with the wisdom and contemplative practices of Interspirituality. Phase Three of the grant included beginning to train facilitators who can then bring this methodology into the larger world. Indeed, the first two facilitator training cohorts included participants from six countries. ProSocial Spirituality brings cohorts of people from all over the world to meet at the convergence of three major wisdom streams:

- evolutionary science and contextual behavioral science
- wide-ranging, welcoming spirituality
- contemplative, trustworthy community building

ProSocial Spirituality continues to build upon Wayne Teasdale's interspiritual legacy and Lin Ostrom's Nobel Prize-winning life's work, along with Parker Palmer's "circles of trust" methodology, exploring and studying the ways these streams can flow together for the betterment of the world. If your interest is sparked and you want to follow this evolving journey of science and spirituality in community, please search online for ProSocial Spirituality and ProSocial World. We welcome diverse perspectives to this transformational work.

Endnotes and References for this Feature[viii:4]

Politics of Being: An Interspiritual Development Paradigm for Our Societies

by Thomas Legrand[1]

In 2012, I embarked on a 10-year journey to develop the vision of a wisdom-based approach to development, a new understanding of how societies should organize themselves that the interspiritual and interreligious movement could endorse. Thus, I looked for the positions and perspectives of spiritual traditions and found this sentence from the Earth Charter, in the interreligious statement at the Rio + 20 Conference[2]: *When basic needs have been met, human development is primarily about being more, rather than having more.*

I understood quickly that even to meet everyone's basic needs, we need to "be more" as expressed in this sentence from the same statement: "To make development truly sustainable, our economic, scientific, and technological accomplishments should assist the processes of individual and collective, psychological, and spiritual development. We must reorient our economic bottom line to support this full human development if we wish to live in a flourishing Earth community." This also echoes the views of Indian spiritual and humanitarian leader Amma: *In today's world, people experience two types of poverty: the poverty caused by lack of food, clothing and shelter, and the poverty caused by lack of love and compassion. Of these two, the second type needs to be considered first — because, if we have love and compassion in our hearts, then we will wholeheartedly serve those who suffer from lack of food, clothing and shelter.*[3]

I knew in this "being" bottom line, I had found the basis for the new development paradigm our societies desperately need. It was clear to me, from my work as an environmentalist, that little can be achieved within our current system prioritizing economic growth ("having more") over everything else. We need to redefine our priorities, our lives' purposes, not only as individuals but also as societies. To my great surprise, I found out that this "being" agenda had not been defined yet, neither in theory, nor in practice. This is what I did through my book *Politics of Being: Wisdom and Science for a New Development Paradigm* published in 2022. The politics of being aims simply at aligning our institutions with our true reason to be here on Earth: becoming who we are, the best and most complete version of ourselves.

The primary objective of governments should be to provide the means for each being to express its full potential, achieving its deepest healthy aspirations, while cultivating human qualities and virtues. The latter echoes the conclusion of American political economist Elinor Ostrom, who at the moment is arguably the most influential scholar in institutional analysis. In her lecture for the reception of her Nobel prize in economics in 2009, she summarized the most important lesson she drew from fifty years of research: *Designing institutions to force (or nudge) entirely self-interested individuals to achieve better outcomes has been the major goal posited by policy analysts for governments to accomplish for much of the past half century. Extensive empirical research leads me to argue that instead, a core goal of public policy should be to facilitate the development of institutions that bring out the best in humans.*[4] Instead of assuming and activating our selfish and competitive nature, we should rather organize societies to bring out our capacity for goodness and cooperation. For example, the dominant paradigm of retributive justice builds upon and strengthens our instinct for retaliation, while the practice of restorative justice allows all those involved to cultivate human values and qualities such as understanding, deep listening, compassion, healing, inclusivity, courage, and responsibility.

Spiritual values — such as the understanding of our interconnectedness, life, happiness, love, peace, or mindfulness that lie at the core of spiritual teachings — can serve as the foundations of this new politics. Indeed, they constitute new fields of scientific research that can tell us how to cultivate them at the individual and collective levels. The scientific literature and social change initiatives associated with these values allow us to identify concrete public policies with existing examples of applications in many sectors. Together, they constitute an actionable agenda for the politics of being.

This policy agenda represents a "second-stage" investment in human development, emphasizing its inner dimension, replacing or complementing more traditional policies. These investments can be direct — for example, through education, mental health, and childhood well-being policies — or indirect, addressing concrete social needs through institutions that cultivate human qualities, as in the case of restorative justice mentioned above.

The politics of being is based on a dialogue between wisdom and science. Scientific knowledge per se cannot determine what we should strive for, the values we should hold, and the desirable direction of our societies' evolution. Hence, we have lost our ways in the blind pursuit of economic and technological development as ends in themselves. We need wisdom to guide our nations, and the role of knowledge is to validate or reject (as erroneous applications or interpretations), specify, and operationalize wisdom's general orientations.

This wisdom is to be found in spiritual traditions that have been cultivating it over centuries and millennia. Through the interspiritual movement, representatives of these different traditions are now sharing their teachings, insights, and experiences, polishing their understandings in light of the latest scientific findings. As Wayne Teasdale said: "Interspirituality is the foundation that can prepare the way for a planet-wide enlightened culture. [...] It will be an enhanced understanding of the inner life through assimilating the psychological, moral, aesthetic, spiritual, and literary treasures of the world's religions."[5] He predicted that the Interspiritual Age we are entering will see the formation of "a universal civilization," a global culture based on common spiritual values.

Humanity is one tribe and the Earth our sacred territory. Now is the time to live accordingly.

POLITICS OF BEING: 10 CORE MESSAGES

1. **We need a collective shift of consciousness, a cultural evolution of a spiritual nature, to address our current challenges.** It is already ongoing, and we are currently facing an evolutive crisis, which requires individuals and societies to look inward and transform.

2. **As a wisdom-based, science-informed approach, a politics of being can support this evolution.** Its main goal is to support the fulfillment of all beings, that is to say the realization of our truest and highest being. "Being" is a wiser and more adequate development objective than "having"; it applies to the whole Earth community.
3. **Cultivating our fundamental "interbeing" or relational nature is instrumental to allow us to live in harmony with one another and the Earth community.** Our spiritual nature makes us interconnected at the level of being with everything that is. Only by recognizing their interconnectedness and sustaining the whole can each part thrive.
4. **Societies progress as they increasingly honor the highest values, qualities, and ideals, such as freedom, goodness, beauty, truth, understanding, life, happiness, love, peace, etc.** These are spiritual qualities in the sense that they reflect an awakened human being or divine perfection. Science and practical initiatives shaped around these universal values can help us design a politics of being. Cultural development relates fundamentally to an evolution of our values, which shape our worldviews and institutions.
5. **The focus on being and the highest values provide a simple conceptual framework for a politics of being, which can integrate all relevant claims and initiatives.** As such, it can help unify this vision and strengthen this movement.
6. **Our institutions should help cultivate human virtues.** They should acknowledge and facilitate the expression of our potential for goodness, cooperation, and intrinsic motivation.

7. **Concrete and actionable policy recommendations supporting this agenda already exist in many sectors.** A politics of being can bring them together and scale them up, articulating them in a coherent and meaningful narrative.
8. **Spiritual teachings and Wisdom Traditions, through dialogue among them and with science, have much to bring to inspire, help design, and implement a politics of being.** They are our most valuable common heritage, able to offer a profound understanding of human nature, as well as practical knowledge and tools for inner, and ultimately social, development.
9. **Each nation needs to reconnect to its own soul and wisdom to develop its version of a politics of being that can support its development and help it bring its unique contribution to the world.** Unity in diversity is the key to harmonious coexistence of nations in a globalized world.
10. **Healing trauma is, for individuals and societies, the gateway to being.** It is fundamental in order for new ways of being and living together to be possible, and for the whole Earth community to flourish.

Endnotes and References for this Feature[viii:5]

A Prophet of the Interspiritual Law of Love

Beinsa Douno (Peter Deunov, 1864-1944)

by David Lorimer

Humanity is moving towards collaboration, mutual aid and union. The question is knowing how to harmonise liberty and the collective, liberty and solidarity. At

> first sight these seem to be mutually exclusive — their harmonic coming together is the higher idea of humanity that can only be attained through Life for the Whole. ~ Beinsa Douno (Peter Deunov, 1864-1944).
>
> We have a choice before us: either to continue [our] predatory policies of individual and tribal selfishness that leads to inevitable doom, or to embark upon the policies of universal solidarity that brings humanity to the aspired for heaven on earth. ~ Pitirim Sorokin (1889-1968).

Last night, my wife and I watched a moving documentary about Thomas Keating entitled *The Rising Tide of Silence* — for him, silence is the first language of God, which we can all access by going within using what he called Centering Prayer. Silence — like Love — brings us together beyond words and ideas that can also divide. And in this silence, we can open up to the possibility of experiencing Divine Love, as have mystics of all traditions. I myself have had this sublime experience on a very few occasions, including listening to Albert Schweitzer playing Bach's Dorian Fugue in D minor and when standing beside the grave of Peter Deunov when I was suffused with a powerful sense of Divine blessing that I felt was coming from him. Incidentally, there is no name and no dates on his headstone — just a pentagram inscribed Love, Wisdom, Truth, Justice, Goodness. More on this below.

The opening quotations above describe our overall evolutionary trend, and also the crucial moment of choice that we face as individuals and collectively as a species. As thinkers like Arnold Toynbee and Vaclav Havel have argued, nothing less than worldwide spiritual revolution of consciousness will be sufficient to alter our self-destructive trajectory — despite the dazzling wizardry of technological progress. We have forgotten what Aldous Huxley pointed out in his arresting remark to be found in his book *Ends and Means* over 80 years ago: "In the world in which we find ourselves, technological advance is rapid. But without progress in charity, technological advance is useless. Indeed, it is worse than useless. Technological progress has merely provided us with a more efficient means for going backwards."

Arnold Toynbee made a similar observation in 1975: "Technology gives us material power — the greater our material power, the greater our need for the spiritual insight and virtue to use power for good and not for evil. The 'morality gap' means that, since we first became human, we have never been adequate spiritually for handling our material power. Today it is greater than ever.' And now it is greater and more perilous than even. The key element here is moral and spiritual advance, which can only be achieved at the inner level by individuals and in communities. In his final book, Albert Schweitzer reflected that 'three kinds of progress are significant for culture: progress in knowledge and technology, progress in the socialisation of humanity, and progress in spirituality. The last is the most important — technical progress, extension of knowledge, does indeed represent progress, but not in fundamentals. The essential thing is that we become more finely and deeply human."

For this reason, we must ask ourselves: what is real progress in fundamentals? It is the understanding, embodiment, and application of universal interspiritual principles. We are currently posing this question in the context of understanding the cycles of rise and decline of cultures and civilizations, where the initial spiritual impulse is gradually undermined by inner decay. As Sir John Glubb observes, self-sacrifice is gradually replaced by self-indulgence; or, in the words of Edward Gibbon (quoted in William Ophuls' *Immoderate Greatness*), who wrote that the decline of Rome was the natural and inevitable effect of what he called immoderate greatness, whereby "prosperity ripened the principle of decay." Similar thoughts were expressed by Rudolf Steiner 100 years ago when he spoke about the iron necessity of cycles of the creation and destruction of civilizations. And as it happens, I am currently reading Robert Lawlor's *The Geometry of the End of Time*, where he refers to Ma-Kali as the cosmic mother / destroyer, and expresses the view that we are in the closing phases of the Kali Yuga, faced with a descent into darkness and destruction followed by eventual renewal.

This brings me to a powerful 1944 prophecy by the Bulgarian sage Beinsa Douno (Peter Deunov — see link for full text at the end), from which the following extracts are taken:

> Some decades will pass before this [Divine] Fire will come that will transform the world by bringing it a new morality. This immense wave comes from cosmic space and will inundate the entire earth. Although the inhabitants of this planet do not all find themselves at the same degree of evolution, the new wave will be felt by each one of us. And this transformation will not only touch the Earth, but the whole of the Cosmos. The best and only thing that man can do now is to turn toward God and improve himself consciously, to elevate his vibratory level, so as to find himself in harmony with the powerful wave that will soon submerge him.
>
> The Fire of which I speak that accompanies the new conditions offered to our planet, will rejuvenate, purify, reconstruct everything: matter will be refined,

> your hearts will be liberated from anguish, troubles, incertitude, and they will become luminous; everything will be improved, elevated; the thoughts, sentiments and negative acts will be consumed and destroyed.
>
> The earth, the solar system, the universe, all are being put in a new direction under the impulsion of Love. Most of you still consider Love as an insignificant force, but in reality, it is the greatest of all forces! Money and power continue to be venerated as if the course of your life depended upon it. In the future, all will be subjugated to Love and all will serve it. But it is through suffering and difficulties that human consciousness will be awakened.

Readers can appreciate his archetypal and apocalyptic message of death and rebirth, decay and renewal. Central to this is the new direction under the impulsion of Love. Our existing global system is based on a love of power, wealth, profit, greed, and exploitation. The rich elites exemplified by the policies and pervasive influence of the World Economic Forum advocate a "Great Reset" whose fundamental basis and modus operandi involves the continued weaponization of fear (deployed through behavioral psychology), propaganda, manipulation of public opinion, control, exploitation, separation (divide and rule), violence, militarism, war, and an ultimate aim of the systematic suppression of freedom of speech and expression, culminating in digital planetary servitude. This view is informed by a mechanistic understanding of the human being and an agenda of evolution through transhumanist upgrades and implants, leading to what Lewis Mumford presciently called mechanical uniformity.

On the other hand, Peter Deunov advocated the Power of Love expressed in harmony with each other and the Earth, community spirit, service, mutual aid, the Golden Rule, nonviolence, freedom, justice, peace, life for the whole, and overcoming evil with good, leading to a natural organic "unity in diversity" (Lewis Mumford's contrasting phrase). This is the kind of life to which we all aspire, summarized by Deunov when he stated, "The supreme goal of human life is that people should be free and to serve Love, Wisdom and Truth." These three principles are central to his teaching, along with Justice and Goodness. He wrote that the whole of humanity needed to know, study and apply these three central principles:

> The first principle on which the whole of existence is based is Love; it brings the impulse to life; it is the compass, the stimulus within the human soul.
>
> The second principle is Wisdom, which brings knowledge and light to the mind, thus enabling human beings to know the laws and use the energies of Nature harmoniously and constructively.
>
> The third principle is Truth; it frees the human soul from bondage and encourages her to learn, work effectively and make efforts toward self-sacrifice.
>
> **There is nothing greater than these principles; there is no straighter or shorter path. In these three principles lies the salvation of the world!** (emphasis added)

Love eliminates hatred, violence, murder.
Wisdom eliminates ignorance, error, darkness.
Truth eliminates lies, slavery, sin.

The world will not be saved by orthodoxy and belief, which lead to division and separation; but rather, as Deunov stresses, through the understanding, embodiment, and application of Love, Wisdom, and Truth manifest in Justice and Goodness or moral virtue. The application of these principles is what he calls the Third Testament, and he further embodied them in his sacred dance movements called Paneurhythmy (universal harmony of movement), for which he also composed the music. The larger evolutionary context of these principles lies in his scheme of four phases of human development, all of which we see in operation in the world today:

- Violence – using force, domination, power
- Law – using external threat (fear), and control
- Justice – which is universal, and excludes privilege
- Love – as life for the Whole

It is also important to understand that Love is not a mere personal sentiment, but rather, in its higher manifestations, is understood as what he calls "Love as a Force in the Mind," as exemplified in the lives of great saints and sages, and "Love as a Principle in the Spirit," which harmonizes differences and resolves contradictions. These higher senses of the word Love were also understood by Gandhi when he remarked, "Love is basically not an emotional but an ontological power, the essence of life, the dynamic union of the separated." Think about this and its implications: **Love as an ontological power**. Deunov also understood the phases of the evolution of human consciousness through individual and collective consciousness to the mutuality and reciprocity of Cosmic Consciousness, and finally to Divine Consciousness — characterized by a seamless spirit, where unity is known and felt, and we naturally apply the Golden Rule as an expression of our realization of Oneness and hence that we are one another; I call this an ethic of interconnectedness.

Deunov's (unheeded) 1919 message to the Versailles Treaty is only too relevant today in a world still torn apart by geopolitics, violence, and war: those who love their enemies are people of the new future culture. And if those who are attending the conference in Versailles love their enemies, a real peace can be established between the peoples. If they do not love their enemies and peace is re-established, it will be temporary. Real peace is one that brings in the future culture of work, life, and Love. If the peace which contemporary people expect rests on the Law of Moses — an eye for an eye and a tooth for a tooth — the future will prove what kind of peace this is and what culture it will bring.

We are still applying the Law of Moses rather than Christ's Law of Love, with the same predictable outcomes — as Desmond Tutu famously stated, there is no future without forgiveness. The Russian sociologist and author of *The Ways and Power of Love,* Pitirim Sorokin, wrote, "Hate begets hate, violence engenders violence, hypocrisy is answered by hypocrisy, war generates war, and love creates love. Unselfish love has enormous creative and therapeutic potentialities, far greater than most people think. Love is a life-giving force, necessary for physical, mental and moral health." This is a modern expression of the nonviolent message of the Sermon on the Mount so deeply understood by Leo Tolstoy, who was a mentor of Mahatma Gandhi.

Already 100 years ago, Deunov was saying that the aim of contemporary society should be "TO UPLIFT WOMEN." Women have to be raised up to the status they used to occupy in the past! Put the woman on that level where she originally was, and you will see that in 125 years the world will improve. The salvation of the world is in the uplifting of the woman. The salvation of our contemporary humanity lies in "**the elevation of the heart**." He continued: "I say there is only one power in the world that is able to annihilate war and to bring in peace. What is that power? — The woman. Women have to direct their power to the entire world and say: 'No more wars!'" Such an uprising of the Divine Feminine is now an urgent evolutionary imperative, so as to make the transition to a Culture of Love, Wisdom and Truth through widespread spiritual awakening, rather than through the devastation of catastrophic breakdown and consequent extreme suffering. This is our existential choice and predicament.

The sciences are now coming to understand a core principle of the perennial wisdom, that of wholeness, Oneness and, therefore, intrinsic connectedness. Deunov noted, "The part cannot detach itself from the whole. In Nature one cannot detach a part from the whole. All human faults arise from wanting to come out of the whole. People must come to understand that the part cannot exist outside the whole. Humans are a part of the whole and it should live in the whole and for the whole — the basis of this is an inner union with all beings. Hence, the whole lives for us and we must live for the whole." To live for the whole is not just to live for oneself, which Deunov calls the law of the part; nor is it to live for society—the law of the majority, of the neighbor; but rather, it is to live life for the Sublime Principle, for the Divine. This is the Law of the Whole, the Law of the Divine.

Writing about the life review, which one finds both in near death experiences and post-mortem communications, Deunov observed: "One day, when you return to the invisible world, you will be examined on how you have applied the law of Love … you will find yourself confronted by the film of your earthly life, you will see the smallest details and notice the tiniest errors and you will have to reform yourself. You must therefore reflect and concentrate on what you are saying and how you are saying it. Here, you are an actor on stage, being photographed and recorded all the time." The argument in my book *Resonant Mind: The Near Death Experience and the Ethic of Interconnectedness* is that if everyone realized that they were going to face a life review at death in the course of which they come to experience directly both the sufferings and joys they have elicited in others, this would represent a revolutionary insight with profound ethical implications whereby people would come to realize that the Oneness of Life and Mind entails that we are each other and are obligated to apply the Golden Rule. Just imagine if understanding and applying this Law of Love was a central component of contemporary education!

Looking through the lens of Interspirituality, Douno's prophecy of and advocacy for a future Culture of Love reflects many of the principles of religion and spirituality expressed in multiple declarations to be found in Universal Principles and Action Steps. He wrote that "Love is necessary for the transformation of the world. It is the only force which can bring peace between the nations, each of which has a mission to accomplish on earth. Love is beginning to appear; goodness, justice and light will triumph; it is simply a question of time. Religions need to be purified; they all contain something divine, but this has been obscured by the repeated addition of human conceptions. All believers will have to get together and agree on one single principle: to make love the basis of any and every belief. Love and brotherhood, that is the common basis."

In a conversation with his followers about the future order of Love, Deunov remarked that "when the heart is set in order, half the world will be set to rights. When the mind is set in order, the whole world will be set to rights." This is not an external, structural process, but rather originates in the inner development of a higher consciousness and understanding: "The most direct way is for people to understand the great truth that they are one and that they shall act according to the law of Love." Without the advent of Love, the ego principle will continue to dominate whereby the strongest prevail and might is right. He explains that the external manifestation of Love is the application of four virtues: honestly, justice, purity, and selflessness. He notes that the Oneness of life in the divine is already the Lord's Prayer with its aspiration for the Kingdom of God to come on Earth. To this end, we can repeat three times the following two formulas:

> Lord, may Thy Love, Thy Wisdom, Thy Truth, Thy Justice, and Thy Goodness dwell within me.
>
> May we sanctify the Name of God.
> May we seek the Kingdom of God and His Righteousness.
> May we fulfil the Will of God.

By way of conclusion, I append two of my poems expressing the theme of this essay:

We are Here to Love

We are here to love and not to hate,
To seek the paths of peace, not war,
To forgive and not to avenge,
To learn deep life lessons
From each other.

We are here to learn the laws of Love,
The laws of Wisdom,
The laws of Truth,
The laws of Justice,
The laws of Goodness,
The laws of Beauty,
The laws of Freedom.

We are here to learn the practice of kindness,
The practice of compassion,
The practice of empathy,
The practice of trust,
The practice of reconciliation.

We are all here for each other,
Entwined with the whole of Life –
With animals, with birds,
With insects, plants and fungi –
Here for a short time together,
Here to awaken,
Here to be, here to act together.

Not in Our Name

In my name, I want no vengeance – Michal Halev, a mother whose son was murdered by Hamas[1]

The mothers, the grandmothers
Carry each generation in their wombs,
They nurse, they cherish,
They love, they sacrifice,
They support, they comfort and console

In the hearths of home and community,
Their hearts aglow with warmth,
Their eyes shining with radiant kindness.

But now they can only weep and wail,
Their sons lie lifeless before them
In pools of seeping blood,
Their lives shattered,
Their hearts wrenched in agony.

Who will hear their piercing screams?
Who will hearken to their searing cries?
Who will listen with their souls ajar?

Between their heaving sobs,
Angels of Peace alight on their shoulders,
Whispering oh so softly in their ears.

"Gentle mothers and grandmothers,
Forgive them for they know not what they do,
Blinded by the rage of oppression and injustice,
Living by the sword, they can only die by the sword,
For violence begets violence,
Hatred begets hatred,
War begets war."

So dare to declare this unthinkable wisdom:
"Love your enemies and pray for those who persecute you,
Do good to those who hate you,
For love begets love,
Forgiveness begets forgiveness,

Understanding begets understanding –
Such is the strength, the vision and courage of Love.

This dreadful cup of bitterness
We have drained to the dregs
To the depths of our broken hearts.
We cannot wish such crushing anguish
As we have endured to be visited
On other mothers and grandmothers,
Not in our name.

In our name we want no vengeance,
This deadly poisonous pattern
Of reciprocal pain and mutual reprisal
Perpetuated down the echoing centuries,
Not in our name.

We lend our name instead to healing,
We lend our name to care and love,
We lend our name to peace:
Shalom, Salaam, Shalom,
Salaam, Shalom, Salaam."

Note: The "unthinkable wisdom" reflects Jesus's words on the cross, and The Sermon on the Mount; and, the thoughts and experience of Pitirim Sorokin (1889-1968) on self-perpetuating cycles of violence and love.

Endnotes and References for this Feature[viii:6]

The Monomyth as Unitive Narrative and Blueprint for a Universal Spirituality

by Robert Atkinson

The First Peoples understood that the power of narrative is to reflect the reality of the unity and wholeness of all things. They gathered to share stories that embodied the values and principles of reverence, harmony, and interconnectedness. These stories held the community together and gave them a shared purpose. They were unitive narratives, essential to their individual and collective well-being.

As the storytelling species, we think in story form, speak in story form, and bring meaning to our lives through story. Telling our stories in a recognizable narrative form and structure is central to our collective human identity.

When communities expanded, spread out, became more diverse, and experienced conflict and disorder, divisive narratives emerged, creating and maintaining separation. With this fall from wholeness, a process of transformation was initiated leading us back to a re-union with our inherent unitive consciousness.

After many millennia, we are remembering who we are. Our challenge now is living by a healing vision that restores the wholeness of all things. Unitive narratives are more needed than ever to help us live in harmony with the unified nature of reality.

The One Myth Common to All

Following the division and destruction of WWII, in 1949, at a time when humanity was just approaching a consciousness of global integration, mythologist Joseph Campbell introduced into public awareness a universal, timeless pattern found in the world's myths that he called the *monomyth*, because it represented the essence of the one myth common to all cultures.

The pattern of archetypes and motifs he identified not only told the story of the journey of the hero, *and* decoded an innate pattern of transformation that is available to everyone, it also verified humanity's common spiritual heritage by identifying the process at the mystic heart of all sacred traditions by which humanity moves closer to the Source of all life.

The monomyth lays out a journey consisting of the three primary archetypes (universal types of experiences) of *departure, initiation,* and *return*. Each of these contain smaller elements, or motifs, that ensure the completion of each archetype in the journey of transformation.

Beginning with a *call to adventure*, the process led to entering the unknown where *aid and assistance* is received, a *challenge* is encountered, a *withdrawal* is needed, and the *road of trials* is undertaken, where a *guide or mentor* is found, and an *inner test* occurs just before *renewal and rebirth* is experienced, which is followed by *crossing the return threshold* where our challenge is becoming the *master of two worlds* by *giving back* what we have been given and *sharing a new message with others*, remembering we are always in a process of becoming.

Yet, as Campbell's *The Hero with a Thousand Faces* became more and more popular, an emphasis was put on the call to adventure and the return as a hero, overlooking the essential middle phase, or *muddle*, consisting of essential challenges bringing about the process of inner transformation that led to a resolution and a higher, more unifying level of consciousness.

A gender-based split also developed in the way it was understood. Many men took it literally as a "hero's" journey that became a great adventure story with overwhelming odds to beat, while many women saw it as missing what their experience is really about; distinct versions of a "heroine's" journey followed.

This resulted in an unintended continuation of the illusion of separation this pattern was meant to heal. It also weakened the impact of the transformational nature of the pattern by keeping separate the potentialities and archetypes we all have access to as human beings.

Variations on the Whole

Long before Campbell had identified the monomyth, this archetypal pattern of transformation was also at the heart of many other ways of knowing. In 1911, Evelyn Underhill described this same process as "the mystic way," a universal journey of spiritual transformation found in the world's mystic traditions that followed a pattern from *awakening* to *purification* to *union*.

Built-in to Indigenous Peoples rites of passage was a process leading to and through transformation as well. In 1909, Arnold van Gennep identified this pattern as a core process taking the initiate through the three phases of *separation, transition,* and *incorporation*. This ritual process guided the young person from a dependent state through independence and on to interdependence within one's community.

This pattern of transformation also finds its way into the psychology of Carl Jung as the "individuation process." It consists of archetypes we are born with in our unconscious being released by life experiences that enable the merging of opposites into a new whole. This inner struggle takes in the stages of *birth of the ego*, *death of the ego*, and *birth of the whole self*.

This central pattern of transformation can also be uncovered within the basic structure of story itself. Beyond the popular story pattern of beginning, middle, and end, there lies a deeper, more meaningful level of *beginning*, *muddle*, and *resolution*, another formula for transformation. The muddles, or challenges, we face represent the core of the pattern that brings the process of transformation to its completion, or resolution.

All these versions of the universal pattern of transformation can also be seen as unitive narratives. What we end up with when we merge these ways of knowing and practices into one is a blueprint for living into the wholeness that culminates in a unitive consciousness. This blueprint consists of the three main parts, *Call to Wholeness*, *Path of Purification*, and *Return to Wholeness*, as described in *A New Story of Wholeness* (2022).

This book also re-unites the hero's journey and the heroine's journey into a single human journey that illustrates how this pattern, in its essence, is designed to return us all to our inherent wholeness.

The Interdependence of All Spiritual Traditions

The emergence of a universal, whole human in harmony with all others is what Brother Wayne Teasdale envisioned in 1999 when he saw a shift in consciousness making possible the interdependence of all spiritual traditions, a new interconnected, universal civilization, and an emerging unitive consciousness available to all.

A universal spirituality rests upon finding the roots of human identity, or what unites us as male and female expressing the same human potentialities and as members of the same global family. As Brother Wayne put it, "the forces of… the masculine and the feminine… are complementary to each other."

The universality of the way of transformation and its various versions further shows, as Brother Wayne said, "the paths are many but the goal is the same." Whatever path we take, it is ultimately meant to lead us back to the wholeness we were created with and most deeply want to recover.

This is the path that begins with a commitment to "spiritual practice," recognizes that "transformation is the reality of inner change," and culminates in "solidarity with all living things." Once there, our focus shifts to being "out in the world," newly committed to "the spirituality of action," or "selfless service and compassionate action." If we all followed this path, we would arrive at "a universal communal spirituality" which would "open the heart of the world," becoming "a spirituality that promotes the unity of the human family."

This life path that Brother Wayne so clearly addresses throughout *The Mystic Heart* represents "an intermystical bridge" across all spiritual traditions that perfectly parallels the monomyth, the mystic way, rites of passage, the individuation process, and the deep structure of story to confirm that in the universal pattern of transformation lies the spiritual DNA that leads us back to our wholeness.

A Blueprint for Restoring the World to Wholeness

Most important in all this is that embedded in the universal process of transformation is a three-part blueprint readily available to all that culminates in an awareness of the responsibility to "give back" to others in whatever ways we can.

With the completion of the process of transformation and a conscious understanding of its full impact and intent for us comes a heightened desire to reciprocate or "pay it forward" so that others can experience, learn from, and benefit by what has so greatly served us.

This is what truly makes our lives heroic, discovering that our purpose, our new-found mission, is to give back to the world what we have learned and gained from the process itself. Kabbalists call it Tikkun Olam, or the work of repairing and restoring the world to wholeness.

This blueprint within us is designed to lead to a unitive consciousness that not only fulfills our innate potential, but also connects us with all others in a realization of our collective wholeness-in-motion.

This means showing up for all our new responsibility demands of us, lifting up others along their journey, and linking up with others to serve the evolutionary impulse and the good of the whole.

Seeking to maintain a holistic view of reality, we take on a wider, all-inclusive identity, integrating unitive qualities, characteristics, and virtues into our thoughts and actions. We strive to live as the whole being we are, lighting up the path we walk, and looking upon all things with the eye of wholeness.

The universal pattern guiding our living into wholeness is a roadmap for achieving the greatest expansion of consciousness that is humanly possible; it also transforms the world in the process while providing us with the sense of union with creation that comes through service to, and deep interpersonal relationships with, others.

Endnotes and References for this Feature[viii:7]

Oneness on the World Stage

by Kabir Helminski

In considering how the world works and what a program for a more harmonious Oneness might entail, what would a spiritual solution be?

Operating within a realistic view of the world, is there any strategy for how to attain a conscious transformation of societies?

The political obstacles are great; to describe them in detail is far beyond the scope of this piece. Amidst what seems like a cacophony of voices, of arbitrary violence, of staggering hypocrisies, we have to keep our hearts intact. To redeem such a many-layered system of ignorance and corruption by focusing on the symptoms would do little to disempower the primary force causing those symptoms. And strategies aimed at the many individual political, social, academic, corporate, and institutional structures that comprise the dominant system would not change the vibrational nature of their activities. The system is locked within a frequency range that resists meaningful transformation.

But there is no force stronger than spiritual realization. And there is reason to be hopeful that enough people will awaken from the narrowly egoic station, and graduate to the level of true individuality, an individuality in resonance with a higher order reality, a connection to the sacred.

The egoic condition of humanity is one in which people are afraid of giving up a position they have adopted as a defense, afraid that something will be imposed on them, taken from them, or that they will be harmed or violated by another.

The tenderest souls fear that if they open to love, their love will be betrayed. The psychopaths, on the other hand, whose souls have withered almost to nothing, totally lacking in empathy, act upon others without regard for the suffering they cause.

The common response is to first of all look out for oneself and one's family, and if that involves competition with others in a zero-sum game, so be it.

The “lovers,” in contrast, are less dominated by self-interest and competition. They keep faith and do the work, and existence mysteriously supports them. Because they are aware of the reciprocal, interdependent nature of reality, they benefit from a collaboration with the Unseen.

The lover is always asking, “What shall we do with the Oneness?” The unrealized human being is responding with various defenses like: You’re not of my race, my ethnicity, my culture. I don’t like your name for God. You’re wearing strange clothes. Don’t get so close. What do you want from me? Or: Look how special I am. Pay attention to me. Why aren’t you behaving as I want you to?

What shall we do with the Oneness? The dimension of ourselves that “knows” is informed and guided by the awakened heart and by higher consciousness. It is an intelligence beyond the limited self; it is a territory of the mind that is vast; and it is the servant of cosmic love. The awakened heart can gain some perspective on the false self and moderate its demands. It stands on a spiritual promontory that can transcend the drama; it can laugh and let go.

It’s all well and good to say we will love humanity, but the awakened heart forges the bonds of oneness one person at a time. Every time we can see another as our self, every time we see others’ needs as important as our own, we are bringing heaven down to earth.

And if the awakened heart must confront the depths of the principalities of evil, it will be given the wisdom and the courage required, for there is no circumstance that does not ultimately serve the unfolding and manifestation of Truth.

The Custodians of Consciousness

There have always been mystics, "knowers" of all traditions, who have been among the "custodians of consciousness," those who maintain and benefit from an awareness of higher levels of Reality. They have perceived that everything in existence reflects consciousness, intelligence, and eternal Life. As custodians of consciousness, they move through life with humility, patience, intuitive awareness, and love.

The custodians of consciousness bear a special responsibility. There has always been a certain portion of humanity whose level of consciousness is relatively free of the biases, superstitions, jealousies, and self-righteousness that enslave so much of humanity. These custodians are the mystics, the gnostics, the peacemakers, the wise, whose hearts and minds are less contaminated with the toxins of egoism. If the custodians of consciousness increase in number, humanity might be turned in a different direction.

In a world where so many billions of humans lack the basic conditions for a healthy and honorable life, what justification is there for the pursuit of more and more wealth only for ourselves and *our* families?

The systems and structures of competition, exclusion, privilege, and domination only compound the world's miseries. Eventually, more of those who have been invested in the false reality will simply see the suffering they are creating for themselves and others, and simply walk away from it all.

Whether you identify with Buddha, Jesus, or Muhammad, you have an exemplar that did not make material accumulation a priority. The way of voluntary simplicity is the best road to health, happiness, justice, and humanity's survival.

It should not be unrealistic for nations and communities to live and function without making self-interest into a primary strategy, and instead seeking the benefit of all.

If, on the other hand, nations exclusively pursue their own national self-interest, resorting primarily to force, subterfuge, and information dominance, then we will continue to create a world like the one we have. We will continue to be dominated by a hidden elite, those who have mastered the strategies of control and power.

The activist who becomes enraged by the abuse of the truth they see and who self-righteously adopts an aggressive, oppositional stance in the argument will inevitably create an opposite reaction. Blinded by self-righteousness, which is a merely self-satisfying aspect of ego, they fail to see that he is driving away exactly the unity he intends to achieve. It must be remembered that our struggle is not against people but against those forces that facilitate the control system that continually divides and oppresses humanity.

> "Them and us" is a dangerous concept. There's only us. We are one human family. We are all the "children of Adam (and Eve)."

The control system has increasingly maintained its power through the omnipresent great Lie: mind control, in its many forms, the debt-based economic system, tactics of "divide and conquer," leading to perpetual war. The primary strategy in confronting the dominant culture would be to remove its primary weapons of control. Foremost among them is the fiat monetary system that has created a monopoly of money creation. Not only has this allowed a group of insiders to profit profligately, but it is also the mechanism by which perpetual war can be financed. Certain governments would not be able to spend virtually infinite amounts of money to finance the military machine if it were not for the ability to create "money" out of thin air and make future generations pay.

The Laws of Reality, however, will not permit an egoic system to survive indefinitely, but unfortunately, its end may be painful for the innocent as well as the guilty. On the one hand, it may appear, if we take a hard, honest look at those who maintain such strategies, that they seem to be ruthless, heartless, without empathy, virtually human in form alone. On the other hand, we cannot discount the possibility that there are enough people, even among those serving a control system, who have hearts, no matter how cold they may be, and that these hearts can be awakened.

The strategic question then becomes, how do we place ourselves beyond the argument, beyond the clash of opposites? How do we become the unifying solution?

Keeping our spirits up is a spiritual practice. No matter how dark it may seem, the light is growing. Deaths by war and oppression during the 20th century were estimated at 203,000,000. Despite the horrors of the present moment, the human situation is improving. Instead of being shocked at the obliviousness of many, we can keep a sense of humor, laugh at the stupidity of evil, keep striving, and keep our spirits up.

Sufis will recall the story from the time of the Prophet Muhammad of a crude Bedouin who relieved himself in the mosque causing a disruption among the companions who then wanted to give the Bedouin a thorough thrashing. But Muhammad ended the argument by cleaning up the mess himself, telling his companions, "We have been sent to make things easy, not difficult. Make it easy, don't make it difficult."

The question remains: how do we place ourselves beyond the argument? How do we move beyond the predator / prey syndrome? How do we bring wisdom and spiritual reconciliation into a world like ours?

Might it be possible to live in such a state that we can say, "We are the enemy of no one." Those who appear to be our enemies are actually enemies of themselves, for they are creating their own suffering, imprisoned in their own illusions and negativity.

The Divine Way should be a way of mutual support, human solidarity, sharing, and true happiness. If enough people can step into this reality, it may become clear that this happiness and virtue is a better strategy than seeking self-interest and power over others. But above all, it will become clear that spiritual laws exist and those who violate them will face consequences. Spiritual laws have a power of their own, greater than the powers of manipulation, exploitation, and domination.

As we step out into the world, as we take a stand for Truth, for Justice, let us not forget what we hope to represent. Even when we are face-to-face with Evil, we represent the power of Witnessing. If the times are "biblical," apocalyptic, terminally insane, we represent the Human vis-à-vis the anti-human. Against all the strategies of the Empires of Lies, we call to witness the vast agencies and angelic powers of the Sacred.

Endnotes and References for this Feature[viii:8]

Conscious Evolution: Our Salvation[1]

by Ervin Laszlo

QUO VADIS HUMANITAS? Where are we headed, humankind? Are we staying on the traveled path, or do we have the vision and the courage to find a better way to live and act? The time has come to reflect on this existential question, the contemporary variant of Hamlet's famous "to be or not to be." Can we shift to a path leading to a peaceful and sustainable world? That is now the question.

With the roadmaps suggested by our world-renowned contributors, we have a set of alternatives in our hand. The suggested roadmaps are bold and daring, yet they are intrinsically feasible. They show the way to a better world, but they do not guarantee that we will take it. Entering on the paths envisaged here calls for a major change in our world — above all, in our thinking. It calls for a veritable revolution in our concept of the real world, and of our ideas of our place and role in that world.

The world that makes up the woof and warp of our everyday experience, and is implicit in the reports of the international media, is a world of real and foreseeable crises. It is unstable and unsustainable. It appears to head toward ever greater breakdowns and raises the specter of an ultimate breakdown. It is very different from the upshifted world of the roadmaps. It appears that an upshift from today's chaotic and crisis-prone world to a world of peace and harmony is plain delusion — mere wishful thinking.

This is not a correct assessment of the situation. We are in the midst of a fundamental and radical systems-change, known in the systems sciences as a "bifurcation." A bifurcation is not only danger — it is also opportunity. It is the opportunity for a new system to be born. Today, the new system is foreshadowed, but not yet in place. How it will be born is yet to be decided. One thing is certain — a new world will be born. It will bring fundamental change in the way we relate to each other and to the world around us. This could be a change for the better, or for the worse. If it is to be better, we need to interact with the process of its birthing. We must make our evolution on the planet conscious.

The presuppositions for conscious evolution are given. We have the human and the material resources as well as the technology to live and thrive on the planet. There is nothing holding us back but our obsolete vision — or lack of vision.

There have been crises in the world before the current one, with revolutionary tipping points and unforeseen consequences. The current crisis is not the first in history, but it is more embracing than any of its predecessors. Our problems and the challenge of coping with them are now greater than ever. Will we rise to meet them? We live in a global crisis in a globalized world. We could rise to the more limited crises of the past — we are still here. But will we rise to the current crises? This is not clear. The current path of our evolution would be a dead-end.

The outlook for the future is not entirely dark, however. There are signs that we are waking up. A spirit of cooperation and solidarity often arises in chaotic times.

We must not discount the evolutionary factor. The evolutionary impetus in the universe, the "holotropic attractor" is an ever-present factor orienting the evolutionary process toward integral systems change. It made the universe into what it is, a coherent and complex whole, rather than a cloud of randomly interacting plasma, as it was at its birth in the aftermath of the Big Bang.

The great upshift can be and must be attempted. There is no time to waste and prevaricate. The chances of success are good. We have practicable roadmaps in our possession — those described in this book and a plethora of others. We are in the midst of a systems bifurcation, and there is growing openness to alternatives. We need not descend into terminal chaos. We can rise toward the wholeness that characterizes fundamental processes in nature.

Recognizing the existence of an evolutionary impetus is not a warrant for complacency and inaction. The response to the survival challenge may manifest independently of our conscious efforts, but how soon will it manifest — and at what cost? Clearly, the longer we wait, the greater the challenge and the higher the cost of meeting it. The naïve attitude of "just wait and see" would take us down the wrong path. The comforting belief that "in the end things will take care of themselves" could be suicidal.

The crisis we experience is deepening and spreading. We need to address its causal core and not its symptoms and corollaries.

We need to change the way we evolve on this planet. But how can we do it? There is no moral authority on Earth that could command or even recommend taking another path, nor is there any legal authority that could enforce it. The power to change does not lie above or beyond us. It lies in us. We must rethink and revise the narrow, materialistic, and exploitative way of thinking that still dominates the modern world. The root problem of our time is the obsolescence of the way we think.

Fortunately, the prevalent mindset is not engraved in stone, nor is it encoded in our DNA. It is subject to change. It has been changing throughout recorded history — every crisis brought a revised mindset. Today's crisis is no exception. Under the impact of mounting crises, more people are questioning the wisdom of continuing to live and think the way we do. But the new mindset that will take place of the old is not yet decided.

Changing the way we think and act is a realistic enterprise. It does not call for changing the mindset of every person on the planet, or even of a significant majority. It is sufficient to shift the mindset of a critical mass. The upshifted mindset of a small group of awakened people can spread and generate a growing wave of change that would constitute a new path for the evolution of humankind on this planet.

The steps we need to take are clear. We need to upshift our physical and mental health and heal ourselves and our fellow beings. We must upshift our thinking to embrace the factors that are crucial for our well-being and even for our survival. We must deepen our intuition so that we are able to apprehend the evolutionary impetus and allow it to guide our steps. The alternatives before us are crystal clear. We either upshift to peace and harmony on the planet, or we downslide to conflict and chaos. Which will it be? On the surface, it appears that we are headed toward a world of conflict and chaos. But underneath, there is a deeper evolution unfolding: a great upshift toward peace and harmony on the planet. The great upshift is before us. It is up to us to enter on the path that leads to it. The vision and the courage to do so could be, and will be, our salvation.

Endnotes and References for this Feature[viii:9]

THE DIALOGUE CONTINUES

Regarding the urgency of this inevitable convergence of science, spirituality and futurist vision, the next three Features briefly summarize three important initiatives and activities, upcoming at the time of these Volumes, that continue this critical dialogue into the future.

Spiritual Experience: A Scientific, Philosophical and Theological Retreat

June 22–29, 2025

by John Calvin Chatlos

This retreat and conference were held on Star Island, New Hampshire, USA, where conveners spent the week informally engaged in multidisciplinary sharing.[1] A pre-Conference paper (Chatlos 2025)[2] and Commentary are published in *Zygon: Journal of Science and Religion* December issue. The Conference reviewed current knowledge about spiritual experience and expanded on three new ideas for future development.

Notably, the conference was uniquely organized around a "Framework of Spirituality" (FOS) presented by Dr. Calvin Chatlos, an addiction psychiatrist. This FOS uses a cognitive behavioral theoretical (CBT)[3] perspective to explore how spiritual experience is phenomenologically and subjectively organized in the human experience. This research model has been demonstrated to intentionally promote spiritual awakening in a short-term group setting.[4] The FOS identifies self-worth and dignity as operationalized experiences that are keys to opening our spiritual core. This resides human awareness in what Sigmund Freud popularized as our "unconscious" and Carl Jung expanded to our "collective unconscious."

Informative graphics ("Framework of Spirituality," "Proposed Biopsychosocial-spiritual Model," and "Development of a common worldview for science, philosophy and theology to promote a 'Worldview Studies'" are cited and linked in the Endnotes hereto).

The first new idea recommended was using the FOS to guide future research in spirituality, psychedelics, and consciousness studies. The FOS identifies a spiritual core that is opened and associated with mystical-like experiences. This spiritual core is the healing element of spiritual experience suggesting that medicine and mental health should recognize the religious / spiritual domain as central to healing.

The second proposes a Biopsychosocial-spiritual Model for medicine with large central religious / spiritual determinants including religious practices with a sociological overlap, and spiritual practices in combined biological and psychological. The opening of the spiritual core is a center of the healing component of medical and mental healthcare. This multiple domain overlap with an ontological and science-grounded understanding suggests development of a larger *common worldview* for science, philosophy, and theology and promotion of a "Worldview Studies."

Thirdly, there should be developed a multidisciplinary Worldview Studies with inclusion of ontology as part of each major discipline. Focus should include the functional aspects of the "soul experience" as identified by the FOS to include the creative forces of a moral core, unconditional love (compassion), and an indomitable faith (not as a belief but as a courageous action). Initial suggestion is to have (1) an employment of Theology and Philosophy focused on spirituality, (2) an employment of Theology and Science focused on the landscapes of creativity and the metaphysical, and (3) employment of Science and Philosophy in the study of mind. Employment of all these elements highlights an emergent common ontological worldview.

Presenters at this conference included noted authors and authorities on emergent phenomena; cognitive behavioral theory; neuroscientific and psychedelic research; Default Mode Network; cosmology, co-creativity and futurism; process philosophy and process theology; cultures and practices of Indigenous Peoples; and Interspirituality and integrative modes of spiritual and psychological practice. Results from these many participants are being published in *Zygon: Journal of Science and Religion.*

Endnotes for this Feature[viii:10]

Faith and Science Rome Conference 2026

by Robert J. Hesse

The first regularly scheduled interfaith, Faith and Science Conference is being planned for 2026 in Rome. *The Faith and Science Conference Enhanced by Art, Music and Interfaith Mysticism* is sponsored by Houston-based Contemplative Network (CN at contemplative.net) and Rome-based Fondazione Pro Musica e Arte Sacra. The theme is "A Journey into God's Mystical Love." The goal is to show how faith, current science, and art reinforce each other and encourage respectful dialogue between laity, clergy, scientists and medical professionals. The strategic aim of the conference is interfaith loving service to those suffering from debilitating illnesses, poor quality of life, and lack of love.

Importance: There is much interest in faith and science (F&S) but an urgent need for a less disparate, broader dialogue. Typical F&S conferences are siloed by faith denominations and scientific disciplines, thus missing their wider ranging asymptotic (close) convergence. Their language often conflates mythology and poetry with faith and science, which confuses non-scientists and non-theologians. The meetings tend to be clubby groups of returning registrants, with little cross-fertilization dialogue. There is a keynote speaker then breakout sessions with less qualified speakers whose topics are often unrelated to each other and the conference theme. The planned Rome conference is organized to address these issues.

Description: Speakers include interfaith contemplative clergy and renowned scientists, three of whom studied under or are working with Nobel Laureates. Cardinal Turkson, Chancellor of the Pontifical Academy of Science, will open the conference, and pending availability, the Pope will close the conference with a private audience. It will culminate in neuroscientific medical research on interfaith contemplative prayer's improvements in quality of life for various illnesses. Clergy from diverse faith traditions will lead meditative experience. The conference is dedicated to the memory of Trappist Fr. Thomas Keating, who said, "In the silence, there is no dogma." It will be a call to love and service.

Presentations: Presentations will cover four main subjects based on chapter titles from CN's book *Faith and Science: A Journey into God's Mystical Love*: Physics to Creation, Chemistry to Life, Biology to Consciousness, and Psychology to Mysticism. Each day of two days will cover two subjects. Each subject will have two distinguished speakers with seamless transitions between them. The final session will show the asymptotic coherence between the four subjects and end with neuroscientific research on improved quality-of-life from practicing interfaith contemplative practice. Presentations will be understandable by non-scientists and non-theologians. Each presentation ends with a Q&A and then a dialogue between the two speakers on that subject. Each day ends with a panel discussion by that day's clergy and scientists.

Offsite Art and Music: This will provide tangible enhancements of the four subjects. Physics to Creation: Vatican Observatory virtual tour. Chemistry to Life: private sacred music in the Sistine Chapel focusing on Michelangelo's painting of *Creation of Adam*. Biology to Consciousness: Borghese Gallery, focusing on Bernini's sculpture, *Apollo and Daphne*, symbolic of the birth of the consciousness. Psychology to Consciousness: St. Maria della Vittoria Chapel, focusing on Bernini's sculpture *Ecstasy of St. Teresa of Avila*.

A Next Conference: A future conference is planned for Houston, Texas, home of the largest medical center in the world. Medical professionals will participate in discussions offering interfaith contemplative practice as an optional physical therapy. Participation will be from volunteer patients from the some 80+ percent of the hospital population who have some form of religious affiliation or spiritual life practice. An Endnote summarizes more and provides various detail.[1]

Endnotes for this Feature[viii:11]

ProSocial Spirituality Initiative toward a Framework for "True Union" of Science, Spirituality and Religion

by David Sloan Wilson and Jeffrey Genung

Quoting from earlier in Volume 2 of these Volumes:

> *ProSocial Spirituality* began in 2019 as an evolutionary research, training, and technology partnership between two nonprofit organizations, the Evolution Institute and Contemplative Life, made possible by a grant jointly sponsored by the Templeton Religion Trust and the Issachar Fund. Contemplative Life's Director of Content, Kate Sheehan Roach, and One Spirit Learning Alliance Founder and Spiritual Director, Rev.

> Diane Berke, took the lead in co-developing a program inspired by a question being asked, independently and quite simultaneously, by two interspiritual trailblazers who were close friends and colleagues of Wayne Teasdale in the final years of his life — Dr. Kurt Johnson and Jeff Genung, Contemplative Life's founder. In January 2019, Johnson published in *Kosmos Journal* "Evolving Toward Cooperation: David Sloan Wilson's [ProSocial's founder] New Evolutionary Biology." Johnson and the ProSocial Spirituality team were asking the same question: "What would happen if a new group framework was formed by combining Wayne Teasdale's Nine Elements of Interspirituality and, from Prosocial Nobel Laureate Elinor Ostrom's Core Design Principles, modern evolutionary science, and contextual behavioral science?"
>
> And so, a field study was born. A team of educators and researchers led by ProSocial World founder and evolutionary biologist Dr. David Sloan Wilson built an experimental framework and methodology designed to explore how variation in understanding and implementation of core spiritual principles and social design principles impacts group function and adaptability.[1]

In 2025, and going forward, ProSocial spirituality aims toward a *Framework for "True Union" of Science, Spirituality and Religion* in a new initiative. From the proposal by David Sloan Wilson:[2]

> One question in particular attracted my interest: The puzzle of how altruism can evolve. [Religious] believers are confronted with the problem of evil: Why does evil exist in a world created by an all-powerful and beneficent god? Evolutionists are confronted with the problem of goodness: How can helping others survive and reproduce evolve, when natural selection inherently favors individuals who survive and reproduce better than other individuals?
>
> ...Darwin described his theory in terms of three simple ingredients: Organisms vary in just about everything that can be measured about them (variation), their differences make a difference in terms of survival and reproduction (selection), and offspring tend to resemble their parents (replication). When these three ingredients are combined, the properties of organisms change over time in the direction of becoming better adapted to their environments. Never was such a powerful theory also so simple!

Of course, since then, the Darwinian framework has been much more fully and elegantly elaborated.[3] Ultimately, Wilson continues his Proposal in this light:

> Nothing about humanity makes sense except in the light of evolution [but has] Darwin's theory [been] making sense of biology but was not yet making sense of humanity! For me, extending my study of altruism to the human realm led directly to the study of religion, starting with my 2002 book *Darwin's Cathedral:*

Evolution, Religion, and the Nature of Society, and continuing to the present.[4]

Working from this legacy of David Sloan Wilson's pioneering work in the sociology of religions and particularly his 2019 dialogues regarding this with His Holiness the 14th Dalai Lama,[5] the new initiative presents a detailed framework for how Science, Spirituality, and Religions might find one framework for a "True Union" satisfactory, especially for contemporary academia, and the boundaries and constraints of multiple, and often conflicting narratives. The framework asks how the behavioral and global change-related elements so desperately needed in our severely challenged modern world might find the same transformative results even within significantly different philosophical, religious, and scientific narratives.

ProSocial Spirituality announced additionally visioned future activities at the 2025 "Wave" event of The Holomovement (at holomovment.net) whose vision is also featured in these Volumes by Featured Authors Emanuel Kuntzelman and William Keepin.[6]

Endnotes and References for this Feature[viii:12]

Endnotes and References for "Science and the Future" Section[viii]

REFLECTIONS AND POINTINGS

On Spiritual Life ~ On Interspiritual Pioneers ~ ~ On the Global Challenge

In this next Section, we share "Reflections" Features from eminent Featured Authors who have centered their Interspiritual messages, first, on profound and numinous matters of the Spiritual Life and the phenomenon of spiritual awakening. We recall once again the words of Br. Teasdale: "We need to understand, to really grasp at an elemental level that the definitive revolution is the spiritual awakening of humankind" (MH p. 12). We are so grateful for these key commentaries on awakening consciousness in the Interspiritual Age. We then celebrate pioneers of this global awakening in the Features subtitled "On Interspiritual Pioneers." Therein, seventeen iconic interspiritual pioneers are honored by Featured Authors deeply familiar with them personally, and/or their life's work. Following thereafter are six important reflections on various and vital aspects of our current global challenge and what the awakening of a profound partnership consciousness in humankind might bring to that in this critical time. We deeply honor the counsel of these gifted Featured Authors — all leaders in the global interfaith and interspiritual communities, as well as within the root traditions from which they come. We begin with the Features on the Spiritual Life.

ON SPIRITUAL LIFE

Camille Hamilton Adams Helminski - Michael Holleran - Kurt Johnson - Karuna Loch Kelly - Audrey E. Kitagawa - Shannon Marie Winters

The Light of Awareness: A Journey with Divine Mother

by Audrey E. Kitagawa

I entered a mystical path that led to the mysteries and wonderment of the Divine from the moment I first met Divine Mother. She riveted me, enchanted me, and immersed me in her love that filled me with an unspeakable peace and quietude that were previously unknown to me. There are divine mysteries that have the power to transform, and are authenticated by one's own direct experience. I traveled this mystical road for twenty years with Divine Mother before she left her body. I have a photo of us on my desk sitting side by side on a couch taken shortly before she passed. I look at this photo every day; a commemorative moment in time of the deep love between us that would signify our last photo taken together. Shortly before she left her body, she told the group of us gathered around her not to cry because she would be "closer to (us) than ever in Spirit." I did not cry when she departed her body because she was fully alive in my heart, and is vibrantly alive in me to this day.

It was a warm August day as I climbed an outside staircase to meet Divine Mother for the first time at her home, not having a clue who she was, or knowing anything about her. She opened her door, took one look at me, pointed her right index finger at me and said,

"You cannot serve two masters." In my heart, I knew exactly what she meant, although I really could not fathom at the time how those words would unfold in my life. We sat down, and I hardly said a word about myself other than I was on my way to law school in Boston.

She launched into the most powerful, exquisite exposition on the Divine that anyone could have the privilege to hear. It was new, vibrant and so alive! She was speaking a language of the Spirit that was transporting, transforming, and immersed me in a profound, pure love that made me feel completely understood and nurtured. She told me the beginning and the end of her life, except she left out one thing, though I was unaware of it at the time. This one thing I was meant to discover on my own, which I eventually did, much to Divine Mother's joy which she expressed to me in one of her letters.

She spoke rapidly and probably reading the concern registered on my face said, "Don't worry. I am transmitting to you Spirit to Spirit, Heart to Heart, Infinite to Infinite and not mind to mind. Whatever you may need of what I have transmitted to you will spontaneously arise when you need them." She was true to her word, and over the years, I was able to verify the truth of these Sacred Transmissions, which spontaneously arose whenever I needed them.

I fell in love with her, this petite, Japanese lady, who spoke "Pidgin English" from a small sugar town in Waipahu, Hawaii, with an eighth-grade education, married, and the mother of five children. She told me that she came for the householders, who carry the challenges of work life, family life, and the many attachments which these can bring. She shared how she met a messenger in 1972 named Jennifer, who came to help an "orphan child" (meaning she had no formal religious affiliation), who taught her how to "work with the light" in the jungles of Waikiki, at the home of a lady named Elsie Locie. For the favor of using Elsie Locie's home, the messenger told her she would take twenty years off her chronological age.

Divine Mother told me that the messenger showed her different aspects of God. The messenger seemed to know exactly what Divine Mother would do, even leaving a written message that said, "Don't be so nosey," when she peeked into something that belonged to the messenger.

In one of the teaching sessions, Jennifer threw a fork against the wall in a seeming rage. This surprised Divine Mother as she thought all spiritual beings were supposed to be placid and calm. Jennifer was teaching her about the "wrath of God."

The messenger gave her several prophecies, which I am seeing fulfilled, and have no doubt that those that have yet to come will certainly come to pass at some time in the future.

When Jennifer touched her shoulder, Divine Mother was immersed in this unspeakable love, and felt she could follow Jennifer to the ends of the earth. The last time she saw Jennifer, she appeared to Divine Mother with a crown on her head dressed in beautiful garments, as the "King of kings." She was looking for every opportunity to see Jennifer again after her training had ended.

One day, she thought she saw Jennifer at a bus stop, but she would not see her again, except that Jennifer told her that she would pick her up "in seven days," at the time that Divine Mother was meant to leave her body. I was trying mightily to figure out seven days from when, as Divine Mother became bedridden from her metastasizing cancer, and it became obvious that her departure was near. I did not have to try to figure anything out in my mind, as Divine Mother announced, "I have to go now," and requested that she be changed into a special blue and white "muumuu" (a Hawaiian dress for women).

Once she was changed into that muumuu, she stopped talking, her arms fell to her sides, and we silently watched as her chest just moved up and down for several hours. I thought Divine Mother had gone into a coma. After several hours, she waved her hand in the air as if to say, "Goodbye," breathed her last, and all that was left was the chrysalis of her body lying there. Divine Mother was not in a coma after all, just in her kindness, giving us time to prepare and accept her departure.

That first meeting changed the trajectory of my life though I did not know it at the time. I was born and raised in Honolulu, Hawaii, and attended a high school right across the street from Divine Mother's home, though her home and who lived in it had no significance to me then.

At that first meeting, Divine Mother became firmly embedded in my heart, and I began writing to her when I reached Boston. She would occasionally write back. There were no computers back then, or email, so everything was handwritten. There were no cell phones either, so I had to be very circumspect on making long distance phone calls that could be very expensive, especially from Boston to Hawaii. In short, long distance phone calls would be made only in emergencies, as funds as a law student were tight. I saved all of her letters to me. They were my treasures.

She was kind and motherly, and she sent me vitamin supplements to improve my health as I seemed to catch colds and the flu often. My health improved with the supplements that she sent, and catching colds and the flu became few and far between by many years. As I write this, I frankly cannot remember the last time I had a cold or flu. Little did I know that she was giving me insights into the importance of taking steps to ensure the quality of my life, body, mind and spirit through proper nutrition, meditation, and undertaking a spiritual life. She even taught me stretching exercises which I continue to do today.

I could not wait to return to Hawaii to see Divine Mother every chance I had during the summer and Christmas breaks from law school. I was able to fly home inexpensively thanks to my sister, Dianne, who was a stewardess at Pan American Airways. I paid full fare from Boston to New York, but was on Pan Am employee benefits from New York to Fairbanks, Alaska, Seattle, and finally, Honolulu. At that time, they were building the Alaskan pipeline, and it seemed every person wanted to return home for the holidays. Several people had been waiting at the airport for many days with no luck of getting a seat. Miraculously, I was always able to secure a seat, often the very last available seat.

I learned many things from Divine Mother by observing her. I was a chronically tardy person. My friends over time adapted to my tardiness by telling me that an event was actually an hour or more before the actual start time so I would show up on time. However, Divine Mother was always mindful about people's time, and never kept anyone waiting. Her mindfulness of others, showing respect for them by respecting their time, being careful not to create unnecessary anxiety and worry in others turned me into a prompt person.

Shortly before she left her body, Divine Mother chose me to head the spiritual family that had grown around her over the years; seekers after God, hungry and thirsty for spiritual food, which she freely gave. At the time that she chose me, I had an active law practice, and I eventually closed my law practice to fulfill my promise to Divine Mother to take Sri Ramakrishna's Light to the world for her. Sri Ramakrishna, considered the "Avatar of the Century" by *Time* magazine, was that one thing that she never told me about during my first meeting with her. I had to find him on my own, which I did. That alone is a beautiful but long story to be shared at another time.

When I closed my law practice, I chose the master which I would serve for the rest of my life, and Divine Mother's words when she saw me at our first meeting, "You cannot serve two masters," came to pass. US Supreme Court Justice Joseph Story characterized law as a "jealous mistress (who) requires long and constant courtship. It is not to be won by trifling favors, but by lavish homage." My law career was demanding, a career that I loved and chose to pursue from the time I was a young girl, knowing that I wanted to be a lawyer, and became one. I chose my law career, but I was suddenly chosen to undertake this sacred global mission.

I was shown in my first year of law school that the day would come when I would have to give up my law career. I was not told exactly when this would happen but was left with the knowing that when that time came, I would be absolutely clear that it was time to leave it behind. Thereafter, I would have to live by the Will of God alone, and be willing to move throughout the world, like a leaf in the wind, not letting any attachments impede my ability to do so. I was indeed absolutely clear when it was time to close my law practice, and I closed it with breathtaking speed. Her words, "Go forth and don't look back," have stayed with me throughout, even as my skills learned while practicing law still remain with me.

I cannot possibly convey all that Divine Mother transmitted to me in my twenty-year journey with her, nor describe all of the sublime, inspiring, extraordinary experiences she conferred on me with such great love. Each experience spawns another deep dive into the divine mysteries, the exploration of which cannot be covered in this short contribution.

I end here with the following powerful snippets of what she transmitted to me when I first met her.

> "The mind is not Real, only God is Real;
> The body is not Real, only God is Real;
> Anything that changes is not Real,
> only God, the Changeless Changer is Real;
> Everything in creation changes.
> Our true purpose in life is God Realization.
> The greatest gifts from God are free.
> God is Love."

Shortly before she left her body, she waved her hand, seeming to sweep across creation and said, "This is just a dream. All a dream."

Intelligent Awareness (IA) is the Next Stage of Human Development

by Loch Kelly

> ***Two Kinds of Intelligence***
> *There are two kinds of intelligence: One acquired,*
> *as a child in school memorizes facts and concepts*
> *from books ...*
> *There is another kind of tablet,*
> *one already completed and preserved inside you.*
> *A spring overflowing its springbox. A freshness*
> *in the center of the chest.*
> *It's fluid, and it doesn't move from outside to inside*
> *through the conduits of plumbing-learning.*
> *This second knowing is a fountainhead*
> *from within you, moving out.*
> ~ Rumi

Two of the most important aspects of human development are the ability to think and the ability to *grow beyond thinking*. Right now, you might be wondering what I mean by "beyond thinking." That's OK. As you move through the exercises and engage with the material in this book, you can begin to experience this new kind of knowing for yourself.

Thinking Is the Sixth Sense

Our senses are the way that we receive information and connect with our bodies and the world. We all know the basic five senses: hearing, seeing, touching, tasting and smelling. In Buddhist understanding, thinking is considered the sixth sense. Each of the six senses is set up to receive a particular kind of information. For instance, the ears hear sound but cannot perceive light. The kind of information that the thinking mind receives is thoughts and images.

Thinking is a complex sense with several roles. One of its functions is to mediate between the other senses by categorizing: we hear a sound with the ears and then thinking labels it "a car horn." The thinking sense uses memory to find a match for what it's experiencing, and then uses language to communicate. The most fundamental function of the thinking sense is to make dualistic distinctions, meaning dividing choices into either/or. It is important for our physical safety that our brains make quick, simple distinctions. If you are driving, your eyes see what is happening and then the images you see go to the thinking sense, which organizes information for a quick decision: stop *or* go, right *or* left, and if a light is yellow, right *or* wrong to go through it.

We have spent a lot of time training the thinking mind, and this is important for functioning in the world. But the thinking mind is not meant to be the central way of knowing. When we look to the thinking mind we are reflecting, which means creating a conceptual picture of what is happening. But here is the key: the reflection or conceptual picture is one second removed from the Now — we are not directly perceiving or connected to what's happening. This self-reflection process alienates and separates us from what we perceive.

Brain research shows that the same parts of the brain fire if you are imagining doing something and when you are actually doing it. Through use of imagination, self-reflection builds a self-image through constructing a conceptual model of reality and of ourselves. This is why we often feel a little alienated or disassociated from life, as though we aren't part of it, or as though our experience is an object and we are a separate subject. When we imagine scenarios from this illusory sense of self, the models tend to fall into the extremes or grandiosity or low self-image. With awarenessing, we may directly experience what's happening as it's happening.

This thinking sense is important, but it cannot know awake awareness or our true being. Can the eyes see the car, *yes or no*? Yes. Can the eyes know thinking? No. Can the thinking sense know our true being? No.

Eventually, we will find out that thinking cannot know awake awareness. In making this important distinction, thinking can return to its natural role. We can then go beyond thinking to discover and use this second kind of non-conceptual knowing we can call awake awareness. Because thinking plays an organizing role, in Western psychology, we have elevated it out of the realm of the senses — but we went too far. None of us would take ourselves to *be* our hearing, but we routinely take ourselves to be our thoughts or our thinking mind. We made thinking the center of our identity rather than part of the process.

From Thinking to Thinker

When thinking is not regarded as one of our senses, it joins with ego function to become ego-identification. This identification with thinking creates a *thinker*, which is at the core of our mistaken identity. This quote, which we've all heard, "I think, therefore I am," sums up this way of perceiving. In order to grow beyond this, we need to experience the "I am" that is not based in thought. Intellectually understanding this can be a helpful first step, but because intellectual understanding is still the first kind of knowing, we have to use it as a stepping-stone. When the thinker is who is looking through our eyes, it uses the bifocals of dualism. The thinker's way of knowing is limited to the senses and tied to the survival function and to the reptilian brain.

When the identity is built on this dualistic, discriminating foundation, it becomes limited. When the thinking becomes the thinker, it becomes reflective and is outside of reality. We *think up* a sense of subject / object separation that is not really there. There is always one right answer or way, and we are limited by the pressure to always decide which is right. This is why people fear being "dead wrong."

We can begin to wake up out of identification with the thinker by directly experiencing another way of knowing. If thinking is actually one of the senses, then who or what does this sense report *to*? Where do the six senses go? We will come to see that they appear to awake awareness.

The Second Kind of Knowing

Awake awareness is the source of the "second knowing" that Rumi talks about in his poem above. In the Western tradition, this kind of intelligence is sometimes called wisdom, but wisdom is often mistakenly understood to mean a highly developed intellect, or wise sayings of the first kind of intelligence. As we all know, someone who is very smart is not necessarily wise. There is a kind of wisdom, a next level of development that releases thinking from being central to ego-identity and frees us from the limited perspective of the small self. Thinking mind is no longer the subject but becomes the object and function of awareness — the observer becomes the observed.

Western thinker Eckhart Tolle writes of "A knowingness that does not destroy the sacredness of life but contains a deep love and reverence for all that is. A knowing of which the mind knows nothing."

Other cultures agree with this distinction of two kinds of knowing. Zen teacher D.T. Suzuki says there are two forms of knowing: The first, discriminating intelligence, is called *vikalpa* in Sanskrit, and the second, called *prajna,* is wisdom or direct realization. Suzuki said it was "most essential" to distinguish these two forms of knowledge.

As the Dzogchen Ponlop Rinpoche explains, "The nature of our mind is completely enlightened right from the beginning, and it is known as ordinary mind." He goes on to say, "Ordinary mind refers to mind that is not fabricated in any way. It is the natural or fundamental state of our mind, totally free from all conceptual elaborations... Whether our thoughts and emotions are positive, negative, or neutral — that mind, in its essence, is totally free from all dualistic fixations."

When you experience this second kind of knowing, you will notice that it does not actively use thoughts as building blocks to construct ideas. You'll notice that self-judging and self-consciousness are absent. There is a more fluid sense, as if information processing is naturally happening on its own, in the background. It's not esoteric or something out of the ordinary, like channeling or a special skill — instead, it's an ordinary human capacity. It is not a gut feeling or intuitive flash that happens occasionally, but an ongoing way of knowing.

Moving from the first kind of knowing to the second kind of knowing is similar to learning to ride a bicycle, drive a car or type. When you first learned to type you had to look at your fingers and consciously remember which finger went to each letter. This is called "hunt and peck." Everyone who learns to type goes through a shift where we *grow beyond thinking* about what we are doing. Now when we type, we don't have to self-monitor or consciously remember the keys. In the same way, thinking becomes an instrument of awake awareness. The second kind of knowing is awake and aware, though not necessarily consciously thinking about each action.

Identity

The conceptual mind cannot know awareness or our real nature. When the thinking mind tries to know our *true Being*, the best it can do is create an imaginary picture, concept, or image. This self-image is a false self or a persona, which means a mask. Not knowing our true Being creates confusion. The thought that arises, "I will never understand this," is actually correct! The thinker cannot ever know our true Being. Transitioning from the thinker identity to abiding as Being can be a frustrating period. The feeling of frustration during this time is normal and is actually a sign that you are going in the right direction. Stay with it and remember that the goal is for awake awareness to shift out of the thinking bandwidth of consciousness, the very bandwidth that is trying to understand it. To know Being, you have to let go or surrender.

If there is another way of knowing available, then thinking can relax into the background. When this happens, what is revealed is awake awareness — an intelligence that is alert, clear, spacious, and connected. Awake awareness is like the autonomic nervous system in that it is happening by itself without any conscious effort, just like our own breathing or our heart beating.

When we rest as awake awareness, the thinking mind is discovered to be more like the ears, which are always open, receiving information and passing that information along. If thinking cannot know our true identity, then which of the senses can? None of the six senses can know our true identity, but with awarenessing as a kind of seventh sense, another way of knowing is possible.

Beyond the Thinker

Information moves through our five senses to thinking, where it is recognized and then labeled or categorized. The information is then processed through memory and past storehouse consciousness in order to orient us. The ego function seeks to relate past experience to what is happening now to this particular human organism. Ego function is the part of consciousness that says, "What does this have to do with this body?"

For example, we may see a car and our sixth sense of thinking labels it as a "car." If the car is moving toward us, ego function organizes information about what's happening and decides to move out of the way. When information from the world comes in contact with thinking and our ego function, it can loop around and create an ego identity or it can continue on to a more inherent dimension of consciousness, awake awareness.

Ego function is a natural, important cognitive process that does not need to change when we awaken beyond ego identification. Instead, sensory information doesn't get caught in our representational, mental loop but continues through to awake awareness. Awareness receives information without coloration or obsession, and remains awake. Ego function is returned to its natural job, rather than trying to be the manager, or an entity on its own. We can learn how to perceive from awake awareness rather than the thinking mind through Effortless Mindfulness with small mindful glimpses so this becomes not just a meditation state but a trait and the next natural stage of human development.

The Intersection of "Direct Paths" in Interspirituality[1]

by Karuna and Kurt Johnson

Br. Wayne Teasdale, in his seminal work on Interspirituality, *The Mystic Heart: Discovering a Universal Spirituality in the World's Religions*, wrote that encounters between and among the world's religions would further amplify with the expansion of the interspiritual experience and the inevitable process of multiculturalism and globalization. Dr. David Sloan Wilson, noted evolutionary biologist, co-founder of Prosocial World, and champion of unfolding paradigm change in evolutionary science, noted that Interspirituality would be the natural direction of the world's religions if what we know today about evolutionary process is true.[2]

In the last decades of our work across multiple spiritual traditions worldwide, we have encountered these intersections between traditions again and again. Not only is the term "intersection" apt for these convergences but also the phrase "crossing-over." In evolutionary science (one of Kurt's areas of expertise, and the specialty of his PhD), the intersection of biological lineages in genetics is also termed crossing over. In the natural world, the actual cross-overs are of genetic material — DNA sequences and their mathematics —

crossing, backcrossing, in a web of exchanged genetic material. This kind of evolution is one of the primal causes of nature's entangled diversity and is called "reticulate evolution" (meaning arranged like a net or network). Analogously, as Kurt and David Robert Ord portrayed in their book, *The Coming Interspiritual Age*, our *future* worldviews, *and* spiritual practices, will emerge from this inevitable, expanding, intimate global contact among and across all the world's spiritual traditions. This sharing of mystical resources was a part of Br. Teasdale's very definition of Interspirituality. And it will continue to increase as the global intercultural evolution of our species continues.

Looking at any current multicultural world map, we see this convergence of worldviews and practices, each offering distinct cosmologies and spiritual technologies. As integral philosopher Ken Wilber has said, having all of these resources available in our time is one of the hallmarks of our current Age. Br. Teasdale characterized this as a natural evolution — departing from the past, and often still prevailing "religious culture[s] of fragmentation and isolation" [MH p. 12] and moving toward *Interspirituality* — be it as "Spiritual but not Religious," "Global, Universal, World-centric or Trans-traditional Spirituality," "Multiple Belonging," or whatever characterizations are made.

We have written about this previously, particularly in two articles originally published in *Contemplative Journal* — both no longer extant and from which we draw here, in brief, for these Volumes. There are two important points.

First, the Intersection of "Direct Paths"

Across most of the traditions to date, particularly with regard to the unfolding of Awakened (or Nondual) Consciousness, there has been the identifying of "direct paths," as it were, "*express trains*" to that awakened "destination": in the West, spiritual awakening, self-realization, inner peace, transcendence, awakening of consciousness, higher awareness, illumination, awakening, nirvana, etc.; in the East, vimoksha, vimukti, kaivalya, apavarga, mukti, nihsreyasa, and nirvana etc. [In Indigenous Traditions, synonyms become difficult because they are generally rendered back to "lst world" languages.] Such awakening metaphors, as travel and destination, are in one sense apt since, at face, all religious narratives and spiritual methods are actually *cosmologies*. That is, they act as *maps*, in this case — especially and ultimately — maps *toward* that realization, awakening, enlightenment, salvation, or these other terms related to profound transformation. These direct paths inevitably intersect in the global environment of Interspirituality.

This is the upside but there is also a potential downside. The downside of this global convergence is what Ken Wilber calls "Myth of the Given" — that it is also utterly natural that each tradition will believe that *its* particular cosmological map is not only *true* but perhaps also better, best, or even *solely* true, and recognizing this potential pathology as one of the great "Aha's" of the interspiritual landscape. It was, in fact, the subject of Br. Wayne Teasdale's writing — republished in these Volumes after being "lost" — concerning the famed interspiritual pioneer Abhishiktananda's own experience of deep-seated fears arising in the exploration of seemingly very *different* contemplative cosmologies and claims, both Christian and Vedic.

As Abhishiktananda recorded, compelling but differing claims of a direct path can be disconcerting to the deeply serious spiritual voyager. There is not only the differences in the cosmological maps of the path, but also how it is coupled with a call to allegiance to the spiritual teacher or guru, asking "complete surrender," or complete "belief." To these also add the classical, even clichéd, caution (attributed to multiple historical "enlightened ones") that regarding the entire map and destination metaphor, "the finger pointing at the moon" (i.e. realization) is not the moon itself (the common parlance is "The Tao that can be spoken of is not the eternal Tao," etc.). It is easy and common for spiritual seekers to simply chase experience — but never find the deeper realization — be it the "unstruck melody" of Kundalini Yoga or the "silent song" of Advaita.

In the message of his spiritual classic *Atma Darshan*, Krishna Menon sought to remind all the traditions, and particularly their technologies "*toward*" realization or awakening, of the trap of casting the journey as one of any kind of attainment. Instead, Menon reminded that the natural state of everything is "already awake" and only because of the veils obscuring this is there a utility to methods and practices themselves. Ultimately, as in our appreciations of the inevitable intersection of direct paths in Interspirituality, we can see that we have side–by–side, and at this time, multiple spiritual technologies that can be direct paths, "Raj Yogas" (royal, titular, direct Yogas) — the "one mountain, many paths" phrase, itself attributed to multiple traditions beyond just that of Miyamoto Musashi in his *The Book of Five Rings*.

Discovering the Natural Unity in Diverse Direct Paths

In our earlier publications on this, we devoted a number of pages with side-by-side examples of celebrated Seers across the many traditions, essentially saying *all the same thing*, across each of these general categories: on the Awakened State; on the Absolute; on the Spiritual Search; on Knowing; on The Body; on Karma; on the Personal Journey; on Spiritual Discipline; on Lifestyle; on Yogic

Practice. Across multiple sages, their words, transcribed from their direct speaking, match up clearly and poignantly, side by side, in often nearly identical phrases. We don't see the need, particularly within the richness of the present Volumes and attention to space, to repeat these here. We have, however, added a few more details in the Endnote to the Title of this piece.

Likely the Direct Path of the future is whatever truly works, from across all the wisdom resources global spirituality now makes available for any particular individual. And, it appears this will inevitably involve the ongoing crossing-over [crossing, back-crossing, etc.] of spiritual paths that we elaborate further below.

Second, Today's "Cross–Over" Phenomenon in Interspirituality

A second major point of our writings in the past has been to provide some actual statistics on the crossing-over phenomenon in spirituality that is unfolding in the interspiritual experience. In biological evolution, diversification happens by the emergence of what are called "new adaptive zones," that is, new situations that create entirely new possibilities and potentials for emergence and diversity. In nature, these most often result precisely from the crossing–over, crossing–back, etc. of information in the mathematical sequences of genetic material. In cultural evolution, it is the exchange of information as ideas and technologies. In both cases, it is simply information exchange. What happens in nature is that evolution's paths, that is, biological lineages, generation to generation intersect, interact, and unfold into new combinations — new "things."

To illustrate the universality of this, the same phenomenon is widely recognized in popular music. Today we see what are actually called cross–over music styles: blues fusion, jazz fusion, world fusion, electronica fusion, reggae–rock, folk–rock, country–rock, etc. In fact, in the last decades, whole new popular music charts have been created to track the success of cross–over music styles. This is a result of our globe's emerging multiculturalism. The same phenomenon is going on now in our planet's interspiritual unfolding. To illustrate this, here are some statistics. They show that many, in some cases most, teachers in the West today — representing myriad traditions — and many in official capacities such as "lineage holders," etc. — are *not* from the ethnic group, or cultural identity, from which those traditions originated.

Examples: From Dharma teacher websites: (1) www.satsangteachers.com: 129 teachers (Advaita, Zen, Dzogchen etc.), Western ethnic origin: 96.2 percent; (2) www.dharmaseed.org (Dharma teachers), 311 teachers, Western ethnic origin: 77.8 percent; (3) www.dharma.org (Insight Meditation), 59 teachers, Western ethnic origin: 91.5 percent; (4) www.batgap.com (Buddha at the Gas Pump interviews), 243 teachers, Western ethnic origin: 97.9 percent; and (5) Spiritual teacher associations, The Heart of the Healer (THOTH) (South American Shamanic Traditions), 8 teachers, non-Native ethnic origin: 96.5 percent.[3] Interestingly also, the American Zen Teachers Association (www.americanzenteacher.org) noted it was not posting its rosters until it can revise criteria because of this crossing-over phenomenon.

Conclusions

Our conclusions are threefold. **First**, it is likely these cross–over teachers will initiate further cross–over of paths, practices, and technologies as the interspiritual experience continues to unfold. This is reflected already in the foundational interspiritual literature itself having arisen from such pioneer cross–over personalities as Fathers Henri Le Saux, Mondhanin, Bede Griffiths, Raimon Pannikar, Thomas Merton, and Brother Wayne Teasdale. **Second**, this intersecting of the world's religions, along with the intricacies of their spiritualities, is the direction of current evolution. There appears to be no doubt that in our interspiritual, globalizing, and multicultural world, the trend is toward more and more crossing-over of traditions and paths and — at least among cosmopolitan cultures — also the crossing–over and crossing–back of the ethnic identities in the leaderships of those traditions. **Third**, we must address the question of "why is this happening?" The answer is very simple — both modern evolutionary science and the Great Wisdom Traditions see nature moving toward a planetary altruism. In science, it is because the meta-levels of "Group" and "Multi-level" natural selection in natural "make selections based on the good of the whole." In the spiritual traditions, they (at best) point all the traditions toward the lofty values-related goals professed in all those traditions. And, in the bigger sense, as reflected in the Features in Volume 1 of these Volumes from the Parliament of the World's Religions, our planet is (ideally) in a process of "waking up," "opening up," "growing up," "cleaning up," "showing up," "linking up," and "lifting up." This is all further linked together by intertwined "being" and "doing" — the fundamental message in Br. Wayne Teasdale's coterie of books linking *The Mystic Heart* in all the world's religions to the sacred activism of *A Monk in the World* — contemplative, prophetic voice, and transformative action.

A Final Insight

What is there to say, in sum, about these emergent phenomena: this crossing–over of the world spiritual paths — even the most direct paths?

As in all emergence, be it in biological evolution or in the growth of consciousness, one sees the emergence of things often called "new." Of course, the ingredients are not new, but the combinations and their summed manifestation serve that innovative purpose. In fact, Wayne Teasdale said the Interspiritual Age itself would emerge "because of a new set of historical circumstances" [MH p. 4].

A number of years ago, the late Lucien Stryk (1924–2013) — the poet and major translator of Zen texts — mentioned to Kurt that all of this was summarized, quite surprisingly to many, in Robert Frost's famous poem "The Road Not Taken." Stryk noted no one seemed to comment on two of the most important lines in that poem — the last two lines of the second stanza, recounted here [with our emphasis in italics]:

> Two roads diverged in a yellow wood, And sorry I could not travel both, And be one traveler, long I stood, And looked down one as far as I could, To where it bent in the undergrowth, Then took the other, as just as fair, And having perhaps the better claim, Because it was grassy and wanted wear; *Though as for that the passing there, Had worn them really about the same….*

Perhaps an understanding of the meaning of these last phrases clearly emerges now, at least for spiritual journeyers, in the context of Interspirituality and the complementarity of direct paths. For indeed, if we consider the efficacy of radically different paths, held by the generalities of awakened Spirit across all the traditions, it is clear —

> *Though as for that the passing there,*
> *Had worn them really about the same….*

Endnotes and References for this Feature[ix:1]

God's Ecstasy and Ours

by Michael Holleran

I am ecstatic! Not only because I am writing on such a wondrous topic, and not just because ecstasy is the primary insight of Beatrice Bruteau, but also because it is the inescapable and fundamental feature of human beings, and of all of reality! Fundamentally, of course, and etymologically, it connotes "ek-stasis," standing outside oneself, not just in a momentary swoon, nor a brief intoxication, but in the permanent "sober drunkenness" (St. Ambrose) that signifies we are perpetually and constitutionally thrust outside our limited being and consciousness by the very energy of that being and consciousness itself!

But back to the launching pad: Returning to the original volume of *The Mystic Heart* in preparation for this essay, I discovered to my delight and surprise that Beatrice Bruteau had written the Preface. Perhaps many others, like me, had forgotten, or never really noticed. Such eloquent luminaries as Cynthia Bourgeault and Ilia Delio have penned effusive tributes; but, to this day, she remains unpardonably underappreciated. Her contribution to the volume was doubtless overshadowed by the Foreword of the Dalai Lama; but, she is recognized by Wayne in the Acknowledgments, along with her husband James Somerville, as "friends of many years." One can only imagine the mutual fertilization that must have occurred, and the inspiration they provided for each other! In addition, the publication date was serendipitous: *The Mystic Heart* appeared in 1999, and Bruteau's undeniable masterpiece *God's Ecstasy: The Creation of a Self-Creating World* had appeared only two years earlier.[1]

The content of Bruteau's work is mirrored in the trajectory of her life, which then foreshadows the same insights and themes that pervade Wayne Teasdale's masterwork. She was a pioneer in so many fields, giving us an example and inspiration for such enthusiastic exploration. Her early academic work was in mathematics; but after encountering the writings of Sri Aurobindo, she began study in the Vedanta Society, and was the first woman to enroll in graduate philosophy studies at Fordham University, where she wrote on Aurobindo. She likewise resonated with the mystical evolutionary thought of Teilhard de Chardin, seeing its connection with Hindu thought, and was one of the founders of the Teilhard Society of America. She helped launch what became the *International Philosophical Quarterly* as well as the *Contemplative Review*. One might have created the term interdisciplinary just for her!

She describes her work *God's Ecstasy: The Creation of a Self-Creating World* in its preface as a "book on science for Christians…and especially for contemplatives" [p. 9]. She then proceeds throughout the volume to outline the whole evolution of the universe, in stunning and even breathtaking detail, and thus offers a running proof of her book title's claim: we are part of a self-creating world that is God's Ecstasy. She brilliantly illustrates that even the controverted advents of Life or Self-Awareness fall into this dynamic, requiring no special intervention from "outside" to come to fruition. She offers two main rubrics for this entire process:

Being, as ecstatic, will leap to "Be More" and to "Be in Every Possible Way," ardently embracing both finite and infinite. Once exploding into finitude, it will then function as "Being-communicating," with an exuberance of multiplicity, the one into the many. And in this vibrant and riotous array, there will be incessant Interaction to constitute ever new things, different from the interactors [pp. 54,58]. This irrepressible dynamic is timeless in time.

Never afraid of neologisms (such as "enstasis," the interiority that contrasts with, and makes possible, all the "ecstasis"), Bruteau couches the whole process in Christian theological images and terms: first as the Theocosmic Exegete, offering an exegesis of the Prologue of St. John, in which the Word becomes Flesh. The phrase also recalls Raimon Panikkar's "cosmotheandric," in which God, Humanity, and the Cosmos are inextricably bound and express one another. Consonant with her underlying theme of ecstasy, Bruteau presents it all in terms of a Cosmic Dance, in which a Sufi dervish would doubtless find delight: "The dance movements…are contingent upon the Dancer, and the dancer transcends them all, but the dancer is really present in and as them. The dancer's inside turns into the outsideness of the dance when the dancer dances. This turning inside out is ecstasy. I am suggesting this is God's relation to the cosmos. The cosmos is a kind of dancing revelation of God. It is a kind of offspring of God. It is a kind of speech of God. It is a kind of phenomenalization of God. It is a kind of incarnation of God. God creates the world as a kind of agape-ecstasy"[p. 39].

Yet, this Incarnational imagery is only the first half of Bruteau's cosmic vision. The second half emerges as she follows this wondrous unfolding of the universe into consciousness and self-consciousness. We wake up to our primordial and inalienable value, at least if we are aware, she says, of the Absolute in ourselves, i.e., ourselves as expressions of this theocosmic exegete. But the inevitable consequence of this is to esteem the inalienable value of all the other subjectivities around us. In its most sublime and morally binding expression, this leads to the "interaction" of love, which indeed extends to everything, in which we recognize the presence and energy of the Absolute. This maturity and transformation she evocatively and provocatively calls "Theotokos: The Ecstasy of the Cosmos as God" [p. 163], utilizing an early Christian expression for the Mother of Christ as the "God-Bearer," the one giving birth to Christ as God. Except this time, it is we, and indeed the whole universe, that is called to give birth to God.

Of course, all of this depends on our race's waking up spiritually, through whatever methods and traditions, to be even remotely equal to this task. Yet, this should be something totally natural and even enthralling. This is indeed Bruteau's primary point in her preface to *The Mystic Heart.* In several striking sequences, she asserts that while we can attempt to organize society's energies from without, via legislation, we would do better to rearrange energies from within. This, she claims, is what mysticism does. And "fortunately, everyone is a mystic. At some deep level, we know that we are not mutually alienated from each other... In talking with one another, sharing experiences, teaching and encouraging one another, all the traditions are being enriched, individuals are growing, and mystical realization is rising. We are helping each other know that we are deeply related, that we are all precious and deserving, that the universe is our home. In this mutual support, the sense of oneness that is the hallmark of the mystic is increasing." She concludes: "Wayne Teasdale's instructive, inspiring and beautiful book is a sort of interim report on this work in progress." Beatrice herself movingly concludes her own volume: "And the contemplative?... If you can see the God you love as present in, even as, this world, then feel that union and rejoice in that. And be active in it, contribute to it, participate in the building...You yourself are both a member of the Finite and a member of the Infinite... You are doing the incarnating and the creating and the realizing and the rejoicing. God's ecstasy creates the world, and the world's ecstasy realizes God. And you are right in the midst of it all!"[p. 179].

Brother Wayne concludes his masterwork with a reflection on the providential role of the Roman Catholic Church in the realization of this vision he proposes. The Second Vatican Council had opened the doors, after so many centuries, to a positive assessment of the role of non-Christian religions in the world, so central to our understanding now, and to Brother Wayne's notion of Interspirituality. He cautions, however: "If the Church is willing to trust the promptings of the Spirit rather than listening to the sirens of fear, she can play a major role in bringing all the faiths together by providing a welcoming space for them within herself." Unfortunately, this has not always played out propitiously in the last quarter century. Indeed, one could easily count on one hand the number of Roman Catholic contributors to this anthology. Many ardent contemporary seekers, for example, while starting as Catholics, have taken refuge elsewhere to remain faithful to their inspiration and vision, their integrity and mission. Bruteau herself, after converting to Catholicism, joined just a community in North Carolina in later years with her ex-Jesuit husband. Still, it is worth noting that so many central figures (Wayne Teasdale, Thomas Merton, Pierre Teilhard de Chardin, Ramon Panikkar, Thomas Keating) remained within the ecclesiastical structure they had known. They all transcended it, as indeed we all must do; but, there seem to be profound mystical currents yet flowing in that primordial tradition. Even as fanatical right-wing movements now threaten to engulf not only the churches, but the United States and other countries, let us hope that the original meaning, not only of America, but of Catholic or universal (cf. Ilia Delio), may prevail in our spirits and in our world, to bring about the flourishing of Interspirituality, and therefore of ourselves and of our universe, now in the twenty-first century. That would be an Ecstasy worthy of our times!

Joy in The Mystic Heart, the World's Religions and Contemporary Psychology

[selected from Volume 3 where, as noted in our Introduction, full publication of this piece will allow inclusion of the quotations from the diverse spiritual traditions noted below.]

by Shannon Marie Winters

In *The Mystic Heart: Discovering a Universal Spirituality in the World's Religions*, Brother Wayne Teasdale describes unitive joy as the crown of all of the fruits (or capacities) of interspiritual wisdom: "Joy…comes as an abiding gift when an individual has reached union with the divine. Joy is the presence of God in us."

Paralleling the Golden Rule, recognition of the importance of Joy also unites all of the world's religions and wisdom traditions. [Then follows quotations on joy from the scriptures or other writings of 18 religious traditions (paralleling that of the Golden Rule for which Wikipedia cites from some 20 world religions and 5 secular values- or ethical-based traditions)].

We can see that the world's religions and spiritual traditions agree on the importance of joy, and it may be surprising to learn that joy is one of the few areas where spirituality and secular psychological science have merged into agreement together. If The Golden Rule is the thread that weaves together the moral code of spirituality in the nonsecular world, then joy is the desired essential state of inner life experience of all souls regardless of secular or nonsecular beliefs. …

Joy's Ascending Trend in Contemporary Psychology

Over the last 100 years, since the first iteration of psychiatric classifications were incorporated into the American Medical Association's (AMA) Standard Classified Nomenclature of Disease Manual, the American Psychiatric Association then began publishing a separate manual for mental disorders that is currently in its 5th edition: *The Diagnostic and Statistical Manual of Mental Disorders*, more well-known as DSM-5™.

The DSM-5 is the principle authority used by clinicians in the United States to diagnose mental health conditions. A host of disorders are included as having symptoms of a lack of or inability to experience joy, or experiencing symptoms that are in opposition to happiness and joy, including: depressive disorders; anxiety and panic disorders; posttraumatic stress disorder (PTSD); acute stress disorders; and bipolar and related disorders. It is important to note only licensed mental health professionals can diagnose any of these disorders in accordance with current medical practices. …

Interestingly, western medicine's approach came to this conclusion from the opposite side of the spectrum from what we see in sacred writings. Instead of joy being the desired state, the scientific view came around from the negative. That was as a missing component or a "lack thereof." American psychologist Abraham Maslow, best known for his hierarchy of needs, recognized this and pioneered discussion of the importance of focusing on the positive — in a book published in 1954, *Motivation and Personality*:

> "The science of psychology has been far more successful on the negative than on the positive side; it has revealed to us much about man's shortcomings, his illnesses, his

> sins, but little about his potentialities, his virtues, his achievable aspirations, or his full psychological height. It is as if psychology had voluntarily restricted itself to only half its rightful jurisdiction, and that the darker, meaner half." ...

This direction was noted by Maslow as "Positive Psychology" and sought to move beyond a focus solely on mental illness and dysfunction, and instead explore the positive aspects of human experience and the pursuit of a fulfilling life.

Today, seventy years later, search of PubMed, one of the preeminent databases for scientific papers and research published in peer-review journals, indicates more than 129,000 publications on Positive Psychology while another 23,000 are cited as referring to the words "joy" or "happiness."

These databases also track conclusions from the professional psychological literature. In current psychological literature, "Joy" is noted as important — irrespective of any particular demographic — in relation to confronting or managing stress, avoidance of "burnout," and as a powerful factor in both physical and emotional healing, in restoring self-confidence and giving hope and a sense of meaning in life. These attributes are further judged as essential elements for well-being, the feeling of success in life, and as one of the optimal conditions for full moral and ethical capacity. "Actualizing full moral and ethical capacity" is Br. Teasdale's first element of his Nine Elements of a Universal Spirituality.

It's all about joy!

The Call of Love

by Camille Hamilton Adams Helminski

A rose by any other name would smell as sweet.
~ Shakespeare, *Romeo and Juliet*

Sometimes names get us into trouble, causing separation, even animosity, when none is due and the whole point is the Love, Compassion that unites and uplifts us all into the fragrance, the Radiance of the Rose. As the Sufi mystic Jalaluddin Rumi once said, "If your thought is a rose, you *are* the Rose Garden." In another moment he reflects:

Open the window towards God
and begin delighting upon the Face.
The whole business of Love is to make this window in the heart.
For the breast is illumined by the Beauty of the Beloved.
[Rumi, *Mathnawi* VI 3095-3096]

Years ago now, in a moment of Grace, Ed Bastian, of the Spiritual Paths Foundation, reached out to my husband, Kabir, and this one, to invite us to participate in a new endeavor of Interspiritual collaboration and education. Having been raised in Christian families, journeyed a while through Eastern traditions, and in our adulthood found our home within the Islamic mystical path of Sufism, we were not unfamiliar with other expressions of spirituality than the path of Sufism in which we had deepened, yet we had spent over thirty years immersing in the Way opened by Mevlana Jalaluddin Rumi.

We are eternally grateful for those moments that followed, of union of heart and mind with our brothers and sisters of Spirit, with whom we began to form a process of Interspiritual education — Rabbi Rami

Shapiro, Swami Atmarupananda, Cynthia Bourgeault, and others who came from time to time to join us, among whom were Chief Jake Swamp, Sister Tessa Bieleki, the Venerable Tenzin Priyadarshi, and of course, Father Thomas Keating. It had been the inspiration from Father Thomas and the Snowmass Dialogue process that had originally thrust Ed along this particular journey, gathering all of us into his emerging vision. We were tied together for some years of work, in a bouquet of hearts, co-creating an instructional and transformational journey of Spirit for several cohorts of students. Then we were released by the Beloved to immerse again fully within our individual Traditions, following the Paths we had come to so deeply value, but ever inspired and renewed afresh by having come to know such dear souls of Spirit, each in their own precious alignment with Truth.

Over the years, it has become more and more apparent to us that the Qur'an, itself, is a document of Interspirituality, recognizing all the prophets and messengers that have come to humanity, and continually reminding us of the Book of nature, all its signs and lessons for us — if we would look and listen, we might live every day in awe. How is it that the tree knows where it is that it should stop growing, in what shape? Or a single leaf, reaching toward the light? We have mirrors everywhere of the elegance of patterning of the Creative Force, and examples of diversity of being in the bird songs with which we awaken. It is obvious that we should honor each expression of Being. Throughout human history, ways of comprehension of Spirit have been opened by beings who have immersed in the Light of the Source of Creation. And people continue to be drawn to follow them. Birthing continues with love. As it is expressed in the *Hadith Qudsi*, a saying conveyed from Divine Reality through the heart of Prophet Muhammad, peace and blessings be upon him:

God says, "I was a Hidden Treasure, and I so loved to be known
that I created the two worlds, seen and unseen,
in order that My treasure of generosity and loving-kindness might be known."

We individual expressions of humanity are not really so different at our core. It is this yearning to open a window to Love that is essential . . . have not all the prophets and spiritual leaders found this intimacy with Truth? Buddha sat under a tree for days awaiting; beloved Mary prayed in her sanctuary and was nourished by the fruits of spring in the midst of winter[1], and received the "Word" within her; the wife (or some say, the daughter) of Pharoah was drawn to the Truth radiated by Moses:

And God sets forth as an example to those who have faith
the wife of Pharaoh:
witness, she said, "O my Sustainer!
Build for me in nearness to You a mansion in the Garden
and save me from Pharaoh and his actions
and save me from those who do wrong";
also Mary, the daughter of 'Imran, who guarded her chastity,
and We breathed into her of Our spirit,
and she witnessed to the Truth of the words of her Sustainer
and of His revelations and was one of those devoted.
[Qur'an, *Surah at-Tahrim* 66:11-12]

See how God has purchased of the faithful
their lives and their possessions;
in return, theirs is the Garden,
and so they intensively strive in the Way of Ultimate Reality.
[Qur'an, *Surah at-Tawbah* 9:111]

Truly, Beloved Mary herself is a ready companion of loving tenderness and strength, during these intense times, encouraging us all to resonate from our deepest, truest self, in alignment with the Heart of Creation. One never knows when we will be called Home; Beloved Mary can assist us in readying ourselves and in simultaneously living our life most fully now, with vibrant Truth and Love.

As it says in the Qur'an, *He loves them, and they love Him* (*Surah al-Maida* 5:54). Through that One we are. Through Him/Her we breathe. The unveiling of secrets is who He/She is; that One is both the Manifest (az-*Zahir)* and the Hidden **(***al-Batin***).** As Prophet David sang in the Psalms: "I have hidden your Word in my heart" (Bible, Psalms 119:11).

And as Shams of Tabriz, the beloved mentor of Jalaluddin Rumi, reminds us, "Every human being is a Word spoken by God." A dear Sufi mentor in Istanbul, Cahit Hoca, once said, "He is always together with us. Wisdom is being able to sense His Presence."

Within Islamic tradition and the universe of the holy book of Islam, the Qur'an, which is as the root of Sufism, God, Divine Reality, is without gender, far beyond anything by which we may attempt to describe that Reality, that Truth. The pronoun of Divine Presence, "Hu," is like the breath, a breeze blowing through every chapter (*surah*), but one of the Qur'an begins with the phrase, *Bismillah ar-Rahman ar-Rahim* ("With the Name of Divine Reality, the Infinitely Compassionate, the Continually Merciful"), reminding us that we are held within the womb of Compassion and Mercy, breathed by it into existence and returned to it.

Recitation of the Divine Name, remembrance with the breath, *Zhikrullah*, is a basis of practice: *Remember Me; I remember you* (*Surah al-Baqarah* 2:152); *Surely remembrance is the greatest* (*Surah al-Ankabut* 29:45). And as Shams of Tabriz deeply lived, "One remembers often the one whom he or she loves. I remember You all the time, and am filled with Your love."[2]

We have long appreciated the saying of St. Teresa of Avila encouraging us to spend time within the Center, toward which we turn in remembrance:

> Turn your eyes towards the center, which is the room or royal chamber where the King stays, and think of how a palmetto has many leaves surrounding and covering the tasty part that can be eaten. So here, surrounding this center room are many other rooms; and the same holds true for those above. The things of the soul must always be considered as plentiful, spacious, large; to do so is not an exaggeration. The soul is capable of much more than we imagine, and the sun that is in this royal chamber shines in all parts. It is very important for any soul that practices prayer, whether little or much, not to hold itself back and stay in one corner. Let it walk through these dwelling places which are above, down below, and to the sides, since God has given it such dignity.[3]

Mary, the mother of Jesus, is such an example for us of one who was profoundly receptive to Spirit, in love with That which was loving her. There is a wondrous verse of the Qur'an that is often seen inscribed in the *mihrab,* the prayer niche toward which one turns for the ritual prayer in Islam, oriented toward the Kaaba, the central focal point of prayer, in the holy city of Mecca. The verse refers to Mary and her receptivity in the sanctuary sometime before the visit of the Angel Gabriel:

> *In the Name of God the Infinitely Compassionate and*
> *Infinitely Merciful*
> *Whenever Zachariah visited her in the sanctuary,*
> *he found her already provided with food. He would ask,*
> *"O Mary, from where did this come to you?"*
> *She would answer: "It is from God;*
> *see how God grants sustenance to whom He/She wills,*
> *beyond all reckoning."*
> [Qur'an, *Surah 'Imran* 3:37]

Ruzbihan Baqli, an Iranian Islamic mystic of the twelfth century, offers us a beautiful reflection on Mary's intimacy with God, in recognition of her intrinsic spirituality as the purest of souls intimately trained by *Haqq* (the Real).

> The true indication here [of *Surah Maryam* 19:16] is that the essence of Mary is the essence of the holy *fitrah* (primordial soul nature). And her essence was trained by "the Real," by the light of intimacy. And in all of her respirations (every breath) she was *majdhuba* by the attribute of the closeness and intimacy to the Source of Divine Illumination. She became constantly in a state of spiritual vigilance (*muraqaba*) for the manifestation of the illumination of the World of Sovereignty (*jabarut*), from the point of the rising place of spiritual orientation (*mashriq*) in the realm of the Kingdom (*malakut*). And she withdrew from the world through spiritual resolve (*himma*) of the highest category, characterized by the Light of the Unseen. And she approached the rising-places (*mashriq*) of the Illumination of the Essence (*Dhat*), and she inhaled the Attributes — fragrances

> from the Eternal World without beginning (*'alam al-azal*). And the gift reached her — the communion with the Pre-Eternal (*azaliyya*). And the Illumination of the witnessing of the Eternal (*mushahadat al-qidamiyya*) shone upon her. And when she experienced the vision of the illumination of the Manifestation of Eternity, Its Lights flashed, and Its Secrets reached her spirit (*ruh*), and her spirit became impregnated with the Divine Secret, and she became the bearer of the glorious Word and the light of the spirit of the Most High.[4]

In the purity of her heart, beloved Maryam was prepared; one might say the Names or Attributes of God of *Al Quddus* ("The Most Holy and Pure"), *Al Wadud*, ("The Infinitely Loving"), and *An Nur* ("The Light") were already brightly illuminating her heart. Her abode was within the abode of God; it was there she rested, there she found refuge. Truly, for the Prophet Muhammad, the example of Mary, Maryam, must have been a great support of heart. He must have felt her as a companion of Spirit, an inspiration, in her devotion to God, her surrender, her compassionate Love.

Completely, beloved Maryam surrendered, in full trust, to the unfolding of what was to come, which she alone would bear. This surrender of the self is, essentially, what "Islam" means — surrender to what Is, knowing we could not design a better portion than the One who created us and seeks the best for us, even more than we are seeking Him — the Source of All Subsistence. We have been given will to accompany the unfolding with the best effort, eyes to discern the best way to proceed, hearts to know by longing, and ears to hear the Words of guidance that have been given through all manner of beings — the angels, the bees, the intimations of roses and wild flowers, the roar of the lion and the song of the nightingales of God, the saints and illuminated ones, calling us to let go of the baggage weighing us down — the encumbrances of the wayward, resistant ego. So many have shown us that it is this surrender into the arms of the Beloved that opens the door for *Salaam* (the Peace of God) to pour through, that we might be recreated by Love.

Nothing would exist
without Your Love.
Bees find
their way
to sip
a flower's fragrance;
we find
our way
to nestle
in
Your Sanctuary,
everywhere,
abundant,
pouring sustenance,
through the smallest keyhole
to Your Refuge.[5]
Light finds
its way
through every crack
in our defenses;
the door,
You set,
we forget

to open,
flies wide
to welcome
all souls
who turn
in recognition
of the Source
of all that nourishes,
all that heals
our riven bones,
our fractured hearts,
our complicated minds,
untangled; restored,
stretched, we rest,
in the shade of Your Love,
in the sunshine of Your Grace,
upon the grass,
soft as a willow's down,
along the river's side
where the table is set
and all
are invited,
always, and now.[6]

As the Prophet David expressed it:

The Lord is my shepherd; I shall not want.
He makes me lie down in green pastures: He leads me beside tranquil waters.
He restores my soul: He guides me along the paths of righteousness for His name's sake.

Even though I walk through the darkest valley, I will fear no harm:
for You are with me; Your rod and Your staff, they comfort me.
You prepare a table before me in the presence of those who challenge me:
You anoint my head with oil; my cup overflows.
Surely goodness and love will follow me all the days of my life:
and I will dwell in the house of the Lord forever.
[The Bible, 23rd Psalm of Prophet David: 1-6]

In *Surah Maryam* we are encouraged:

Truly, those who have faith
and do the deeds of wholeness and reconciliation
the Infinitely Compassionate will endow with love.
[Qur'an, *Surah Maryam*, 19:96]

And again, we are reminded:

And as for those who have attained to faith in God and hold fast to Him/Her —
He/She will cause them to enter into His/Her Compassion
and His/Her abundant blessing.
[Qur'an, *Surah an-Nisa* 4:174–5]

Solomon, the Wise, intimated that Holy Wisdom is always waiting for us:

Wisdom shines without dimming.
All who love Her, see Her,
All who desire Her, embrace Her.

She rushes to reveal Herself,
to those who yearn for Her;
No matter how early you arise to meet Her,
She is already waiting for you at the gate.
[Bible, Wisdom of Solomon 6:12-14][7]

We hear echoes of the Truth of this All-Pervading Presence everywhere, including in the words of the Turkish mystic, Zeynep Hatun:

I am a fountain, You are my water.
I flow from You to You.

I am an eye, You are my light,
I look from You to You.

You are neither my right nor my left.
You are my foot and my arm as well.

I am a traveler, You are my road.
I go from You to You.[8]

May the House of the heart be filled with Light! May our journeying be blessed. May peace be with you!

Endnotes and References for this Feature[ix:2]

Endnotes and References for "Spiritual Life" Section[ix]

ON INTERSPIRITUAL PIONEERS

Bede Griffiths (Andrew Harvey) - **Raimon Panikkar** (Kurt Johnson) - **Thomas Keating** (Edward Bastian, Cynthia Bourgeault, et al.) - **Wayne Teasdale** (William Howell, Gard Jameson, Jamal Rahman) - **Wayne Teasdale, Rabbi Zalman Schachter-Shalomi, Cynthia Bourgeault** (Gordon Dveirin, Joan Borysenko) - **Thomas Berry** (Emily A. DeMoor) **Sharafuddin Maneri** (Joseph Victor Edwin S.J.) - **Swami Shraddhananda** (Sacred Feet Dharma Heirs) - **H. H. Baba Virsa Singh** (Ralph Singh) - **Max King** (Doug King) - **Edgar Mitchell, Willis Harman** (Claudia Welss) - **David Loye** (Galia Benartzi, Riane Eisler and Kurt Johnson) - **Diane Berke and One Spirit Interfaith Seminary** (Leslie Reambeault, Melissa Stewart) - note the special Features in Volume 1 on **Thomas Merton** (James Finley p. 326) **Edward Bastian** (John A. Wilde p. 322) and **Br. Teasdale** (Jeffrey Genung p. 265)

Fr. Bede's Great Gift to Me
The Vision of Sacred Activism

by Andrew Harvey

The seeds of the vision of sacred activism were planted and deeply took root in my soul when I met my great teacher, Fr. Bede Griffiths. One of the greatest mysteries of the path is that the Divine will guide you to meet, at the time when you are ready and receptive, the beings who can lead you forward. I came to meet Fr. Bede through an invitation from a friend who wanted to make a documentary about the life of this interspiritual visionary and mystic, and asked me to be the interviewer for the film.

For ten days, I had the amazing, illuminating, and transformative experience of being with this extraordinary, radiant, funny, wise, humble man at his ashram in Southern India, only fifty miles from where I was born. At the time, Fr. Bede was eighty-five years old, and I was forty-one. In his presence, I felt I had met a true spiritual father, who set me on the path of what I consider my true life's work: the vision of sacred activism, doing everything I possibly can, through passion and grace, to help to birth a new, Divine Humanity.

On the last day of filming, I went in to see him before the film crew arrived, and he looked up at me and said, "You know, Andrew, we are in the hour of God." I asked him what he meant by "the hour of God," and he responded, "We're in the hour of God because we are coming quite soon to the moment in which we will have to decide between adoration and suicide."

He went on, "There are three possibilities before the human race. The first one is that we'll wake up, fall on our knees, beg for grace, and God will transfigure us and make us instruments of a great revolution of peace in action. That is highly unlikely at the moment. Human beings change slowly, and even in desperate circumstances cling to their pride and ignorance. I certainly know that I have."

"The second possibility," he continued, "is that we'll continue in our mad addiction to greed, power and domination, and engineer a crisis that will destroy us and take a great deal of nature with us. That's what seems likely many days as I sit in this hut meditating on what I've known and experienced during my life." He paused to let that sink in.

Then he smiled — he gave this tremendous, radiant smile — and said, "But that's not what is going to happen, I think. You see, Andrew, the God that I have come to know is a God of infinite love, infinite mercy, and infinite resourcefulness. I have been saved again and again from the worst in myself. Even my worst mistakes and most destructive and stupid thoughts and actions have turned out to create, through some mysterious paradox, doors into deeper compassion for all beings and into action born from this compassion."

He continued, "What I believe is going to happen is what happened to me. Three years ago, I was sitting on my balcony meditating, and suddenly I was struck by a tremendous force that seemed to be coming from my left and pulled me out of my chair. It was terrifying. I had had a stroke. I thought I was going to die, and I prepared myself for death saying all the traditional prayers. I felt bewildered and disturbed, as if my whole being had been plunged into chaos. Suddenly, the inspiration came to me to surrender to the Mother; I heard an inner voice say quite clearly, 'Surrender to the Mother.' And somehow, without really knowing how, I did."

"Instead of dying, I had an experience of being invaded and overwhelmed by waves and waves of love, a power and passion of love that I had never experienced before. I found myself crying out, *I am being overwhelmed by love! I am being overwhelmed by love!* And I *knew* that the love that I was being overwhelmed and possessed by was the love of the Mother — the Mother of All, the Mother of the Universe, the great embodied Godhead glowing in and through everything. Through it, my being was being opened to the radiance of the Mother alive in every tree, plant, rock, and sentient being, and in this very body."

"The consciousness I am being brought into since this experience is unlike anything I experienced up until the time of my stroke. It is a non-dual *embodied* consciousness in which I experience a profound and mysterious unity with everything and everyone. Distinctions are not lost in this awareness; in fact, everyone and everything becomes more individual, sacred, precious, and holy because I am seeing that every sentient being and every pebble and fern is a unique creation of the Divine Light, infinitely loved and cherished, and entirely inhabited by the Light. I have come to believe that what is beginning to happen in me is destined to happen on a growing scale in humanity."

"And this, Andrew, is the third possibility before us, the one I believe will happen. I believe that the world will be taken into the depths of a global dark night crisis, which at many times as it gets more and more intense will feel like the end — the end of every possibility. But it will not be the end … because, just as in the inner path of the mystic, the dark night is actually — if you can stand it and live through it with grace and joy and faith and the capacity to surrender both to the suffering it brings and the resurrecting power of the Divine — the dark night is the birth canal of an unimaginable transformation into embodied divine consciousness."

"So I believe that the world is in a vast evolutionary crisis which will go through a terrifying dark night. But that will not be the end, it will be the beginning of something absolutely extraordinary, and amazing, and unimaginable, through the extravagant grace of the One. God is everywhere working a massive Resurrection, and it is the destiny of our time to be the birthing-ground of this Resurrection."

I took that in, and then he said words which he wrote with a diamond pencil on my soul forever. He said, "You know, Andrew," — and he was gleaming, because he was very mischievous; he was a very holy, grand being but at eighty-five he was also a divine child — "I think that I'm at last understanding the Second Coming. You know what's going to happen, I think. It's certainly not going to be the return of Christ as a *person.* Jesus in time and history opened this path for us, irradiating the entire universe by the resurrection light, and I think we can say that that job was well done. But what's going to happen, I believe, because of the agony and difficulty and wildness and horror of the dark night, many of us are going to be sent on a journey in which we discover in ourselves an unimaginable passion and energy of hope and joy and hunger to recreate the world in justice, and kinship, and celebration, and peace."

"The birthing of a Divine Humanity on a large scale, this rising of the golden yeast of love consciousness at its most impassioned and beautiful and focused and holy and clear in millions of people — *that* will be the Second Coming, the Great Healing that leads to the Birth. This is a miracle greater than any 'outer' rescuing by God could ever be. We are going to be rescued from 'within' though a massive alchemical process in which the whole of history will take part as a midwife of the new."

"What is going to be very difficult for human beings to accept and manage is that this Great Healing will have to manifest first as an immense crisis or series of crises that will plunge all previous human agendas into chaos. For the Birth to take place, there is a necessary death of all previous visions and ways of acting, a deconstruction of the false self and a dying to the tyranny of the ego. This is not punishment but the fiercest and ultimately most merciful grace, which is known in all mystical traditions."

"Knowing this mystery and that it ends, not in annihilation but in the birth of the Divine in matter, in the body, is, I believe, the greatest imaginable source of hope."

We ended our conversation as we heard the film crew shuffling and coughing outside the door. They had been waiting patiently for us to finish, to begin the final day of filming for the documentary.

A week later, back in Paris where I was living at the time, I learned that Fr. Bede had suffered two more strokes and was dying. I felt a great need to see him one last time, and within a few days was by his bedside. He was in a terrible state. One side of his body was paralyzed, and the intellectually brilliant part of his mind had been largely shattered. Yet despite great pain, he was also, for long moments, in a state of grace, overflowing with love for all those around him. He would hold the hands of his disciples and friends and weep with joy, gazing into their eyes with pure and luminous wonder and childlike trust.

On the last night I was with him, I sat alone by his bedside in the early hours of the morning, watching him toss and turn in half-sleep. At around 2 o'clock, he awoke, reached for my hand, and caressed it. Then, quite suddenly, as if commanded by someone I could not see or hear, he sat straight up in his bed and said loudly, over and over again: "Serve the growing Christ! Serve the growing Christ! Serve the growing Christ!"

I experienced these four simple words, which crystallized for me everything he had said in our conversation in his hut, as a direct transmission by Divine Love itself. I knew, through the grace I felt pouring down on us both in that moment, that "serve the growing Christ" meant that our terrible and wonderful time was the destined birthing ground of the Divine Human (the growing Christ). And I realized that anyone who was brought by grace to the realization of this truth was called upon to do three related things: to serve the growing Christ in themselves through meditation, prayer, and surrender to the Divine; to serve all other beings as growing Christs; and to serve the growing Christ in history through sacred action.

This profound understanding of our time — the vision of the birth of a Divine Humanity emerging from the Dark Night we are experiencing individually and collectively — and his own humble yet powerful embodiment of this amazing possibility for all of us were Fr. Bede's great gifts to me. My profound gratitude and love for him inspired me to dedicate the remainder of my life to serve this vision through teaching and inviting others to the path of sacred activism.

We are now among those millions of beings who are being crucified *and* resurrected by the tremendous ordeal the whole of creation is going through. So the worst of times is potentially the best of times, the dark night is a savage grace and a birth canal, and our job, it seems, is to go through whatever we need to go through to be able to find in ourselves the courage, the hope, the joy, the power we never imagined ourselves capable of, together, inspiring and encouraging each other.

Who Could Have Known? A Tribute, and My Unusual Relationship with Raimon Panikkar

by Kurt Johnson

I feel some responsibility to provide tribute and much more information on one of Interspirituality's most beloved pioneers, Fr. Raimon Panikkar [aka Raimundo, Raymond]. As is perhaps not well known, his book *The Intra-Religious Dialogue* which offered that name for the interspiritual paradigm, was published in its most well-known form (the American imprint from the Paulist Press) just four months after Br. Teasdale's popular *The Mystic Heart* appeared from New World Library in 1999. *The Intra-Religious Dialogue had* been published earlier, in 1978 by a British publisher, but it had not reached a large public audience. More will be said about this below, since Panikkar's iconic contributions to comparative religion, and trans-disciplinary polymathy in general — which included over 40 books and 900 articles (in several languages) — had an inherent marketing complication of being vended by multiple large and small publishers. Thus, Panikkar — *so* well known, especially in Europe and India, as a scholar, prominent figure in the Monastic Interreligious Dialogue [see that element in the History sections of these Volumes] and friend of the equally iconic pioneer of Interspirituality, Abhishiktananda (see Br. Teasdale's article on him published also herein) — was much less known to the book-buying public, especially of America.

In scholarly circles, the book most noted as Panikkar's most famous today, was published only later — in 2010 around the time of his passing as *The Rhythm of Being: The Gifford Lectures* [delivered in 1989]. It distinguished him as an unusual polymath of religion, philosophy, science, and the arts. In fact, Panikkar's first published book was *The Concept of Nature* (El concepto de Naturaleza), published in 1951. Originally, it was his doctoral dissertation from the University of Madrid (1946) and received the distinguished Premio Menéndez Pelayo award. It was in this context that I first met him, in meetings from 1975-76 in the context of science. We served together on a Board of Directors of a foundation pursuing scientific and medical elements of the "Foundationalist Discussion" (see that element in the Introduction to Volume 1 of these Volumes). I detail this co-work more below — but who could have known that *much later* his own part of the interspiritual legacy would further clarify, with his now well-known standing, side by side, with Br. Wayne Teasdale and others as a foundational "namer" of the interspiritual paradigm, along with Fr. Matthew Fox, author of the Foreword to these Volumes.

In 1969-1979, I was both part of the Anglican Order of the Holy Cross and a resident Research Associate of the American Museum of Natural History in New York City, specializing in evolution — the area in which I received my PhD degree. I was recruited into the founding members, along with Panikkar, of the Society for Systemology, a then Washington, D.C. based nonprofit exploring foundational elements of the relationship of science and religion, and also medicine (which, with regard to Indian Ayurveda was part of Panikkar's interests across his polymathy of the Wisdom Traditions). The founder was another Indian — the late Benedict Victor Arul — author of *Systemology* (a pioneering work on wholistic science and holistic medicine). The book seems to no longer be in print, and current internet search indicates the Society seems no longer extant. However, the internet records remnants of its work as late as 1980 through another Indian member of that Board, Suvarna Nalapat MD (specialty Pathology), recording presentations of the group, and Arul on "Cancer-A Prohomeostatic Systemal Strategy" at the American Psychotronics Association's meetings at that time, again in Washington, D.C.

My tasking, as a staff member of a major scientific institution, was to arrange the levels of scrutiny, study, and discussion needed for an exploration of the kinds of foundational ideas that were being discussed across science and religion at that time. When Panikkar would come to New York City, where Arul also resided at that time, we would have both informal meetings and also Board meetings as required by law. Interestingly, we often met at the New Yorker Hotel, where Nikola Tesla had lived out his life, as Arul felt a particular bond to the Tesla legacy and would arrange our meetings there, where he also resided. Another member of the group, also traceable on the internet to recent times was the New Zealand cosmologist Brian St. Clair Corcoran, since that time author of *The Shape of a Stable Society, The Objective Mind Universe,* and *Harmonising Quantum Mechanics with the General Theory of Relativity*. A major colleague of mine at the American Museum of Natural History, as you will see through my own writing on scientific inquiry and methodologies[1] was the distinguished scholar of the Philosophy of Science, Dr. David Hull, then at the University of Wisconsin. You see him cited in my scientific writings as the scholar most consulted at the time on emerging paradigms. Arul, Panikkar, Corcoran, and myself in 1976 worked with another well-known wholistic scholar, Dr. Stanley Salthe, then of the City University of New York and American Museum of Natural History (where I did my doctoral work), on a Symposium on scientific elements of the Foundationalist discussion, part of whose work was rigorous assessment of emergent views like those in "Systemology."

We forget sometimes that in the 1970s, what we take for granted today as Interspirituality, wholistic science, or holistic medicine were *very* new. It was at least two decades before Pannikar's own works became more publicly well known, especially on "Intra-religious Experience," one of the foundations we know today as Interspirituality. In this context, one can understand that the extent to which Pannikar and I spoke about what later became Interspirituality, was limited to us both acknowledging that we were both in Religious Orders and that the then emergent Monastic Interreligious Dialogue (see that element in the History sections of Volume 1 and the extensive Feature by Fr. Matthew Cobb therein) was of great interest to both of us. The literature on what has become Interspirituality and wholistic science was only emergent in the 1970s (as seen from such dates as Merton's initial books regarding Zen (*Zen and the Birds of Appetite*, 1968) and those of Fr. Bede Griffiths' speaking tours of the United States on the East-West Dialogue (from 1963). In fact, Pannikar's short popular book *The Unknown Christ of Hinduism* (1964) also appeared in that early time, and I remember noting to him that American monastics *were* familiar with that book.

Panikkar's Iconic Contribution to Interspirituality

Panikkar's own work is now renowned as iconic in the history of Interfaith and Interspirituality, and fortunately, there is a extensive body of work on its importance, especially in the scholarly realm (see in the following Endnote an extensive bibliography of his work).[2] His legacy not only figures prominently across the realms of discussion contained in the paragraphs just above but also in the New Monasticism discussion (see Features on that element in Volume 1). In 1982, the Seabury Press published his *Blessed Simplicity: The Monk as Universal Archetype*. Particularly important to the publication of this book was the Holyoke Conference of global monastics, organized by North America predecessor of what later became the Monastic Interreligious Dialogue (see that entry in the History sections of Volume 1). Scholarship around the New Monasticism discussion, especially that of Fr. Francis Tiso, on the origins of the "new Monk" movement, further elaborates this part of Panikkar's legacy. Tiso's scholarship[3] particularizes the dynamism of discussions on monasticism among the Monastic Interreligious Dialogue, especially that between East and West, between the "grassroots" and "elites" of the denominational monasticism, and the interesting roles of Thomas Merton in those discussions, particularly just before the time of his tragic passing at an East-West dialogue in Thailand in 1968.

Also, Panikkar was a close friend of the iconic East-West cross-over [see the Feature on cross-overs herein by me and Karuna] Benedictine Fr. Henri Le Saux, also known as Swami Abhishiktananda, about whom Br. Teasdale also writes in detail in his "lost" treatise on Abhishiktananda republished, after many years, in Volume 1 of these Volumes. Expressly, Panikkar wrote that he kept his friendship with Abhishiktananda quite confidential as he felt only history could make some sense of all that was unfolding across the spiritual traditions of the world at that formative time. Echoing the equivocations noted by Br. Teasdale in his piece on Abhishiktananda and challenges of an emerging Interspirituality, Anglican theologian James Stuart, wrote:

> One of the very few theologians — perhaps the only one — who in Abhishiktananda's view was addressing the problem, was his friend Raymond Panikkar. They had now been sharing their thoughts for the past ten years. He had welcomed Panikkar's book, *The Unknown Christ of Hinduism*, and felt that his friend had written far more boldly than he had so far dared to do."[4]

By the time one includes into one's understanding of Panikkar's work even the twenty or more of his books still available at online booksellers (the way books are harvested in these days), one has added other important and influential works as: *Christophany: The Fullness of Man*; *The Experience of God: Icons of the Mystery*; *A Dwelling Place for Wisdom*; *The Cosmotheandric Experience*; *Myth, Faith and Hermeneutics*; and many more. It is a masterful landscape to say the least and one whose contribution to the evolving future of global interfaith and Interspirituality will undoubtedly continue to unfold into the future. It is wonderful, and fitting, to see that acknowledged by so many authors, and references, in these Volumes. At the time of the Barcelona Parliament of the World's Religions, the Interspiritual Dialogue made the effort to contact Fr. Pannikar for a reconnection but between Br. Teasdale's last-minute absence from the event (see the History sections in Volume 1) and Panikkar's own busy schedule, it did not occur.

Endnotes and References for this Feature[x:1]

Fr. Thomas Keating: Memorial Tributes and Legacy Event July 12-14, 2019

by Edward Bastian, Cynthia Bourgeault and Journalists[1]

Our Thomas Keating Aspen gathering has left me wordless. The multi-leveled elements of our program settled deeply within me and others. It melded us into a state-of-being that words cannot touch. We experienced the sacred silence of Thomas' ongoing presence that forever connects us all. It is futile to conceptually reify that which is the foundation of reality and which precedes all concepts. Attempting to describe this presence is to push it away. Thomas brought us together from all spiritual and secular perspectives to jointly experience this sacred silence, to become permeable, to dissolve our rigid identities, to relinquish our false sense of self, and to connect with each other at the deepest level of our being. All of us who connected with Thomas tasted this and will forever savor its flavor. Father Thomas led us into this sacred silence. Now it is our turn.
~ Edward Bastian[2]

Thomas Keating has been my teacher, friend, and spiritual mentor for more than thirty years. It is he who laid the spiritual foundations of both my teaching and my practice and who launched me on my own path as a spiritual teacher and writer. He will be remembered as one of the giants of contemporary contemplative spirituality, not only for his groundbreaking work in

> Centering Prayer — which made contemplation truly accessible to Christian lay people for the first time — but also for the breadth and depth of his interspiritual vision, which kept growing in luminosity and compassion right up to his very last breath. I have never witnessed a more triumphant and powerful conscious death, modeling for us all the wingspan of spirit that can dwell in a life courageously and recklessly tossed to the winds of God.
>
> ~ Cynthia Bourgeault[3]

Life-long interfaith and interspiritual colleagues from around the world, and diverse spiritual traditions, gathered at The Aspen Chapel in Aspen, Colorado, July 12 – 14 for a weekend-long tribute to the life and work of Fr. Thomas Keating O.C.S.O. The three-day program also focused on how to continue the change-making global work of this renowned ambassador of interfaith and Interspirituality and of our world religions' understanding of their shared contemplative heritage.

Fr. Thomas was one of the most celebrated of contemplative writers and known worldwide for his role in founding Contemplative Outreach (contemplativeoutreach.org), the Centering Prayer Movement, and the decades-long work of his Snowmass Inter-religious Dialogue — today the Snowmass Interspiritual Dialogue — (see the extensive Features on The Snowmass Dialogues in Volume 1 of these Volumes). A Roman Catholic monk and priest, he had joined the Order of Cistercians of the Strict Observance (also called The Trappists) in 1944 and served as Abbot of two of its monasteries in the United States, returning to the Abbey in Spencer, Massachusetts, before his passing on October 25, 2018, at the age of 94.

He was the author of over thirty books, many which were highly influential. These, along with extensive audio and video presentations, and even a feature film, *The Rising Tide of Silence*, propelled his prominence as a pioneer for our modern-day understanding of the contemplative experience around the world. His decades-long programs at the St. Benedict's Abbey in Snowmass, Colorado, where he became Abbot after retiring from the same position at the St. Joseph's Abbey in Massachusetts led to the publication in 2007 of "The Nine Points of Agreement Among The World's Religions" in a book entitled *The Common Heart*. This global view of the message of the world's religions, along with those called "The Nine Elements of a Universal Spirituality" by a monastic colleague Br. Wayne Teasdale, have become recognized "Foundational Documents" for the interfaith and interspiritual communities, committees and caucuses across the United Nations community.

Members of the global interfaith and interspiritual communities remember Fr. Thomas as a mentor. Continuing the work of Western monastics who were instrumental in creating the East-West and North-South dialogues among our world religions' mystical traditions (through the Monastic Interreligious Dialogue and other seminal networks) but who had passed before him — Thomas Merton, Bede Griffiths, Raimon Panikkar, and Teasdale — Fr. Thomas continued to gather the many pioneers of this growing universal spirituality through his auspices and encouraging and helping organize their work. From these gatherings came a pivotal international conference on Interspirituality in 2013 and the founding of networks and media which have continued this important work (see interspirituality.com). Teasdale, in his most well-known work *The Mystic Heart: Discovering a Universal Spirituality in the World's Religions*, had considered both

Fr. Thomas and Bede Griffiths as his mentors and had coined the now widely used terms Interspiritual and Interspirituality.

Organizers of the event at the Aspen Chapel were well-known interfaith authors, educators, and retreat leaders Edward Bastian and Cynthia Bourgeault in collaboration with Nicholas and Heather Vesey who lead the chapel. For the event, they gathered over two dozen world interfaith leaders who had been a part of Fr. Thomas's work, along with young contemplative leaders. Interviewed by *The Aspen Daily News*, Rev. Vesey reflected the group's view of today's global spiritual community, saying: "It's a sense of community that's important. That's the direction it's going: toward realizing that we are one community, that China's problems are America's problems, and America's problems are China's problems. If we can help solve each other's problems through developing the wisdom to do that, that will be a major shift. We can model that in the traditionally divisive area of religion, and I think that's what we're trying to do: to model community." The newspaper also pointed out the words from a flyer for the event, from Bede Griffiths' *Return to the Center*: "The goal of each religion is the same."

As summarized in the Endnotes to this piece, press and internet coverages of the event and related activities have been appreciatively extensive, contributing to the synthesized content of this memorial piece. Wisdom Waypoints (wisdomwaypoints.org) has also since released the "Thomas Keating: An Interspiritual Celebration ~ and Online Public Video Archive." Dr. Kurt Johnson, co-founder of Light on Light Publications and Media, and the Light on Light Press, was an attendee and later in 2019, facilitated by the late former Br. Erik Keeney, monastic assistant to Fr. Keating, facilitated a memorial written communication from Fr. Keating to His Holiness the 14th Dalai

Lama, with whom Fr. Keating had shared a deep friendship and many international events. Kurt Johnson delivered this communication in person to His Holiness when Kurt was a part of a conference on science and religion with the Dalai Lama, at his residence in Dharamsala, India, late October to early November 2019 facilitated by the Mind & Life Institute.

Endnotes and References for this Feature[x:2]

A Monk in Every Heart — A Teasdalean Tale

by William Howell (aka Swami Vishnu Datta)

It was a blazingly clear Colorado morning, still early summer (which most everywhere else is known as Spring) when my wife and I brought Cynthia Bourgeault up the winding road climbing to our small dream house, with Wayne Teasdale pulling into our one extra parking place atop our mesa overlooking the valley of Old Snowmass. We'd all just attended Mass at St. Benedict's Monastery, where our mutual mentor and friend, Fr. Thomas Keating, had just delivered one of his stunning homilies whose crescendo led to pin-drop silence.

The deck of our house celebrated the sweep of forty miles of the Little Elk Range, from Aspen Highlands north to Mt. Sopris, still resonant with snow. Fr. Thomas, celebrant at our outdoor wedding a handful of years before, had pointed out that Sopris, from our vantage point, boasted three peaks, which the original ancestors (whose arrowheads I was yet to find) took to be the head, belly big with child, and knees up of a mother ready to give birth.

As my wife poured lemonade and made a foursome, the day would prove a birthing one, with vast blue sky as our fitting witness.

Wayne was brimming with Bede Griffiths, one of his dearest teachers, along with Fr. Keating and the Dalai Lama. Wayne shared how he still hoped Fr. Thomas would don the sun-bleached ochre robes that he himself was wearing — to symbolize East-West connectivity, an energy to unite Christianity and Hinduism, toward which Fr. Bede was ardently working, but also to serve the inter-religious inner embrace that would center Wayne's all-too-short time with us.

Cynthia was fast becoming an adept spokesperson for Centering Prayer, the meditation method Thomas Keating had founded and the four of us shared. She skillfully brought Raimon Panikkar to our discussion, his *The Intra-Religious Dialogue* (1978) having pronounced impeccable guidelines for authentic interfaith conversation.

And I, having recently met Lex Hixon, was beginning a love affair with Plotinus, the central Christian exemplar in Lex's spiritual classic *Coming Home: The Experience of Enlightenment in Sacred Traditions.* Often called the world's finest philosopher, the third-century founder of Neoplatonism had inimitably located in "The One" *all* the tendencies in and by which Creation gets expressed.

Thus, with Oneness as inspiration and the great Wisdom Traditions intersecting our collective imagination, the seed was watered for Wayne's inter-spiritual work to blossom as *The Mystic Heart* just before the millennium, and fruit in *A Monk in the World* (2002). Cynthia's first book, *The Wisdom Way of Knowing: Reclaiming an Ancient Tradition to Awaken the Heart*, would come out a year later. While I was way behind these two vanguards, I now reap the joy of recalling that pregnant day.

My wife and I had been with Wayne in the remarkable gathering called "Harmonium Mundi" in Orange County, beginning on St. Francis of Assisi's feast day in 1989, where adepts of the world's great religious traditions came together to mentor with those fortunate enough to participate. Though we had spent our last $700 to be there, our risk was amply rewarded. Thomas Keating, the adept representing contemplative Christianity, told us, "Here's a feast of spirituality; don't hang around me!" (which we did back in Colorado during his thirty-five years as our spiritual advisor). Culminating the final convocation was HH Dalai Lama, who that morning had received the Nobel Peace Prize. Our prize was bestowed by His Holiness (Wayne instructing us, "Once he finishes his dharma talk, run to the stage") grasping our outstretched hands — to this day one of my deepest, most indelible, poignant, and mystifying moments.

Wayne was a simple man, a brother whose vision was clear and simple. His closeness with Fr. Bede rubbed off in the simplicity of monkhood and Christian–Hindu unity, and his closeness with Fr. Keating supported the vision that made Wayne's *The Mystic Heart: Discovering a Universal Spirituality in the World's Religions* (1999) inevitable.

Wayne's seed-term inter-spiritual has centered the prayer of our global family living meaningfully in harmony. Wayne sensed every heart housed a monk, however silent. He knew religion to be the deepest — ergo, most powerful — urge in the human breast. He also knew that this most verdant territory was also the most fragile and, at the same time, the most defended. I sense that made him, to complement of his visionary innocence, a passionate fighter.

I'll not forget the 1993 Parliament of the World's Religions in Chicago, toward the end of a breakout group headed by Wayne's friend, teacher and ally, the Dalai Lama, the energy with which Wayne read out a forceful statement he had written about the necessity of a free Tibet.

Here was Wayne's heft. His demonstrable commitment. His growing maturity that was still nearly a decade from *A Monk in the World*, wherein he named the call I have long felt. Wayne, still cultivating his spiritual life, spoke on that Colorado day in 1991 as if the seeds of all his ministerings were already in hand.

I feel akin enough to Wayne and his inner monastery to suggest where the arrow he shot into the mist of a new day for humanity might land. Brother Wayne moved "inter-religious dialogue" to "inter-spiritual dialogue"…and I think he would support moving "God" into "Wholeness."

While I delight in the possibility of "G-O-D" being an acronym for Generation / Operation / Destruction (the three timeless mathematical operators that describe every possible wave and event), God shall not be an admired universal term, given its historical specificities and misuses. However apt, its baggage is overweight for the twenty-first-century flight that humanity needs to make. Besides, it's hard to take Wholeness' name in vain.

Wholeness is both abstract enough to carry the necessary feeling-tone of absolutely unbounded and eternal vastness and at the same time offer a felt-sense of presence, of embrace in which all things, places, events, dimensions, strata, and beings reside. Wholeness feels a bit cloudlike, the cloud that contains all the moisture that ever was-is-will be: the Original Calm before the original storm (which, of course, is also ever within Wholeness). For me, it's so much cleaner and easier to grasp the unbeginningness and unendingness of everything in Wholeness…because the questions always arise: *Where did God come from*? and *Who made God?* For me, and I'm betting for Wayne, human beings can better grok the truth that in Wholeness there is no beginning or end. After all, Wholeness is whole. Wholeness is whole, and nothing sticks to it, especially since Wholeness is the only non-it. Wholeness is fresh, carries zero baggage, offends no one. Wholeness is Unity beyond all notion of parts. There is no partial wholeness, and so it will always be copacetic with whatever quantum physics might reveal.

Wholeness unites the absolute of Pure Existence (exemplified in Meher Baba's assertion, "To say that God was, is and will be, is wrong. All eternity is now present at this moment. So I say, God IS.") with Plotinus' all-encompassing The One, and also with all notions of sovereignty, glory, and majesty, which I like to call The Supreme.

You can picture this by imagining a circle standing for, and compassing, this Trinity of Being — Unity, and highest Potency / Capacity / Capability. Wholeness not only unifies all three expressions of The Trinity, but also the whole idea of number, of division, of three-ness, of elements, of circle, of meaning, of language, of words, of page, of space, of time.... You get the idea: Whatever can be exists in and by virtue of Wholeness.

Let's call The Wholeness "Cosmic Being," given that you are a being, and are Being…as am I. Ergo, we automatically and intrinsically have some familiarity with Wholeness.

Now, one step more, one Brother Wayne would likely have found obvious:

- You and I both have a mind. As does the Cosmos…the Cosmic Mind being omniscient Pure Intelligence whereby Nature is Nature and the various realms fit together like Russian dolls.
- You and I both have a heart. As does the Cosmos…the Cosmic Heart being omnipresent Love and Light whereby life is clearly alive and necessarily relational.

- You and I both have a body. As does the Cosmos…the Cosmic Body is the Universe, being the omnipotence of Wholeness made manifest.

Cosmology and philosophy and theology get so much simpler when we peer through any of the infinite "eyes" of Wholeness. Clarity of Being, clarity of thinking, clarity of relating, and clarity of embodiment nicely explicate Gen 1:27 ("So God created man in his own image, in the image of God he created him").

I imagine Wayne's smile at inter-cosmic inter-spirituality.

There is heft in wisdom and power in clarity. There is beauty in elegance. And there is lightness and innocence in simplicity.

I sense Brother Wayne's nod. Wholeness is all-One, and Wayne understood that being a monk meant being heartfully alone with the All-One. And that the alone place in each of us required expression — as united the four of us that sacred Colorado morning.

Had I had the opportunity to remind Brother Wayne of the inter-relatedness of Wholeness and holiness, I would expect his characteristic knowing gaze, communicating, "Why else would the Holy Spirit come about?"

Memories of Wayne

by Gard Jameson

Gurdjieff wrote a wonderful text: *Meetings with Remarkable Men*. For me, my life has been a series of meetings with remarkable men and women. In 1993 at the Parliament of the World's Religions in Chicago, I had my eyes opened very wide as I gazed upon a galaxy of awe-filled men and women, from His Holiness the Dalai Lama to Sister Jayanti of the Brahma Kumaris. I experienced utter bliss as Sister Jayanti led the entire Parliament Assembly in meditation, transported by the awareness of individuals who carried Presence wherever they turned. In the hallways, my consciousness would be powerfully drawn as a Holy One passed by.

One of those beings whom I met was Wayne Teasdale. I had been familiar with Bede Griffiths and his amazing life through video and text. Now, I was blessed to meet one of his students, Brother Wayne. For those who have been blessed by Wayne's person, there is a delight in the grace of his words, the strength of his character, and the clear vision of his imagination. He led conversations at that Parliament which were an epiphany for this young aspirant.

What followed the 1993 Parliament in Chicago was the Cape Town Parliament where I really got to know Wayne personally. One encounter was particularly enchanted, for I got to be with him one-on-one for an extended period of time. The flight was fifteen hours from Cape Town to Atlanta… while everyone was fast asleep, I got to see Wayne dancing, dervish that he is, through the isle of the airliner, visiting, sharing his matchless goodwill and humor. When I got my time with Wayne, it felt like I had known him my entire life. He was so at home in his soul, so friendly, so joyful that any apprehension of being in the presence of a spiritual master was soon gone.

We spoke of many things, stories of our lives, our commitment to an interspiritual way of being, the recognition of the pain of the planet and the opportunity to invite others into the balm of personal spiritual experience, cosmic awareness, and spiritual perception. Since that flight, I did not have much contact other than diving into his wisdom through his writings, *The Mystic Heart*, *A Monk in the World*. Only recently, through my brother, Jeff Genung, have I been delighted to learn more of Brother Wayne and his inspired life.

At the recent Parliament of the World's Religions, we were provided an opportunity to put up four yurts in the middle of maelstrom of cordoned areas where presentations were going on. The yurts were dedicated to the realization that the journey requires "all of our heart, mind, body, and soul." Jeff Genung and Kate Roach were the co-Captains of the first yurt which faced the Parliament's labyrinth, "Wayne's Yurt." Jeff, who cared for Wayne during his final years, provided a loop of amazing images of Wayne's labyrinthian journey. There was continuous interspiritual dialogue filling the walls of that yurt, music to Wayne's ears.

When we see the Contemplative Life incarnate, as with Wayne, we are given the gift of the Light of Love, Compassion, and Hope to guide our own pathway. By these three values, cosmogenesis is propelled. I close with a wondrous passage from *The Mystic Heart*:

> Daily Contemplative Practice soon lends a genuine perspective on life, people, God, nature, and oneself. When we enter a place of solitude, all the things that seemed so important to us recede in significance; what is truly important emerges in clarity.

May we each take seriously, with great joy, the invitation to a daily immersion in our contemplative practice, knowing that the world craves what you, and you alone, are incarnating!

Conversations with Brother Wayne Teasdale

by Imam Jamal Rahman

I first met Brother Wayne Teasdale when he visited Seattle in early 2001 to promote his book *The Mystic Heart.* We became friends, and he visited us in our 1890 historic church building. He marveled over the fact that since 1997 the building is home to an interfaith community of about 150 members who espouse a variety of traditions including those called "spiritual but not religious." He expressed immense joy over our insight that interfaith is not about conversion; it is about becoming a more complete and developed human being. He promised to visit us again in the future.

Br. Wayne returned to our community in the next few months following the horrific events of 9/11. He was eager to talk about spiritual teachings at the heart of every religion and especially looked forward to meeting the Muslim members of our community to learn about spirituality in Islam. Amazingly, between 2001 and 2004, he came to our community seven times to deepen the conversations he initiated!

The remarkable meetings, some of which lasted several hours, are deeply etched in my memory and my scribbled notes. The conversations have profoundly impacted my being and my ministry.

In our first get together, Br. Wayne, reflecting on excessive political and military reactions to the terrorist attack of 9/11, offered a primary teaching from Taoism: we humans tend to overreact in speech and action to difficulties in our lives. Knowing when to stop is a profound art. Stretching the string of a bow sends the arrow further but overstretch, and the string breaks.

How do we learn not to overreact with someone we consider an enemy? It behooves us, he explained, to truly listen to the other. An adversary is someone whose story we have not fully listened to. Br. Wayne shared a definition by the 13th century sage Rumi: metaphorically speaking, listening is akin to putting one's head on a person's chest and sinking into the answer.

We all realized that, ultimately, we need to listen to the wisdom of our heart. We meditated on an insight emphasized by the Prophet Muhammad: "No matter what the expert or authority advises, first consult your heart. Consult your heart!"

The next meeting started with a Christian centering prayer. Br. Wayne explained that the practice of silence is universal, and he encouraged us to weave into our daily hectic lives some regular moments of silence where we experience expanded awareness, nourishment, and peace. He related the Hindu story of a child who asks his father about the origin of the fruit tree. The father encourages him to look inside the fruit, and then inside the seed. The son exclaims in astonishment that there is nothing in the interior of the seed. The father explains that from the empty silence of nothingness has emerged everything that exists.

This beautiful story encouraged conversation about the story of the Night of Destiny mentioned in the Qur'an. Muhammad, not yet a prophet, despaired of the savagery of his 7th century society and retreated often in the caves of Mecca to find comfort and regeneration in meditation. On one fateful night in the year 610 CE, Muhammad was wrapped in deep silence in a Meccan cave when the angel Gabriel appeared and revealed to him the first verses of the Qur'an. Thus, say the mystics, the Qur'an has its roots in the womb of silence, and the holy book reveals that in the mystery of silence, "angels and the spirit descend."

During a third session, Br. Wayne told the story of the Buddha who was asked if he was a wizard, sage, or deity. The Buddha replied, "I am awake! The truth is that we live in a hypnotic trance, unaware of the astonishing mysteries swirling inside and outside of us."

The subject of bewildering existential questions led to lengthy conversations about God. Of Brahman, the Hindus say that "the mind cannot think it, but it is that by which the mind thinks; the tongue cannot utter it, but it is that by which the tongue utters; the eyes cannot see it, but it is that by which the eyes see…" Taoists explain that knowledge of the Tao is unattainable: "Those who say do not know; those who know do not say." The Buddhists do not mention God in their texts but explain that using human faculties to comprehend mysteries of the invisible world is like using a bamboo stick to measure the depth of the ocean. The Qur'an reveals that "Everywhere you turn is the face of Allah."

In our fourth session, Br. Wayne explained that the problems of social injustice and planetary degradation would be resolved primarily by raising our consciousness. From a Christian perspective, become more Christ-like; from a Buddhist perspective, more Buddha-like. Can we overcome in our lifetime our conditioned biases, and embrace love and compassion in our being? It is highly significant, he explained, that the last words of the Buddha on his death bed were, "Be a lamp unto yourself. Work out your salvation with diligence." We simply must, over a lifetime, engage in what Islamic mystics call "the inner inconvenient work." This essential work is embodied in a verse by the 19th century Sufi mystic Mirza Ghalib: "Your face was unclean, but you were obsessed with polishing and polishing the mirror."

The next gathering focused on the topic of suffering. Br. Wayne pointed out that all religions explain that we live in a world of opposites. High is defined by low; long by short; joy by sorrow. Buddhism states that some suffering in our lives is inevitable. How we respond to our suffering impacts the course of our life. It is critical not to avoid or deny the pain or wounding. Little by little, nurse the pain and allow it to heal. In good time, the blessing of some precious wisdom will emerge from within.

Br. Wayne talked candidly about his personal pain. His mother was toxic and abusive. He left home at an early age to live with his uncle whom he adored. He explained that he developed the gift of empathy and compassion for those who suffered because of dysfunction or abuse in their family. Afflicted people whom he met remarked to him that his mere presence was healing to them.

The session concluded on the topic of forgiveness. Br. Wayne was able to forgive his mother but only after he, over the course of time and with help of spiritual practices, was able to heal his pain. To forgive a perpetrator without tending to one's wound is unwise. To quote the Buddha, "it is like whitewashing a burning house."

In a subsequent session, Br. Wayne brought up the critical need to be of service to God's creation. This constitutes a major reason for our existence on earth. The most important point to take to heart about service, he reiterated, is to offer our righteous deed without attachment to the prestige or prize it brings us. Be of service for the sake of God — this precious insight is highlighted in many traditions.

We reflected on an insight of the Prophet Muhammad: "Whosoever of you sees an evil, let him change it with his hand; and if he is not able to do so, then let him change it with his tongue; and if he is not able to do so, then with his heart-and that is the weakest of faith."

In a final session, Br. Wayne stressed the need for community and diversity. On the topic of community, we reflected on metaphors uttered by Rumi. A wall standing alone is useless; add to it other walls, and it can support a roof. Only when ink joins with a pen can the blank paper say something.

Br. Wayne predicted that over the coming decades, we humans would move beyond tribal affiliations and create community based on "kinship of spirit." One aspect of this kinship is to bond with people who espouse love of truth. This foresight reflects the wisdom of ancient sages and holy texts. When the Buddha was asked about sangha or community, he advised, "Find friends who love the truth." The Qur'an counsels us to create community with those with whom we can grow with teachings of patience and truth.

On the topic of diversity, Br. Wayne was familiar with a verse of the Qur'an that was repeated countless times by Muslims in the wake of Islamophobia following the event of 9/11. The holy book reveals that Allah created diversity out of a cosmic design so that we humans might get to know one another. This sacred task was not meant to be easy.

In conclusion, I often contemplate the priceless wisdom Br. Wayne shared with us. In his short span of life, he opened countless hearts and minds globally. In cherishing his memory, I am reminded of a saying of the Prophet Muhammad: "When you arrived here, everyone around you was smiling and laughing but you were crying and weeping. Live such a life that when you depart, everyone around you is crying and weeping but you are smiling and laughing."

Wayne Teasdale, Rabbi Zalman Schachter-Shalomi, Cynthia Bourgeault

by Gordon Dveirin and Joan Borysenko

[Excerpted for honoring these pioneers from "The Claritas Institute for Interspiritual Inquiry" by Gordon Dveirin and Joan Borysenko in Volume 3]

In 2004, Joan and I had the joy of spending an inspiring week in Vancouver in close, spiritual companionship with our friends Brother Wayne Teasdale, Cynthia Bourgeault, HH the Dalai Lama's brother, Tenzin Choegyal, and others who had arrived to take part in a city-wide process of interfaith sharing: churches, temples, and mosques opening their doors to share their contemplative practices, along with representatives of First Nations people indigenous to that land.

Joan had been chosen to serve as master of ceremonies for a daylong conference that was part of this larger event. The conference occurred during the same week in April that HH the Dalai Lama, along with two fellow Nobel Laureates, Desmond Tutu and Shirin Ebadi, were awarded honorary Doctor of Laws degrees from the University of British Columbia (UBC). The award ceremony took place beneath a huge banner that read: *Balancing Educating the Mind with Educating the Heart*, the subject of a roundtable dialogue that took place the following day at UBC.

In his seminal book *The Mystic Heart*, Brother Wayne Teasdale wrote that "Interspirituality — the sharing of ultimate experience across traditions — is the religion of the third millennium." That is what we saw in action that wonderful week in Vancouver.

Joan and I returned home inspired to create the Claritas Institute for Interspiritual Inquiry to promote dialogue and understanding between different spiritual traditions though workshops, retreats, and educational programs that explored the essential unity that lies at the heart of all spiritual traditions, no matter how they may differ in external belief and ritual. This venture is recounted in more detail in Volume 3 of these Volumes, which details and celebrates specific interspiritual communities.

...Our yearlong training program was comprised of three weeklong, in-person retreats, and a series of online sessions featuring presentations and conversations with spiritual luminaries including Fr. Thomas Keating, Rabbi Rami Shapiro, Episcopal priest Cynthia Bourgeault, Rabbi Zalman Schachter-Shalomi, Chief Jake Swamp of the Wolf Clan-Mohawk nation, Sister Rose Mary Dougherty, and a splendid group of Sufi, Buddhist, and Hindu teachers — all interspiritual pioneers.

...True leaders that increase the personal and greater good call for mindful reflection and retrospection. ...When we interviewed Rabbi Zalman Schachter-Shalomi for our book *Your Souls Compass: What is Spiritual Guidance*, we asked him how he differentiated true guidance from egoic desire. He laughed uproariously and replied, "If you can answer that, I'll become your disciple."

..."Contemplation and action are really the same," Reverend Cynthia Bourgeault told us when we interviewed her for *Your Soul's Compass.* She said, "as one meditates deeply, contemplation narrows the distance between prayer and life because your action is always an immediate and integral response to what's in your heart."

Thomas Berry, the Cosmic Mother, and Renewed Wholeness

by Emily A. DeMoor

I had the incredible honor and pleasure of knowing cultural historian and geologian[1] Thomas Berry, as his student and friend, when he taught courses in Religion and Ecology for the Loyola Institute for Ministry (LIM) in New Orleans. I remember one Saturday, after he had taught an all-day class, a small group of us took him to a cozy, uptown restaurant. It was raining, and the closest parking spot we could find was over a block away. A couple of us approached him to share our umbrellas with him as we walked toward the restaurant, but he declined, saying, "I *like* the rain!" He happily walked in the rain, without cover. This simple, carefree act brought his teachings about being in communion with the universe alive in a vivid, joyful and embodied way, becoming part of our collective spiritual experience.

In *The Dream of the Earth* (1988), Thomas Berry argues for the recovery of the Earth's psychic energy to heal and renew our planet, which has suffered from misguided dreams of progress. He encourages us to create a sustainable human culture by tapping into our instinctive, pre-rational resources. (Perhaps walking in the rain is one of these?) Berry emphasizes that visionary experiences, often revealed through dreams, should guide our recovery efforts, as these experiences are universal and vital to both individual and community psychic life. He explains that the word "dream" here not only refers to the psychic processes that occur during sleep, but also to "an intuitive, non-rational process that occurs when we awaken to the numinous powers ever present in the phenomenal world about us, powers that possess us and our high creative moments."[2] For the radiance of the natural world awakens us intellectually, aesthetically and emotionally.

In *The Great Work: Our Way into the Future* (1999), Berry again draws upon the concepts of dreaming and awakening to urge humanity to usher in an Ecozoic Era in which humans act as a benevolent force on Earth in a relationship of reciprocity. He asserts that this role is not chosen by us but assigned by a higher power. Berry emphasizes that our life's nobility depends on how we understand and fulfill this role, with guidance and support from the same powers that brought us into existence. He calls for a new revelatory experience in which human consciousness awakens to the Earth's grandeur and sacredness. He emphasizes that this awakening is crucial for our future and the entire Earth community.

In Berry's view, the universe that birthed us is the primary referent in the phenomenal order and the primary sacred community. The universe has been a spiritual and physical reality from the beginning, carrying the primordial energies with it throughout its emergence. In its sequence of transformations, it continues to carry the comprehensive meaning of the phenomenal world within it. Moments of transformation are of great significance, thus, the natural world is "the primary source of religious consciousness"[3] — a consciousness characterized by an ecological Interspirituality and intersectionality, although Berry did not use these terms. Berry tells us that as humans we bear "the impress of every transformation through which the universe and the planet earth have passed" within us.[4]

Just as we bear the mark of our cosmic origins, Earth's children also carry the imprint of their human mothers and leave a part of themselves within her. This biological exchange happens in the womb through fetal-maternal microchimerism. Research indicates that microchimeric cells can aid in a mother's healing process long after childbirth.[5] On a larger scale, Berry tells us, that "…we need to understand that the Earth acts in all that acts upon the Earth. The Earth is acting in us whenever we act. In and through the Earth, spiritual energy is present."[6] Thus, our language and imagery need to acknowledge "the numinous maternal principle out of which all life emerges."[7] Berry's writings suggest that reconnecting with Mother Earth can help us achieve greater wholeness through a renewed relationship of intimacy, reciprocity, and potential healing.

For Berry, this renewal requires re-envisioning education as a universal endeavor. He articulates his vision in *The Dream of the Earth* when he writes, "All human professions, institutions, and activities must be integral with the earth as the primary self-nourishing self-governing and self-fulfilling community. To integrate our human activities within this context is our way into the future" (p. 88). This type of education is taking many forms that are bearing fruit throughout the world, as you will see in the essays that follow.

I remember, many years ago, Thomas Berry gave a public presentation in a large, new, university performance hall, rather than the usual lecture hall. The audience did not fill the space, as it typically did in the smaller venue. At a reception afterward, a student reporter walked up to him and, within earshot, asked him if he felt like a failure. While I was very embarrassed by this, Berry very calmly and directly responded, "It doesn't matter whether I succeed or fail. What matters is that I do what is needed." To do what is needed — this is our way forward as we birth the future together.

Endnotes and References for this Feature[x:3]

Cherishing the Spirituality of a Sufi

by Joseph Victor Edwin S.J.

Reading and meditating *Sharafuddin Maneri: Hundred Letters*, translated and introduced by the Jesuit Paul Jackson, I was wonderstruck by the interspiritual depth of the Muslim Sufi Saint Sharafuddin Maneri. I was particularly moved by his spiritually-enriching teachings on repentance.

Maneri, the Pilgrim

Sharafuddin Maneri was born about the year 1290 to a pious couple. From his infancy, the fact that God reigned in the lives of his parents made an indelible impact on him. He spontaneously accepted God's reign in his own life. Maneri began his education when he was four years, four months and four days old. The first lesson was traditionally learning and writing a few alphabets. Later, he went to Sonargaon in Bengal for his further studies. There, he attended the lectures of many Islamic scholars.

Maneri returned to his hometown in 1323. His father had died before he returned. Maneri did not stay home for long. The yearning of his heart was too great for him to settle down quietly in Maner, in Bihar, in eastern India. His need for guidance along the Path to God became compelling for him. He set out for Delhi with his elder brother, Khaliluddin. There, he met Nizamuddin Auliya, the famous Sufi of his times. Maneri was impressed by the holiness of Nizamuddin. However, he did not feel called to become his disciple. Maneri called upon Bu Ali Qalandar of Panipat and found this Sufi was lost in ecstasy most of the times. Maneri was not keen on taking him as his guide. Maneri was disappointed and almost decided to return home. His brother, however, encouraged him and took him to Sheikh Najibuddin Firdausi. Out of consideration for his brother, he agreed to visit him as a last attempt to find a spiritual guide for himself in Delhi. He was quite unexpectedly overcome emotionally at this meeting and was deeply affected by it. Without the slightest hesitation, he asked to become his disciple. Maneri stayed in Delhi about eight years. He remained with Sheikh Najibuddin Firdausi till the latter's death.

Shortly after the death of his guide, Maneri left Delhi. On the way back home, instead of entering his hometown, he veered off into the jungle of Bihia. He wanted to give himself wholly to the pursuit of union with God. After living a brief period of complete isolation, he moved to a cave in Rajgir, in Bihar, besides a spring. This spring is known even to this day as Makhdam Kund. He began to go to nearby Bihar for Friday congregational prayers that enabled people to meet him easily. At times, he felt it irksome to receive many visitors requesting his intercession with the local administrator. A visiting *shaikh*, however, advised him not to hesitate to take up the "burden of people." Maneri eventually moved to Bihar town and helped people by writing recommendation letters on their behalf to administrators and guided many seekers in the ways of God.

Maneri dictated a number of letters on various spiritual topics on the request of Qazi Shamsuddin, the Governor of Chausa in western Bihar throughout the year 1346–1347 CE. These letters were copied and compiled by Zain Badr Arabi. *The Hundred Letters* gained fame within Sufi circles of Bihar and elsewhere. The royals, too, paid attention to the teachings of this spiritual genius. Sultan Muhammad bin Tughluq (d. 1351) asked for further advice on some points that were raised in *The Hundred Letters*. The Indo-Persian Mughal elite read *The Hundred Letters* that had been copied for their reading and thus were undoubtedly influenced by *The Hundred Letters*.

"Seekers of God" as Pilgrims

Maneri portrays "seekers of God" as pilgrims. Pilgrims are on the path that leads toward God. A pilgrim is not a tourist. A tourist stops and often gets lost in the beauty of what he sees on the way. A pilgrim, however, is focused on the destination. The end is of prime importance for him. Pilgrims have to traverse the spiritual wilderness toward their destination all by themselves. Maneri warns seekers to be aware of many obstacles on the way. He compares obstacles to a band of robbers who lie in wait to plunder travelers. He cautions them to keep a sharp eye on the pitfalls. He instructs them not to be lost on what they saw on the way. He advocates the need of a spiritual guide for pilgrims.

Faith that Inspires One to Become a Pilgrim

Why should a pilgrim burn boats behind and take a journey to uncertainty? A pilgrim sets out since he thirsts for more in life. What gives him the assurance to enable him to take such risk, the risk of taking a journey to uncertainty? "Faith," answers Maneri poignantly. Maneri teaches that it is faith that inspires one to become a pilgrim. Faith shows the way to God. The grace of God stirs the heart of persons to don the pilgrim's garb. God alone calls a person for this journey. The initiative lies with God. Only those who yearn for more can respond to the invitation and set out for the pilgrim journey. Once on the pilgrim journey, one never knows for sure when the grace of God will come and sweep the person toward Himself. Anyone who sets upon this journey on his own succumbs to temptations of austerities which may result in pride or even loss of faith. God's invitation never comes to an ignorant person. Maneri tells that all baseness could be traced back to ignorance!

A Pilgrim Should Trust God Absolutely

Maneri teaches that the pilgrim should trust God absolutely. He gives the following graphic illustration to drive home his point. Imagine a person who is fully aware of his sinfulness and hears a heavenly voice that proclaims that only one person would enter heaven. The sinful person believes that he is that only person! That is "trust in God." It is relying upon God fully without any reserve. Maneri explains the more a pilgrim relies on God and not on his efforts, the more he recognizes that he is united with God and shares already, to some degree, in the absoluteness of God's power. In other words, God provides for those whom he called for this pilgrimage. God cares for the pilgrim like a mother cares for her children. God makes the way easy for the pilgrim. Finally, God leads the pilgrim toward total union with Himself. This union is not God sharing his divine life with man. This union is simply an experience of being overwhelmed by God. The gap between the Creator and created person remain unbridgeable in Muslim theology.

An Experience of God Is the Gift from God

Maneri teaches that any form of the mystical knowledge of God or an experience of God is a gift from God. Pilgrims should recognize that their experience of God is not the fruit of their searching. It is not a payment for labor undertaken on behalf of God. It is simply God's gift. Maneri, further, teaches his listeners that a person "sees" God not because he sought God relentlessly, but because God chose to show Himself to the pilgrim. Thus, Maneri urges pilgrims to focus on God, not on oneself. Maneri also reminds his disciples of the human dimension in response to God's call. He relates that the courage of the pilgrim in the face of challenges keeps him/her in good stead in his/her resolve to reach the goal. Maneri advises the pilgrims not to worry too much about what particular state they are in.

Repentance Is "Turning Back" to God

Repentance, for Maneri, is "turning back" to God. Ordinary folk repent out of fear that God may punish them. They turn aside from their sins and observe God's commandments. The pilgrims are more aware of God than the ordinary folk. The pilgrims observe commandments not out of fear but for God's sake. The pilgrims wish to be faithful to the commandments for the love of God. The pilgrims observe the commandments because of a stirring love and reverence for God. Maneri recognizes the touch of divine grace when he highlights "reverence."

Maneri encourages his disciples not to lose heart if they repeatedly fall into sin. He counsels them not to succumb to the satanic deception that repentance is futile. He was able to perceive even a modicum of goodwill and generosity in his disciples to fight evil within oneself. He highlighted that generosity and encouraged them to repent repeatedly. There is no place for complacency; the disciples should press on and remain penitent. God alone, he says, can effect a radical transformation of a person's heart. He alerts pilgrims that humans generally have something "other than God" and they should keep repenting, even if that otherness is their own very self! Beginners should show earnest resolution to abandon sin. This earnestness to abandon sin is achieved not merely by crying for God's forgiveness but also by rectifying the damage that was brought about by one's sin. Repentance also means transforming one's nature with the grace of God.

Spiritual Guidance Is Essential

Maneri insists on the necessity of the assistance of an experienced guide for a pilgrim. How would a pilgrim recognize someone as his guide? Maneri suggests that God, through a special grace of inspiration, will help the pilgrim to identify his guide. Maneri makes it clear that the novice will feel a great attraction toward that particular guide and a confidence to entrust himself to him. An experienced guide will be able to guide the novice since he himself has gone through an orderly progress.

Even a *shaikh's* own mistakes can be helpful in guiding others, for he himself can learn valuable lessons by wandering off the Way for a time. The sureness with which Sharafuddin describes some of the dangers along the Way, particularly the most subtle imaginable, indicates he had learnt his lesson the hard way.

Maneri makes an insightful comment saying that a man attains freedom in service for others. A servant is a free person. A free person can experience the joy of union with God. As long as one considers oneself as somebody, he is nobody in the eyes of God. Maneri's idea of service is intimately joined with self-negation. A person's service for others is tried and found sound only when he considers himself to be rejected and valued useless. Maneri stresses that one can belittle oneself in one's own estimation by denying oneself and serve others.

Genuine Service Trains the Religious Person to Be Humble

Maneri affirms that genuine service trains the religious person to be humble. It makes the person radiant both internally and externally. A pilgrim in authentic service to the other would learn that such service is impossible unless he entirely abandons his own wishes, desires and control over others. If a pilgrim progresses in authentic service in the way Maneri indicates, he will be able to deal with inordinate self-love effectively.

Pray Without Ceasing

Maneri emphasized that "prayer without ceasing" is at the heart of a pilgrim's devotion to God. Prayer should be embellished by other forms of spiritual exercises, like restraining one's speech, praying for others, spiritual conversation, and instructing someone who is in need of religious knowledge. Maneri also recognized that an unexamined life is not worth living and stressed that pilgrims should carefully examine their life: their thoughts and actions.

Service, Devotion and Mystical Experience

A pilgrim is focused toward attaining the mystical experience of God. The motivation for God experience is often tinged with lesser motivations. Man's worth is measured according to his purity. It takes time, patience, and guidance to purify one's intention. Purity of heart is the prerequisite of the mystical experience of God. Actions born of pure intentions will bring one closer to union with God. Actions bereft of purity of heart are utterly useless. The whole purpose purifying one's heart is to seek God.

After the initial preparation, a pilgrim has a long way to go. Maneri emphasizes that pilgrims have some provisions for the journey. First, Maneri recommends a forty days' retreat, which will bring about an overwhelming change in the very nature of the person. After this, the retreatant will emerge completely a new man. The retreat helps him to live a humble, self-disciplined, and God-oriented life. At this stage, the pilgrim will experience an attraction to God and experience mystical illumination. Second, Maneri recommends listening to or singing spiritual hymns that would bring out the spirituality of a pilgrim that is hidden in heart. Singing would be of no spiritual consequence if heart is empty. Thirdly, Maneri recommends begging to foster the pilgrim's trust in God.

Begging is a good form of asceticism and helps to acquire freedom of heart. Begging also helps one to become aware that all belongs to God. When the pilgrim begs, he is begging from God. God provides the pilgrim through other people. Fourthly, Maneri warns pilgrims not to become proud. All mystical experiences are due to God's grace. Fifthly, Maneri reminds the pilgrim that contentment is one of the signs of a sincere pilgrim. The sincere pilgrim is contended with whatever comes from the grace of God, including disappointments. A sincere pilgrim is fully aware even the most disappointing moment could be the most graceful moment of his life. Sixthly, Maneri encourages pilgrims to deal with fear along with hope. Finally, Maneri encourages pilgrims by emphasizing time and again the eternal covenant which exists between God and the entire human race. “Am I not your Lord?”: this Qur’anic verse is at the heart of Maneri’s conception of the Way to God.

Maneri’s life is marked with hunger: hunger for knowledge and hunger for experience. He traveled considerably in search of knowledge and experience. Throughout his search, his gaze was fixed on God and longing for union with God. He was enlightened with a deep experience of God. He felt a call to guide others in the ways of God.

Conclusion

I salute Paul Jackson for rendering the spiritual treasures of Maneri that were locked in the fourteenth-century Persian into modern English. What impressed me first and foremost is the “God-consciousness” of Maneri. He was so focused on God; he saw everything from the optic of God. Maneri challenges every reader to organize one’s life around the word of God that is given to each community. A Muslim grows in God-consciousness through reflecting on the Qur’an, the word of God and living out the demands of the holy book. A Christian is challenged to be faithful to the Word of God that became human in Jesus Christ. A Christian grows in God-Consciousness by an act of love that orients him/her toward Christ.

Secondly, Maneri the pilgrim reminds me of my own Christian tradition, and for me as a Jesuit, one of the important elements of the Jesuit spirituality. The founder of the Society of Jesus, Saint Ignatius of Loyola, considered himself a pilgrim, always discerning the will of God in his life and the lives of his companions, the Jesuits. Maneri takes up the faith-inspired pilgrimage. Faith in God guides one to draw strength and consolation from God. Trusting God becomes part and parcel of the life of a pilgrim. The spirituality of Maneri is illuminated by his deep trust in God. The light comes from that illumination (certainly from a different source, a Muslim source) amazes and energizes me, a Christian who seeks to follow the spirituality of Saint Ignatius.

Thirdly, the mysticism of service that is found in the spirituality of Maneri astonishes me. A service that is faith inspired enriches the journey of a pilgrim. There is an adage in the Tamil language that instructs a pilgrim, "If you pray ... you go close to God ... If you serve the poor and sick, God comes close to you." I feel I easily resonate with the spirituality of Maneri as a Christian. Maneri not only challenges me but also consoles me as a co-pilgrim.

The Interspiritual Legacy of Swami Shraddhananda

by the Dharma Heirs of Sacred Feet Yoga

Sacred Feet Yoga Creed

> *We honor the basic truths found in all religions. In our view, truth and dogma are not synonymous, and we do not seek to impose a belief system on practitioners. Ours is a yoga that focuses on sacred energy.*
>
> *We seek to develop the Christ Spirit or Guru Spirit in those who practice Sacred Feet Yoga. We do not consider any one teacher to be Lord of the Universe*

> *but look to all legitimate teachers for wisdom and guidance.*
>
> *Our major focus is on the Holy Spirit or Maha Kundalini Shakti. It is She who leads us to freedom from the vicissitudes of the human ego. In Sacred Feet Yoga philosophy, freedom is possible in the life we are living if we are willing to work for it.*

Sw. Shraddhananda (1948–2021), aka Rev. Dr. Sonya L. Jones, was a highly regarded Spiritual Teacher who studied with key enlightened teachers of classical tantra for thirty years. In 2012, she took *Sannyas*, or monastic vows in the Saraswati Order of Monks and Meditation Masters in the sacred village of Ganeshpuri, India, and she was a Successor in the lineage of Shri Bhagavan Nityananda of Ganeshpuri. She was also lineage holder and Preceptor for the Community of the Mystic Heart, an Interspiritual monastic group founded by Br. Wayne Teasdale who coined the term Interspirituality with publication of *The Mystic Heart* in 1999. She was ordained as an Interfaith minister in 2013 by The New Seminary in New York City, the oldest Interfaith institution in the world, and was drafted onto the Seminary faculty and served as its first Dean of Graduate Studies.

Sw. Shraddhananda (bliss of faith) was the Preceptor of Sacred Feet Yoga, an Interspiritual system which she founded in 2010 in Somerset, KY, USA, upon receiving The Five Teachings of Sacred Feet Yoga Level One by transmission from her Siddha guides. A second transmission for Level Two was received by her in 2017. A third transmission for Level Three was received by Dharma Heir Sw. Prakashananda upon Sw. Shraddhananda's transition in 2021. The spine of Sacred Feet Yoga rests in The Third Teachings of Level One (see below) which encourage seekers to open to *Shaktipat*, the awakening of the sacred energy known across spiritual traditions as Maha Kundalini Shakti, the Holy Spirit, Windhorse, Tara, Ruah, Ruh, etc. Indeed, the sole purpose of all levels of Sacred Feet Yoga Teachings is to kindle and facilitate the blaze of the sacred energy within that frees us from the behavioral and emotional patterns which no longer serve us and allows us to "hold our seat" along bumps that rise in the road until we are able to live every moment from our natural, innate, steady state of divinity, leading us to what many call liberation, enlightenment, luminous emptiness, *moksha*, or freedom.

1.3.1 Honor the sacred energy at the core of your being.
1.3.2 Nurture the Holy Spirit's bright and faithful fire.
1.3.3 Digest the knowledge that leads unfailingly to freedom.

A life-long educator and scholar, Sw. Shraddhananda's prior thirty-five years of service in the academic world as an author, journalist, and professor of Classics, World Literature, and Comparative World Religions (tenured professor at Allegheny College in Meadville, PA, and, subsequently, "Teacher Who Makes a Difference" in the Honors Program at the University of Kentucky) set the stage for her establishing The Sacred Feet Publishing Imprint for Interspiritual books. Its inaugural edition was her widely acclaimed *Jesus Was a Shaktipat Guru* in which she explores the context and mission of Jesus the Christ, placing him alongside the Buddha and other Jagadgurus on the collective world stage of Master Teachers and discussing the inner meaning of his teachings, his role as a Shaktipat Guru, how a Guru works with his or her students, and how modern spiritual teachers are deeply connected and supported by their own "enlivened" lineages. Sw. Shraddhananda also was a Book Review Editor for Light on Light through her work with Dr. Kurt Johnson, who is known internationally as a scientist, comparative religionist, social activist, spiritual teacher, former monastic, and leader in the consciousness and world shift movements and is co-founder of ISD (Interspiritual Dialog, Inc.) with Br. Wayne Teasdale, an original co-founder of the Community of the Mystic Heart, and co-author of *The Coming Interspiritual Age* with David Robert Ord.

Although she had lectured on six continents, nothing was of more importance to Sw. Shraddhananda than bringing Interspirituality to her small town of Somerset in Kentucky, "on the buckle of the "Bible Belt" as she would often say, holding numerous meditation / yoga retreats at the Slate Branch and Boat Dock Road retreat houses before establishing Anugraha House across the street from St. Patrick's Episcopal Church where she honored the Christian elements of her faith. As she said in *Jesus Was a Shaktipat Guru*, "After all, the good ole' Christian revival may not be that different in intent from the Shaktipat Intensive. The Vajrayana Buddhist Retreat may not be that far removed from the mystical Jewish group meeting in Dr. Steinbaum's den to ignite the Sephiroth… *Jaya Jaya Amrita Guru*, praises are due to all the Shaktipat Gurus who have set the Holy Spirit free to do her liberating work…" (p. 134).[1] Sw. Shraddhananda was tenacious and fearless in her efforts to bring everyone together on the common ground of the heart through the grace of the sacred energy that joins us as One:

"Interfaith / Interspiritual / Intra-Tantric Studies can be useful in helping to diminish the sense of spiritual superiority which often accompanies entrenchment in dogma. By promoting the virtues of intra-religious dialogue, the Interfaith Movement has assisted many people in the process of learning how to think across religious boundaries, thus avoiding the traps of fundamentalism. When individuals step outside their story lines, or personal narratives partially constructed by religious upbringing, they usually are able to develop more expansive perspectives" (p. 25).

In Somerset in April of 2016, Sw. Shraddhananda and Sacred Feet Yoga hosted a retreat for the Community of the Mystic Heart in which Teasdale's "Nine Elements" by which any spirituality could be examined for durability were explored. A mature spirituality, or Interspirituality in Teasdale's view, would integrate all Nine Elements. Lead presenters were Dr. Kurt Johnson and Mirabai Starr along with Sw. Shraddhananda, and participants came from various parts of the United States, Canada, and the United Kingdom. Among the attendees were Fr. Giles Spoonhour, co-founder of The New Seminary, whose contribution, according to Kurt Johnson, like that of other early pioneers in the Interfaith / Interspiritual / Trans-Theological Movement has been enormous and Dr. M. Darrol Bryant, who was considered by Professor Huston Smith (1919–2016), author of *The World's Religions*, to be his "heir apparent."

As you can read in Dr. Bryant's Afterword in *Mature Interspirituality: Wayne Teasdale's Nine Elements – and Beyond* (2017), the compiled and published presentations and commentaries from this retreat, it had been a "living example of Interspirituality" where Yoga teachers, ministers, a doctor, seekers, and teachers shared experiences, practices, meals, and silence. He shares: "There was an utter absence of any sense of uneasiness arising from diversity or difference. And an openness towards one another that made the retreat so rich and enriching" (p. 124).[2]

Dr. Bryant's experience is exactly what Sw. Shraddhananda hoped would be lived by all participants at the retreat (and all beings in this life), a space fostering a welcoming atmosphere of community akin to the very well-known words of Rumi (excerpt taken from *The Essential Rumi*, published by HarperCollins. Copyright © 1995 by Coleman Barks) where people could meet, soul to soul, with respect and appreciation for differences and celebration for the deep undercurrent of divine connection:

> Out beyond ideas of wrongdoing and rightdoing,
> There is a field. I'll meet you there.
> When the soul lies down in that grass,
> The world is too full to talk about.
> Ideas, language, even the phrase *each other*
> Doesn't make any sense.

Sw. Shraddhananda was that "living example of Interspirituality," whether meditating, chanting, leading a Sacred Feet Yoga retreat, participating in a Christian church service, writing a book, or teaching a life lesson to students as she navigated nature in her pontoon boat on Lake Cumberland. Regardless of your spiritual tradition, you felt the sacred energy, her very soul, radiate from her and the unspoken invitation to open your heart and go deeper within (although the invitation was often spoken as well). The sacred light in her was always reaching out to the sacred light in you. She focused on being a conduit for that light, so that it would shine as brightly as it could for you, until you could find the light within and make your own way out of the darkness.

That is her legacy, a calling to share the light with all beings — regardless of spiritual tradition — who are poised and open to receive it. Carrying on her lineage, through the grace of the divine, we Dharma Heirs of Sacred Feet Yoga gratefully continue her work for the spiritual awakening and Oneness of all. Our Interspiritual *seva* is very clearly stated throughout the Sacred Feet Yoga Teachings, but certainly the directive is clear in the final trio of teachings of Level Three:

3.5.1 Recognize the Divine Essence in all.

3.5.2 Serve unconditionally. Love all, reject none.

3.5.3 Merge in the heart of the universe.

With reverence, we join in service with the divine hearts coming together in this Interspiritual anthology to, as Ken Wilber says, "Wake Up, Grow Up, Clean Up, Show Up, Link Up and Lift Up" until we all, indeed, merge into the heart of the universe.

Sw. Shraddhananda entered mahasamadhi on Feb. 16, 2021. She is survived by three ordained Dharma Heirs: Jenny Williams (Amrita) of Somerset, KY; Sandra Simon (Chamatkara) of Pittsburgh, PA; and Sw. Prakashananda (The Right Rev. Bishop Christine Deefholts) of the United Kingdom. She is also survived by hundreds of former students and colleagues worldwide who remember her good heart, keen intellect, and abiding sense of humor.

Endnotes and References for this Feature[x:4]

Spiritual Transformation Moving from Self-conscious to God Conscious

Demonstrating God's Power to Heal a Broken World - A Testimonial to HH Baba Virsa Singh ji of Gobind Sadan, "God's House without Walls"

by Ralph Singh

The Guru can turn us into angels in the blink of an eye.
—Guru Nanak Dev ji

Baba Virsa Singh ji's life was dedicated to demonstrating God's power to heal a broken world. Tirelessly, he would plow the fields transforming barren land into productive crops to feed the poor, reclaiming lost souls and eradicating poverty in the process. He showed how to overcome religious hatred, brought peace to strife-torn areas of India by changing the terrorists' minds through his love, and guided his devotees to overcome hatred and transform the lives of the arsonists following the post 9-11 hate-inspired attack on Gobind Sadan, USA, North of Syracuse, NY, through his powerful message of forgiveness that still resonates today.

Most importantly, he showed that true social transformation grows out of our change of consciousness, and healing starts with spiritual vision. The ultimate move from "me to we" is when we recognize we are one with everything and everyone. Spiritual growth does not occur in a vacuum. As we grow in our love, the world around us is changed in the process.

While the human soul is thirsting, starving for spiritual sustenance, our minds are constantly bombarded by the external stimuli which leave us empty. The lack of spiritual practice has created a loneliness pandemic that's eroding the mental health of not just our children but adults around the world, as well, leading to increased drug use and suicide at truly frightening levels. While the cure is "free," we are so busy fulfilling our material desires, we lose sight of our spiritual needs.

To those of us fortunate enough to meet and serve a spiritual Master, we learn that all life is a spiritual quest. And this quest is fueled by love — by a longing to meet one's beloved which is so deep and so powerful that no worldly love or attachments can even come close. *Vairag* drives us beyond our worldly bonds. The desire to serve our spiritual master then translates into a commitment to serve humanity, the expression of God's love through his devotees.

There is something which we love even more than we can love ourselves — and which loves us, guides us, and empowers us in all aspects of our lives. For we are simply actors in the Divine Play of life — While we must quest — *He* ultimately finds us. He knows where we are, at all times of our lives, and when He is ready, He appears to us and calls us to Him.

> While the cure is "free" *Nam is the food for the soul*
> *— keep it close to your heart —*
> we are so busy fulfilling our material desires, we lose
> sight of our spiritual needs.

All Gurbani, revelations within Guru Granth Sahib, speaks about the core spiritual practice of reciting ***Nam, (God's holy name)***. Attuning our minds to the Voice of the Infinite and grounding us in the bedrock of God within us. As HH Baba Virsa Singh ji used to remind us constantly:

> *In this age of darkness — the one gift Guru Nanak brought to the world was NAM, God's Holy Name.*

And for this time, it is spoken *Ek Onkar Satnam Siri WaheGuru* (There is One God, whose Name is Truth, Praise the Ever Greater, Beyond Wondrous God) as Baba Virsa Singh ji received directly from Guru Nanak Dev ji and spent his entire life sharing with everyone who came to him in need.

Sometimes in endless song, as he would stand for hours singing with his devotees gathered around him, and sometimes in quiet lessons, he would simply say "repeat after me." But whichever way he transmitted Nam, that transcendent seed would grow within us, and link our consciousness to God — the ineffable — and expand our consciousness to accept the endless power that lies within.

Without Nam expanding our consciousness, experiencing the power of God would be overwhelming. Through Nam, our entire beings, from the circuitry of our minds to every chemical structure, are tuned to the frequency of God's order, and the resistance of our egos is melted away. As is said, "Every hair on our body reverberates in divine remembrance. With each breath let us recite His Holy Name, and all our cares melt away." So, it becomes the very rhythm of our lives. Waking or sleeping, it goes on continuously.

Babaji continually reminded us that God is closer than our very hands and feet — quoting the Gurus that the curtain that separates us from the spiritual dimension is "thinner than a butterfly's wing."

While sorting our way through the tests of the material world, we often take on more karmic debt. In meditation, we are clearing away the dirt from our past lives. Like cleaning the soot from an oil lamp reveals the light within, so meditation cleanses our minds and allows the light within us to shine. Then everywhere we go, we carry the light to brighten each encounter.

> *Oh my mind — you are the form of God's light — recognize your value / worth.*
> —Guru Nanak

The True Purpose of human life is devoted to finding God — the Ultimate Truth — *Koi jan har sio devai jor* "there must be someone in the world who can link me to God."

If during our lifetimes we are fortunate to find a Divine teacher, shouldn't we surrender everything in His service? After all, we compete to attend the best schools to learn from outstanding professors and practitioners, shouldn't we devote even more effort to finding one who can lead us to God?

Such was my life and my quest, that drew me from my Upper West side apartment outside Columbia's (University) back gates to the feet of HH Baba Virsa Singh ji in February 1971. I had never seen a Sikh, nor even knew that such a tradition as Sikhism existed. But in August of 1970, Baba ji appeared to me in Spiritual Form and literally drew me to His feet. It was as if the Voice which had been speaking to me since childhood suddenly manifested. I deferred my admission to graduate school, having been shown a higher path of "study" awaited, and took off on a quest following the Voice that called me.

It led me across Europe, through Turkey, Iran, and Afghanistan. Then across the Khyber into the subcontinent, the Voice calling loudly, "My son you'll be home in seven days," and ending in Amritsar, at the Golden Temple. This was my first encounter with Sikhs, but the one who was calling was not there.

Finally, I was led to Delhi where at last, in a compound behind a small village on the outskirts of Delhi, I was brought face-to-face with the one who had appeared to me in New York. His eyes lit up the room (as well as the heavens) with endless love. Dressed all in white, his turban framed his dark beard.

He welcomed me, though speaking no English, and addressed me through a translator, "You're a student; have you found God in your books yet?" then broke into his wonderful laugh. "Why do you think it should be so easy to find God, when it takes thirty to forty years to become a doctor, lawyer, or engineer? You should find God without any effort? Just as we have basics of our worldly studies, 'reading, writing, and arithmetic,' so, too, in God's school meditation is the basic lesson."

When I asked what he meant by meditation, Babaji replied: "This is God's school. You've come in search of God, and tomorrow God will come and take your final exam. You're way behind in your studies. Now repeat your first lesson: *Ek Onkar Satnam Siri WaheGuru.*"

"Go to your room and recite it like you're cramming for your final! And ask God, that you've come so far in search and please answer your prayer." So, I wrote these "foreign" words on a slip of paper and began reciting my lesson that would guide my whole life. And within a short time, those words which I'd never heard before, began to echo throughout my being. I couldn't sleep; I had lost my appetite; and I felt like I was three feet off the ground.

By the third day, waves of *Ek Onkar Satnam Siri WaheGuru* were pounding my mind into submission. Finally, the Voice within just said, "Why are you fighting? Just accept it." And as I did, my mind stilled into an ocean of endless peace. Nam was still echoing, but everywhere there was just peace.

When I returned to the compound that evening, I was met with a message, "Babaji is calling you." I rushed to the receiving room, and on seeing me, he simply looked over the heads of the group who were seeking his guidance, and said directly to me, "Now do you accept it or not — that God exists?" The exact words that had calmed my mind.

Then smiling, he asked, "Now what do you want?" I just laid out in front of him and asked, "I have no desire but to know what is God's order for me. You picked me up from New York, brought me here, and brought me face-to-face with God at age twenty-two."

I had realized the Power that was controlling my life, in fact all life, was sitting right in front of me! "All right; you can stay; and we'll teach you!!"

Babaji allowed me to serve him for six years in Gobind Sadan during the early phase of its development. He himself would be out plowing, saying, "A person who believed in God should work ten times harder." He felt people lost faith because those who represented God took money from the poor. I would move from early morning meditation and prayer, into the fields to work alongside the incredibly strong village farmers with Babaji often standing supervising the whole day. He once was known to stand for thirty-six hours to keep everyone's spirits up. After a long day cutting fodder by hand with a sickle, Babaji smiled at me and said, "After this, you'll never feel any job is too hard!" Throughout my life, he would call me back, or when he stayed with us on visits to the U.S., but His voice was my constant companion and guide. Everything was a lifelong lesson that work is just an extension of spiritual practice.

Besides Nam, *Jaap Sahib* of Guru Gobind Singh ji attuned my mind through its endless Praise of the One who is formless beyond any description — even beyond religion. Babaji would offer Jaap Sahib almost as a doctor issues a prescription, and everyone from around the world finds strength to overcome even the most difficult tests and challenges. Chanting its 199 verses surrounds us with a protective force field as it lifts our minds toward God. My dear wife, Joginder, who Babaji blessed with a gift of singing, leads the congregational chanting of Jaap Sahib whenever she's present. Guru Gobind Singh ji had declared, "'Recognize all people as one human race!"

Babaji says, "Jaap Sahib is a mighty ocean of God's grace and compassion. I encourage you to plunge into it and enjoy its bliss. You will emerge transformed and rejuvenated. Your anxieties, fears, and afflictions will drop away like dead leaves in autumn, replaced by fragrant spring breeze which will sweep through you, bringing the blossoms of strength, courage, and tranquility. With this transformation, you will find the worldly challenges and problems so puny that you will sail through them smoothly, successfully, and as if effortlessly, because God's grace and power will be operating through you. What is more, your spirit will be constantly soaring upwards toward its ultimate goal of union with God."

Despite the scientific advances and the advent of AI, the world today still needs to discover the Spiritual realm and turn inward for peace to dawn.

As Babaji would say, the darkness is just a background for the light to play upon. And the darker it becomes, the brighter the light will shine to lead people home. At an early interfaith Thanksgiving service in 1980 (Syracuse University, Hendrik's Chapel), everyone gathered at the end to sing God's praises. And God was so happy that the Vision was so powerful:

> Tell all those who have cursed their fate that they were born at this time, that they will live to thank God that they were born at this time.

And I know the more we celebrate the Transcendent 1 — that peace will emerge. May it be so!!

Additional Resources for this Feature[x:5]

The History Leading to an Integral Approach to Theology

And a Challenging Proposal for the Future of Spirituality

by Doug King

Like so many others who are contributing to this Volume, my journey has taken many twists and turns. It began in the late 60s with my father, the most unlikely person to begin the journey. Max R. King grew up on a farm in the hills of West Virginia. He and his three siblings were born in the same farmhouse, which was definitely off the grid. He was that guy who actually did homework by a kerosene lamp and walked a mile or so down the mountain to catch the school bus to a one-room schoolhouse.

He did well in school, becoming one of the first in the family to graduate from high school. He was president of the local chapter of the Future Farmers of America and even won a state essay contest, earning him and his teacher a trip to the national convention in Kansas City. The convention featured all of the amazing farming technology under development, but his greatest memory was an encounter with J. C. Penny on his farm outside Kansas City. There's no time here to share the complete anecdote, but Penny did prank my father into opening a newly developed electric fence. It was truly a shocking experience that left Penny laughing at Dad's expense!

Even though he went to work for Wetzel County after graduation, he continued to use his speaking talent on Sundays at small country churches that couldn't afford a pastor. And as a result of his love for nature, he began to raise questions in his mind about all of the apocalyptic interpretations of the Biblical narrative. He couldn't understand why God would want to destroy such beauty.

These life experiences led him to leave government work and become a full-time pastor / preacher. To use the language of Spiral Dynamics, he was moving from a Blue Traditional worldview into an Orange Modern worldview. When theology is interpreted through the Blue Traditional lens, it is simply passed down from generation to generation. One did not question long-held interpretations. But Max King began to question, and his questioning was followed by deconstructing previously held doctrinal positions of his denomination with regard to the subject of eschatology. His work was immediately categorized as heresy.

His last writings moved into the Green Postmodern space of inclusivity. His last two books, *The Cross and the Parousia of Christ* and *Irrevocable* represented a proposal for nothing less than a paradigm change in the interpretation of Christology. Rather than following the traditional interpretations of Christology as a religion, he proposed Christology as *movement* from a paradigm of religious doing / law / dogma to a paradigm of universal being. The setting for Christology was the first century, wherein came its completed role and function. The radical consequences of this approach meant that Christology wasn't meant to be carried through history as a particular religion (Christianity), nor was the function of the church to continue as an ongoing institution. Rather, Christology was a *movement* revealing the universal Spiritual identity of all humans.

Although he never knew anything about integral theory or Spiral Dynamics, his theology was following a trajectory moving from ethnocentric to world-centric in terms of spiritual identity. Those who were following his work were looking for a post-Christian, trans-religious path. As the audience for his work grew, we formed a nonprofit *presence.tv*.

My journey began with a dual degree in Theology and Biblical Languages from a fundamentalist college. I intended to go on for a PhD in theology and began study in a Master of Divinity program. However, it soon became apparent to the Administration that I was following the same theological path as my father, and they took away my scholarship. At that time, I didn't know which direction to take. It was a very difficult period of my life.

Eventually, I took a job in the fast-growing telecom industry and found some surprising success. In fact, I became part of a start-up in 1989 and became president of that company for 20 years. However, my involvement in Presence and theological studies never ceased during that time. When our company was sold in 2009, I then joined Presence full-time. I had been introduced to Spiral Dynamics and Integral Theory around 1999.

I took the principles of evolutionary growth and worldviews and began to apply them to the trajectory I was seeing in the Biblical Narrative.

In that sense, I began to take the theological principles from my father's work and expand them in a cross-disciplinary approach. I initially used the Spiral and stages of growth as outlined by many others in the field of integral consciousness. I began podcasting and videocasting, as well as speaking at various venues. The next step in my work came as a result of an invitation to join Evolutionary Leaders (evolutionaryleaders.net).

In addition to the historical and philosophical models in the integral arena, I became acquainted with the holomovement concept of science. The ideas of David Bohm regarding implicate and explicate orders flowed nicely into my work in Biblical Cosmology. I then produced theological material comparing the function of the holomovement in our universe with the function of Christology in Biblical Cosmology. This approach further reinforced our proposal for a radical paradigm shift. We continued to challenge the long-held interpretation of Christology as a religion or institutional form. We proposed a trajectory instead of form, transform, and formlessness.

The result is a new way of seeing the narrative or story of God and humanity beyond religion. These new cross-disciplinary principles transform the Biblical Narrative from a story whose outcome is the conflicting, fixed-identity, silos of the religion of the past to the story of the evolution of spiritual consciousness with regard to *universal* God identity.

There is obviously so much more to say, but this brief overview of the approach taken by Presence illustrates why a new audience of followers is emerging. The growth of the Spiritual but not Religious (SBNR) and the non-affiliated (NONES) points to new directions of understanding. At the same time, the world's most read wisdom narrative is finding new fertile ground by applying a new lens that goes beyond 2,000 years of traditional interpretations. Our tag line is "A Global Conversation For a New Earth." And our work is built on all that came before — even from the most unlikely places.

Edgar Mitchell, Willis Harman, and the Noetic Roots of an Interspiritual Future

by Claudia Welss

If Interspirituality is a movement toward a shared mystical core beyond doctrine and dogma, then certain pioneers can be seen not only as visionaries but also as early emissaries of a spiritual commons. Among these are Apollo 14 astronaut Edgar Mitchell and Stanford futurist Willis Harman — not only for their individual achievements in space exploration and social innovation, but also for their combined effort to birth a science of inner knowing: the noetic sciences. Together, they planted institutional, intellectual, and experiential seeds for a future in which science and spirituality might no longer be in opposition, but allies in a new human paradigm.

Mitchell, the sixth man to walk on the Moon, experienced a life-changing epiphany on his return, later known as the Overview Effect. Gazing at Earth suspended in the vastness of space, he felt a visceral, ecstatic sense of unity with the cosmos — an unshakable knowing that he and everything else was part of a single living, evolving system. Rather than intellectual, it was an experience of direct knowing. Later, he would learn that this state mirrored descriptions from the world's mystical traditions: a dissolution of the separate self, accompanied by feelings of awe and unconditional love.

This experience became the genesis of the Institute of Noetic Sciences (IONS), which Mitchell founded in 1973. His intention was to investigate scientifically what mystics had long described: that consciousness is not confined to the brain, is nonlocal, and is fundamental to the true nature of reality. In this way, Mitchell advanced the heart of Interspirituality — not focusing on any one tradition, using the tools of science to validate their shared truths and thereby dissolve the boundaries between science and spirituality.

Willis Harman, who served as IONS' foundational president until 1997, also embodied this integrative vision. A systems scientist, futurist, and Stanford professor, Harman had previously led social policy research at SRI International, where he explored the future of humanity under conditions of rapid technological and social change. Like Mitchell, Harman believed that no amount of external innovation could solve humanity's challenges without a fundamental shift in human consciousness. The deepest crisis was not economic, ecological, or political, but epistemological, manifesting as a narrow materialist worldview shaping modern civilization.

His legacy was calling for a Global Mind Change — with subjective inner knowing valued alongside objective observation, and humanity's spiritual potential regarded not with skepticism but as a legitimate frontier of scientific inquiry. At IONS, he championed a "gentle revolution" toward a science that could hold noetic insight, psychic phenomena, alternative healing, intuition, and altered states — not as anomalies to ignore, but as windows into the fuller nature of consciousness.

IONS took on rigorous studies of meditation, intentionality, mind-matter interaction, and spontaneous healing long before such topics were considered worthy of mainstream investigation. It soon earned a reputation as a safe, credible space for notable scientists to study what they couldn't explore elsewhere. Like Interspirituality, IONS stood for openness and dialogue across boundaries — between academic disciplines, cultural traditions, and spiritual ways of knowing.

Both Mitchell and Harman were influenced by mystical and interspiritual traditions. Mitchell explored Vedanta, Taoism, and Indigenous wisdom, seeking resonance between ancient cosmologies and quantum physics. Harman drew inspiration from Sufi teachings, Christian mysticism, and the perennial philosophy. They understood that the transformative experience of unity at the heart of all authentic spiritual paths was well within the reach of scientific understanding when approached with appropriate humility. In this way, the rise of Interspirituality grew from the seeds they planted.

Today, the relevance of their work is only deepening as their legacy lives on in a new generation of noetic pioneers — researchers, activists, and experiencers — dedicated to this gentle revolution. Mitchell and Harman saw the systems breakdown we are currently facing fifty years ago. But they also saw the possibility of breakthrough. Their example offers both guidance and optimism for evolving into the next level of human maturity — one capable of recognizing our oneness with all life and becoming coherent co-creators with it.

As scientists of the sacred who dared to explore the essential relationship between outer space but the vast interior cosmos of the human spirit, Edgar Mitchell and Willis Harman — and the Institute of Noetic Sciences — can rightly be called interspiritual pioneers.

Love: Our Evolutionary Imperative

Honoring David Loye's Scientific Legacy of Moral Transformation in a Time of Global Crisis

by Galia Benartzi, Riane Eisler and Kurt Johnson

A Turning Point in Human History

As our world convulses with war, ecological collapse, and rising authoritarianism, the question is no longer whether our systems are broken. It is whether we can evolve — ethically, emotionally, collectively — in time to survive them. In this liminal hour, we must ask not just what is to be done, but who are we, really?

David Loye spent his life answering that question. He saw that beneath the machinery of modern collapse lies a deeper malfunction: a false story of human nature. And he spent over four decades retrieving its forgotten alternative — not from myth, but from science. In David's work, love is not sentiment, but biology. Moral sensitivity is not weakness, but evolution's gift. And cooperation is not utopian fantasy, but our species' deepest instinct — and mandate — for survival.

He did not live to see the world heed this truth. But we write now so that it may.

Reclaiming Darwin's Lost Legacy

At the heart of David Loye's life's work was an astonishing recovery: that Charles Darwin, long invoked as champion of cutthroat competition, actually believed love and moral development to be evolution's highest goals. In *The Descent of Man*, Darwin used the word "love" 95 times, "moral" 92 times, and "survival of the fittest" only twice, and one of those in doubt.[1]

Loye painstakingly traced how these humanistic insights were erased by later theorists who aligned with empire, industry, and domination.[2] In place of Darwin's moral compass, a different myth took root — one in which evolution meant "red in tooth and claw," progress required conquest, and human beings were defined by selfishness.

Correcting that error was not just a scholarly task. It was, for Loye, a civilizational emergency. "If we tell ourselves the wrong story about our nature," he warned, "we build the wrong world [to nurture it]."

Changing the Story of Who We Are

Loye understood that culture is built on narrative, and that the story we tell about human nature determines everything from how we raise children to how we wage war. He wrote to replace the myth of separation, scarcity, and domination with a science-backed story of partnership, empathy, and evolutionary love as key to long-term survival.

This wasn't wishful thinking. It was grounded in neuroscience, systems theory, chaos dynamics, and the biology of cooperation. Loye's insights echo those of Riane Eisler, whose partnership-dominator social scale maps the structures that either nourish or suppress moral sensitivity.[3]

Today, biologists like David Sloan Wilson,[4] theorists like co-author Kurt Johnson,[5] and interdisciplinary leaders around the world affirm that "the best cooperator" — not the fiercest competitor — is evolution's new hero. Loye saw it coming long before the data caught up.

He asked us to imagine: what if we built our future on that truth?

David Loye as Scientist, Visionary, and Mentor

A lifelong integrator, David Loye was not only an evolutionary theorist. He was a journalist, policy analyst, political psychologist, poet, and author of over thirty books ranging from *The Healing of a Nation* to *The Sphinx and the Rainbow*. He studied the impact of media violence, modeled the dynamics of moral development through chaos theory, and co-founded the General Evolution Research Group with Ervin Laszlo.[6]

Yet, he also wrote children's books and love poems. He lived what he taught: that full human flourishing requires both intellect and emotion, science and spirit. His 45-year partnership with his beloved wife, co-author Riane Eisler, was itself a living embodiment of the evolutionary ethos he championed.

To many, he was also a mentor — generous with time, encouragement, and connection. He built communities, launched journals, and opened doors. He was a visionary in every sense: someone who lived in devotion to humanity's next great leap.

Crisis He Saw — and We Are Now In

What David Loye foresaw is no longer theoretical. The dominator systems he warned of — militarism, patriarchy, extractive capitalism, social Darwinism — are now tearing at the seams of human civilization. The empathy gap is widening. The story of separation has gone viral.

Loye's writings, some of them decades old, describe with uncanny accuracy the moral and ecological disintegration we now face. Yet, he never surrendered to despair. He believed that humanity was in a transitional crunch — a phase between breakdown and breakthrough — and that our survival would depend on our ability to recover what he called our moral sensitivity.

In today's crises, his voice is not only relevant — it is necessary. Rather than break, we need not only to bend, but also to bow — in reverence to each other and to all that is.

Religion, the Grand Sounding, and the Evolutionary Sacred

David Loye saw religion not as enemy to science, but as its forgotten twin. In his later writings, he called for what he termed the "Grand Sounding" — a convergence of science, ethics, and spirituality that could guide humanity through its current moral emergency.

He critiqued the way organized religion, especially when aligned with domination systems, too often became a vehicle for patriarchy, nationalism, violence and repression. But he also believed that the world's wisdom traditions held deep evolutionary truths — especially in their emphasis on love, compassion, and justice.

The Grand Sounding was his name for an evolutionary spirituality rooted not in hierarchy, but in partnership; not in fear, but in moral imagination. It invited all people — believers, scientists, secularists, seekers — to co-create a new covenant with life, built not on creed, but on conscience.

In a time of rising theocracy and moral confusion, David's call still rings out: to reclaim the sacred as a force for moral evolution, and to sound it — not with trumpets of conquest, but with the resonance of truth, empathy, and joy.

Love as Biological and Civilizational Mandate

In David Loye's vision, love is not an abstraction. It is a biological design — a scaffold for the moral development of both individuals and societies. It is the connective tissue of our species: from parent to child, partner to partner, citizen to citizen.

He called on scientists, educators, and policymakers to build with this in mind. He worked with the Montessori Foundation, whose 22,000+ schools globally now integrate partnership values.[7] His influence extends to healthcare, public policy, peacebuilding, and trauma healing — fields now recognizing what he declared long ago: *that empathy is infrastructure.*

For Loye, evolution was not finished. It was waiting on us, and within us.

Closing: Let This Be the Time

There are many ways to honor a legacy. Many beautiful pieces honor David Loye with essays, testimonials, and the voices of those he inspired. But he would have wanted more. He would have wanted us to rewrite the story. To teach children that love is strength. To lead with moral imagination. To build systems aligned with our deepest evolutionary truths.

He saw the species we could still become. Let this be the time we become it.

Endnotes for this Feature[x:6]

Rev. Diane Berke and a Posse of Like-hearted Souls

by Leslie Reambeault and Melissa Stewart

[Selected here from Volume 3 of these Volumes' "Interspirituality — In and Out of the Classroom" by Leslie Reambeault and Melissa Stewart, a detailed Feature on multicultural community and the exemplar of One Spirit Interfaith Seminary]

In July 2023, we, Leslie and Melissa, began our tenure as Co-Directors of the current iteration of the One Spirit Seminary. After traveling circuitous paths, we each found our way to One Spirit where we have reaped the treasures of both its overt and "deeper" curriculums developed and nurtured by Rev. Diane Berke and a posse of like-hearted souls who are our spiritual elders and revered ancestors.

The work we do expands outward through the evolving framework of Interspirituality, supporting and requiring as essential that we engage with and reimagine all Seminary activities as anti-oppressive. This requires that we acknowledge the various influences of our social identities and our personal histories as well as the dominant culture of Whiteness / White Supremacy on our interpersonal, educational, professional, and religious / spiritual experiences and perspectives… to the understanding that we are all One, that there is no support for stratification by age, class, race, cultural or ethnic heritage, geographic location, religion, sexual orientation, gender identity, ability, neurodiversity, or other discriminators. In aspects of our social identity, particularly that we are both dis-gendered and white-bodied, we are privileged and still have places of deep unawareness. We learn from our colleagues and students who teach us, for example, where we have ableist expectations.

…We are sensing into and becoming increasingly aware of a world-wide palpable Interspirituality that informs those of us who imagine that there is a sane and spiritual way to move through these times of climate catastrophe, sociopolitical upheaval, and transition. …Our work is both visionary and filled with minute details. Collaboration, embodied relationship, and responsiveness to the demands of the moment, both within and outside of the Seminary, are cornerstones of an Interspiritual way of teaching, learning, and living. From an interspiritual perspective, all of life is inextricably interdependent and interconnected. It informs all else and provides direction for what we do and, more to the point, how we do it. Interspirituality is both ancient and newly emerging. It promotes deep reverence for the history and cultures that have gifted the world with so many meaningful spiritual practices. The interspiritual perspective encourages sincere, non-appropriative spiritual exploration and makes room for a reimagining of spiritual experience in *this* time and place. It does not ever authorize the misuse or exploitation of spiritual practices and traditions for personal or organizational gain.

…The interspiritual paradigm births a truly collaborative form of co-leadership that requires patience and emotional honesty, grounded in spiritual practice and deep inner work. …. Listening for another person's sacred truth is a core aspect of interspiritual ministry. In support of this, we have intentionally engaged in what has become a "living laboratory" for the co-creation of the interspiritual space that we are both remembering and dreaming into being for and with our colleagues and students. We experience Interspirituality as embodied. Embodiment asks for an exquisite self-perception that is other than recognizing our thoughts and beliefs.

…The interspiritual paradigm births a truly collaborative form of co-leadership that requires patience and emotional honesty, grounded in spiritual practice and deep inner work. As co-directors, we have embraced a "shared lift." … an example of … the evolution of a responsive curriculum, the development of a reinvigorated Seminary culture…the active engagement of students and administrators of the One Spirit Interfaith Seminary.

Endnotes and References for "Interspiritual Pioneers" Section[x]

ON THE GLOBAL CHALLENGE

Robert Atkinson - Richard Bowell - Emanuel Kuntzelman - A. K. Merchant - Deborah Moldow - Elena Mustakova - Nicholas Vesey

Each of the Featured Authors below brings a leadership background with a major global constituency contributing significantly to the growing landscape of worldwide transformational change. Richard Bowell combines decades-long contributions to dharma and awakening teachings with multiple books centering on spiritual dimensions of transformational change, especially regarding the United Nations' Sustainable Development Goals and Conscious World Citizens. Emanuel Kuntzelman, with his partner Laura Rose and a global community, is co-visioneer of the burgeoning Holomovement, whose vision of joining cosmic implicate and explicate order, from famed physicist David Bohm (also reviewed above in the Feature by integral theologian Doug King) has launched a formidable — and much needed — new movement for transformational change. Dr. A. K. Merchant is a fixture in the interfaith history of Asia, indeed the world, and is head of the Baha'i Foundation of India. Rev. Deborah Moldow is Director of the Evolutionary Leaders Circle, an initiative of the Source of Synergy Foundation, joining nearly 500 influential thought leaders in both vision and action. Their members include dozens of the Featured Authors to these Volumes. Rev. Nicholas Vesey is Rector of the iconic Aspen Chapel in Aspen, Colorado, famous for the programs of its Wisdom School. Join them below for their Reflections on the Global Challenge. The section closes with a Reflection by Drs. Elena Mustakova and Robert Atkinson from their recent award-winning books on peace and global healing.

It's All Connected: The Science and Spirit of Oneness

by Emanuel Kuntzelman

Our Ancestors and Universal Experience have always known it to be true, and now science confirms: Everything is connected. It's a bold statement juxtaposing a definition of Oneness with our current planetary crisis of polarization. If this is indeed our true definition of our Cosmos, how can we recover the thread of our interconnectedness? Where is the common ground that we can return to as a global family?

To find our shared essence of both the physical and spiritual world, we must start at the beginning — in Source. There are infinite names and definitions used for this primordial starting point. American physicist David Bohm, a contemporary of Einstein, described it as an ontological pilot wave giving rise to a living, interconnected universe defined as the "holomovement."[1]

Bohm believed there is an Implicate Order, which is the source of consciousness and the field holding the infinite potential of the universe. The Implicate Order, via the holomovement, expands and grows into the Explicate Order as manifest reality. It's an unbroken wholeness, the unbounded consciousness of the universe, and the holomovement is what ties it together. This theory offers an explanation of how we can all be One despite what appears to be a reality of separate beings.

Bohm's theory of quantum mechanics, first proposed back in 1951, has since been vindicated by the Nobel prize in physics of 2022. The award establishes non-locality, which Bohmian mechanics requires, as a fundamental feature of the universe. It further validates this concept of universal Oneness, bridging ancient spiritual wisdom with modern science and offers a sociological model for uniting humanity in our many pathways toward higher consciousness.

For most of us, this theory is nearly impossible to comprehend intellectually, yet we inherently sense that everything is interconnected. Within the holomovement's "wholeness-in-motion," our many spiritual and material manifestations, in all its rich diversity, comes from the same Source.

In the beginning, there were not simply elementary particles bumping around like billiard balls, but rather an initial primordial vibration. Something in the depths of the infinity of the Cosmos sent out a wave, the Source of all, that has carried us through both physical and cultural evolution in its undulating flow. In the flow of the holomovement, the Big Breath of the Implicate Order *unfolds* into materialism (Explicate Order). However, in Bohm's theory, not everything was left to chance.

He proposed that an ontological pilot wave giving rise to the universe begins as deterministic but also allows for free will, a concept known as "compatibilism," allowing the two seemingly opposed concepts to intertwine. Thus, we venture to say that the Implicate Order coded the universe with a general plan, one that sometimes tends to meander as much as it progresses.

The process of creating our human civilization follows the same unfolding process that produced the physical nature of the universe. Just as the universe erupted into supernova explosions and convulsed into black holes in the process of creating our universe, the unfolding of human civilization mirrors this bumpy and dramatic ride into the Explicate Order of now. Humanity's own evolution follows similar peaks and troughs emitted from that first primordial vibration of our ontological pilot wave. We could even say that in our current moment in human history we've swerved off our evolutionary course as materialism overpowers the free will of human consciousness.

This downward trajectory of the wave is represented in most religious and spiritual stories as a fall from grace, the declaration that we're all born sinners, that life is suffering, that we've strayed from God, Allah, right livelihood and so on. This separation complex we all suffer within the human psyche is because of the nature of the wave. It is the flow of the descending wave pattern that makes us think we have "fallen from grace." Allowing our spiritual nature to be intoxicated by materiality and fear, we move deeper into our evolutionary wave trough. The temptations of materialism are many, and it is this downward flow of our evolutionary wave that has given rise to the divisiveness among so many religious and cultural beliefs.

Gurdjieff described the difficulties of passing through intervals. This is especially true when it is a great turning, when the large-scale process needs to reverse direction. That is the case now. We are nearing a stagnation and breakdown of civilization, requiring a new way forward, based on unifying principles, to build collective momentum and ascend to higher consciousness.

In attempting to take on this singular challenge, however, we do need some pilot wave orientation of our own, ignited by peace and love and manifested in purposeful social action. Despite the illusion that we are all separate, the Implicate Order is wholeness, and there is an attraction to bring us back to wholeness, or a "holotropic attractor."

It is what creates order when chaos is involved, the impetus to lead civilization out of chaos and back to our natural state of harmony.

Cosmologically, psycho-spiritually, and sociologically, the holomovement is quite literally a movement of the whole toward truth, beauty, and goodness. Our earliest ancestors, with their close connection to the natural and spiritual world, understood the essence of unitive consciousness, based upon a purposeful universe. Now is the time to merge the understandings of our wisdom traditions with our knowledge of quantum reality such as proposed by David Bohm, and fuse it into a worldwide movement for social renewal.

Perhaps as we are nearing the bottom of our evolutionary wave, we instinctively understand the urgency of weaving our many interspiritual pathways into a collective ascent back to wholeness. We are beginning to recognize the call to serve in healing humanity and facilitate its transformation into a higher level of consciousness. The holomovement, along with acting as the cosmic flow of the quantum field of existence, also represents the sociological phenomenon that heralds the convergence of individuals, organizations, and movements around the globe into a worldwide movement, one being called the Holomovement (with a capital "H").

The Holomovement, a social movement awakening our interconnectedness and inspired by Bohm's holomovement, recognizes this diversity and asks for all to heed the call — back to the cooperative, loving and altruistic nature of the human spirit. It is a call to unity, but not uniformity. Just as the call for honoring an interspiritual experience is vital for our global family to thrive and evolve, it is imperative that we form and nurture relationships across all divides and belief systems if we are to rediscover our collective sense of purpose and spiritual potential.

Love and compassion are not finite resources. In fact, the more we connect with others through goodwill, compassion, joy, and curiosity, the more abundant these qualities become. And just as there seems to be a universal story describing our fall from Source, there, too, is a powerful vision for a collective journey toward ascension. It's a beautiful, universal through-line we share within so many diverse spiritual pathways.

It is an act of surrender to open to the field of higher consciousness in how we can each be of service, beyond material wealth or achievement. The more we are willing to surrender to the good of the whole, the more enhanced our individual consciousness becomes. In the same way Bohm described the Implicate and Explicate Orders moving in an unbroken whole, each of us are entwined as co-creators within our evolutionary flow. We must move beyond the transactional nature of relationships and embody the transformative power of deep, interspiritual connection.

The good news is that the holomovement is endemic to everything we do. It is consciousness flowing in the universe, through us and the manifestations of our souls. Thankfully, we don't have to "find it" but rather slow down and drop into a mindful place of deep knowing and feel the force of love that weaves our humanity together.

Just as a rising tide lifts all boats, the upward flow of the entrained frequency of our ever-higher states of consciousness leads us to an ascendancy of spirit over materialism. All religions, all creeds and cultures, merge like streams into the oneness of the Holomovement. This holotropic attractor calls us back to the original unity from whence we came, forming an energetic wave that propels us upward. It reveals to us the interconnectedness of all that exists and ushers in a new era of human understanding and interspiritual harmony. It fuses science and spirit into the grand unified field. It is our destiny to all meet there together as one.

Humanity in Transition: The Emerging Global Spirituality

by Deborah Moldow

If we were to take the spiritual pulse of our planet in 2024, we would diagnose a world in transition. For the past 3,000 years, many places on Earth have been aligned with the major religious groups: Christianity, Islam, Buddhism, Hinduism, the smaller religious groups such as Judaism, Jainism, Paganism, Sikhism, etc., and the traditional animist beliefs still prevalent among Indigenous Peoples, often in remote areas.

But the emergence of a globally-connected society linked by rapid communication and travel, along with international commerce, has given rise to something new: a growing recognition of the spirituality that is common to all faiths and the values that so many share. This phenomenon, coined Interspirituality by Br. Wayne Teasdale in the 1990s, is an outgrowth of all of the above, plus the interfaith movement that arose during the late twentieth century. In the United States, a country committed by law to pluralism, interfaith services became the norm in times of national tragedy — sadly correlated to the rise of mass shootings in schools and houses of worship.

Another pertinent trend has been the so-called "woke" culture of the early twenty-first century, where it became unacceptable to use discriminatory language on campuses or in public discourse. Women gained equality in the workplace, the unfinished business of the Civil Rights Movement expanded into Black Lives Matter, and gay marriage was widely normalized, just as those with non-binary gender identifications began to demand rights, too. It seemed that society, at least to some measure, had moved on from overcoming religious prejudice to a more expansive view of equal rights for all.

Yet this growth of acceptance of differing views did not come without a price. Just at the time when it looked as though a more liberal approach was gaining traction, the political right began to rise across the U.S. and Europe, evidenced by the election of right-wing leaders with strong nationalist leanings and populist demonstrations. This pushback could be seen as an expected result when a society is embracing change at a pace that is too rapid for the population.

Many who embrace a right-wing political worldview also cling to fundamentalist views of their own religions, sometimes to the point of embracing violent suppression of other beliefs. At the same time, others have joined the "nones," who identify with no religion and consider atheism to be most consistent with modern science — even though the latest discoveries in quantum physics are more closely aligned with the ways in which mystics see the world.

And so, while it appears that the interspiritual movement is no longer progressing, it is more likely that the opposite is true and that those surfing its wave must wait for this rather new stage in the evolution of consciousness to catch on gradually. My belief is that it cannot be stopped.

In an increasingly globalized world, the commonality of human experience cannot be denied, including a pervading sense that there is more meaning to our existence than what can be perceived through our ordinary senses. We are becoming more and more aware of the harm we are doing to nature and the rise of an overload of information that accompanies significant screen time. The decline in attendance at churches and other houses of worship, along with a freedom of opportunity and movement that has fractured the traditional extended family unit, is contemporaneous with an upswing in depression, isolation, and general malaise or even despair.

This naturally fuels the flames of political unrest as ambitious politicians seek to scapegoat marginalized groups. In a time of increased global south to north migration, which is only likely to worsen as the effects of climate change inflict ever greater impact on the global south, there will always be desperate, impoverished people of different cultures upon whom to cast blame.

The good news is that as much as this darkness is rising, the light is rising up to meet it across the globe. The characteristics of the emerging global spirituality include a wide range of values that point toward our Oneness, as expressed through such principles as nonviolence, compassion, tolerance and the dignity of each human being. Although slavery was eradicated by law in most countries centuries ago, economic inequality has increased, with a handful of billionaires holding as much individual wealth as most countries. The wealthy are still held in high regard among the masses, whether they come from the business world, sports, or entertainment. Yet it is Bill Gates himself, near the top of the global wealth pyramid, who has been known to say, "I believe that every life is of equal value." This in itself is revolutionary — or perhaps better described as evolutionary.

And this points to a very dramatic shift in views on war. In an attitude of blame and judgment coupled with righteous superiority, conflict can easily escalate into violence. But in a community that takes responsibility not only for its actions but for its circumstances as well, there is much greater willingness to sit down with people of differing views with respect to arrive at mutually beneficial solutions, however challenging the situation may be. With this mindset, war is as criminal as murder and cannot be justified without a clear case of self-defense.

It is interesting to note that during the time when most people on the planet identified strongly with one of the major religions, there was constant warfare. Many armed conflicts were the result of animosities between people of different faiths. In the emerging Interspiritual Age, war is only a last resort, and the use of nuclear weapons capable of annihilating all life on Earth is completely unthinkable.

New threats are appearing on the horizon in this transitional time before humanity has reached a point where we can face them together. Climate change can no longer be denied, even if the term "global warming" is still not acceptable, and while the wealthier nations are still not prepared to make the most meaningful investments of funds and changes in their reliance on fossil fuels, the prospects ahead are dire indeed. While we humans are naturally most concerned with how extreme weather may affect our own families, homes, and communities, we are more informed than ever about natural tragedies affecting others across the globe. We are more likely to respond as one human family as the values of Oneness and compassion take hold.

Artificial Intelligence, or AI, is also looked upon as a looming threat, as it becomes more and more challenging to attribute any information to its original source. We are inundated daily by "fake news" and reports that cannot be confirmed. AI appears to have limitless capabilities to infiltrate information systems and wreak chaos accordingly — and yet it will also be able to solve heretofore intractable mysteries, particularly in the field of medicine and other sciences. Who will reign in this beast and direct it toward the greater good? We can only hope that it will be people of the highest values.

And what of the possibility that we will at long last find proof of intelligent life beyond our planet? If beings from outside our solar system have the technologies to pay us a visit, it would be of the utmost importance that they be greeted as friends and brothers rather than hostile invaders! If such entities exist, perhaps they are waiting for us to give up our ways of war before they approach us in friendship, maybe even with solutions to some of our present problems.

At present, however, we need to find our own way forward, and this is taking place in many ways. Human ingenuity continues to seek answers to such thorny issues as how to clean up our polluted waterways, how to grow healthy food without relying on chemicals, how to transition to new sources of electrical power, and how to re-vision so many of our obsolete systems of education, finance, governance, health care, and many more. The approaching crises can be powerful motivators, and it would clearly be preferable to walk through the challenging times ahead as one human family. This will require innovative new ways of working together, rather than relying on the old model of individual achievement leading the way. We need leaders, but of a new kind: leaders whose success depends on their ability to empower others. These are evolutionary leaders, forging a path to a different kind of future based on our interdependence.

Evolutionary leaders look to nature for guidance, understanding that her systems are mutually supportive so that many diverse life forms can co-exist in harmony and sustainability. They understand that the modern world is seriously in need of balance between the masculine and the feminine, the powerful and the disenfranchised, the mind and the heart. In this way, domination becomes a way of the past, with each individual finding his/her purpose within the pathway to the greater good. Spiritual leaders will arise, not out of the study of dogma, but from their experience of a greater power that moves them to listen to the voice within that can help each one to find their way as a light that adds to the rainbow tapestry of humanity's will to good.

These new leaders are finding one another across the globe through the internet and social media. They are building new forms of partnerships and learning to co-create in teams where every member has a chance to shine. They are not motivated by the glories of personal achievement as much as by finding ways to make their personal contribution to the beauty of what is emerging. These are the visionaries helping to birth the new Interspiritual Age.

No, we do not wish to go back in time. Yet, we do wish to honor the wisdom of the people who have kept alive their native traditions that showed them how to live in sacred reciprocity with the Earth and its abundant life. We need to approach the wisdom of our faith traditions with the humble eyes of seekers, instead of the arrogance of those who think they have the only way. We need to open our minds to new possibilities that may be radically different from the habits to which we are accustomed, especially learning from the young people who will lead the way.

And most of all, we need to learn to love — to love ourselves, to love one another, to love the Earth, to love life with all its joys and sorrows. This love transcends our preferences for comfort and safety and instead prioritizes a radical new culture where every child is as precious as our own and every adult is a vital component of a vast living wholeness. This is the love that can finally unite all peoples in a thriving, abundant culture of peace.

True Happiness Is Linked to Divine Purpose & Selfless Service[1]

by A. K. Merchant

Reviewing the latest World Happiness Report 2025, it was quite enlightening how cultural and social elements shape perceptions of happiness and well-being. Living in times of great uncertainty and turmoil, how can every individual ensure healthy relationships and a sense of purpose? India ranked 118th in the list of 147 countries. India's ranking reflects both strengths and challenges. The country scored well in social support due to strong family structures and community bonds but ranked lower in perceived freedom, indicating limited individual choice satisfaction.

Commissioned by the United Nations, the data is collected by Gallup, and analysis is conducted by the Wellbeing Research Centre at Oxford University. The top countries have not changed significantly from last year: the happiest people still live in Northern Europe. Finland has held the top spot for eight years in a row. It is followed by Denmark, Iceland, Sweden, and the Netherlands. Interestingly, Mexico and Costa Rica have made it into the top ten.

Contrasting the UN commissioned report with Ipsos Global Happiness Survey suggests a different perspective, ranking India as the happiest country in the world with 88 percent of Indians reporting they are happy. Such an anomaly highlights how different methodologies can yield varying results. For the uninformed, let me explain. The Ipsos Global Happiness Survey is an annual study conducted by the French research firm Ipsos. It gathers responses from thousands of people across multiple countries to assess global happiness trends. The survey typically explores factors such as personal well-being, financial security, social relationships, and life satisfaction.

In the 2025 edition, Ipsos surveyed nearly 24,000 adults across 30 countries between December 2024 and January 2025. The results often differ from other happiness rankings, as Ipsos focuses on self-reported happiness rather than broader economic or social indicators such as caring, sharing, and social connections, selfless service, kindness, and community-building.

Although resources are important, happiness is not dependent on how much wealth a person has. The survey shows that well-being is heavily influenced by people's perception of kindness from those around them and the actual benevolence they experience. This is amply confirmed by what different religions have to say about true happiness. Since humans are a gregarious species, social connections play a crucial role. For example, research shows that people who live alone and rarely share meals with others feel significantly less happy. However, this trend has a limit; when more than four people live in the same household, happiness levels begin to decline. To assess kindness, people from different countries were surveyed about how often they engage in charity, volunteer work, or helping strangers. The top rankings in different categories went to relatively less wealthy countries: Jamaica (helping strangers) and Indonesia (charity and volunteering).

No research or survey can capture the full spectrum of the complexity inherent in human society. Researchers of the Happiness Index analyze six key variables: GDP per capita, social support, expected healthy life expectancy, freedom to make life choices, generosity, and perception of corruption. How accurate the methodology is can be debated. There are indications that not everyone is truly happy in the top ten countries. Cultural differences can also distort the results of the research. Different cultures interpret the concept of "best possible life" in different ways, which affects their ratings. In some countries, happiness is closely linked to personal success and achievements. In other cultures, people tend to underrate their own happiness if those around them are also unhappy.

Studies suggest that belief and association with religion or *dharma* can enhance happiness. Different faiths offer unique perspectives on happiness, often blending spiritual fulfillment with ethical living. Here are some insights:

- **Christianity**: Happiness is often linked to faith in God, love, and service to others. The teachings of Jesus emphasize joy through compassion and righteousness.
- **Islam**: True happiness comes from submission to God *(Allah*) and living a life of balance, gratitude, and moral integrity.
- **Hinduism**: Happiness is tied to *dharma* (duty), *karma* (actions), and *moksha* (liberation). Spiritual growth and self-realization lead to lasting joy.
- **Buddhism**: Happiness is found by overcoming suffering through mindfulness, compassion, and the Eightfold Path.
- **Jainism**: A restrained and contented life is the basis of a healthy and happy life.
- **Judaism**: Joy is deeply connected to community, tradition, and living a life of purpose and ethical responsibility.
- **Sikhism**: Happiness (*sukh*) is understood as a state of well-being and contentment achieved through a life lived in alignment with the divine will (*hukam*), characterized by gratitude, service, and a focus on present-moment living.
- **Zoroastrian-Parsi**: "Happiness to those who make others happy," states the Gathas. From this, one could infer that happiness comes to those who live in harmony.

- From the perspective of the **Baha'i Faith**, true happiness comes not just from material success but from spiritual fulfillment and contributing to the betterment of society:

> Happiness consists of two kinds: physical and spiritual. Physical happiness is limited; its utmost duration is one day, one month, one year. It hath no result. Spiritual happiness is eternal and unfathomable. This kind of happiness appeareth in one's soul with the love of God and suffereth one to attain to the virtues and perfections of the world of humanity. Therefore, endeavour as much as thou art able in order to illuminate the lamp of thy heart by the light of love.
>
> The more we make others happy the greater will be our own happiness and the deeper our sense of having served humanity.
>
> ...Is any larger bounty conceivable than this, that an individual, looking within himself, should find that by the confirming grace of God he has become the cause of peace and well-being, of happiness and advantage to his fellow men?...

This resonates with the findings of the UN report on how prosocial behavior and trust improve well-being.

While in Chicago, 'Abdu'l-Baha, the son of the Founder of the Baha'i Faith, revealed "one of His most buoyant Tablets" requested by a newspaper reporter. Whenever we feel sad or stressed out, let's sing the verses, and it will surely lift our spirits:

> Be happy! Be happy! The Sun of Truth has shone!
>
> Be happy! Be happy! The Light of the Spirit has surrounded the world!

> Be happy! Be happy! The doors of the Kingdom are opened!
> Be happy! Be happy! The song of the Supreme Concourse is raised!
> Be happy! Be happy! The breaths of the Holy Spirit are life-giving, and the world of man is being quickened.

Endnotes and References for this Feature[xi:1,2]

Interspirituality as the Foundation for Global Citizenship

by Nicholas Vesey

We are all interdependent on each other, dependent also on plants and animals, on the weather, on nature, on the planet. This is the logical understanding that comes from the universal interspiritual approach to religion.

China's problems are our problems, and our problems are China's problems. For countries to be worrying about territorial claims, security, economic prosperity, pride, and empire is not the issue. The issue is that the world has problems, and we need to be big enough to get beyond our own self-interest and solve them.

That is what the leaders of the world need to understand. When we start thinking this way, then we will be able to solve the problems of the world. While we start thinking of our own survival, we will not. Rather than being Americans or British or French, we have to become the Global Citizens realizing that humanity has got so big that no one country can contain it. That is why 82 million people around the world are refugees. Our borders simply cannot contain them, and the only way to start to deal with the problem is to see that this planet is everyone's home; we have to start seeing it that way. That is the logical extension of the interspiritual approach.

Until we take responsibility as individuals for caring for the whole planet, rather than just our little bit, we will not solve the problems that our world is encountering. Because unless we solve problems of a global level, they will just come back to bite us, like the pandemic and climate change. We are faced not with national catastrophes, but global catastrophes: pandemics, climate change, selfish totalitarianism. These are problems that can only be solved from a global perspective, and the sooner we realize that and take up the concept of global citizenship, the better.

We already have the emergence of a global consciousness through television and the internet. Corporations are now global, and it is only a matter of time before politicians begin to think this way. And they will only do so if we, the global citizens on the ground, demand it.

I was wondering what it meant to identify as a global citizen and how it might affect our behavior. I think the first thing that it does is make us identify with the largest grouping that we can. It includes the whole planet with all humanity, with plants and animals and the Earth itself. We see all people as our brothers and sisters in the human family. In fact, we see all things as a part of our family, much as St. Francis did when he referred to Brother Sun and Sister Moon. He was actually identifying as a citizen of the universe. Which is, of course, the next stage up, and actually the rationale for the concept of Global Citizenship.

When you identify as an intimate part of the universe, you are really affirming the idea of the Oneness of all, that we are actually that part of the universe which is conscious of itself. Everything is linked by the "ground of all being" that we can call God, or unitive consciousness, or the primal origin. Hence, St. Francis' idea of Brother Sun, Sister Moon.

This is the essence of Interspirituality. We are intimately in relationship with all elements in the universe as they are of the same Oneness. There is no leap at all to go from this to say that we are all one with our planet, the Earth, and therefore, we should declare our solidarity with all beings and things that make up the Earth, Brother Tree and Sister Cloud.

To be a global citizen is to stand up for the whole planet, not just the bits that we think are "me" and "mine." To be a global citizen is to see that our responsibility is not just to our family, our community, and the people with whom we directly identify. The interspiritual approach must precipitate the emergence of a new consciousness that is demonstrably relevant and practical in solving the world's problems.

All we have is our individual experience of the world, and our willingness to respond in an appropriate way. In an evolved consciousness, this comes with an understanding that what we are required to do is to love. And it is that loving response to all things that qualifies us to be global citizens. We are the present moment, and as such, we are a part of a larger consciousness that is using us for the evolution of all creation. The interspiritual tool we have to use to do that is love, giving with no expectation of a return.

To do this, we have to be living in the present moment. Through this, we see what is sent to us by the universe, and we respond to whatever comes our way with love. That is the mindset we are asked to hold onto as we experience ourselves within this home that is the present moment. We are asked to bring love into our home, to infuse our home with love, to reflect it back into our home, through an interspiritual approach.

We become Global Citizens when we see our lives as part of a complete whole, as the wave in the ocean. And when we realize that we are One with the universe, we immediately recognize that what we do matters, that everything we do matters. Because everything we do in our own lives affects everything else in that whole.

We are the drop of water that contains the ocean, and which is also a part of the ocean. We do not say, "I will identify with only this part of the ocean, or only that part of the ocean." We know that the ocean has no divide within itself, and any divide that we might perceive is only something that has been made up, and shared with others who also imagine it. Through this, we conspire with others to make divisions where no divisions exist.

So, to be a global citizen is not a function of doing, it is a function of being.

It is being able to identify with the seamless reality of the universe, which is the essence of Interspirituality, rather than identifying with artificial ideas and constructs that are merely created in order for individuals to band together with other individuals to make themselves feel better about their situation.

When you realize that there is only your world, that you are completely alone in that world, and that you are relating not to other individuals, but to the entire universe of which you are a part, then you become a world leader, the leader of your own world. As such, you take your place as a global citizen and a portal for love coming into that world — love from within you going out into your world.

At the moment, the world is caught up as an Ouroboros. We are eating ourselves in order to survive. The rich and powerful are literally feeding off the poor and the powerless. In America, the top 10 precent held 69.8 percent of total U.S. net worth. The top 1 percent held about half of that wealth — 32.1 percent.

That is how we have become an Ouroboros, and that is true for the whole world.

In the past, the Ouroboros could regenerate itself and start again. But our world is now in such a place that we are all becoming part of one great Ouroboros, and for that to regenerate will take a shift in consciousness greater than ever before. We have to become a part of a shift in consciousness that breaks the current thinking, the rush to safety, the ghettoization of thought and rush to strong men and women who will protect us at the expense of others.

Interspirituality is part of that shift in consciousness, as is what you do in your life. It has been coming since the First Axial Age, since the emergence of the Buddha, Jesus, Lao Tzu, and Mohammed. We are now in the Second Axial Age with the rise of Global consciousness and the realization of the unified nature of the universe. The rational mind is strong, and the rise of popularism is the rise in the unprotected for protection. We want to know that we will be okay, even if others are not.

This is wrong thinking, and there is an alternative: if you want to put a name to it, it is the idea of Global Citizenship.

Becoming Conscious as Citizens of This World

[Selections from "What Is" as published in full in the Community and Spiritual Modalities Section in Volume 3]

by Richard Bowell

Until we SEE from WHAT IS rather than what 'I' think is the case, we will continue to re-enforce our view of what is and do more of the same. …

Reaching a higher starting point where one can see more requires us to make a specific elevation out of the level of habit (and initiative, as the stretch to see more) that is similar to climbing up a mountain to better SEE the views. In the inner *meaning* of this, climbing upwards is accomplished by shedding the weight of assumptions and opinions, habits and initiatives and letting oneself be released from one's current level to rise to a new starting point. ....

Human development is as much the release from impediments as it is the aspiration to elevate to a higher level. ...

This is initiative. ...

Real lasting change is not a result of the habit-initiative platform....

If we are to transform our world and ourselves in the world it is necessary to SEE the impossibility and ineffectiveness of this level of thinking and to release ourselves from its grip and 'stop the world' as they say.

Even in these times, making collective goals aimed at achieving everything from world peace to ending poverty or achieving climate balance are still the way we approach change, not SEEING that it cannot bring about these outcomes however much we press for change.

Only from a higher level can real change unfold, and to join a new platform where harmony or a state of peace or the sense of inclusion in worlds that one was never meant to be excluded from is possible, one needs to first of all SEE the futility of doing more at the same level. ...

Can you register that who we are is joined to a larger unfolding story in just this one example, that we are both an individual and a part of a larger wholeness? We are growing up to join WHAT IS, and the wire from WHAT IS is a guide leading us back to source.....

Along this wire, new insights and perceptions can flow as the narrative of evolution's unfolding in us in which we can play a part and a purpose. …

Facilitating this realm in downloading new insights into our human situation confirms that we have a part and purpose to play in the evolution story that has been taking place over vast tracts of time and that our purpose is made significant by it taking place inside the larger story of evolution in this moment, in this epoch. …

WHAT IS, is the ground from which all significant inquiry grows and not from oneself thinking about some matter or another that one thinks is important or assumes is important. Real significance emerges form WHAT IS, already….

WHAT IS invites us to SEE our purpose and affirm it as an internal growth sequence within WHAT IS. …

Real knowledge has living presence, whereas seeking answers to problems has taken the place of seeking to understand and join WHAT IS to SEE the whole picture in which our growth is central as an emergence in the whole. …

At a time when our current ways of thinking are no longer sustainable, it is our evolutionary unfolding and SEEING our next steps that join us to a new interconnected level of becoming Conscious as Citizens of this World. …

Our human engagement begins in the calling (not a question to be answered) that evokes in us a human response as a sense of exploration to SEE our part in the unfolding evolutionary story to come closer to the source.

Evolution is an intimacy that culture has managed to distance us from, and the consequence is a world in crisis that seems to matter little, even as it crashes.

At a time when our current ways of thinking are no longer sustainable, is it our evolutionary unfolding and SEEING our next steps that join us to a new interconnected level of becoming Conscious as Citizens of this World.

Closing Reflection — A Wholistic Vision of Evolution and Consciousness

by Elena Mustakova and Robert Atkinson

Dr. Elena Mustakova is author of the Nautilus Award-winning book from Light on Light, *Global Unitive Healing: Integral Skills for Personal and Collective Transformation* (2021) with a Foreword by Ken Wilber and Afterword by Claudia Welss, both Featured Authors in these Volumes. Dr. Robert Atkinson is the author of Light on Light's latest book, *The Way of Unity: Essential Principles and Preconditions for Peace* (2025). Both books are central not only to understanding the landscape of our era's global challenge but also center significantly on the vital historical message of the Baha'i tradition. We're pleased to share this brief closing reflection from them, from their recent article in *Kosmos* journal, "Global Challenges Are Directing Us Toward a Unity of Purpose."[3]

> A holistic vision of evolution and consciousness sees a purpose to these turbulent times. Cycles of transformation and renewal punctuate our evolutionary progress, as we see in these years of lockdowns, demonstrations, and confrontations. Yet, all the divisions that natural differences create are essentially due to an incomplete investigation of truth. This can result in extreme antisocial orientations and behavioral patterns that support separation, create hierarchies,

and endanger our very survival. On the other hand, an unfettered search for truth leads to a prosocial orientation and actions built upon a consciousness of wholeness, which also fulfills our innate potentiality. Consciousness is designed to evolve toward wholeness and unity.

Living by a consciousness of wholeness prioritizes the whole, engenders a response based on harmony and cooperation, and places a unity of purpose above all else. At the same time, a consciousness of wholeness acknowledges our diversity of views, appearances, and contributions to the whole as our sustaining strength.

This consciousness calls for a complete shift in how we relate to reality. If we can see beyond the illusion of separation, we can focus on the one reality which is already a unified whole. Anything currently dividing us is also a catalyst for uniting us. We saw this organic interconnectedness last summer when the streets filled with people calling for racial justice and deep systemic change. A convergence of forces is building like never before. As we join hands across differences, we seek to heal a great divide in the human family.

Endnotes and References for "Global Challenge" Section[xi]

INTERSPIRITUAL COMMUNITY

Opening Features by
JoAnn Barrett - Philip Goldberg - Karuna - Charles Vogl

Subsequent Features and Selections by
DeShannon Barnes-Bowens - Leena Banerjee Brown - Connie Kaplan
Sally Mahé - Yanni Maniates - Matt Mitler - Rajashree Maa (aka Joni Dittrich)
Leslie Reambeault - Bhakti Rasayana Sagara Swami - Melissa Stewart -
Daniel J. Stone - William Thiele - Kim Vanderheiden - Andre van Zijl

As noted in the Introduction to these Volumes, unanticipated by us, and especially key to these Volumes contents, some Featured Authors wrote on very specific interspiritual communities. Others also furnished copious historically valuable photographs and other illustrations with their Features. As well, a number of Featured Authors — writing on very specific interspiritual communities, practices, or modalities — included additional valuable content, including long sections of quotations, practice descriptions, and also poems and prayers. These have considerable historical value but do not technically reproduce or format well for a non-glossy print book. We thus announced the subsequent third volume planned for this series, centering especially on exemplary interspiritual Community around the world and providing a place for the full publication of longer, or illustrated Features.

The contributions for the subsequent third volume are significant in themselves, standing out as rich and inspiring elaborations of specific interspiritual communities, modalities of interspiritual practice, and especially the relationship of these to both sacred activism and the Arts. As well, many key pieces of content from these contributions have already been used as quotations, from these varied Featured Authors, *in* sections of these Volumes 1 and 2. Further, it is in this third volume that we can give deserved space to details from a variety of interspiritual communities, past and present (from Bede Griffiths' Shantivanam Ashram [Saccidananda Ashram] in India, Beverly Lanzetta's Community of the New Monastic Way, Swami Shraddhananda's sangha's Sacred Feet Anugraha House, and Long Island's Gathering of Light [USA], to the diverse experiments of the Community of the Mystic Heart [originally Universal Order of Sannyasa], the recent Charis Foundation new monastic community, and others). Finding a place for detailed comments on their structures, practices, vows, lifestyle, etc. richly deserves that attention and can also be fully illustrated.

Consequently, in this Section on Interspiritual Community, we have created a category, noted as "Selections," wherein we can share in these print-book pages of Volumes 1 and 2 important and inspiring aspects from the submissions of these Featured Authors while still intending to publish their full texts, and historically valuable additional materials, in the subsequent fully illustrated third volume. Thus, we refer to these entries herein as "Selected from…" and then give the full title of the larger pieces from which these materials have been drawn.

Our emphasis on community follows on the Interspiritual Dialogue's special 2018 e-publication, through its Light on Light Press, *Transformational Communities* (at issuu.com/lightonlight). It featured seventeen exemplary global communities, many of which are reprised in the current Volumes, and in our Volume 3. These include elements of our Opening Features below — by JoAnn Barrett, Philip Goldberg, Charles Vogl and Karuna — and subsequently all the authors in our Section: Interspiritual Community. In that light, we begin with the overview of an award-winning author on community — Charles Vogl.

In his award-winning books on *The Art of Community,*[1] Charles Vogl notes that, especially today and particularly for younger generations, "community" is even more important than worldview, belief, or ideology. Community *is* connection, and in community, we have each other to hold at the deepest levels of connection. Vogl's measure of the "success" of a community is how much it really *cares* for its members. He elaborates these criteria for authentic and successful communities — and notes that although they are *the same* whether a community is more "sacred" or "secular," there are dimensions of "sacred community" that are unique — particularly because of the attention to the subtle realms of human experience.

Successful communities always have the following attributes (and in these we add below [in brackets] their even more specific meanings for spiritual communities). The latter notations are from another of our Featured Authors, Karuna, who employs Vogl's categories in her recent book on lifestyle, *Light on Kundalini: Your Lifestyle Guide to Yoga and Awakening*. The attributes are:

- A shared sense of identity [in spiritual communities, a sense of "communing together with the Divine"]
- Shared values and ethical aspirations [in spiritual communities, "practicing goodness"]
- A sense of a higher value to be attained [in spiritual communities, often "the path to Awakening"]

Vogl's list of what characterizes authentic and successful communities becomes even more obvious when we consider other aspects of successful spiritual communities:

- Members join and stay because they deeply feel welcome.
- Members do meaningful things together.
- Members share a meaningful space or place.
- Members embrace shared narratives or stories.
- Members share objects that have deep symbolic meanings.

In his Afterword to these Volumes, Ken Wilber points out how that strength of community also accounts for how both the worst and best in human behaviors have happened in the context of religion. And, he adds, we must hope that the direction of Interspirituality, with its wholism and diversity, can point our world in the direction of the highest and best.

Philip Goldberg's fitting introductory Feature to this section below further elaborates this landscape. It also provides a context for the Selections we can then share, more richly, from Features appearing in our subsequent Volume 3. Most important, these speak not only to the specific traditions or communities about which these authors write, but also to the universality of the Interspirituality that Br. Teasdale visioned in *The Mystic Heart*.

From Inter to Trans, Me to We

by Philip Goldberg

I used to go to interfaith gatherings that resembled the opening of a joke: "A priest, a minister, and a rabbi walk into a room..." only without a good punch line. The clerics would remain in their silos, speaking on behalf of their own traditions about a given topic. Typically, the meetings were warm and friendly, and participants left with better understanding of, and usually more respect for, other religions. But the events were essentially Comparative Religion 101. For me, they lacked depth; they did not get past the doctrines and rituals that comprise what Huston Smith called *exoteric* religion. Absent was the *esoteric* — the transformative inner experience that mystics brought to light. I found myself often bored, sometimes irritated, and usually frustrated. I stopped attending.

In time, the interfaith world evolved, horizontally and vertically. In diverse urban settings at least, the breadth of participation expanded, and the substance deepened. Imams were invited, perhaps a Sufi; sometimes a Wiccan or a Pagan or an indigenous Shaman, or even a Secular Humanist. But the most crucial element in the evolution of interfaith came with representatives of the Eastern traditions: a swami, a Yogacharya, a Hindu scholar; a roshi, a lama, a Vipassana teacher, a practicing Buddhist; more rarely, a Sikh, a Jain, or a Taoist. With those additions came an emphasis on spiritual methodologies — most commonly, some form of meditation or mindfulness — and with it the vital element of shared inner experience.

In this regard, the cutting edge of interfaith mirrored the larger history of American spirituality, which, thanks to penetration from the East, came to resemble a nation of diverse, independent yogis, as opposed to groupings of believers guarding their turf. American spirituality became a living experiment in which the core, nondual premise of the Perennial Philosophy — in Vedantic terms, "Truth is One, the wise call it by many names" — could be tested in the internal laboratories of individual practitioners.

The progress within interfaith was welcome, but the organizing principle remained what standard religious conversation calls "faith traditions," and the subject matter remained focused on beliefs, texts, rituals, and history. The mystics among us — those committed to a particular tradition, lineage, or path as well as the independents, the unaffiliated, the "nones," and the "Spiritual-but-not-religious" cohort that is now larger than many Christian denominations — needed settings in which spiritual development, not faith or doctrine, was the principal driver and experiential, evidence-based, unifying, transpersonal spirituality was the focus. Hence, the emergence of Interspirituality.

What might come next? Perhaps a name change. The prefix *inter* means "among, between, in the midst of." That is certainly appropriate as far as it goes, but does it capture the essence of a movement whose direction is vertically deeper and horizontally more expansive than "inter" might suggest? Would *transpirituality* be more accurate? The prefix *trans* most commonly means "beyond," especially in a spiritual context, as in transcendence, transubstantiation, and transfiguration. It also resonates with the evolutionary and integral emphasis of the interspiritual constituency, which is transtraditional and transhistorical, and valued transparency, transcendence, and transformation. After all, "transcend and include" is one of the guiding principles.

But that's merely a linguistic matter. The future presents more consequential issues. As I view it, perhaps the most pressing concern is community. In my experience, many (if not most) spiritual independents are refugees from spiritual organizations who find freelance inquiry and eclectic exploration more compatible with their personalities and needs — what scholars call questers as opposed to nesters. At the same time, many (if not most) often find themselves craving community. That tension between the desire to belong and the need to be free can be as difficult to navigate as it is easy to joke about. It is also a highly practical concern. One of the great paradoxes of the spiritual path is that we're on our own — captains of our own ships, in charge of all choices and decisions on the winding road to illumination — and yet we can't do it alone: we need companions, guides, teachers, and classmates as we matriculate from one stage of development to the next.

Spiritual community offers well-known advantages: the sharing of knowledge, celebration, ritual, and methods; comfort, support, and tangible help in times of crisis; resources for addressing common concerns, from the care and education of children to the mobilization of service projects. Community also provides a crucible for the relational element of spirituality, a place where ethics and morals are put to the test and flaws and foibles are exposed.

Historically, the mainstream religions have done a decent job of providing community for their adherents. The question arises, will the experience-based, free-thinking, non-dogmatic, pluralistic, spirituality of the future find ways to provide the advantages of community? Are buildings necessary? Institutions with rules, norms, and organizational charts? Scheduled gatherings like worship services? Celebrations of special days? Rites of passage? Or are such elements of religiosity destined to become historical relics? How well can social media and internet resources provide what in-the-flesh communities have traditionally offered? Can informal, leaderless gatherings take the place of ritualized assemblies led by authority figures? Will loosely-knit groups find satisfactory ways to educate, inspire, support, and mobilize their constituents? Will swift, integrated, authentic spiritual development compensate for the absence of traditional forms of community?

However the details shake out over time, the trend lines are clear. I hope I live long enough to see what the younger generations do with the momentum they've inherited.

Endnotes and Reference for this Introduction[xii:1]

DIMENSIONS OF INTERSPIRITUAL COMMUNITY

The spirit and message of Philip Goldberg's introductory piece is echoed deeply in the work of one of Interspirituality's most successful communities — Long Island, New York's "Gathering of Light." This community, formed around Rev. JoAnn Barrett, has been a vibrant and activist community since 1996. JoAnn and members of her community have been featured in national media; JoAnn contributed to the book already oft-noted in these Volumes—*Mature Interspirituality*; and she was part of the panel on Br. Teasdale's interspiritual message at the Salt Lake City Parliament of the World's Religions.

Selected from

Spiritual Community from an Interspiritual Perspective

published in full in Volume 3

by JoAnn Barrett

"…I remember when I first started studying *A Course in Miracles* in 1980. I did not know anybody who was participating in this self-study spiritual psychotherapy. But I happily and diligently proceeded to do the workbook of 365 lessons in the solitude of my basement den. I was struck by what occurred. I was meditating on about lesson fifty, and my whole body began to shake. I knew from the deepest part of my being, 'If I continue to do this work, I would never be the same again.' There was in that moment a sense of exhilaration; a connection so deep and profound that was immediately followed by a sense of panic. And the thought came to me, 'What would I become? What does a spiritual person look like?' …

The nine elements of Interspirituality answer these profound questions in a broad yet kind way. Brother Teasdale wisely formulated these concepts based on dialogues with the Snowmass conference participants. They transcend dogma and doctrine and respond to a very basic need. There is this need to know as a sojourner of the spiritual path, what does the spiritual person look like? The interesting thing about the answer to this question is the idea that the spiritual seeker doesn't look a certain way but has attributes, qualities. What the nine elements provide for us are these universal qualities and aspirations. This is the spiritual person 'look' that Interspirituality creates. …

Spiritual community provides these opportunities. Spiritual communities provide opportunities to learn, grow, and outreach in ways that as individuals we would never be able to accomplish. …

Interspirituality was the brilliant and clear channeled work of Br. Teasdale. The mystical heart was providing a promise of unity into all our consciousness. …

This unity was expressed in the form of spiritual community even in the humblest band of seekers — building on the concepts of Br. Teasdale and making them manifest. …

The promises of spiritual community are the same as the promises that the divine has laid out for us since the beginning of our looking for some aspect of a higher power for guidance. The promise that we have been given all we need to choose to live in the flow of life."

Let's continue, and expand, our discussion of the Dimensions of Interspiritual Community by sharing contributions in four thematic circles:

- Interspiritual Communities — Spirituality and Sacred Activism
- Interspiritual Communities — Healing Modalities
- Interspiritual Communities — and the Arts
- Interspiritual Communities — and Prophetic Voice

INTERSPIRITUAL COMMUNITIES — SPIRITUALITY AND SACRED ACTIVISM

Selected from

One Spirit Interfaith Seminary Interspirituality — In and Out of the Classroom

published in full in Volume 3

by Leslie Reambeault and Melissa Stewart

We have already had the privilege of sharing excerpts from this detailed Feature on multicultural community, and the exemplar of One Spirit Interfaith Seminary, under "Interspiritual Pioneers" in our interspiritual "Reflections and Pointers" Section. We look forward to sharing the entire Feature in Volume 3. Following on that section earlier in this Volume 2 and emphasizing its important content here, we summarize:

"…the One Spirit Seminary experience is the aforementioned 'deeper curriculum,' which refers to the process of self-discovery and enhanced awareness, and the development of community among the cohort. This rests on the belief that each group of people are brought together by Spirit — perhaps experienced by some as an Unnamed Force — and 'for a reason.'"

Selected from

United Religions Initiative's Global Community Lives into the Interspiritual Age

published in full in Volume 3

by Sally Mahé

Following on United Religions Initiative's founding Executive Director, Rev. Canon Charles P. Gibbs', Feature on URI, Sally Mahé explores the foundations and praxis of its visions and activism in an important piece shared in its entirety in Volume 3.

"...Over 25 years ago, Brother Wayne Teasdale forecast changes that were afoot regarding people's shift toward inner spiritual life. He predicted, 'The only viable religion for the Third Millennium is spirituality itself.' ...

The Inter-spiritual Age calls humanity to embrace its collective potential to love and serve one another and the Earth in life-giving ways. I believe that the United Religions Initiative, an interfaith organization conceived in the late-90s, is a forerunner showing how cooperation among religions can be the basis for a unified, compassionate humanity. As URI's origin story goes, 'when people from different religions began to speak and listen to each other, there was something there that wasn't there before, a star.'

URI began with an intriguing question — could there be an organization with the stature of the United Nations that brings the peoples of the world's religions together in pursuit of peace? A compelling question, a bold vision, a shared dream, and dedicated work by hundreds of people around the world gave birth to URI in 2000. URI declared itself to be a bridge building organization, not a religion. ...

URI's founding Charter states, *We people of diverse religions, spiritual expressions, and indigenous traditions throughout the world, hereby establish the United Religions Initiative to promote enduring daily interfaith cooperation, to end religiously motivated violence, and to create cultures of peace, justice and healing for the Earth and all living beings.* These groups, called Cooperation Circles, varying in size, experience, and prominence, apply to join URI's global community. In 2024, URI's global community has grown to over 1,200 Cooperation Circles in 112 countries. About 4-6 new groups are screened and selected to join each month."

Selected from

Leadership, Empowerment and Development in the Bhakti Tradition

published in full in Volume 3

by Bhakti Rasayana Sagara Swami

In this selection from Volume 3, Bhakti Rasayana Sagara Swami, an Interfaith Ambassador of the International Society for Krishna Consciousness (ISKCON) explores its, and his, unique background and life's work of deep social engagement.

"...I'm a sannyasi monk in the Bhakti tradition, represented in the Western world by International Society for Krishna Consciousness (ISKCON). I'm engaged in my spiritual practices since my childhood, being born in a Muslim family from the former Soviet Union. But I often wanted to learn more about other spiritual paths as well and, despite of the communist persecution existing at the time, aside from Koran I managed to read Torah, New Testament, and the Lotus Sutra. Later I came across the Hare Krishnas and got their main text, Bhagavad Gita, which impressed me the most with its clarity and the depth of wisdom. It helped me to understand the unifying factor behind all the religious and spiritual diversity and introduced me to the powerful spiritual practices I pursued ever since. Thus, the very first purpose of ISKCON, founded by His Divine Grace Bhaktivedanta Swami Prabhupada, became my life and soul."

This transition moved Bhakti Rasayana Sagara Swami from life as an armed Muslim freedom fighter in the former Soviet Union to a life in sacred activism as an international leader in Sannyas.

Selected from

Sourcing Our Service is the Future of Interspirituality

published in full in Volume 3

by William Thiele

Rev. William Thiele, PhD, founding spiritual director of the School for Contemplative Living, pastor of Parker United Methodist Church, and Adjunct Professor at Loyola University in New Orleans writes intimately on the interspiritual grounding of one of his books, *Monks in the World: Seeking God in a Frantic Culture*, paralleling the activist message in Br. Teasdale's *A Monk in the World.*

"... Mary and Merry found themselves called to make friends with people from the streets of New Orleans in our School for Contemplative Living's weekly street ministry. They also felt called to take a knee at a busy street corner each week after the murder of George Floyd. They were living the reality that Black Lives Matter. They were being contemplatives in action. They were acting out our motto to 'Let Love Rule.' The service was never easy or comfortable, but they were compelled to practice Sourcing themselves in the Great Love both 'on and off the cushion,' as our Buddhist friends say. Staying in perpetual contemplation was just not enough.

The twin contemplative practices of Sourcing and compassionate serving go hand in hand as fundamental to the Interspirituality of the future. In fact, I believe there is no such thing as Interspirituality without some form of expression in compassionate service *with* the world. This union of contemplation and action proves our spirituality to be real."

Also in Volume 3, Dr. Thiele shares a moving story of community: "Oneing: How Friendship Between a Quaker and a Vietnamese Buddhist Monk Became a Model for Transformation."

Selected from

A Full Circle from Interfaith Pioneering to Interspiritual Fulfillment

published in full in Volume 3

by Yanni Maniates

Yanni Maniates, a prominent visioneer of the UNITY EARTH network widely featured in these Volumes comments on his over fifty years of interfaith and interspiritual engagement and the dramatic changes that have occurred in that near half century.

"Today I work with UNITY EARTH, an impact network prominently featured in these Volumes.... Nearly fifty years ago, in late 1978, I found myself asked to help with the expansion of a nascent, ecumenical, interfaith organization — (New ERA) The New Ecumenical Research Association and (IRF) The International Religious Foundation. I agreed, and to my surprise, in a few short years, it grew exponentially and brought together many theologians, academics, spiritual leaders, ministers, and students of religion from all over the world and from all the major faith traditions. The timing was right; there was a hunger and clear need for this. A very solid groundwork of interfaith cooperation and dialogue was seeded by these organizations, and an enduring foundation was created.

During the time frame I was involved, more than one hundred and twenty events were held all over the world.... many thousands of people were involved in the actual events. The ripple effect of both the events and the New ERA Books publications program reached far and wide and left a lasting legacy of dialogue, mutual trust, concrete positive actions, and programs. A significant foundation was created for the subsequent international, interfaith, ecumenical work that grew out of all these encounters. ...

...As Br. Wayne Teasdale said, we are at a major juncture in the evolution of humanity, 'We are at the dawn of a new consciousness...' [MH p. 4]."

INTERSPIRITUAL COMMUNITIES— HEALING MODALITIES

Selected from

The Universal Energy of Healing Touch: Reiki as an Interspiritual Practice

published in full in Volume 3

by Rajashree Maa (aka Joni Dittrich)

In an important contribution, Rajashree Maa (Joni Dittrich, PhD [Psychology]) elaborates the significance of her 2023 book establishing a new lineage of Reiki healing based on the Divine Feminine: *May the Loveforce Be With You — Kali-Ki Reiki: Healing Through Divine Mother & Yogic Wisdom*. The Foreword is by Sadhvi Bhagawati Saraswati, recipient of the Lifetime Achievement Award (2021) awarded by United States President Joseph Biden for her lifetime of commitment and achievement in social service.

"Giving touch to heal, protect, soothe, console, calm, nurture, steady, empower, pleasure, love, and even bless is natural to human beings. Touch is part of our preverbal communication system. While acknowledging that touch can also hurt, dominate, control, and even kill, the focus here is on the universality of healing energy conveyed through touch and how reiki healing is a practice that spans interspiritual dimensions. …

Every wisdom tradition refers to a universal life-giving energy, or lifeforce. This lifeforce in humans goes by various names in world cultures: Prana and Shakti in Hinduism; Chi and Ki, respectively, in Chinese and Japanese Buddhist and shamanic cultures; Nyama and Ase in African cultures; Wakan Tanka and Great Spirit in Native American cultures; and Holy Spirit, Rhu, and Ruah, respective to Christianity, Islam, and Judaism. In all these traditions, it is through somehow activating, re-directing, and balancing this animating lifeforce within that healing takes place. …

It would seem the only healing tradition that doesn't directly talk about lifeforce energy is that of western allopathic medicine. Western science, under the influence of the church, and later Newtonian physics, historically threw the proverbial baby out with the bath water by patently discarding pagan, shamanic, and herbal healing practices as religious or scientific heresy. But current science, recognizing that there is no real difference between matter and energy, has begun embracing the unseen quanta of existence and thereby acknowledging the healing possibilities…"

Selected from

True Light — The Healing Modality of Sukyo Mahikari

published in full in Volume 3

by Leena Banerjee Brown

In this selection, Leena Banerjee Brown PhD (psychology) details the effectiveness of the Sukyo Mahikari practice of "True Light," another healing modality similar to Reiki and Therapeutic Touch, as elaborated in her book *True Light: Ordinary People on the Extraordinary Spiritual Path of Sukyo Mahikari.*[2] *True Light* is an important print book companioning the widely read international publication on Sukyo Mahikari's vision and praxis: *God's Light and Universal Principles for All Humanity: An Introduction to Sukyo Mahikari* by Sidney E. Chang PhD (Ansembourg, Luxembourg: LH Europe (2007)). From Dr. Leena Banerjee Brown:

"...The spiritual path of Sukyo Mahikari is compatible with many religious paths. If one meets the practices of giving and receiving True Light as a Christian, one may remain Christian along the path. If one meets the practices of giving and receiving True Light as a Hindu, one may remain Hindu along the path. If one meets the practices of giving and receiving True Light as a Muslim, one may remain Muslim along the path. If one meets the practices of giving and receiving True Light as a Buddhist, one may remain Buddhist along the path. And so it goes for all spiritual paths and practices. If one meets the practices of giving and receiving True Light with no specific religious or spiritual path, one need not adopt a specific tradition to encounter God on the path of Sukyo Mahikari.

Giving True Light is the most direct way to cut through from the conscious, to the subconscious, to the deepest consciousness and vibration of the true self. It leaves people energized, takes away the static of the mind, and epiphanies arise, giving people realizations and insight-strengthening intuitions. Giving and receiving True Light, engages a spirit-mind-body principle, deepening the mind's reflective capacity.... likely the physical benefits that are obvious in so many cases come from the elimination of accumulated toxins in the bodily system. ...

We focus our attention on improvements in well-being, including both physical and mental health, combining these Sukyo Mahikari spiritual practices with medical science. ... We combine the practice of True Light with professional medical recommendations, as is encouraged in Sukyo Mahikari practice."

Endnotes and References for this Feature[xii:2]

Selected from

Ground

published in full in Volume 3

by Kim Vanderheiden

In a selection entitled "Ground," used as a verb, activist Kim Vanderheiden, of Roman Catholicism background, and active in its association Pax Christi, addresses social justice as healing — from the perspective of an interspiritual activism based simply on Love. It is an insightful and inspiring piece, powerfully expressing the Heart of the grassroots activism also championed in Br. Teasdale's now classic work: *A Monk in the World*. From Kim Vanderheiden:

"… I sat in the dirt in the middle of the street in meditation, before a protective mandala beautifully drawn with thousands of black and white beans by an ally who shared her Indigenous spirituality and healing with Wood Street Commons. My rosary rested in my open hand. The mandala's creator tended the burning medicine plants in its center. A drummer beat cadence around us and the circle. …

What if we had learned each other's spoken languages as well as spiritual languages, and brought them together? Rather than a legacy of destruction, dominance, and death, my culture might have had restorative justice practices centuries sooner, different legal frameworks, parenting practices, and attitudes toward caring for the earth. For those of us who call ourselves Christian, I think we would have understood Christ better, too. …

What does it look like if the law of our lives is love, and love is the measure we use to discern what to do, and what is just? …

A community, a country, a world in a state of justice is one in which all are in healthy relationship of interbeing with each other. …

Injustice is caused by violence, and is fundamentally a tearing in relationship. The tear must then be mended, reconciled. The practices of restorative justice, including self-opening, witnessing, truth-telling, accountability, compassion for all beings, reparation, and reconciliation are some of our most important tools for justice and peace."

Selected from

The Importance of Direct Access to Personal Spiritual Information

published in full in Volume 3

by Connie Kaplan

In this selection from the full Feature in our Volume 3, Connie Kaplan, a globally acknowledged specialist on dreams, shares how that landscape informs Br. Teasdale's famous words "We are all mystics…." [MH p. 3] and how these deepest mystical unfoldings are part of our healing process into a global Interspiritual Age. In the fuller Feature, she recounts in detail how this dimension helps us also understand the variety of mystical "personages" ["deities"] that typify the literature of the Great Wisdom Traditions.

"…I've become increasingly interested in how spiritual practitioners are finding each other outside of traditionally structured religious organizations and creating small pods of mutual support and encouragement in their desire to fully understand human incarnation. In these next few pages, I … invite you to explore your personal contribution to answering the Great Question: Why are we here? ...

While I do have several academic degrees (a bachelor's in education, a master's in television production, a master's in psychology, and a doctorate of ministry), my more fundamental credentials come from direct access — from mystical experiences and otherwise unexplainable events during which I received information from somewhere / someone other than (or perhaps more than) human….

My books, *The Woman's Book of Dreams* and *Dreams Are Letters from the Soul*, provide specifics about the dream teachers and the content of the recurring dreams I had while 'dreaming myself awake.'…

These dream teachers assured me that while the Jungian style of dream analysis holds important psychological value to an individual, the deeper collective truth about dreaming unveils amazing skills that most humans don't acknowledge in themselves. Those skills involve an inner knowing that every person has direct access to *truth* through the agency of dreaming. …

Our job as awake humans is to hear others' dream stories and mine them for the cosmic and evolutionary information and deeper verity to which they point. These dream stories, more often than not, point us to what is about to happen in waking reality.

…as dreamers we see the coming of a new consciousness that no longer clings to antiquated beliefs about time, space, gender, age, polarity, and emotional stuckness. It's a beautiful New Story, and it's a possible New Story. Let's dream it from the 'not-yet' into the Now, shall we? …"

"For 'What did the Angels say?' see Volume 3. And, if you are interested in discovering what this body of information defines as your spiritual signature, I refer you to my book *The Invisible Garment*.[3] While there may be other paths to finding out 'who you are,' this body of work teaches a specific mathematical approach to that discovery."

INTERSPIRITUAL COMMUNITY — AND THE ARTS

This is a special subject, well represented in the contributions to these Volumes, and especially to be highlighted in our Volume 3. The Arts are crucial to the needed global journey of our collective human consciousness to what Br. Teasdale called "a civilization with a heart" [MH p. 5]. Modern neuroscience affirms that, except perhaps for scholars and other professionals who are trained to be fact and information oriented, humans more naturally learn, and are induced by, feelings. And the strongest of these are compelling emotions related to beauty, awe, sympathy, empathy, compassion, inspiration, revelation, vision, muse, and so on. And, on the other side of this — echoing Wilber's note that the best, and worst, human behaviors have occurred in the context of religion—is hate, vengeance, and the like. The arts, be it visual arts, music, poetry, theatre, cinema, and evocative voice of all kinds, are pivotal. Readers of *The Coming Interspiritual Age* [p. 248 f] will remember the extensive discussion of such "archimedean," or fulcrum points, that will be critical to whether humankind is able to ascend from domination cultures to a planetary altruism based on partnership consciousness and partnership cultures. The Arts appear to be the most direct fulcrum, or archimedean, point for influencing human behavior.

Selected from

Dzieci Theatre
A Creative Experiment in Interspirituality

published in full in Volume 3

by Matt Mitler

We have already noted Dzieci Theatre throughout these Volumes, in Volume 1's Benchmark sections, on the Snowmass Dialogues, the 2004 Parliament of the World's Religions in Barcelona, and the Tribute Event to Br. Wayne Teasdale, 2005. In the latter section, we quoted directly from earlier sections of *this* Feature, which will be published in its entirety in Volume 3. Below is this further excerpt emphasizing community and the arts. As noted in our History section, at Br. Teasdale's invitation, Dzieci accompanied Br. Teasdale's "association" to the Barcelona Parliament of the World's Religions where the first program on Interspirituality at the Parliament was held in 2004. From Matt Mitler and Dzieci Theatre:

"…My own work has been entwined with the cumulative efforts of a community, and that community is Dzieci, an ensemble dedicated to a search for the 'sacred' through the medium of theatre, which as a work not only of the mind and heart, but also of the body, serves us well as a vehicle for transformation. …

Members come to Dzieci from a variety of spiritual and religious orientations, but there is an agreement to seek that which is essential, beyond (and beneath) any specific doctrine. We prefer our workshops and training sessions to be non-verbal, allowing us to interact without typical definitions, labels, histories, not bringing our past or projections of the future, but who we are in the moment. …

Through eleven years of offerings, still asking questions — *What is this work? Who am I in relation to it? And what is necessary?* We are not looking for answers, only to see if questions still exist. …

We are still in process. Our endeavor does not preclude conflict and struggle; strong work is hard work, but we have a few guidelines that help keep us in balance.

To assist our mutual arising, we have committed to following twelve basic principles:

1. We do not work alone. Only through the strength of community are we able to break through personal barriers and venture beyond self-perceived limitations.
2. We wish to be brought to a more complete awareness of ourselves, even if that awareness shows us what we are not. In

community, through the efforts of others, we can be reminded to remain attentive and awake.

3. Dzieci is a school, and transmission is fundamental to our practice. We are all teachers. We are all students.
4. Here there are no labels, no divisions — whoever you are, wherever you come from, we share a common aim: to be able to be.
5. We make a commitment to be responsible for each other together in the workspace. All struggles are accepted and integral to the working of the group. However, should anyone step away during a period of personal struggle, they are on their own path.
6. We do not wish to abandon ourselves for the sake of changing others, nor become lost in self-absorption. Rather we strive to direct our attention equally — without and within, that we may simply see and be seen.
7. Leading non-verbally through action and gesture is our preference. Silence is a quality to be honored, and a practice not only for outer work, but for inner work as well.
8. We begin from where we are.
9. Our endeavors are self-initiated. We establish conditions, which may appear insurmountable, in order to expose our fear, refine our attention, and strengthen our resolve. The group can only provide guidance and bear witness, not help.
10. What someone knows is not of interest to us, only their willingness to leap into the unknown.
11. If there is a way to do something more humanely, more organically, or more adventurously, we make every effort to do so. We also welcome the participation of tricksters and fools.

12. The form of our work is not the work; it is only a context for revealing what is true."

Selected from

Interspirituality, Catastrophic Change, Creativity & The Arts

published in full in Volume 3

by Andre van Zijl

Andre van Zijl is an accomplished visual and musical artist, art historian, interfaith studies professor and interfaith seminary founder. He and his wife Debrorah are esteemed elders and counselors across the global interfaith and interspiritual communities. In his piece below, which we are so happy to publish in full in our Volume 3 dedicated in part to the Arts, he plumbs into the depths of the artistic nexus of Interspirituality, an element Br. Teasdale also enfolded and elaborated, as van Zijl notes in his opening quotation:

"The arts are one of the ways in which we connect
with the inner life of the soul."
— Br. Wayne Teasdale

"Art is an essential pathway of connecting to the deepest aspects of our soul, and with it, life becomes a creation of legacy in how we express and embody these deeper soul essences. We all become expanded, more capacious versions of ourselves by meeting the most challenging life changes. …

Br. Wayne Teasdale wrote about the awakened heart, 'It is the heart awakened to its divine essence, to the presence of the sacred in all creation, that can offer a universal religious dimension to this global vision.' …

Art is a whole body language. It bypasses the cultural and intellectual filters of the conditioned mind and strikes the heart directly. Only later reflection expands into the mind's musings, which, ideally, have been offered more intriguing questions to consider than answers. Viewing a magnificent work of art is like meeting a fascinating stranger. We feel the whole before we start noticing the parts. …

All great art is revolutionary in that it is usually in the vanguard of society, alerting us of any transformational crises / opportunities coming into view…. and a clear understanding of what transformational paradigm we stand for. …

Artists are the shamanic midwives of the unseen; so are the mystics, each performing the rituals of purifying the collective body of consciousness until they become fit vessels for the expression of the divine. Art can bring people together and create a sense of community. It allows us to connect on a deeper level, amplifying the experience of our undividedness and oneness as a human family. Through art, we can explore our shared experiences, emotions, and values and find common ground despite our differences. …

'The mystic sees the world as a manifestation of the divine and lives in service to the divine in all things.' — Br. Wayne Teasdale.

'Art is a language of the heart, and it speaks to us in ways that words cannot.' — Br. Wayne Teasdale. …

Art is a means of accessing the wordless language of the heart, of making the invisible visible, of being in the flow of intuitional apprehension of the rhythms of the divine as it reveals itself in human experience."

INTERSPIRITUALITY COMMUNITIES — AND PROPHETIC VOICE

Br. Teasdale in his Nine Elements of a Universal Spirituality ended his nine principles with that of "Prophetic Voice," in its current common parlance "Empowering the prophetic voice for justice, compassion, and world transformation." Of course, this voice has been echoed throughout these present Volumes.

Eloquent submissions from our Featured Authors include a number of important pieces, or elements within their contributions, regarding the following vital observation. If Interspirituality itself is part of the process of "gathering" our global community into a cooperative and peaceful collective, would we not expect the message of "universality" to be inherent within *all* of the world's traditions — the very "universal spirituality in the world's religions" that Br. Teasdale pointed to in his now classic book *The Mystic Heart*?

This is something for us to share in much more detail as we move toward the future additional publication which will center *on* Community in much more detail, and in a format allowing active linkages to elements of the arts, spiritual practice, and other transformational modalities.

As we have said, many if not most of the Features in these Volumes touch on diverse elements of this universality. These enliven some final comments on this world of the Heart, and the forming of a global community in that awakened light — what Br. Teasdale called "preparing the way for a universal civilization, a civilization with a heart." "Such a universal society," he said, "will draw its inspiration from perennial spiritual and moral insights, intuitions, and experiences. These aspects of spirituality will shape...politics and education...our economics, media...and how we develop our relationship with the natural world, while pursuing our quality of life" [MH, p. 5].

As clarioned therein, Teasdale's visioning elicits echoes from across all of the contributions to these Volumes. Furthering this point with some added selections from our Featured Authors, we can look forward to the further development of this theme of the universality of spiritual experience in the direction of our global prophetic voice.

We have already shared from DeShannon Barnes-Bowens' contribution in the Section on First Peoples and foundational cultures — it again pointing to this universality in spiritual experience. Below are further selections from her insightful and inspiring piece.

Selected from

What We Seek is Already Here: The Pluralistic & Interspiritual Nature of Ifá-Òrìṣà Traditions

published in full in Volume 3

by DeShannon Barnes-Bowens

"One of the most profound and impactful cultures on the world spiritual landscape is the Yoruba people of southwest Nigeria. Yoruba culture gave birth to a religious tradition that many people refer to as Ìṣẹ̀ṣe (*tradition*) and more commonly known as Ifá. Some people refer to Ifá as a spiritual tradition that is at least 8,000 years old. ...

Regarding Interspirituality, it is important to look at how Ifá and the spiritual traditions that grew from it, became a collective of Ifá-Òrìṣà traditions comprising at least 100 million practitioners estimated to be anywhere between the 8th to 10 largest world religions according to various scholar-practitioners.[1] ...

We can surmise the purpose of this spiritual tradition to spread beyond the continent of Africa was to demonstrate how characteristics of compassion, benevolence, and generosity naturally develop when we open ourselves to sharing our wisdom with others. These values are similar to what Wayne Teasdale expressed in *The Mystic Heart* when he wrote about the Interspiritual concept of sharing commonalities across religious practices and how that can lead to, '*the ultimate goal of more human responsibility to one another and the planet as a whole.*'[2]

The pluralistic nature of Ifá-Òrìṣà traditions promotes religious integration (*equal value of incorporating religious beliefs*), over acculturation (*assimilating or conforming to the religious beliefs of a dominant group or culture*). …

Harvard Divinity School professor, Dr. Tracey E. Hucks, highlights African American Ifá-Òrìṣà devotees with Interspiritual beliefs and pluralist practices in her groundbreaking book, *Yoruba Traditions & African American Religious Nationalism*. …

When Dr. Hucks interviewed Chief Olomo about her practice of Christianity and Islam before she came into the Ifá-Òrìṣà tradition she said, 'I did not have to throw away or completely ignore the religious tenets that had given my family spiritual solace for generations. Because of ancestral veneration I could integrate them into my African spirituality. …'

These devotees never used the word 'Interspiritual' to describe their beliefs and practice, yet it is what they embody and live. …

My spiritual godfather in Ifá-Òrìṣà tradition would often share the adage, '*S/he who knows one book, knows none*,' emphasizing the importance of becoming familiar with the views of other religious traditions to combat ignorance and realize our connection to each other. …[It] personifies the inclusive tenets that Ifá-Òrìṣà traditions and Interspirituality promotes. …

In *Practical Foundations of Ifá*, Oba Ifágbemi shares an Ifá divination verse of the scripture Ose Osa offering sage guidance, '*Love is the most superior. Let us show love to each other.*'[3] May it become our reality in this lifetime and the next. Ase."

Regarding the universality of that experience of prophetic voice in religious leaders, it has already been mentioned as well in the context of Br. Teasdale's legacy in the remembrance of him by his friend William Howell (Swami Vishnu Datta) — in attribution to Meher Baba's "Wholeness unites the absolute of Pure Existence." In Kurt Johnson and Karuna's piece "The Intersection of Direct Paths in Interspirituality," it is noted that the original longer version in *Contemplative Journal* featured columns of side-by-side quotations of multiple historical seers and gurus "all saying the same thing."

Below, Daniel J. Stone, a strategic change consultant by profession, follows on William Howell's comments on the relevance of this prophetic voice in the Interspiritual Age.

Selected from

Meher Baba and the Coming Interspiritual Age

published in full in Volume 3

by Daniel J. Stone

"Meher Baba is a spiritual master dedicated to this shift in consciousness from reason to intuition that is fundamental to bringing about the feeling of oneness that will underlie the birth of a true Interspiritual Age. …

In one of his most seminal statements, Meher Baba said: *'I have come not to teach but to awaken. I lay down no precepts. When I release the tide of Truth which I have come to give, men's daily lives will be the living precept. The words I have not spoken will come to life in them.'...* — the initiation of the Interspiritual Age, in which all religions and paths find their commonality and are brought together in a harmonious and creative interplay. …

He said that this would usher in a long period of happiness, in which all would have ready access to a living spiritual experience. Beginning in the 1930s, Meher Baba referred to this coming age as the New Humanity. …

However, given all that, what are we then to make of the current cacophony and disharmony we find in our world? Here are Meher Baba's words:

> *All this world confusion and chaos was inevitable and*
> *no one is to blame. What had to happen has happened;*
> *and what has to happen will happen ...*

This all seems like a metaphor for what is happening in our world today; our collective 'boil' is ripening to the point where it is sufficiently 'black,' ready to be lanced. …those who are already experiencing a degree of awakening must continue to spread whatever light has been given to us to participate in bringing about this great event — an event about which Meher Baba said would be something that has never happened before. This great event will be the awakening throughout humanity to the awareness of God as the ever-present reality within each one's heart — the essence of the Interspiritual Age."

Interspiritual Communities Scaling-Up for Real Global Change

Let's conclude with final attention to this vision of our planet being able to "scale-up" to a global partnership culture held by the values that characterize the foundational messages of all our spiritual traditions. It would fulfill the very quotation that opened these Volumes:

> We are at the dawn of a new consciousness, a radically fresh approach to our life as the human family in a fragile world. This journey is what spirituality is really about. We are not meant to remain just where we are. We cannot depend on our culture either to guide and support us in our quest. We must do the hard work of clarification together ourselves. This revolution will be the task of the Interspiritual Age. The necessary shifts in consciousness require a new approach to spirituality that transcends past religious cultures of fragmentation and isolation. We need to understand, to really grasp at an elemental level, that the definitive revolution is the spiritual awakening of humankind [MH pp. 4-12 sequence].

Recently, on September 19, 2024, the day before the historic United Nations "Summit of the Future" and its visioned "Pact for the Future" ("Pact 2030"), leaders of interspiritual and transformational organizations and networks from around the world, including dozens of Featured Authors from these Volumes, gathered at the Synod House of the Cathedral St. John the Divine in New York City for a day-long "Deep and Rapid Transformation Convergence Event." Answering the call of the United Nations Secretary General for action by civil society toward the Summit of the Future, and sponsored by The Evolutionary Leader's Sustainable Development Goals Thought Leaders Circle and others, it (and its gifted facilitators) brought to the Summit of the Future an emergent and powerful unitive and transformational vision (see unitivenarrative.org and "A Radical Guide to Reality" at YouTube), especially aimed at the successful scaling up of global activities toward real transformative change.[5]

Deeply coherent with "the Ups" discussed and detailed throughout these Volumes — "Waking Up, Growing Up, Cleaning Up, Showing Up, Opening Up," etc. — also the centerpiece of Ken Wilber's Afterword to these Volumes, the daylong event brought forward guidelines of principles and praxis by which Interspiritual and transformational communities can effectively support action toward significant global change. As Ken Wilber contexted in his published comments in *The Coming Interspiritual Age*, a book also celebrating its tenth anniversary with the publication of these interspiritual Volumes: "Interspirituality is part of the larger global intersubjective discussion that our world so desperately needs but to a great extent has never had." And, further, "the coming Interspiritual Age has its basis in a background coming transformation — that of an Integral Age."[6] This echoes again Br. Teasdale's words: "We are at the dawn of a new consciousness…" [MH p. 4] and "The Interspiritual Age will require institutions and structures to carry, express, and support it" [MH p. 248].

The principles for vision and praxis advanced by this international event addressed what is truly needed for transformational communities, leaders, and networks to scale up toward truly effective activism. These were:

For something to scale-up to a transformational or paradigm shift, first there must be a *real need*, and in that real need a gravitas and energy that naturally generates direction toward change. To that criterion we answer: "Yes, we address a landscape of real global challenges." What then is distinctive in *our* approaches that may lead them to succeed? "Our approaches are spiritually grounded, vision driven and holistic."

What is uniquely required of our transformational approaches for them to scale-up and actually succeed in real change?

Our praxis approaches must:

(1) Simultaneously serve the individual activist, community, network, or organization *and* the larger surrounding collective landscape of communities and networks;

(2) Be coherent but also adaptable to the diversity of vision and passions of the involved communities and the larger landscape;

(3) Aim to enable empower participation, creativity, innovation and trusted leadership;

(4) Nurture individuals and groups able to "lean-in" deeply for compromises and finding "win-wins" together;

(5) Be result- and process-focused but always appreciative; and

(6) Generate radical collaboration and, in the context of all the above, thus enable structures that are scalable.

And lastly, our work must be persistent and courageous.

In thinking about how to conclude these multi-faceted Volumes, it may serve best to remind of the millennial dilemma of our species — living on this goldilocks (habitable zone) planet somewhere in the Milky Way galaxy, somewhere in the universe. We are a story-telling species, and our planet is elegantly awash with myriad stories of its origin and destiny.

After the vast content of these Volumes, perhaps this can be served by simply repeating the first and last paragraphs in the book *The Coming Interspiritual Age*. They speak to Br. Teasdale's notations:

> "We can integrate all of these insights into human identity, into the *who* of experience, into a reconciling understanding that more deeply comprehends the nature of the human with the matrix of the divine, cosmic and earthly reality" [MH p. 64]; and
>
> "The Interspiritual Age will focus this prophetic function for us as a collective responsibility…concerned with the planet in its entirety" [MH p. 164].

The Opening Challenge
in *The Coming Interspiritual Age*

The dawn of the Third Millennium presented humankind with a dilemma. Will the skill that has characterized our species and propelled its development continue to sustain us, or will competition for power and resources lead to escalating conflict and our eventual extinction? [p. 1]

The Closing Challenge

in *The Coming Interspiritual Age*

After billions of years, there's still a society on this planet participating in the decisions that will ultimately decide our destiny. This is why Interspirituality is so important and so timely. This is ultimately what propels the tale — not this group or that, this citizen or that. The message is always about unity, about ultimate togetherness — earth and cosmos, earth and animal, animal and animal, animal and human, human and human, religion and religion. In the end the message is about the end of separateness, as in all the myths and sacred texts. This is the heart of unitive consciousness [p. 371].

Endnotes and References for "Interspiritual Community" Section[xii]

AFTERWORD

A Truly "Inclusive" Spirituality

by Ken Wilber

One of the greatest breakthroughs in the understanding of world religion is the recent discovery that human beings have at least two quite different, but equally important, types of religious or spiritual engagement. One has been understood for several centuries or even millennia, is found in some form in most of the world's great religions, and can be referred to as "Waking Up." The other is much more recent — so recent, in fact, that it is found in none of the major world religions themselves —and can be called "Growing Up."

Waking Up is generally understood to be the very deepest core of most of the great wisdom religions. It is marked by a direct religious experience of an Awakening to, or Realization of, what is said to be an ultimate Reality (Spirit, Godhead, Ground of All Being, Tao, Brahman, Allah, Great Perfection), an experience known around the world as Enlightenment, Metamorphosis, Satori, Moksha, Fana, the Great Liberation, the Supreme Identity.

Although there are certainly differences in the ways that realization is experienced by different cultures, as well as different genders, different languages, different historical periods, and so on, there are some general family resemblances that make them all generically recognizable. There is almost always a sense of an expansion of self-identity from an isolated, separate self-sense to a Oneness with this ultimate Reality, and therefore also a sense of being one with the entire universe. This is often described as an "awakening" or "enlightenment" because, by comparison, a person's typical pre-awakening consciousness was felt as being lost in a "dream world," a world that is, by comparison, fallen, alienated, and fragmented, marked by inherent suffering (e.g., dukkha) or original sin. The realization of this Supreme Identity is usually said to be the *summum bonum*, the ultimate good, of humankind.

Many of the great traditions have specific systems of meditation, contemplation, deep prayer, yoga, or voyaging that, through a specific set of steps or injunctions, are designed to help move a person from their limited and narrow identity with the separate self-sense (often called the "ego") to a deeper and wider self (generally described as one's "True Self" or "Real Self") that is said to be one with Spirit or ultimate Reality itself. For example, both Vedanta Hinduism and Tibetan Buddhism describe five major states of consciousness possessed by all humans.

They are 1) the waking state (which is said to be an example of the "gross state" of consciousness); 2) the dream state (an example of the "subtle state"); 3) deep dreamless sleep (an example of the "very subtle" or "causal" state); then 4) turiya (which is simply the Sanskrit term for "fourth," and is given that name simply because it is the fourth major state — after the gross, subtle, and causal — and it indicates a pure content-free Awareness, also called the Witness or True Self); and finally, 5) turiyatita ("beyond turiya," which is beyond pure Awareness because the Witness itself becomes one with, or nondual with, everything that it witnesses — in other words, a type of "ultimate Unity consciousness" or "nondual Oneness," the home of one's "True Self"). Similar states to these five major states can be found in many of the world's great mystical and spiritual traditions. The first three states are said to be relative and the home of the ego; the second two states are ultimate and the home of the True Self and its nondual Suchness or ultimate Oneness.

For these traditions, when a person first takes up an effective meditative or contemplative practice, they are usually only fully conscious of the first major state — the waking state, marked by the separate self or ego. As meditation progresses, they will move through each of the five major states (not like rungs in a rigid ladder but as flowing states of increasing expansion), until they have a fully conscious realization of the highest or ultimate state itself (turiyatita or nondual Oneness), which is then said to be the Enlightened or Awakened state. In other words, the major states of consciousness become major stages of development in the overall process of Awakening, or a general process that is called simply "Waking Up."

So compare the names of those major state-stages — the gross (such as waking), the subtle (such as dreaming), the causal (such as deep formless sleep), the Witness, and nondual Unity consciousness — with the following names: the archaic, the magic, the mythic, the rational, the pluralistic, and the integral. They don't sound similar at all, do they?

It's because they are not. The first set of names refers to some of the major states of consciousness that can become some of the major stages of meditation (on the way to Enlightenment). In other words, they are the names of some of the major state-stages of Waking Up. The second set of names, on the other hand, refers to some of the major stages of the process of Growing Up. Whereas Waking Up refers to an overall process that is said to result in the ultimate transcendence of the relative, conventional self (in a selfless True Self and nondual Ground of Being), Growing Up refers to the actual development of that relative self itself — the specific stages that it goes through as it grows and develops and evolves in the conventional relative world.

And why is this important (especially for spirituality)? One of the most profound of the recent discoveries about this Growing Up process is that, no matter what type of immediate awareness or experience that a person has (sensory, mental, or spiritual experience), the stage of Growing Up that they are at will be the primary interpreter of that experience. And this means that no matter what state of Waking Up a person is at, they will interpret that state using the stage of Growing Up that they are at.

One way to explain this is that Waking Up consists of major states of consciousness (we gave five of them according to Hinduism and Buddhism — gross, subtle, causal, turiya, and turiyatita) while Growing Up consists of major structures of consciousness — not states but structures — the archaic structure, the magic structure, the mythic, the rational, the pluralistic, and the integral. Both of them unfold in stages (which are often called state-stages and structure stages, resp.), but otherwise they are quite different. States are immediate, first-person, direct experiences or direct awareness; when you have a state experience, you are directly and fully aware of it. But structures are not like that at all; they are more like grammar — they are third-person rules and patterns that cannot themselves be experienced, but govern how experience is interpreted, edited, parsed — and, most significantly, they cannot be seen by introspecting or looking within or meditating. Most people don't even know that they are actually following an entire system of grammatical rules, let alone what those rules are. Thus, for example, if you look within right now, you won't see anything like the rules of grammar in your awareness, although every time you think and speak you are following those rules quite accurately. (And notice that no amount of meditation will show you those rules, either.)

The various structures of Growing Up (such as magic, mythic, rational, pluralistic, integral), are very much like grammar — when a person is following a particular structure of Growing Up, they will follow its rules and patterns quite accurately, but have no idea that they are doing so. For this reason, these structures were not even discovered until around one hundred years ago — quite unlike most of the major states of consciousness (including unitive states), many of which (precisely because they are direct and immediate first-person experiences) were discovered thousands of years ago (and almost all of the great religious traditions have some sort of reference, often quite detailed, to these higher states of enlightenment, awakening, or metamorphosis and how to attain them).

This is why, as we noted, that most of the world's great religions were founded by individuals who had experienced some of these higher states, and they began teaching others how to attain or Wake Up to these enlightened states. But not a single great religion or meditative spiritual system anywhere in the world has any understanding of the stages of Growing Up. In ancient times, knowledge of those Growing Up stages was like the knowledge of quarks, atoms, molecules, or cells — they were completely unknown at the time during which most of the great religions were first codified (and they remain unknown to this day in virtually every major spiritual system worldwide) — which is one of the major deficiencies of typical religions.

Similarly, James Fowler empirically discovered this when he studied the spiritual belief systems of thousands of people. Let me preface this by pointing out that many psychologists today do not believe that humans have only one type of intelligence, usually called "cognitive intelligence" and measured by an all important IQ. Humans rather possess what Howard Gardner referred to as "multiple intelligences." However important cognitive intelligence certainly is, there is also emotional intelligence, moral intelligence, aesthetic intelligence, mathematical intelligence, interpersonal intelligence, spatial intelligence, verbal intelligence, and so on — and this definitely includes a spiritual intelligence as well. The discovery of this spiritual intelligence is the second major form of spiritual engagement that human beings have. Notice that this specific spiritual intelligence, as one of several multiple intelligences, is not the same as a direct Waking Up or personal experience of anything claimed to be an ultimate reality; these multiple intelligences are all aspects of relative mental growth and development, they are lines of development in the Growing Up process; they all consist of structures, like grammar, not states, or direct first-person experiences.

There is another major dimension that, like the path of Growing Up, was only discovered in a serious way by the modern West, also around just one hundred years ago, and thus does not clearly or fully show up in any major spiritual system anywhere in the world, and that is what we call "Cleaning Up."

Cleaning Up refers to the general processes whose discovery is most often associated with the name of Sigmund Freud and his inner circle (all of whom were bona fide geniuses — Carl Jung, Alfred Adler, Otto Rank, Salvador Ferenczi), but actually includes an entire panoply of folks such as Janet, Binswanger, Sullivan, Perls, Kernberg,

Kohut, and so on. It deals with the fact that human beings can, under extremely stressful and traumatic conditions, deny or repress or split off or alienate significant facets of their own being, pushing them from consciousness into an unconscious state. Denying or repressing these aspects — often known as "shadow" — does not actually make them go away, but instead forces this shadow material to create warped, disguised, and painful symptoms (of anxiety, depression, obsession, and so on), a dysfunction usually known as neurosis or a more serious psychosis. The cure — according to Freud et al. — is to contact the alienated, unconscious, shadow material and make it conscious again, rejoining and integrating it with the rest of the conscious mind.

This repression of shadow material is an extremely serious matter when it comes to religious or spiritual issues, because, first, virtually everybody has some sort of shadow material, and second, the religious drives that a person has are almost always infested with shadow material. Shadow driven desires, on the one hand, and the search for God, on the other, are almost always deeply intertwined. And teasing them apart — engaging the process of Cleaning Up to at least some degree — becomes a crucial component of any serious spiritual path, or the seeker might find, when they think they have discovered God, that they have only come face-to-face with their own shadow. And even a profound Waking Up will not necessarily get at this unconscious material — the specific practices found in psychotherapy or Cleaning Up are required (and are profoundly different from those of Waking Up).

So it's important to note that Cleaning Up is a process that in itself is profoundly different from both Waking Up and Growing Up. It has different causes; it produces very different results; and it is addressed by very different practices and techniques. And they are all relatively independent — Growing Up and Waking Up and Cleaning Up — you can progress incredibly well in any one of them and still be totally lagging in the others, and this can happen in any combination. But it seems undeniable that many, perhaps most, individuals on a spiritual path seem on occasion to be infected with significant amounts of shadow material, and the drive to (unconsciously) deal with that shadow material can become disguised as the drive to find Spirit — with the added disaster that most spiritual paths teach very little, if anything, about Cleaning Up and ways to both recognize and treat shadow material. If severe, this shadow material can derange the spiritual journey in profound ways, including completely derailing it.

Let me briefly mention one more such area, and then I'll draw a few important conclusions. We call this domain "Showing Up," and it refers to being fully open to, or showing up for, the major fundamental perspectives available in a person's life. There are many different and equally legitimate ways to refer to these basic perspectives. The Greeks called them "the Good, the True, and the Beautiful." Virtually all languages around the world contain pronouns that refer to first-person, second-person, and third-person perspectives (with first-person being defined as the perspective of "the person who is speaking," an "I" or "me" — and this includes aesthetics or the Beauty that "is in the eye — the 'I' — of the beholder"; second-person is "the person being spoken to" — or a "you" or "thou" — with the Good (as with the Good, the True, and the Beautiful) being the ethical ways that "I" should treat "you"; and third-person is "the person or thing being spoken about" — which includes the objectively True of the natural sciences). These are Karl Popper's "Three Worlds" (subjective, sociocultural, and objective). They are Jürgen Habermas's "three validity claims" (aesthetics / truthfulness, goodness, and objective truth). They are

Immanuel Kant's three major critiques: of Pure Reason, Practical Reason, and Judgement.

These perspectives directly apply to spirituality as well, because Spirit itself can legitimately be viewed through all three of them. Notice, as but one example, that Christ spoke ABOUT God (that's third-person), he spoke TO God (that's second-person), and he spoke AS God (that's first-person). As usual, it's fairly rare that an integral approach is taken and all three perspectives are realized to be equally valid so that all of them are fully embraced — usually just one perspective is chosen and proclaimed the only correct view.

Thus… Waking Up (including all states of consciousness and Enlightenment), Growing Up (including all structures or levels of vertical growth and development), Cleaning Up (including and integrating all shadow material), Opening Up (to all of one's multiple intelligences or lines of development), and Showing Up (including all three or four quadrant perspectives of one's being and awareness) — these are simply ways to embrace the very important and equally necessary dimension / perspectives that any spirituality would want to fully incorporate if it wants to be truly healthy and authentic. Notice that both Growing Up and Cleaning Up are areas that were only recently understood to be found in any of the major religious systems anywhere in the world, many of which are a thousand years or older. This lack has increasingly become truly a cultural disaster of worldwide and global proportions, because research continues to demonstrate that success in any one of these five major areas (Waking Up, Growing Up, Cleaning Up, Opening Up, and Showing Up) does not guarantee success in any of the others, and thus not only can a person have a very high degree of Waking Up yet remain at very early and relatively low stages of Growing Up (often egocentric magic and ethnocentric mythic), they also often have very serious shadow issues that need horribly to be dealt with in Cleaning Up; and, to really drive in the last coffin nail, they could also not be aware of the 1-2-3 of Spirit, thus failing to Show Up fully for the many faces of God in their own lives.

In other words, due to ongoing research and metatheoretical work — or, we could say, due to the ongoing evolution of Spirit in the manifest world — we of today have a much broader understanding of the dimensions or components that a fully enacted spiritual awareness ideally involves. We have also seen that leaving out any one of these dimensions results in a demonstrably crippled spirituality, offering considerably less than we already know can in fact be achieved.

I think we've seen enough of even some simple and short explanations of why all five of those dimensions — Waking Up, Growing Up, Cleaning Up, Opening Up, and Showing Up — are so crucial and indispensable to any authentic spirituality, and certainly any Religion of Tomorrow (which is the title of a book I wrote on just this topic). The point of that book is that traditional religion as we know it is declining quite rapidly; polls show that the number of northern Europeans who seriously believe in orthodox religion is now only 11 percent. My point is that since most modern Western religion tends to neglect Waking Up as a central practice, has absolutely no Growing Up and no Cleaning Up, and seems to poorly grasp Showing Up — it's no surprise that such a deficient system is in decline, and such a defective religion will very likely not survive into the future if it does not become truly integral and begin including all of those areas it now severely neglects. A truly comprehensive spirituality today contains a wealth of different dimensions that none of the traditional religious approaches came anywhere near understanding or including.

The point of all of that is simply that Spirit itself continues to unfold and evolve in numerous ways in the manifest world, and any authentic spirituality needs to stay on a path of genuine inclusiveness just to keep up. A thousand years from now — given how incredibly fast culture evolves, including spiritual culture — do we really think that the Bible or the Upanishads or Sutras will describe absolutely everything that there is to know about Spirit and how to realize it? Of course not. So why wait a thousand years to start including?

A truly Integral Spirituality — including Waking Up, Growing Up, Cleaning Up, Opening Up, and Showing Up — will almost certainly be the religion of tomorrow. The wise will therefore surely start now on this path of genuine spiritual inclusion.

ENDNOTES
Volume 2

i: Endnotes and References for Opening Message

[1.] H. H. the 14th Dalai Lama authored the Foreword to Br. Teasdale's *The Mystic Heart* and for his Opening Message in the current Volumes we thank him, his staff, the creators of *The Wisdom of Happiness* film, the Oneness of Humanity Awards and Olivia Hansen for arranging this Opening Message.

ii: Endnotes and References for "Introduction to Volume 2"

[1.] Friends of the Institute of Noetic Sciences (fions.org): Statement of the reorganized Board of Directors, 2013. **[2.]** National Public Radio (NPR) account (npr.org), October 23, 2022. **[3.]** Same source as Endnote 1. **[4.]** *Waking Up, Growing Up, Cleaning Up, Showing Up, Lifting Up, Linking Up*. [hereafter "2018 Publication for Parliament of the World's Religions"] 2019. Preview Issue for the 2018 Parliament of the World's Religions. Johnson, K., S. M. Winters and R. Ulfik (Eds.). New York, NY: Light on Light Publications. https://issuu.com/lightonlight/docs/the_convergence_special_edition_preview. **[5.]** Endnote 4 citation, p. 6. Published in full in: *Waking Up: The New York Convergence* [*Convergence* Special Issue] 2019. Winters, S. M., and K. Johnson (Eds.). New York, NY: Light on Light Publications. **[6.]** Wilson, David Sloan. 2015. *Does Altruism Exist? Culture, Genes and the Welfare of Others*, from Foundational Questions in Science Series, 1. New Haven CT: Yale University Press / Templeton Press. Program partnerships between the interspiritual community and the mainstream evolutionary science community began in 2015 with programs between the Interspiritual Dialogue Network and the Evolution Institute of the State Universities of New York (https://evolution-institute.org/). Kurt Johnson also summarized the backstory in the oft-cited publication "Evolving Toward Cooperation: David Sloan Wilson's New Evolutionary Biology" *Kosmos Journal* 2022: Vol 18, Issue 3, now at https://www.kosmosjournal.org/kj_article/interspirituality-and-evolutions-direction-toward-cooperation/ Later there was a transition to named partnerships with Prosocial.world which was a new entity that evolved out of the Evolution Institute in 2020. **[7.]** Originally published online in 2015 by Evolution Institute (https://evolution-institute.org/steering-toward-the-omega-point-a-roundtable-discussion-of-altruism-evolution-and-spirituality/); archived on line in 2022 as https://davidsloanwilson.world/online-content/steering-toward-the-omega-point-a-roundtable-discussion-of-altruism-evolution-and-spirituality-with-kurt-johnson/ with these participations: Table of Contents: – Introduction: Science in a Spiritual Key, by David Sloan Wilson and Kurt Johnson – Synopsis of Does Altruism Exist? Culture Genes and the Welfare of Others, by David Sloan Wilson; – Commentary 1: The Sacred and the Secular Can Unite on Altruism, by Kurt Johnson; – Commentary 2: When It Comes to Climate Change, Altruism Better Exist, by Richard Clugston; – Commentary 3: The Wolves of Wall Street and Superorganisms: How Social Justice Should Mimic Our Cells, by Barbara Marx Hubbard, Zachary Stein, and Marc Gafni; – Commentary 4: "Does Altruism Exist?" Wrong Question; Right Answer, by David Korten; – Commentary 5: Insects Model their Societies on Altruism. We need to become Planetary Altruists, by Rev. Mac Legerton; – Commentary 6: Altruism Comes with Age, by Kevin Brabazon; – Commentary 7: Altruism's Path and the Rebirth of Spirituality, by Doug King and Mike Morrell;– Commentary 8: Altruism and Integral Spirituality, by Ken Wilber; – Discussion Questions about Does Altruism Exist?; – Reply to Commentaries on Does Altruism Exist?: Integrating Science and Spirituality through Action, by David Sloan Wilson; – References. There is then the long history of shared events in the texts of these Volumes, beginning with the citations in Endnotes 8 and 9 and, ultimately the discussion with H. H. The Dalai Lama, David Sloan Wilson, Kurt Johnson and others facilitated by Mind & Life Institute in India (see Endnotes viii: [12]:5). **[8.]** Videos of these Conference's Panels at "Altruism Roundtables to Date," Panel 1-3, http://www.thecominginterspiritualage.com/initiatives and "Roundtable Discussions on the Evolutionary Altruism Paradigm" [same 3 panels] at https://www.selfcaretoearthcare.com/resources. **[9.]** *Does Altruism Exist?* [*Convergence* Special Issue]. 2017. Winters, S. M., K. Johnson and Y. Maniates (Ed.). New York, NY: Light on Light Publications. https://issuu.com/lightonlight/docs/the_convergence_oct_2017. **[10.]** **(i)** Two sequential special issues of *Light on Light* e-magazine [2018] and **(ii)** one of *Convergence* e-magazine [2017] record these ongoing activities (with subsequent shorter articles in *Convergence* and *Light on*

Light emags [2017-19] all at issuu.com links below: 1. Activities of the Interspiritual Dialogue Network (https://issuu.com/lightonlight/docs/lightonlight_issue_1); "Transformational Communities" (https://issuu.com/lightonlight/docs/lightonlight_issue_2); 2. *The Road to 2020* [*Convergence* Special Issue]. 2018. Winters, S. M., B. Bowler, K. Johnson and Y. Maniates (Ed.). New York, NY: Light on Light Publications. These were followed by, up to, or reporting on, the noted Crestone Leadership Conference by **(iii)** the previously noted 2018 Publication for Parliament of the World's Religions [Endnote 4]; **(iv)** the first annual *Yoga, Healing and Peace* [*Light on Light* Special Issue] 2018. Winters, S. M., D. Scotto and Karuna (Ed.). New York, NY: Light on Light Publications. **(v)** *UDay Festival at African Union for UN World Interfaith Harmony Week*. [*Convergence* Special Issue] 2018. Winters, S. M., M. Hailu and B. Bowler (Ed.). New York, NY: Light on Light Publications. **(vi)** *Waking Up: The New York Convergence* [*Convergence* Special Issue] 2019. Winters, S. M., and K. Johnson (Ed.). New York, NY: Light on Light Publications. **(vii)** *Waking Up and Growing Up: The Conscious Business World Summit*. 2019. *Convergence* [*Convergence* Special Issue] 2019. Winters, S. M., and K. Johnson (Ed.). New York, NY: Light on Light Publications. **(viii)** *Sacred Sites and Spirituality in Nature*. 2019. [*Light on Light* Special Issue] 2019. Winters, S. M., Karuna and K. Johnson (Ed.). New York, NY: Light on Light Publications. **[11.]** Aspen Chapel quotation from original ms. of Kurt Johnson's presentation; second quotation from "The Interspiritual Paradigm: Legacies and Horizons" by Kurt Johnson, pp. 55-56 in Sw. Shraddhananda [Ed.]. *Mature Interspirituality*. 2017. Somerset, KY: Sacred Feet. **[12.]** From "Steering Toward the Omega Point: A Roundtable Discussion of Altruism, Evolution and Spirituality" with Kurt Johnson (2015) from This View of Life ("Interviews": https://davidsloanwilson.world/online-content/). **[13.]** See Snow, C.P. *The Two Cultures*. London UK: Cambridge University Press, [1959] 2001; Snow, C. P., and Stefan Collini. *The Two Cultures* [Commemorative Ed.]. London UK: Cambridge University Press, 1993; and Brockman, John. *The Third Culture: Beyond the Scientific Revolution*. New York, NY: Simon & Schuster, 1995. **[14.]** Familiar and popular phrase from public presentations by Dr. David Sloan Wilson; for example in "Picking Up Where Darwin Left Off," Andi Publisher, pitchforkeconomics.com (June 18, 2019), drawn from his Wilson, David Sloan. 2019. *This View of Life: Completing the Darwinian Revolution*. New York, NY:

Pantheon Books. **[15.]** See Endnote vii: 21 in Volume 1. Quoted from the ms. of Kurt Johnson's presentation at Science and Nonduality Conference (SAND), 2014 (Conference Theme: "Entanglement"). **[16.]** Hellmich, P. and K. Johnson. "Sacred and Secular Activists are now Joining their Strategies for Peacebuilding," pp, 27-41 in Cook, B. L. and M. C. Azcona (Eds.). 2016. *Strategies for Peace*. Rochester NY: Cook Communication. **[17.]** Hellmich, P. 2012. *God and Conflict: A Search for Peace in a Time of Crisis*. Berkeley, Ca: Spirit of Peace Press. **[18.]** "Towards a Global Ethic: An Initial Declaration" The Parliament of the World's Religions (wikipedia.org/wiki/Towards_a_Global_Ethic:_An_Initial_Declaration). Toronto Parliament theme: https://parliamentofreligions.org/parliament/2018-toronto/#. **[19.]** See Volume 1, Endnote vii: 14. **[20.]** "The Growing Edge of Interspirituality" by Kurt Johnson. *The Interfaith Observer*, originally published, Oct. 2017, now at http://www.theinterfaithobserver.org/journal-articles/2017/10/2/the-growing-edge-of-interspirituality.

iii: Endnotes and References for "History" Section

[1.] Wikipedia re: Max King https://en.wikipedia.org/wiki/Max_King_(theologian). **[2.]** Sw. Shraddhananda [Ed.]. 2017. *Mature Interspirituality*. Somerset, KY: Sacred Feet. **[3.]** *The Convergence* radio series on VoiceAmerica (see history and program chronology at lightonlight.us/voice-america) was founded in 2016 by 1God.com and the Interspiritual Dialogue as they joined as UNITY EARTH (unity.earth). Since 2022 the program has been dedicated to activities of the Evolutionary Leaders under the theme "Humanity's Moment of Choice" following on the award-winning book by the Evolutionary Leaders *Our Moment of Choice*. The program moved to a new platform in 2025-2026, with all previous programming available in an Archive, and this can be tracked at lightonlight.us/voice-america. **[4.]** Abridged from p. 3; pp. 7-9 in *U Day Festival at African Union for UN World Interfaith Harmony Week*. [*Convergence* Special Issue] 2018. Winters, S. M., M. Hailu and B. Bowler (Ed.). New York, NY: Light on Light Publications. **[5.]** Abridged from pp. 25-27 in source in Endnote 4. **[6.]** The series of free e-magazines and e-publications from Light on Light Publications is at https://issuu.com/lightonlight. As of 2025 there are 23 issues, including those under the banners of the *Convergence* magazine, the *Light on Light* magazine and various free-standing e-publication titles. Interspiritual Dialogue

(ISD) (a religious 501c3) is the parent of Light on Light, under the auspices of ISD's mandated education programs. **[7.]** *Waking Up, Growing Up, Cleaning Up, Showing Up, Lifting Up, Linking Up*. [aka "2018 Publication for Parliament of the World's Religions"] 2019. Preview Issue for the 2018 Parliament of the World's Religions. Johnson, K., S. M. Winters and R. Ulfik (Eds.). New York, NY: Light on Light Publications. https://issuu.com/lightonlight/docs/the_convergence_special_edition_preview. **[8.]** Where these authors' pieces are published in full online (Citation and then names and paginations of relevant authors): *Waking Up: The New York Convergence* [*Convergence* Special Issue] 2019. Winters, S. M., and K. Johnson (Ed.). New York, NY: Light on Light Publications (Deepak Chopra, Dena Merriam, Ken Wilber); *Waking Up and Growing Up: The Conscious Business World Summit*. 2019. *Convergence* [*Convergence* Special Issue] 2019. Winters, S. M., and K. Johnson (Ed.). New York, NY: Light on Light Publications (Patrick Carolan, Duane Elgin); *Sacred Sites and Spirituality in Nature*. 2019. [*Light on Light* Special Issue] 2019. Winters, S. M., Karuna and K. Johnson (Ed.). New York, NY: Light on Light Publications (Duane Elgin, Llewellyn Vaughan-Lee); *Change Makers*. 2019. [*Light on Light* Special Issue] 2019. Winters, S. M., Karuna and K. Johnson (Ed.). New York, NY: Light on Light Publications (Michael Bernard Beckwith, Deepak Chopra). **[9.]** See Endnote 8, first citation. **[10.]** We are so pleased to publish in full this piece submitted to Light on Light Publications by the late, beloved, Terry Patten. Learn more about Terry Patten here: https://awholeheart.com/2021/11/02/the-brightening-of-terry-patten/. **[11.]** See "Opening Up" in the contributions by Ken Wilber to Light on Light Press books: "Foreword" in *Global Unitive Healing* (2021), "Special Commentary" in *Science, Being, & Becoming* (2022); "Interval" in *The Holomovement* (2023), all at lightonlight.us. And, in references noted: Wilber, Ken. 1977. *The Spectrum of Consciousness*. New York, NY: Quest Books; he has also featured "Opening Up" as one of five key dimensions of human wholeness (or transformation) in his recent book *Finding Radical Wholeness: The Integral Path to Unity, Growth, and Delight*. 2024. Boulder, CO: Shambhala Publications. See also *The Religion of Tomorrow: A Vision of the Future of the Great Traditions — More Inclusive, More Comprehensive, More Complete*. 2017. Boulder, CO: Shambhala Publications.

iv: Endnotes and References for "Global Ethic" Section 2

[1.] See Endnote vii: 21 in Volume 1. Quoted from the ms. of Kurt Johnson's presentation at Science and Nonduality Conference (SAND), 2015 (Conference Theme: "Living Transformation"). **[2.]** See Endnotes ii: 6-9 in Volume 2 re: same information, citations, quotations and paraphrases as referenced in this speech. **[3.]** Re: Crestone Leadership Conferences (aka "Crestone Convergences"), see details and citations in Endnotes ii: 10 (i-iii) in Volume 2. Re: Rome-Assisi Conferences—2017: Forum 21 was a major cosponsor of the 2017 "Rome and Assisi Conference on Spirituality and Sustainability (S&S)" (June 27-July 4, 2017) that brought together 60 lead organizations and individuals. UNITY EARTH joined as a cosponsor. For photos of this conference, see https://forum-a6mp.squarespace.com/assisi-media; 2018: Forum 21, along with UNITY EARTH and other co-sponsors, hosted "The 2018 Rome and Assisi Conference on Spirituality and Sustainability" May 25 – June 1, 2018. **[4.]** Re: the Crestone conferences and First Peoples see *Sacred Sites and Spirituality in Nature*. 2019. [*Light on Light* Special Issue] 2019. Winters, S. M., Karuna and K. Johnson (Ed.). New York, NY: Light on Light Publications. **[5.]** See Volume 2 Endnote iii: 3, just above. **[6.]** A photo, and the letter are both shared on pp. 40-41 at the citation in Volume 2 Endnote iii: 4, just above, and, among other places at One Earth: https://www.oneearth.org/vatican-renounces-doctrine-of-discovery-in-support-of-indigenous-rights/. **[7.]** General context: "google" "The Emerging Inter-Shamanism Inherent in the Emerging Interspiritual Age". The original Interspiritual Network "Subtle Realm Activism" Circle had fifty members identifying the Interspiritual experience within First Peoples traditions and their shamanic heritage; it was associated with Gaiafield.net (https://gaiafield.net/gaiafield-allies/) in 2015. The tele-summit hosted by this group was recounted at the isdna.org's "Interspiritual Multiplex" website which, due to now obsolete web-hosting is no longer on line. These activities were a precursor to the Crestone events of 2017 and 2018 detailed in these Volumes and the Endnotes in Volume 2, iii: 3-6 above. **[8.]** Detailed at https://gaiafield.net/ following on the book: Nicol, David. 2015. *Subtle Activism: The Inner Dimension of Social and Planetary Transformation*. Albany, NY: State University of New York Series in Transpersonal and Humanistic Psychology. **[9.**] See pp. 52-54 in *Sacred Sites and Spirituality in*

Nature. 2019. [*Light on Light* Special Issue] 2019. Winters, S. M., Karuna and K. Johnson (Ed.). New York, NY: Light on Light Publications. **[10.]** See Volume 2 Endnote ii: 3.

v: Endnotes and References for "Indigenous Peoples" Section

[1.] Selected from event compositions of Patricia Anne Davis, Jon Ramer, and Chief Dwaine Perry from the Solstice Unites initiative (https://solsticeunites.earth/); summary of initiative (https://us5.campaign-archive.com/?u=18513a22108989dad7e255cfd&id=25ef34ba00) and re: in relationship to the Ramapough Lenape First Peoples [see Chief Dwaine Perry below, Endnotes 6,7] and https://oneworld.earth/posts/many-peoples-one-nation-the-enduring-story-of-the-ramapough-munsee-lenape-nation-83548839. **[2.]** Following on this solicited Feature, see also re: Mindahi sources, Volume 2, Endnotes ii: 10 (i, v, vii); Volume 2, Endnotes Iv: 3, 4, 5, 6; Volume 2, Endnote v: 11). **[3.]** Excerpted and abridged from article and interview with Geraldine Patrick Encina at The Institute of Natural Law: https://instituteofnaturallaw.substack.com/p/waking-up-to-the-new-dawn-in-2025. **[4.]** Excerpted and abridged from article and interview with Geraldine Patrick Encina at Earth Timekeepers: http://earthtimekeepers.org/. **[5.]** From Four Winds International Institute (of Hereditary Chief Phil Lane et al.): sequentially subtitled sections at Four Winds International Institute Home Page https://www.fwii.earth/; for additional vision and information see the rest of that site and https://www.linkedin.com/pulse/dawning-new-global-civilization-phil-lane-jr-; https://www.4worlds.org/. **[6.]** Podcast: https://www.buzzsprout.com/1827447/13710848 or YouTube "Crossing the Boundary" (https://www.youtube.com/watch?v=xwCj57Qo61c) led with the commentator's note: "At the center of these activities is the man who since 2007 has been the elected Chief of the Ramapough Munsee tribe, Dwaine Perry. It was an honor for me to record my recent conversation with Chief Perry for my podcast and YouTube Channel "Crossing the Boundary." **[7.]** The Film *American Native* (https://www.imdb.com/title/tt2734708/). **[8.]** Adapted from two recent presentations by Oscar Miro-Quesada: "Taripaypacha: The Prophesied Era of Re-Encounter" and "Shamanism and Generative AI: Unveiling Shared Potentials for Planetary Survival and Human Evolution" provided in manuscript form. **[9.]** [1]Tracey E. Hucks, *Yoruba Traditions and African American Religious Nationalism*

(Albuquerque: University of New Mexico Press, 2012), 240. [2]Ibid., 241. [3]Kọ́lá Abímbọ́lá, *Yoruba Culture – A Philosophical Account* (Birmingham, United Kingdom: Iroko Academic Publishers, 2006), 102-103. **[10.]** Ywahoo, Dhyani. *Voices of Our Ancestors: Cherokee Teachings From the Wisdom Fire*. Shambhala Publications, 1987. **11.** Bastida, Mindahi. *Ancestors: Divine Remembrances of Lineage, Relations and Sacred Sites*. Sacred Stories. 2023.

vi: Endnotes and References for "Sacred Activism, Holism" Section

[1.] References: Bullard, R. et al. (2007). *Toxic waste and race at twenty.* NRDC. https://www.nrdc.org/sites/default/files/toxic-wastes-and-race-at-twenty-1987-2007.pdf. Carson, R. (2017). *The sense of wonder: A celebration of nature for parents and children.* Harper Perennial. Teasdale, W. (1999). *The Mystic Heart: Discovering a Universal Spirituality in the World's Religions.* New World Library. Davidson, R. (2023, August 8-10). *Climate change and the psychology of resilience* [Conference presentation]. Resilience in the Anthropocene at the Rita Summit, online. Kimmerer, R. W. (2021). White Pine. In J. Ryan, P. Vieira, & M. Gagliano (Eds.), *The Mind of Plants: Narratives of Vegetal Intelligence.* Synergetic Press. Li, Q. (2018). *Forest bathing: How trees can help you find health and happiness.* Viking. Kimmerer, R.W. (2015). *Braiding sweetgrass: Indigenous wisdom, scientific knowledge and the teaching of plants.* Milkweed Editions. Krenshaw, K. (1989). Demarginalizing the intersection of race and sex: A Black feminist critique of antidiscrimination doctrine, feminist theory and antiracist politics. *University of Chicago Legal Forum: Vol. 1989, Article 8.* https://chicagounbound.uchicago.edu/uclf/vol1989/iss1/8. *Treaties still matter: The Dakota access pipeline.* (2018). https://americanindian.si.edu/nk360/plains-treaties/dapl#:~:text=Many%20Native%20Nations%2C%20along%20with,at%20the%20camp%20became%20intense. **[2.]** [1]Chief Si'ahl also known as Chief Seattle (Chief of the Duwamish and Suquamish tribes) *Letter to All.* December 1854. [2]Vaughan-Lee, Llewellyn. *The Return of the Feminine and the World Soul.* California: The Golden Sufi Center, CA. 2009: 47. [3]Quoted. in Mathew Fox, "Hildegard of Bingen's Vision of the Divine Feminine." *Daily Meditations with Mathew Fox*, March 15, 2019. https://dailymeditationswithmatthewfox.org/2019/05/15/hildegard-of-bingens-vision-of-the-divine-feminine/. [4]Johnson, Kurt & Ord David R, *The Coming of the Interspiritual Age*. Canada: Namaste Publishing Inc, 2013: 322. [5]Teasdale, Wayne. *The Mystic Heart: Discovering a Universal Spirituality in the World's Religions*. Novato, CA: New World Library, 1999:268. [6]Borysenko, Joan. *What is Interspirituality?* (2023) https://joanborysenko.com/spirituality/what-is-interspirituality/. [7]Kourie, Celia. *Abhishiktananda (Henri le Saux, O.S.B) 1910-1973: Pioneer of interspiritual mysticism*. HTS/ Theological Studies. Original Research: SPIRASA Spirituality. Aosis Publishing: 2018 https://hts.org.za/index.php/HTS/article/view/5132. [8]Teasdale, Wayne. *The Mystic Heart: Discovering a Universal Spirituality in the World's Religions*. Novato, CA: New World Library, 1999: 4. Teasdale, Wayne. *The Mystic Heart: Discovering a Universal Spirituality in the World's Religions*. Novato, CA: New World Library, 1999: 27. [0]Teasdale, Wayne. *The Mystic Heart: Discovering a Universal Spirituality in the World's Religions*. Novato, CA: New World Library, 1999: 28. **[3.]** [1]Sri Aurobindo. "Essays in Philosophy and Yoga," CWSA Vol. 13, p. 211. [2]Wikimedia Foundation. (1/17/24). Religious war. Wikipedia. https://en.wikipedia.org/wiki/Religious_war. [3]Lurie, R. A. (2012, June 10). Is religion the cause of most wars? HuffPost. https://www.huffpost.com/entry/is-religion-the-cause-of_b_1400766. [4]Sri Aurobindo. "Essays on the Gita," CWSA Vol. 19, p. 4. [5]Sri Aurobindo. "Savitri," Book 6, Canto 2, CWSA Vols. 33-34, p. 459. [6]Sri Aurobindo. :Savitri," Book 1, Canto 4, CWSA Vols. 33-34, p. 68. [7]Sri Aurobindo. "Savitri," Book 6, Canto 2, CWSA Vols. 33-34, p. 460. [8]Sri Aurobindo. "The Human Cycle," CWSA Vol. 25. Sri Aurobindo. "The Human Cycle." CWSA Vol. 25, p. 19. [10]Sri Aurobindo. "The Ideal of Human Unity," CWSA Vol. 25, p. 566. [11]Sri Aurobindo. "Savitri," Book 5, Canto 1, CWSA Vols. 33-34, p. 390. [12]Sri Aurobindo. "The Human Cycle," CWSA Vol. 25 p. 184. [13]Sri Aurobindo. "The Human Cycle." CWSA Vol. 25, p. 77. [14]Sri Aurobindo. "Karmayogin," CWSA Vol. 8, p. 11. [15]The Mother. "Questions and Answers (1957-1958)" CWM Vol. 9, p. 78. [16]Zukav, Gary. "The Seat of the Soul." New York: Simon & Schuster (A Fireside Book), 1989, pp. 13-21. [17]Hawkins, David. "Power Versus Force: An Anatomy of Consciousness. The Hidden Determinants of Human Behaviour." Sedona Arizona: Veritas Publishing, Second Edition, 1998, p.67. [18]Sri Aurobindo. "Savitri," Book 7, Canto 2, CWSA Vols. 33-34, p. 484. **[4.]** Diogo Ponte and Lothar Schäfer. 2013. "Carl Gustav Jung, Quantum Physics and the Spiritual Mind: A Mystical Vision of the Twenty-First

Century." *Behavioral Sciences* 3 (4): 601–18. https://doi.org/10.3390/bs3040601. [2]Ponte and Schäfer, Carl Jung, p. 611, 602. [3]According to the online Oxford Reference, intersubjectivity is "(1.) the process and product of sharing experiences, knowledge, understandings, and expectations with others…; (2.) the mutual construction of relationship through shared subjectivity." Philosopher Edmund Husserl defined it as "the interchange of thoughts and feelings, both conscious and unconscious, between two persons or 'subject,' as facilitated by empathy." In this experience, the person or subject loses him- or herself in the experience of connection. From Roberto S. Goizuetta, *Caminemos Con Jesús: Toward A Hispanic / Latino Theology of Accompaniment.* Maryknoll (New York: Orbis Books, 1995), 91. See José Vasconcelos, Obras Completas, 4 vols (México, DF: Libreros Mexicanos Unidos, 1958–61), 4:16. [4]Raimon Panikkar. 2013. *The Rhythm of Being: The Unbroken Trinity*. Maryknoll, New York: Orbis Books, p. 34, 55, 277. [5]Loren Eiseley, L. C., "The Dance of the Frogs," *The Star Thrower*. New York: Harcourt Brace & Company, 1978, 112. [6]Loren Eiseley, "Dance," 114. [7]Loren Eiseley, "Dance," 114. [8]Loren Eiseley, "Dance," 114. [9]Loren Eiseley, "Dance," 115. [10]In Greek mythology a chimera was a "fire-breathing she-monster," with the head of a lion, the body of a goat, and the tail of a serpent; "an imaginary monster compounded of incongruous parts." *Merriam-Webster.com Dictionary*, s.v. "chimera," accessed November 11, 2022, https://www.merriam-webster.com/dictionary/chimera. [11]Olav Lapaire , Irène Hösli, Rosanna Zanetti-Daellenbach, Dorothy Huang, Carmen Jaeggi, Susanne Gatfield-Mergenthaler, Sinuhe Hahn, & Wolfgang Holzgreve, "Impact of fetal-maternal microchimerism on women's health–a review," NIH National Library of Medicine, Nat. Center for Biotechnology Information. https://pubmed.ncbi.nlm.nih.gov/17437192/. [12]Jose Vasconcelos proposed coined the term "'empathetic fusion" to describe an encounter in which a person or subject loses him or herself in the experience of connection. Roberto S. Goizuetta, *Caminemos Con Jesús: Toward A Hispanic / Latino Theology of Accompaniment*. Maryknoll (New York: Orbis Books, 1995), 91. See José Vasconcelos, *Obras Completas*, 4 vols (México, DF: Libreros Mexicanos Unidos, 1958–61), 4:16. [13]Human Energy. "Singing the Universe into Being: Ritual and Creation of a Global Community." *YouTube*, 2 Aug. 2021, https://youtu.be/iiZzPV8wyc0?si=jjjH64Xx36jo_hQW. **[5.]**

Fr. Thomas Keating on the Spirit of Interreligious Dialogue, presentation at Naropa University, 2010, online, https://www.youtube.com/watch?v=H0QKupTCWMA. [2]For examples of teachings across the religions that encourage respect and love for the other religions, here are some key passages from various scriptures: *Christianity:* And Peter opened his mouth and said, "Truly I perceive that God shows no partiality, but in every nation anyone who fears God and does what is right is acceptable to God." (*Acts* 10:34-35). *Islam:* "Those who believe in the Qur'an, those who follow the Jewish scriptures, and the Sabeans and the Christians — any who believe in God and righteousness — on them shall be no fear, nor shall they grieve." (*Qur'an* 5.69) "We believe in what has been sent down to us, and in what has been sent down to you. Our God and your God is one, and to God we surrender." (29:46). *Hinduism*: "As seekers approach Me, so I receive them. All paths, Arjuna, lead to Me." (*Bhagavad Gita* 4.11). "The wise person accepts the essence of different scriptures, and sees only the good in all religions." (*Srimad Bhagavatam* 11.3). "Truth is one; sages call it by many names." (Rig Veda *Samhita* 1.164.46). *Confucianism:* " In the world there are many different roads but the destination is the same. There are a hundred deliberations but the result is one." — *I Ching* (Appended Remarks 2.5). *Sikhism:* "The Hindus and the Muslims have but one and the same God." (*Adi Granth*, Bhairo, p.1158). *Buddhism:* The Buddha says, "To be attached to a certain view, and to look down upon other views as inferior; this the wise call a fetter." (*Sutta Nipata* 798).

vii: Endnotes and References for "Sacred Activism, Education" Section

[1.] [1]Some people have chosen to take these aspirations as *vows* by which to guide their lives: I vow to fully actualize and live my moral and ethical capacity. I vow to live in solidarity with the cosmos and all living beings. I vow to cultivate and live a life of deep non-violence. I vow to cultivate and live in humility. I vow to embrace a regular spiritual practice. I vow to cultivate mature self-knowledge. I vow to live a life of simplicity. I vow to engage in selfless service and compassionate action. I vow to empower and embody the prophetic voice of peace, justice, and world transformation.

viii: Endnotes and References for "Science and the Future" Section

[1.] [1]See, for example, Peter Richerson and Robert Boyd, *Not by Genes Alone* (2005). [2]Although Jean Gebser worked closely with Carl Jung, I can find no evidence that Gebser and Jean Piaget knew each other or were aware of each other's work. [3]Confirmed by the author in correspondence with Merlin Donald. [4]Many other species *use* simple tools like twigs and stones, and teach this to their offspring, so it is often said that other animals have culture. I suggest calling this proto-culture. It is the *making* of tools and the *innovation* of new designs over many generations that defines the emergence of *true* culture that is unique to our lineage. [5]The first toolmakers are thought to have been either *Australopithecus africanus* or *afarensis.* See *Oldest stone tools pre-date earliest humans*. BBC News, May 20, 2015. https://www.bbc.com/news/science-environment-32804177. [6]Wang Jie Hu, et al. *Science*, August 31, 2023. "Genomic inference of a severe human bottleneck during the Early to Middle Pleistocene transition." https://www.science.org/doi/10.1126/science.abq7487. [7]There is no widely agreed upon definition of "human" among paleoanthropologists. They prefer genus and species names like *Homo erectus*, *Homo heidelbergensis*, and *Homo sapiens*. [8]Jared Diamond coined "the Great Leap" in *Guns, Germs, and Steel* (1997). Paleoanthropologists call this the transition to the *Upper Paleolithic* period. [9]This term comes from Stanford Anthropologist Richard Klein. [10] See Eckhart Tolle, *A New Earth.* **[2.]** [1]Currivan, J. *The Cosmic Hologram: In-formation at the Center of Creation* (Inner Traditions, 2017). [2]Currivan. J. *The Story of Gaia: The Big Breath and The Evolutionary Journey of Our Conscious Planet* (Inner Traditions, 2022). [3]Currivan, J. "A Unitive Narrative Cosmology Underpinning the Holomovement," pp. 21-34, in Kuntzelman, E. and J. Robinson. *The Holomovement: Embracing Our Collective Purpose to Unite Humanity* (Light on Light Press, 2023 original pagination version). 4https://sdgthoughtleaderscircle.org/unitive-new-narrative/. 5https://www.unitivenarrative.org/. **[3.]** [1]Karl Glazebrook et al, (2004) "A massive galaxy that formed its stars at z ~ 11." *Nature. 14 February, 2024* DOI: 10.1038/s41586-024-07191-9. On arXiv: DOI: 10.48550/arxiv.2308.05606. [2]Sharov, Aleksandr Sergeevich; Novikov, Igor Dmitrievich (1993). *Edwin Hubble, the discoverer of the Big Bang universe.* Cambridge

University Press. p. 34. ISBN 978-0-521-41617-7. 3Eduard A. Tropp; Viktor Ya. Frenkel; Artur D. Chernin (2006). "The final year." Alexander A Friedmann: The Man who Made the Universe Expand. Cambridge University Press. 4Hurtak, James J., D. E. Hurtak and Elizabeth A. Rauscher (2013) "Examining the Existence of the Multiverse." London: World Scientific in *The Physics of Reality, pp. 364-375.* [5]"Early Universe Crackled With Bursts of Star Formation, Webb Shows" (2023) June 5, 2023, https://www.nasa.gov/universe/early-universe-crackled-with-bursts-of-star-formation-webb-shows/. [6]J.J. Hurtak (1973) *The Book of Knowledge: The Keys of Enoch.* Acad. for Future Science, Los Gatos, CA. **[4.]** [1]Johnson, Kurt. "Evolving Toward Cooperation: David Sloan Wilson's New Evolutionary Biology" *Kosmos Journal* 2022: Vol 18, Issue 3, now at https://www.kosmosjournal.org/kj_article/interspirituality-and-evolutions-direction-toward-cooperation/. [2]A letter from David Sloan Wilson on the Prosocial World website (www.prosocial.world/blog) announcing the release of a documentary, "Evolution of the Heart," about his meeting with His Holiness the 14th Dalai Lama in 2019. [3]For a fuller exploration of Teasdale's Nine Elements, see Diane Berke's article "Becoming Creatures of Boundless Love" in the Heritage Volume of this series. [4]The work of creating circles of trust is articulated in Palmer's book *A Hidden Wholeness*, and extensive information and resources can be found at the Center's website, www.couragerenewal.org. [4]Frances, Shelley & The Center for Courage & Renewal, *The Courage Way: Leading and Living with Integrity,* pp. 42 – 51. [5]Parker Palmer, *A Hidden Wholeness,* pp. 91-92. **[5.]** [1]Holding a PhD in Economics, Thomas Legrand is the author of *Politics of Being: Wisdom and Science for a New Development Paradigm* (Ocean of Wisdom Press, 2021). He is the lead Technical Advisor of the UNDP-convened Conscious Food Systems Alliance. He lives next to Plum Village, the monastery of Zen master Thích Nhất Hạnh, in the Southwest of France. [2]Jacob Soetendorp Institute for Human Values (2012). [3]http://amma.org/, accessed July 27 2020. [4]Ostrom (2009). [5]Teasdale (1999). **References:** Jacob Soetendorp Institute for Human Values. 2012. "Towards RIO + 20 and Beyond—a Turning Point in Earth History." Interreligious statement to the Rio+20 Conference. Legrand, Thomas. 2021. *Politics of Being: Wisdom and Science for a New Development Paradigm.* Ocean of Wisdom Press. Ostrom, Elinor. 2009. "Beyond Markets and States: Polycentric Governance of Complex Economic Systems." Nobel Prize Lecture,

December 8, 2009. Teasdale, Wayne. 1999. *The Mystic Heart: Discovering a Universal Spirituality in the World's Religions.* Novato, CA: New World Library. **[6.]** [1]https://www.youtube.com/watch?v=ERjkto7g4U4. **References:** *Prophet for our Times,* edited by David Lorimer (with Krum Vazharov and Maria Mitovksa, foreword by Wayne Dyer. Hay House, New York and London, 2015. *The Teacher, Volume 1 The Dawning Epoch,* by Beinsa Douno and edited by Maria Mitovska and Harry Carr. Shining World Press 2016, available on Amazon in both hardback and paperback. *Gems of Love (Prayers and Formulas of Beinsa Douno),* edited and translated by David Lorimer in 1994 and available for £7.50 plus p & p. Prophecy (with extensive commentary and other key texts - https://sophiafoundation.org/wp-content/uploads/2020/06/Prophecy-of-Peter-Deunov-Beinsa-Douno.pdf. *Resonant Mind – the Near Death Experience and the Ethic of Interconnectedness.* White Crow Books 2017. *The Ways and Power of Love,* by Pitirim Sorokin. Templeton Press, 2004. **[7.] References:** Atkinson, Robert. (2022). *A New Story of Wholeness: An Experiential Guide for Connecting the Human Family*. Light on Light Press. Campbell, Joseph. (1949). *The Hero with a Thousand Faces*. Princeton University Press. Jung, Carl. (1969). *The Archetypes and the Collective Unconscious*. (Collected Works of C.G. Jung, Vol. 9 Part 1) Princeton University Press. Teasdale, Wayne. (1999). *The Mystic Heart: Discovering a Universal Spirituality in the World's Religions*. New World Library. Underhill, Evelyn. (1911). *Mysticism: A Study in the Nature and Development of Spiritual Consciousness*. Dutton. Van Gennep, Arnold. (1909). *The Rites of Passage*. University of Chicago Press. **[8.]** [1]Population number: http://necrometrics.com/all20c.htm. **[9.]** [1]Reprinted with permission from Laszlo, Ervin and David Lorimer. 2023. *The Great Upshift: Humanity's Coming Advance Toward Peace and Harmony on the Planet*. New York, NY: Light on Light Press. **[10.]** Conference details: [1]https://www.iras.org/2025-summer-conference.html. [2]https://doi.org/10.16995/zygon.17372. [3]Definition from Google AI. [4]https://doi.org/10.15406/ipmrj.2025.10.00390 (Chatlos et al 2025). **[11.]** [1]Out of respect for the Pope's April 21, 2025, passing, the conference founding partners postponed the planned Faith and Science Conference in Rome. This also addresses the uncertainty of accommodations related to the arrival of cardinals for the funeral and conclave during a Jubilee Year, the first time that has happened since 1775. Consult www.faith-science.org for conference updates. **[12.]** [1]See "ProSocial Spirituality:

Evolutionary Science Meets Interspirituality" by Diane Berke, Jeff Genung, Kate Sheehan Roach and Susan Soleil in this Volume. [2]Word(s) inserted in brackets from these Volumes' Editors. [3]Wilson, David Sloan. 2019. *This View of Life: Completing the Darwinian Revolution.* New York NY: Pantheon Books. [4]Wilson, David Sloan. 2003. *Darwin's Cathedral: Evolution, Religion, and the Nature of Society.* Chicago IL: University of Chicago Press. [5] Mind & Life Institute event: His Holiness the 14th Dalai Lama, Dr. David Sloan Wilson: Toward a Whole World Ethic: The Role of Conscious Evolution. Dharamsala, India October 30 & November 1, 2019. General Information: https://www.mindandlife.org/wp-content/uploads/2020/07/Fall19Program_finalSpreads-1.pdf; Videos: https://www.mindandlife.org/media/toward-a-whole-world-ethic-the-role-of-conscious-evolution/; https://www.mindandlife.org/media/2019-mind-life-conversation-with-the-dalai-lama-david-sloan-wilson/. For the film series *Evolution of the Heart* from Mind & Life based on the vision and impact of this event see: https://www.facebook.com/watch/?v=883561322225295. 6. For ProSocial Spirituality at The Wave event of The Holomovement, see https://www.holomovement.net/wave and the free e-magazine https://issuu.com/lightonlight/docs/theholomovementwave entitled *The Holomovement Wave.*

ix: Endnotes and References for "Spiritual Life" Section

[1.] [1]Originally published online in *Contemplative Journal* in a much longer form (no longer extant and thus republished here in shorter form). The original version had extensive column layout of quotations from nondual spiritual leaders and teachers (gurus, seers, etc.) from multiple traditions, also grouped by the "themes" listed the paragraph and of this new version beginning: "In our earlier publications….", to show clearly how nearly identical the quotations across this landscape actually were. [2]Johnson Kurt. 2022. "Evolving Toward Cooperation: David Sloan Wilson's New Evolutionary Biology" *Kosmos Journal* 2022: Vol 18, Issue 3, now at https://www.kosmosjournal.org/kj_article/interspirituality-and-evolutions-direction-toward-cooperation/. [3]Although here highly condensed in this brief paragraph, the original consultation included reference to the websites and other sources for the large number of spiritual teachers noted, and then computation of the percentages. Note that this computation was done approximately 10 years ago [2015]; thus, the trends noted are from that time period. **[2.]** [1]See *The Way of Mary: Maryam, Beloved* *of God*, Camille Hamilton Adams Helminski, Sweet Lady Press, 2021, Louisville, KY, Chapter II, "Within the Sanctuary." [2]*Rumi's Sun, the Teachings of Shams of Tabriz*, translated by Refik Algan and Camille Adams Helminski, Threshold Books, 2017, Louisville, KY, p. 203. [3]*Teresa of Avila, Mystical Writings* by Tessa Bielecki, The Crossroad Publishing Co., 1997, New York, NY, p.41. [4] Ruzbihan al-Baqli, "Ara'is" II, 7 as cited by Kristin Zahra Sands, *Sufi Commentaries on the Qur'an in Classical Islam*, Routledge Studies in the Quran, N.Y., 2000, p. 91-92; See also, Smith, Jane I. and Yvonne Y. Haddad, "The Virgin Mary in Islamic Tradition and Commentary"; Muslim World 79:3-4 (July/Oct. 1989), p.161-87; 183-184 trans. McCarthy of al-Baqli, *Tafsir*, 11, 7. See *The Way of Mary, Maryam: Beloved of God*, op. cit., p. 29-30. [5] See Qur'an, *Surah an Nahl*, The Bee, 16: 66-69: *And your Sustainer taught the bee to build its cells in hills, on trees, and in dwelling places, / then to eat of all that the earth produces and to skillfully find the spacious paths of its Sustainer. / There issues from within their bodies a drink of varied hues containing healing for human beings: / truly, in this is a sign for those who reflect.* [6] "Bees of Your Haven" excerpt from forthcoming *Notes from Love'ville,* offered by Camille Hamilton Adams Helminski .[7]As translated by Rabbi Rami Shapiro in *The Divine Feminine in Biblical Wisdom Literature*, Skylight Paths, 2005, Woodstock, VT, p.65. [8]*Women of Sufism*: *A Hidden Treasure*, Camille Adams Helminski, Shambhala Publications, 2003, Boston, MA, p.87.

x: Endnotes and References for "Interspiritual Pioneers" Section

[1.] [1]See in "Notes" to "Introduction" in Blackwell, Stephen H., and Kurt Johnson. 2016. *Fine Lines: Vladimir Nabokov's Scientific Art*. New Haven CT: Yale University Press: Note 38, p. 26, especially re: philosopher of science Dr. David Hull ("Hull" citations therein). [2]Link to extensive Panikkar bibliography: https://gerardhallsm.wordpress.com/wp-content/uploads/2019/07/hall_panikkarthesis_bibliography.pdf. [3]The important work of Fr. Francis Tiso is worthy of deep study in its own right, for example as in from MID website, Bulletin 74, April 2005: http://monasticdialog.com/a.php?id=513 and MID *Bulletin* 71, Sept. 2003: http://monasticdialog.com/a.php?id=193 and in James Stuart, *Swami Abhishiktananda: His Life Told Through His Letters* (Delhi: ISPCK, 1995). [4]James Stuart, *Swami Abhishiktananda: His Life*

Told Through His Letters (Delhi: ISPCK, 1995), p. 216. **[2.]** [1]Journalist accounts consulted for this Feature are as cited in "Tribute to Fr. Thomas Keating: a Legacy Event July 12-14, 2019" pp. 52-54 in *Change Makers* (*Light on Light* special issue), https://issuu.com/lightonlight/docs/lightonlight_issue_5: *Contemplative Outreach* (https://www.contemplativeoutreach.org/), *The Aspen Times, Aspen Daily News* and Newsletter of The Aspen Chapel (https://www.aspenchapel.org/Groups/1000101780/_Weekly_Newsletter.aspx); Snowmass Inter-religious Dialogue (today the Charis Snowmass Interspiritual Dialogue) then http://www.globalspirit.tv/project/the-interspiritual-dialogue-with-father-thomas-keating/); books: "The Nine Points of Agreement Among The World's Religions" in the book entitled *The Common Heart* in 2006: Miles-Yépez, Netanel [Ed.]. 2006. *The Common Heart: An Experience of Interreligious Dialogue.* Brooklyn NY: Lantern Books (current: https://www.amazon.com/Common-Heart-Experience-Interreligious-Dialogue-ebook/dp/B004WDRW7K/) international significance, United Nations, (http://nationalserviceaeu.org/about-us/executive-committee/kurt-johnson/); Ulfik, Rick, Kurt Johnson and Shannon Marie Winters (Ed.). 2021. *Universal Principles and Action Steps: A Historic Collection Gathered from Organizations, Networks, NGOs and Thought Leaders around the World.* Education Synergy Circle of the Evolutionary Leaders: https://issuu.com/lightonlight; feature film: *The Rising Tide of Silence* (https://www.amazon.com/Thomas-Keating-Rising-Tide-Silence/dp/B014R1TTO0); conference: see www.interspirituality.com. [2]Ed Bastian as quoted in "Tribute to Fr. Thomas Keating: a Legacy Event July 12-14, 2019" pp. 52-54 in *Change Makers* (*Light on Light* special issue), https://issuu.com/lightonlight/docs/lightonlight_issue_5. [3]"Fr. Thomas Keating: Reflection From Cynthia Bourgeault" https://www.cynthiabourgeault.org/blog and https://www.prayingfromtheheart.org/?p=1234 (December 2, 2018). **Additional Resources:** Bourgeault, Cynthia. 2024. *Thomas Keating: The Making of a Modern Christian Mystic.* Boulder, CO: Shambhala Publications. **[3.]** [1]Thomas Berry often referred to himself as a "geologian" to indicate that he was a theologian of the Earth. [2]Thomas Berry. *The Dream of the Earth,* p. 211. [3]Thomas Berry. *The Dream of the Earth,* p. 134. [4]Thomas Berry. *The Dream of the Earth,* p. 138. Berry further explains, "It takes a universe to bring humans into being, a universe to educate humans, a universe to fulfill the human mode of being. More immediately, it takes a solar system and a planet Earth to shape, educate, and fulfill the human" (p. 134). Thus, he sometimes uses the words "universe" and "Earth" interchangeably when speaking of the underlying psychic energy of creation. [5]See Lapaire, Olav, Irène Hösli, Rosanna Zanetti-Daellenbach, Dorothy Huang, Carmen Jaeggi, Susanne Gatfield Mergenthaler, Sinuhe Hahn, and Wolfgang Holzgreve. 2007. "Impact of Fetal–Maternal Microchimerism on Women's Health — a Review." *The Journal of Maternal-Fetal & Neonatal Medicine* 20 (1): 1–5. https://doi.org/10.1080/14767050601144834. [6]Thomas Berry. *The Sacred Universe*, p. 85.[7] Thomas Berry, *The Sacred Universe*, p. 90. **References:** Berry, Thomas. 1988. *The Dream of the Earth*. San Francisco, Calif.: Sierra Club Books. Berry, Thomas. 2000. *The Great Work: Our Way into the Future*. New York: Bell Tower. Berry, Thomas. 2009. *The Sacred Universe: Earth, Spirituality, and Religion in the Twenty-First Century*. New York: Columbia University Press. Lapaire, Olav, Irène Hösli, Rosanna Zanetti-Daellenbach, Dorothy Huang, Carmen Jaeggi, Susanne Gatfield-Mergenthaler, Sinuhe Hahn, and Wolfgang Holzgreve. 2007. "Impact of Fetal–Maternal Microchimerism on Women's Health — a Review." *The Journal of Maternal-Fetal & Neonatal Medicine* 20 (1): 1–5. https://doi.org/10.1080/14767050601144834. **[4.]**[1]Page numbers noted as (p. #) from Sw. Shraddhananda. 2014. *Jesus Was a Shaktipat Guru*. Somerset KY: Sacred Feet. [2]Page numbers noted as (p. #) from Sw. Shraddhananda [Ed.]. 2017. *Mature Interspirituality*. 2017. Somerset, KY: Sacred Feet. Afterword by Dr. M. Darroll Bryant. **[5.] Additional Resources:** Singh, Ralph. 2008. *A Path to Follow, a Life to Lead*. New York: NY: Sterling Paperbacks. For More of Baba Virsa Singh ji's teachings www.gobindsadan.org; Jaap Sahib of Guru Gobind Singh ji - Recite Jaap Sahib – Gobind Sadan. **[6.]** [1]Darwin, C. (1871). *The Descent of Man, and Selection in Relation to Sex*. London: John Murray. [2]Loye, D. (2004). *Darwin's Lost Theory*. Benjamin Franklin Press. [3]Eisler, R. (1987). *The Chalice and the Blade*. Harper & Row. [4]Wilson, D. S. (2007). *Evolution for Everyone*. Delta. [5]Johnson, K. (2023). Personal communication and *IJPS* Vol. 9, Issue 2. [6]Laszlo, E., & Loye, D. (Eds.). (1993). *The Evolutionary Outrider*. Adamantine Press. [7]Seldin, T. (2023). "A World of Partners." *IJPS*, 9(2).

xi: Endnotes and References for "Global Challenge" Section

[1.] [1]David Bohm: *Wholeness and the Implicate Order*, 1980, Routledge. [2] *The Holomovement: Embracing Our Collective Purpose to Unite Humanity* 2023, Light on Light Press. **[2.]** [1]Permissioned by Star News Agency, New Delhi, India; North East Colours, Agartala, Tripura, India. **[3.]** "Global Challenges are Directing Us Toward a Unity of Purpose," Mustakova, E., R. Atkinson, and K. Johnson. 2021. *Kosmos* 21: 1. https://www.kosmosjournal.org/kj_article/global-challenges-are-directing-us-toward-a-unity-of-purpose/.

xii: Endnotes and References for "Interspiritual Community" Section

[1.] Vogl, Charles. 2016. *The Art of Community: Seven Principles for Belonging.* Oakland, CA: Berrett-Koehler Publishers. 2025. *The Art of Community, Second Edition: 7 Principles for Belonging*. Oakland, CA: Berrett-Koehler Publishers. **[2.]** Brown, Leena Banerjee. 2021. *True Light: Ordinary People on the Extraordinary Spiritual Path of Sukyo Mahikari*. New York NY: Light on Light Press. **[3.]** Kaplan, Connie. 2004. *The Invisible Garment: 30 Spiritual Principles That Weave the Fabric of Human Life*. San Diego, CA: Jodere Group. **[4.]** [1]An estimate of practitioners numbering one hundred million was stated on a panel of scholar-practitioners at CCCADI's 2016 conference, Orisha Sacred Traditions, at City College on February 28, 2016, in New York City. [2]See Wikipedia entry on Interspirituality which quotes Wayne Teasdale's work: https://en.wikipedia.org/wiki/Interspirituality#cite_note-2. [3]Oba Ifágbemi Faseye Babatunde, *Practical Foundations of Ifá – A Handbook of Ifá View and Practice* (Oracle Ifá, LLC, 2022), 33. **[5.]** Strategic advisors, including five Featured Authors herein: Daniel J. Stone, Heidi Sparkes Guber, Jude Currivan, Tezekiah Gabriel, Joni Carley, Kurt Johnson, Richard Clugston, Scott Alan Carlin and Gordon Dveirin (http://sdgthoughtleaderscircle.org/hosts/). **[6.]** Ken Wilber, lead blurb in Advance Praise section in Johnson, Kurt and David Robert Ord. 2013. *The Coming Interspiritual Age*. Vancouver, CN: Namaste Publishing.

FEATURED AUTHORS

Robert Atkinson. Robert Atkinson, PhD, is an award-winning author, educator, and developmental psychologist. He is a 2020 Gold Nautilus Book Award winner for *Our Moment of Choice* (co-editor), a 2023 Silver winner for *A New Story of Wholeness*, and a 2017 Silver winner for *The Story of Our Time*. Author or co-editor of nine other books, his works include *Year of Living Deeply*, *Mystic Journey*, and *The Gift of Stories*. Atkinson is professor emeritus at the University of Southern Maine, director of StoryCommons, founder of the One Planet Peace Forum, and a member of the Evolutionary Leaders Circle. See *robertatkinson.net*; *lightonlight.us*.

Jeanette Banashak. Jeanette Banashak, EdD, PhD, is co-founder and co-director of The Spiritual Guidance Training Institute. A bilingual interfaith / interspiritual director and supervisor, she incorporates creativity, Integral Spirituality Mapping (ISM), and mandala work into her teachings and sessions. She facilitates ISM and mandala practices in a variety of settings and uses them as supports on her own path. Banashak serves on the faculty at Erikson Institute, teaching courses in child development and social-emotional learning, and is a visiting professor of spiritual direction at the Graduate Theological Foundation. Outside of work, she enjoys hiking with her partner and sharing stories with friends and family while playing board games. See *spiritualguidancetraining.com.*

DeShannon Barnes-Bowens. Iya Rev. DeShannon Barnes-Bowens is a psychotherapist, professional development trainer, and spiritual counselor. She is founder of ILERA Counseling & Education Services, and her work focuses on spiritual development, healing from sexual abuse, vicarious trauma, and sustainable self-care. An initiated priestess of Ifá-Òrìṣà spirituality, she was ordained in 2010 as an Interfaith Minister and later served as co-director of One Spirit Interfaith Seminary. Barnes-Bowens is author of *Hush Hush: An African American Family Breaks their Silence on Sexuality and Sexual Abuse* and was the first recipient of the Bill T. Jones Award from AASECT. She coordinated CONNECT Faith's Ending Child Sexual Abuse Collaborative and has taught at national and international events, including the Parliament of the World's Religions and the American Academy of Religion. See *ilera.com.*

JoAnn Barrett. Rev. JoAnn Barrett, ordained in 1995 from what is now One Spirit Interfaith Seminary, is the founder and spiritual director of Gathering of Light Interspiritual Fellowship. With degrees in human services, social policy, and substance abuse counseling, she has served on numerous interfaith and state faith-based task forces, including the Interfaith Institute of Long Island and Faith Leaders Task Force for NY State. A long-time student and teacher of *A Course in Miracles,* she founded programs like Voices of Faith for Peace, STARTER Packs for the homeless, and Bedding for Babes. Barrett is also the founder and spiritual director of Lightpaths Wisdom Studies Interspiritual Seminary. She served in pastoral care and clinical roles and contributed to *Mature Interspirituality* and *Guideposts.* See *gatheringoflight.org.*

Edward Bastian. Edward Bastian, PhD, is founder and president of Spiritual Paths Foundation. With a PhD in Buddhist Studies, he has spent over forty years studying and teaching in dialogue with teachers from many faith traditions. He developed InterSpiritual Meditation and Mandala processes, and the well-known books associated with them, and has led retreats and educational programs since 2002. A former co-director of the Forum on Biodiversity for the Smithsonian and the National Academy of Sciences, he has also produced religion-focused documentaries for the BBC and PBS. His most recently premiered film is *The Dalai Lama's Gift.* Bastian is author of *InterSpiritual Meditation* and *Mandala: Creating an Authentic Spiritual Path: An InterSpiritual Process,* and co-author of *Living Fully, Dying Well.* Bastian was also instrumental in forming the Interspiritual Network and its current web resource *interspiritiuality.com.* See *spiritualpaths.net; interspirituality.com.*

Michael Bernard Beckwith. Michael Bernard Beckwith is founder of the Agape International Spiritual Center, a trans-denominational community based in Los Angeles. A sought-after speaker and teacher, he leads retreats and teaches meditation, the Life Visioning Process, and The Mastery of Life Structures. He co-founded the Association for Global New Thought and co-directs A Season for Nonviolence with

Arun Gandhi. Beckwith is the author of *40 Day Mind Fast Soul Feast, A Manifesto of Peace,* and *Living from the Overflow.* He has appeared alongside global leaders such as the Dalai Lama and is a featured teacher in films and media supporting spiritual transformation. See *agapelive.com.*

Galia Benartzi. Galia Benartzi is a systems entrepreneur, economic theorist, and digital currency pioneer working at the intersection of decentralization, moral imagination, and regenerative design inspired by nature. She co-founded Bancor, the first on-chain liquidity protocol enabling permissionless, blockchain-based asset conversions through open-source infrastructure. Her work centers on redefining value and developing tools, narratives, and networks to support cooperative economics on a sustainable planet for all. Galia studied comparative literature at Dartmouth and holds a master's in international economics and energy policy from Johns Hopkins SAIS. She carries forward the legacies of her mentors, Dr. Riane Eisler and Bernard Lietaer, whose work continues to shape her inquiry into money, meaning, humanity, evolution, ethics, and consciousness. Her current projects explore how our stories and technologies can catalyze new architectures for peace, partnership, and wellbeing—both at home and at scale.
See *centerforpartnership.org/about/cps-team.*

Diane Berke. Rev. Diane Berke is the founder and spiritual director of One Spirit Learning Alliance and One Spirit Interfaith Seminary who have played a pivotal role in the development of Interspirituality and interspiritual education. Ordained in 1988, she has trained and ordained nearly 1,500 interfaith / interspiritual ministers. She holds advanced degrees in sociology, psychology, and therapeutic counseling, and is a licensed mental health counselor in New York State. A certified facilitator of Circles of Trust® through the Center for Courage and Renewal, Berke also maintains a private spiritual counseling practice. She is the author of *Love Always Answers, The Gentle Smile,* and *Developing and Deepening Your Spiritual Practice.* She is a founding member of the Contemplative Alliance of the Global Peace Initiative of women, and a core team member of Transformation365 and ProSocial Spirituality. Rev. Berke was also part of the group who created the Interspiritual Network, and its current web resource interspiritality. com. See *1spirit.org; interspirituality.com; prosocial.world/prosocial-initiatives/prosocial-spirituality.*

Ramesh Bijlani. Ramesh Lal Bijlani, MD, also known as R.L. Bijlani, is a medical scientist, author, and retired professor of Physiology from the All India Institute of Medical Sciences, New Delhi (AIIMS). His expertise spans physiology, nutrition, yoga, and integrative medicine. Educated at AIIMS and Massachusetts Institute of Technology, he has published over 200 scientific papers, 250 blogs, and 25 books, including *Understanding Medical Physiology* and *Our Body: A Wonderful Machine.* His spiritual writing is grounded in the Integral Yoga of Sri Aurobindo and The Mother. A resident of Sri Aurobindo Ashram, Delhi Branch, he continues to inspire through writing, teaching, and speaking on holistic health and yoga. See *yespirituality.in.*

Joan Borysenko. Joan Borysenko, PhD, is president and founding partner of MindBody Health Sciences, LLC. A Harvard-trained cell biologist and licensed psychologist, she taught at Harvard Medical School until 1988. She is the author or co-author of seventeen books on integrative medicine, psychology, spirituality, and women's studies. Her work bridges science and mysticism, and she is widely regarded as a pioneer in mind-body medicine. Borysenko lives in New Mexico with her husband Gordon Dveirin. Close friends of Br. Wayne Teasdale, Borysenko and Dveirin co-founded the Claritas Institute for Interspiritual Inquiry and co-authored with Dveirin *Saying Yes to Change* and *Your Soul's Compass: What is Spiritual Guidance?* See *joanborysenko.com; claritasinstitute.com.*

Cynthia Bourgeault. Cynthia Bourgeault is an Episcopal priest, author, and modern-day mystic known for reviving the Christian contemplative and Wisdom traditions. She is founding director of an international network of wisdom schools that blend Christian mystical and monastic teachings with practices of mindfulness and embodied presence. A globally respected retreat leader, Bourgeault divides her time between her seaside hermitage in Maine and an international teaching schedule. She is a faculty member emeritus of the Center for Action and Contemplation and was named one of the 100 most spiritually influential living people in 2021. See *cynthiabourgeault.org.*

Richard A. Bowell. Richard A. Bowell's work is held in trust at the Global Center for Human Change, a New York-based educational charity that makes the work available through the Conscious World Citizen Movement. His body of work includes multiple books on the spiritual dimensions needed to underpin the United Nations Sustainable Development Goals and other global transformational initiatives. His books have been endorsed by internationally renowned philosophers, evolutionary leaders, scientists, and *New York Times* best-selling authors. He and his wife, as featured in a Netflix special, live a large part of the year on an estate on the Greek islands — a sanctuary and harmonious living space — which they have developed and share with the cats of the island. See *richardabowell.org.*

Ben Bowler. Ben Bowler is a unity-activist, spiritual entrepreneur, and founder of spiritual programs that foster interfaith immersion. In 2008, he and his wife founded Blood Foundation to support communities along the Thai-Burma border. He later launched Monk for a Month and Muslim for a Month, immersive spiritual programs in Thailand and Turkey. Bowler founded World Weavers and the U DAY Festival, bringing together spiritual leaders and musicians in global celebration. He co-founded 1GOD.com and *The Convergence* radio series, and helped launch Sacred Australia. A "Social Entrepreneur in Residence" at INSEAD Business School and blogger for *HuffPost,* he is active in building interspiritual unity. See *UNITY.earth; 1GOD.com; interspirituality.com.*

Roger P. Briggs. Roger P. Briggs is an educator, scientist, and author dedicated to uniting science, spirituality, and planetary transformation. Author of *Emerging World: The Evolution of Consciousness and the Future of Humanity* and *Emergence: The Shift from Ego to Essence and Journey to Civilization.* He is the founder of the Planet Project and a core team member at the Light on Light Press and Riane Eisler's Center for Partnership Systems. His work explores how human consciousness and collective behavior can evolve to meet global challenges. A former high school science teacher and musician, member of the Rock Climbing and Boulder Sports

Hall of Fame, Briggs now leads workshops and writes on the intersection of systems thinking, evolutionary spirituality, and collective action. See *rogerpbriggs.org; lightonlight.us.*

Cynthia Brix. Rev. Cynthia Brix, PhD (hon.), is co-founder and co-director of Gender Equity and Reconciliation International (GERI), which has offered more than 280 intensive trainings in 12 countries. She is an ordained interfaith minister and co-director of Satyana Institute. A long-time student of Eknath Easwaran's Passage Meditation, she also leads retreats on interfaith spirituality. Brix co-organized 5 international conferences on interspirituality and produced *Cultivating Women's Spiritual Mastery.* She holds a Master of Divinity from Iliff School of Theology, a double M.A. in wellness management and gerontology, and an honorary doctorate from CIIS. See *Satyana. org, GRworld.org, DawnofInterSpirituality.org; interspirituality.com.*

Leena Banerjee Brown. Leena Banerjee Brown, PhD, is a licensed psychologist and retired professor of clinical psychology at Alliant International University. Born and raised in India, she served children and families in underserved communities across India and the U.S. Brown trained doctoral students, guided their research, and clinically supervised future professionals. A practitioner of Sukyo Mahikari, she co-founded the Circles group to explore Light-giving and spiritual reflection with other leaders. In retirement, she focuses on writing about spiritual experiences and cultivating inner awareness through service. Her first publication, *True Light,* emerged from this journey. See *truelightbook.com.*

Constance Buffalo. Constance Buffalo is co-founder of The Renaissance Project, International, which she established with Jean Houston to take human potential through perception, empowerment, and inspired action to a higher octave. A Chippewa elder and visionary, she brings decades of leadership rooted in sacred values and transformative change. Formerly president and CEO of Intelagard, she recognized that lasting security must emerge from human consciousness, not technology. Her earlier roles include director of promotion for CBS Regional Markets and executive positions in interactive technologies and educational media, where she produced national and international training programs. Guided by indigenous wisdom, Buffalo champions dignity, relationality, and meaningful transformation across cultures and industries. See *forthfire.com.*

Patrick Carolan. Patrick Carolan is a Catholic activist, organizer, and writer who served as executive director of the Franciscan Action Network for a decade. He co-founded the Global Catholic Climate Movement and Catholics Vote Common Good. Carolan's advocacy draws from Franciscan spirituality and centers on the interconnectedness of all creation and the divine. A longtime advocate for social and environmental justice, he works to bridge faith and action in service to a just, peaceful, and sustainable world. He is widely published in activist, religious and interfaith serials around the world and featured extensively at the websites of these diverse venues. See, for instance, *ncronline.org/authors/patrick-carolan.*

Calvin Chatlos. Dr. Calvin Chatlos is an emeritus professor of psychiatry at Rutgers-Robert Wood Johnson Medical School. Certified in adult, child / adolescent, and addiction psychiatry, he has worked in inpatient, outpatient, and intensive care settings treating addiction and psychiatric disorders. His clinical experience and personal spiritual journey led to a framework for understanding spiritual experiences across clinical and community settings. He studies religious / spiritual determinants of mental health and advocates for common language to unite faith and healthcare systems. Chatlos is a Distinguished Life Fellow of the American Psychiatric Association and a Distinguished Fellow of the American Academy of Child & Adolescent Psychiatry. See *chatlosmd.com; IRAS.org.*

Haji Syed Salman Chishty. Haji Syed Salman Chishty is chairman of the Chishty Foundation, based at the revered Ajmer Sharif Dargah in India. A founding member of the Chishty Sufi Family, he has led the foundation for over eight years, promoting the Sufi principles of love, unity, and service to humanity. He travels extensively, engaging in interfaith dialogue, peacebuilding, and efforts to uplift the underserved. His work highlights the Chishty Sufi message of unconditional love and spiritual service, fostering global harmony across religious and cultural boundaries. See *chishtyfoundation.org.*

Deepak Chopra. Deepak Chopra, MD, FACP, is the founder of The Chopra Foundation and Chopra Global, bridging science, spirituality, humanitarianism, and well-being. A clinical professor at the University of California, San Diego, and senior scientist with Gallup, he is a global leader in integrative medicine and personal transformation. For over 3 decades, Chopra has been at the forefront of the meditation revolution. He has authored over 90 books translated into 43 languages, including *Metahuman: Unleashing Your Infinite Potential* and *Total Meditation: Practices in Living the Awakened Life.* TIME magazine named him "one of the top 100 heroes and icons of the century." See *deepakchopra.com.*

Richard Clugston. Rick Clugston, PhD, is co-director of the Association of University Leaders for a Sustainable Future and a member of the Earth Charter International Council. A founding member of the SDG Thought Leaders Circle, he has led sustainability initiatives globally for decades. He directed the Sustainability and Global Concerns program at the Center for Earth Ethics and served twenty years as executive director of the Center for Respect of Life and Environment where he assisted religious and academic institutions in transforming their teaching and practices to support strong sustainability. Clugston holds a doctorate in higher education policy and planning from the University of Minnesota. See *ulsf.org*

Jude Currivan. Jude Currivan, PhD, is a cosmologist, planetary healer, and co-founder of WholeWorld-View. She holds a master's degree in physics from Oxford and a doctorate in archaeology, specializing in ancient cosmologies. Author of 7 books, including *The Cosmic Hologram* and *The Story of Gaia,* Currivan has traveled to over 80 countries working with wisdom keepers to promote planetary healing and conscious evolution. Her short film, *A Radical Guide to Reality,* has been globally influential. Grounded in a unitive vision of wholeness, her work is formative and ground-breaking across diverse international networks, including the United Nations. See *wholeworld-view.org; sdgthoughleadesrcircle.org.*

H. H. the 14th Dalai Lama. His Holiness the 14th Dalai Lama, born Lhamo Thondup and later named Tenzin Gyatso, is the spiritual leader of Tibetan Buddhism. Recognized as the reincarnation of Avalokiteshvara, he was enthroned in 1940 and later fled to India in 1959 following the continued oppression of Tibet, and Tibetan culture, by the Chinese communist regime. He continues to lead the Tibetan government-in-exile and advocates tirelessly for peace, non-violence, and interfaith dialogue. In 1989, he was awarded the Nobel Peace Prize for his dedication to nonviolent resistance against Chinese occupation and for his broader message of compassion, tolerance, and universal responsibility. His Holiness has had close long-term relationships with many key pioneers of Interspirituality, including Fr. Thomas Keating, Br. Wayne Teasdale and others, and has been a major part of seminal interreligious and interspiritual dialogues and initiatives around the world. See *dalailama.com.*

Patricia Anne Davis. Patricia Anne Davis, MA, is a Choctaw- Navajo and Chahta-Dineh indigenous wisdom keeper. As a practitioner, diagnostician, international teacher, and consultant of the Navajo / Dineh blessingway ceremonial healing principles, she spreads sacred earth wisdom for wellness restoration. She translates these principles into appropriate English descriptions to teach the Indigenous Ceremonial Change Process in an all-inclusive, cross- cultural, intergenerational, and universal way. Her teachings offer a win-win, life-affirming way of life for all creatures of Mother Earth. See *nativeamericanconcepts.wordpress.com/about/.*

Emily A. DeMoor. Emily DeMoor, PhD, serves as director of Christophany Groups for the Center for Christogenesis and as director of the Caritas Center at Brescia University. An educational consultant with Human Energy, she brings a multidisciplinary background in musicology, pastoral studies, and environmental education. DeMoor has taught at all academic levels and led liturgical and interfaith worship. Her research focuses on ecotheology, process theology, intersubjectivity, and the noosphere, with a passion for integrating these concepts into K-12 and university curricula and pedagogy. Her work reaches audiences through teaching, retreats, and international presentations. See *centerforchristogenesis.org.*

Gordon Dveirin. Gordon Dveirin, EdD, is an educator, organizational consultant, and spiritual mentor whose work spans systems change and transpersonal development. Educated in literature and the history of ideas at the University of Toronto, and in organizational development at the University of Northern Colorado, he has consulted in both private and public sectors for forty years. Dveirin co-founded the Claritas Institute for Interspiritual Inquiry with his wife, Dr. Joan Borysenko, and co-authored with Borysenko *Saying Yes to Change* and *Your Soul's Compass: What is Spiritual Guidance?* He is a founding member of the Evolutionary Leaders Circle. See *claritasinstitute.com.*

Joseph Victor Edwin, SJ. Fr. Joseph Victor Edwin, SJ, is a Jesuit of the Delhi Province and a scholar of Christian-Muslim relations. He teaches theology at Vidyajyoti College of Theology in Delhi and serves as part of Jesuits Among Muslims in Asia, a network engaged in dialogue, research, and solidarity across faiths. Through academic and interreligious work, he fosters greater understanding between Christians and Muslims.

Riane Eisler. Riane Eisler, JD, PhD (hon.), is a social systems scientist, cultural historian, futurist, attorney, and internationally known author. Her research has transformed understandings of human development and social organization globally. Her groundbreaking books include *The Chalice and the Blade: Our History, Our Future,* and her book on economics, *The Real Wealth of Nations: Creating a Caring Economics,* was hailed by Archbishop Desmond Tutu as "a template for the better world we have been so urgently seeking" and by Jane Goodall as "a call to action." Eisler is founder and president of the Center for Partnership Studies and editor-in-chief of the *Interdisciplinary Journal of Partnership Studies.* She has addressed the UN General Assembly, U.S. Congress, and institutions worldwide, promoting partnership systems as a path to sustainable, equitable, and peaceful societies. See *centerforpartnership.org.*

Duane Elgin. Duane Elgin is a visionary author, speaker, and activist whose work integrates science, spirituality, and social transformation. His books include *Voluntary Simplicity, The Living Universe, Promise Ahead,* and *Awakening Earth.* He co-authored *Changing Images of Man* with Joseph Campbell and worked as a senior staff member of the Presidential Commission on the American Future. He also served as a senior social scientist at SRI International. Elgin holds an MBA from the

Wharton School, an MA in economic history from the University of Pennsylvania, and an honorary PhD from the California Institute of Integral Studies. In 2006, he received the Goi Peace Award for his contributions to a more sustainable and spiritual culture. His work spans voluntary simplicity, media reform, cosmology, and planetary consciousness. See *awakeningearth.org.*

Geraldine Patrick Encina. Geraldine Patrick Encina, PhD, is a consultant for One Earth, executive director of Earth Timekeepers, and board member of the Pre-Columbian Society at UPenn Museum. She is a member of the Grand Council of the Eagle and the Condor, the Otomi Council of the High Lerma River Basin, the Academic and Technical Committee of the Biocultural Heritage Network of the National Council of Science and Technology in Mexico (CONACYT), Land Healers, and Interamerican Society for Astronomy in Culture (SIAC). She is a scholar of Mesoamerican conceptions of time-space and biocultural heritage, and has taught at universities in Mexico and served as a Scholar in Residence at the Center for Earth Ethics. Her publications span sacred ecology, ethnoecology, and Indigenous timekeeping. See *geraldinepatrick.wordpress.com; earthtimekeepers. org.*

Matthew Fox. Matthew Fox, PhD is a spiritual theologian, Episcopal priest, and activist for gender and ecological justice. He has authored thirty-seven books, including *Original Blessing, The Coming of the Cosmic Christ*, and *The Hidden Spirituality of Men.* A pioneer of Creation Spirituality, he founded the Institute in Culture and Creation Spirituality and later the University of Creation Spirituality. He is co-founder of the Order of the Sacred Earth and creator of The Cosmic Mass, a reinvention of Western ritual. Fox has taught at major universities and inspired the rediscovery of mystics like Hildegard of Bingen and Meister Eckhart. His honors include the Abbey Courage of Conscience Award and the Gandhi King Ikeda Award. He is consistently listed among Watkins' Top 100 Most Spiritually Influential People. See *matthewfox.org.*

Ashok Gangadean. Ashok Gangadean, PhD is professor and chair of Philosophy at Haverford College, where he has taught for over forty years. His work explores common ground across worldviews and expands philosophy into global consciousness. He is founder-director of the Global Dialogue Institute and co-convener of the World Commission on Global Consciousness and Spirituality. He is also co-chair of the World Wisdom Council. Gangadean's current work includes deep dialogue initiatives and hosting the television series Global Lens. His most recent book is The Awakening of the Global Mind. See *awakeningmind.org; global-dialogue.com; globalspirit.org.*

Jeffrey Genung. Jeffrey Genung is managing director and chief architect of Prosocial World, a nonprofit advancing global cooperation and well-being. He is co-founder of Contemplative Life, a hub connecting people with transformative practices, and of Transformation365.org, an experiential practice network. His newest initiative, Prosocial Spirituality, integrates evolutionary science with evolutionary spirituality through training and research. A longtime entrepreneur and technology executive, Jeff has developed partnerships with major global companies. He now focuses on the intersection of science, spirituality, art, and technology to help create a more caring and balanced world. Long associated with the Wayne Teasdale legacy, he has now also joined with The Interspiritual Network and Light on Light. See *prosocial.world; contemplativelife.org; interspirituality.com, lightonlight.us.*

Philip Goldberg. Philip Goldberg has explored the world's spiritual traditions for over fifty years as a practitioner, teacher, and author. As an interfaith minister, spiritual counselor, and public speaker, he has presented at major venues and been widely published. He has written or co-written over twenty-five books, including *American Veda: The Life of Yogananda, Roadsigns on the Spiritual Path, and Spiritual Practice for Crazy Times*. He teaches on various online platforms, co-hosts the Spirit Matters podcast, and serves on the board of the Association for Spiritual Integrity. His work bridges Eastern and Western wisdom for contemporary seekers. See *philipgoldberg.com.*

Jonathan Granoff. Jonathan Granoff is an international lawyer, former professor of international law, and a passionate advocate for global peace and nuclear disarmament. A founder of the Global Security Institute, and a Nobel Peace Prize nominee, he serves as senior advisor and UN Representative for the Permanent

Secretariat of the World Summit of Nobel Peace Laureates and is Ambassador for Peace and Security for the Parliament of the World's Religions. He chairs the Task Force on Nuclear Nonproliferation for the American Bar Association's International Law Section and serves on numerous advisory boards, including the NGO Committee on Disarmament, the Jane Goodall Institute, and the Middle Powers Initiative. A Fellow of the World Academy of Arts and Science, Jonathan focuses on the moral, legal, and spiritual dimensions of peacebuilding. He is the recipient of multiple awards, including the Distinguished Alumni Award from Rutgers University School of Law. See *gsinstitute.org; uri.org.*

Mussie Hailu. Ambassador Mussie Hailu is a global peacebuilder and interfaith leader promoting peace, compassion, disarmament, and human dignity. A founding member of the United Religions Initiative (URI), he currently serves as URI's director of Global Partnerships and representative to the African Union and UN offices in Africa and Geneva. He pioneered Ethiopia's interfaith movement and has led peace initiatives across the continent, including the Peace Monument at the African Union and the "Declaration for Peace" for the UN's fiftieth anniversary. He introduced and champions the celebration of Golden Rule Day, now observed globally, and authored its official proclamation endorsed in over 120 countries. Honored with numerous humanitarian awards, he is recognized among 73 global leaders for outstanding contributions to humanity. See *uri.org; au.int; unity.earth.*

Grove Harris. Grove Harris is a global leader in interfaith engagement with connections to the United Nations and Harvard University. Her work bridges spiritual leadership and institutional collaboration, coaching interreligious initiatives in international policy and educational settings. With experience in global diplomacy and academic forums, Harris combines spiritual wisdom with strategic direction to advance understanding among faith traditions. Her contributions focus on embedding sacred values into global institutions and fostering dialogue in secular and spiritual arenas alike. She is recognized for enhancing both policy and practice through integrative interspiritual leadership. See *groveharris.org.*

Andrew Harvey. Andrew Harvey is a renowned religious scholar, spiritual teacher, and author of over forty books, including the critically acclaimed *The Hope, Son of Man*, and *Savage Grace* with Carolyn Baker. Born in South India, he has studied and practiced deeply within the world's mystical traditions, including Hinduism, Buddhism, and Sufism. He is the founder of the Institute of Sacred Activism, an international organization dedicated to uniting spiritual insight with action for justice, sustainability, and planetary healing. Through Sacred Activism, he encourages individuals to become compassionate agents of transformation by fusing inner wisdom with courageous service. His work calls for a collective response to global crises rooted in love and awakened consciousness. See *andrewharvey.net.*

Philip M. Hellmich. The late Philip M. Hellmich was a global peacebuilder and thought leader known for bridging inner transformation with international peace. As director of peace at The Shift Network, he helped create global programs such as the Summer of Peace, Yoga Day Summit, and World Peace Library. A former Peace Corps volunteer in Sierra Leone, he also worked with Search for Common Ground for fourteen years. He authored *God and Conflict: A Search for Peace in a Time of Crisis*, and advised The Global Peace Initiative of Women. Hellmich's legacy lives on through his teachings on the Peace Continuum — from inner peace to international harmony. Hellmich transitioned in 2022. See *theshiftnetwork.com.*

Camille Hamilton Adams Helminski. Camille Hamilton Adams Helminski is co-founder of the Threshold Society and a respected translator, poet, and spiritual teacher in the Sufi tradition. She is the author of *Women of Sufism, The Way of Mary*, and several volumes of poetry, including *Ninety-Nine Names of the Beloved.* She co- translated Rumi's *Sun: The Teachings of Shams of Tabriz* and holds the distinction of being the first woman to translate a substantial portion of the Qur'an into English, published as *The Light of Dawn*. Helminski continues work on a full Qur'an translation and teaches widely on Sufism in interspiritual contexts alongside her husband and collaborator, Kabir Helminski. See *sufism.org.*

Kabir Helminski. Kabir Helminski is a Mevlevi Shaikh in the Sufi tradition of Rumi, a translator of classical Sufi texts, and author of widely respected books on spirituality. His titles include *Living Presence, The Knowing Heart, The Mysterion: Rumi and the Secret of Becoming Fully Human, and Holistic Islam.* His work focuses on spiritual psychology and sacred presence, integrating Sufi wisdom with contemporary spiritual life. Kabir has co-translated volumes of Rumi's work with Camille Helminski, and together they founded the Threshold Society. In 2009, he was named one of "The 500 Most Influential Muslims in the World." See *sufism.org.*

Robert Hesse. Deacon Robert Hesse is a permanent Catholic deacon. He is also co-founder and president of Contemplative Network, promoting interdenominational Christian contemplative prayer, scientific research, and interfaith dialogue. Inspired by Thomas Merton during a retreat at Gethsemani, he was later appointed by Thomas Keating as a Commissioned Presenter of Contemplative Outreach and served as emissary to its first dialogue with the Mind & Life Institute at the Dalai Lama's invitation. A permanent deacon in the Archdiocese of GalvestonHouston with a PhD in physical chemistry, Hesse also teaches faithandscience courses as adjunct faculty at the University of St. Thomas. He is author of *Faith and Science: A Journey Into God's Mystical Love* and continues to speak internationally on the integration of contemplative spirituality and scientific insight. See *contemplative.net.*

Michael Holleran. Fr. Michael Holleran is a retired Catholic priest, former Jesuit and Carthusian monk, and a Zen teacher (Roshi) in the White Plum Asanga lineage. He offers teachings that integrate Christian mysticism and Zen Buddhism through Dragon's Eye Zendo in New York City. Fr. Holleran resides at the Church of St. Monica on Manhattan's East Side, where he continues to offer spiritual direction, retreats, and contemplative practice. Passionate about integrating contemplative traditions, he offers Zen practice both in person and online, and engages deeply with LGBTQIA+ inclusion and interfaith dialogue. His interspiritual work is grounded in a deep commitment to silence, compassion, and the unity of all paths. See *michaelkholleran.org.*

William Howell. William Howell (aka Swami Vishnu Datta) is a poet, author, meditation teacher, and retreat master who has studied deeply with adept teachers across the world's major spiritual and religious traditions. Author of *From the Mouth* *of the Supreme*, in 1992, he founded Sanctuary House, an inter-religious educational nonprofit based in Crestone, Colorado. He later co-founded Crestone Charter School in 1995, and helped establish the Crestone End-of-Life Project in 2007. Currently, he is spearheading the Camino de Crestone, a contemplative pilgrimage initiative rooted in sacred landscape and spiritual practice. Howell served for five years as a khalifa in the Nur Ashki Jerrahi Sufi Order and was later made a swami by Sri Punitachariji Maharaj. His work reflects a life devoted to spiritual integration, sacred community, and interspiritual education. See *sanctuaryhousecrestone.org*.

Desiree Hurtak. Desiree Hurtak, PhD, is a social scientist, futurist, environmentalist, and president of the Foundation for Future Science. She co-founded The Academy For Future Science, an NGO with UN ECOSOC/DPI accreditation active in over fifteen countries. Hurtak's work includes delivering water and education to underserved communities and presenting at the United Nations' Rio+20 focusing on youth and sustainable development. Her presentation focused on The Academy's work with the Indigenous Peoples of Brazil, to give them a voice so they are free to live in harmony with nature. She has conducted acoustic studies of ancient Egyptian sites, participated in the discovery of the "Tomb of Osiris," produced films such as *The Light Body and Initiation*, and co-authored *Overself Awakening* with her husband, Dr. J.J. Hurtak. Her media collaborations include the award-winning documentary Voice of Africa: Credo Mutwa and the Sacred Name Sacred Codes CD with Steven Halpern. See *futurescience.org*.

J.J. Hurtak. J.J. Hurtak, PhD, is a social scientist, futurist, and co- founder of The Academy For Future Science (AFFS), a UN-affiliated NGO promoting the integration of science and consciousness through education, sustainability, and cross-cultural understanding. An author, composer, and researcher, he holds two PhDs and a Master of Theology from Luther Theological Seminary, where he studied ancient languages and early Christian texts. Hurtak was a principal discoverer of the "Tomb of Osiris" in Egypt and has conducted pioneering research using acoustic testing and ground-penetrating radar in ancient pyramids. His work spans archeology, advanced technologies, space law, and environmental science. He is best known for *The*

Keys of Enoch and has composed music performed by the Deutsches Symphonie-Orchester of Berlin. See *futurescience.org.*

Gard Jameson. Gard Jameson holds a PhD from Pacifica Graduate Institute and teaches Chinese and Indian philosophy at the University of Nevada, Las Vegas. A former CPA and financial planner, he is also the author of *Footprints on the Sands of Time*, *Phaethon: Our Mythic Moment*, and *Monkey: Our Mythic Moment.* Jameson co-founded and chairs the boards of the Children's Advocacy Alliance and the Interfaith Council of Southern Nevada. He also serves as treasurer of Volunteers in Medicine of Southern Nevada and helped found the Nevada Community Foundation. He is a board member of Stillpoint Center for Spiritual Development and the Alf Museum of Life, and serves as associate pastor at Grace Community Church in Boulder City, Nevada. See *charterforcompassion.org.*

Kurt Johnson. Rev. Kurt Johnson, PhD, has worked in professional science and comparative religion for more than fifty years. Author, and co-founder of the award-winning Light on Light Press, he is a prominent figure on international committees, particularly at the United Nations. He has published over 200 scientific articles and seven books including co-authoring or co-editing award winners *The Coming Interspiritual Age, Our Moment of Choice, Nabokov's Blues* and *Fine Lines*. Johnson served on the faculty of New York's Interfaith Seminary for fifteen years and was on the staff of the American Museum of Natural History in New York City for twenty-five years. As part of UNITY EARTH and the Interspiritual Dialogue Network, he co-edits two magazines, *The Convergence* and *Light on Light*, and cohosts the Convergence series on VoiceAmerica. He serves on core teams of the Evolutionary Leaders, The Holomovement and Prosocial World. See *EvolutionaryLeaders.net/leaders/KJohnson; lightonlight.us; issuu.com/LightonLight; isdna.org; thecominginterspiritualage.com; sdgthoughtleaderscircle.org; interspiritualitycom.*

Connie Kaplan. Connie Kaplan, DMin, is a spiritual teacher, dreamwork facilitator, and author focused on the intersection of spirituality and consciousness. She founded the Invisible Garment Network, a community centered on sacred dreaming and divine purpose. With a doctorate in ministry and background in television production,

Kaplan offers a unique blend of intuitive insight and grounded scholarship. Her books include *The Invisible Garment: 30 Spiritual Principles That Weave the Fabric of Human Life, Dreams Are Letters from the Soul, The Woman's Book of Dreams, and The Emergence of a New Cosmology.* She is widely known for her teachings on dream guidance and soul assignment. See *theinvisiblegarment.com.*

Karuna (Caroline Ashley). Karuna (Rev. Caroline Ashley), author of the recent *Light on Kundalini: Your Lifestyle Guide to Yoga and Awakening,* is a teacher, actress, event producer, and longtime interspiritual contributor known for her joyful presence and leadership in yoga communities worldwide. Based in Boulder, Colorado, she is Host Editor of *Light on Light* magazine and part of the host team for The Convergence on VoiceAmerica. Karuna pioneered KRI Levels 1–3 Kundalini Yoga Teacher Training in Boulder and offers daily and online classes for all ages, including prenatal and children's yoga. She has hosted retreats and yoga festivals in Costa Rica and Europe and collaborated with master teachers including Snatam Kaur and GuruGanesha. Ordained as a "Wisdom Keeper" in Kundalini Yoga and Lakota Native American healing, she brings compassion and transformation to all she does. See *lightonkundalini.com; lightolight. us.*

Aditi Kaul. Aditi Kaul is a teacher, psychologist, and spiritual practitioner in Integral Yoga Psychology based in India. Her work blends psychology, interspirituality, and feminine mysticism, drawing on traditions of Vedanta, Sufism, and nondual awareness. Kaul facilitates healing through meditation, reflective writing, and dialogue rooted in presence and compassion. She has presented on themes like ego, equanimity, and the search for true self through talks such as "Ego: The Master Storyteller" and "Equanimity as a Doorway to Delight." In 2024, she spoke at the Shakti Kumbh on conscious living and inner growth. She also works as an expressive arts-based therapist with Fortis Healthcare, using visual art, movement, and music in self- care workshops. She is a contributor to interspiritual initiatives and writes on spiritual embodiment, trauma healing, and the evolution of consciousness. See *aditikaul.com; aurosociety.org; instagram.com/ aditikaul1.*

Victor H. Kazanjian Jr. Rev. Victor H. Kazanjian Jr., Mdiv, is a global leader in interfaith and intergenerational peacebuilding. From 2013 to 2021, he served as executive director of the United Religions Initiative, guiding over 1,000 interfaith groups across more than 100 countries and at the United Nations. Prior to that, he was dean of Religious and Spiritual Life and co-director of the Peace & Justice Studies Program at Wellesley College, where he co-founded Education as Transformation Inc., promoting religious diversity and spirituality in higher education. He has also served as Fulbright Professor of Peace & Justice Studies at Banaras Hindu University and Visiting Fellow at Harvard Divinity School. An Episcopal priest and ordained community organizer, his work centers on interreligious dialogue, conflict transformation, and spiritual values in education. He holds degrees from Episcopal Divinity School and Harvard University. See *ulsf.org.*

Thomas Keating. Fr. Thomas Keating (1923–2018) was a Trappist monk and one of the most influential figures in modern Christian contemplative practice. Born in New York, he studied at Yale and Fordham before joining the Cistercian Orders in 1944. From 1961 to 1981, he served as Abbot of St. Joseph's Abbey in Spencer, Massachusetts, later residing at St. Benedict's Monastery in Snowmass, Colorado. A founding member of Contemplative Outreach, he played a central role in developing and teaching Centering Prayer, a method of silent meditation rooted in ancient Christian traditions. Fr. Keating was also a pioneer of interreligious dialogue, collaborating with spiritual leaders from diverse traditions through forums such as the Snowmass InterSpiritual Dialogue. He was closely associated with both H. H. The Dalai Lama and Br. Wayne Teasdale (who considered Fr. Keating a "spiritual father," along with Fr. Bede Griffiths). He, and other contributors to these volumes, were pivotal in planning the 2013 Dawn of Interspirituality Conference. Fr. Keating authored important books, including *Open Mind, Open Heart and Invitation to Love*, and remained a dedicated monastic at St. Benedict's Monastery in Snowmass, Colorado, until his passing. See *contemplativeoutreach.org; interspirituality.com.*

Loch Kelly. Loch Kelly is a contemplative psychotherapist and recognized leader in the field of consciousness and awakening. He is the author of the award-winning books *The Way of Effortless Mindfulness: A Revolutionary Guide for Living* *an Awakened Life and Shift into Freedom: The Science and Practice of Open-Hearted Awareness*. A graduate of Columbia University and Union Theological Seminary, Kelly studied Insight Meditation, Advaita, and Tibetan Buddhism in Asia with teachers including Tulku Urgyen Rinpoche and has served on the Teacher's Council at New York Insight. His work blends psychology, nondual traditions, and neuroscience, and he partners with universities like Yale and NYU to research mindfulness and compassion. Kelly is the founder of the Open-Hearted Awareness Institute, and teaches effortless mindfulness with warmth and humor, supporting others in awakening as a natural stage of development. He lives in New York City with his wife Paige and their cat Duffy. See *effortlessmindfulness.org.*

Doug King. Doug King is president of Presence, a nonprofit research and writing group, dedicated to a reinterpretation of religion and spirituality. He has worked with his father, Max King, who has written since the early 70s in the field of Theology. Doug has a dual degree in Theology and Biblical Languages, and is co-author of *The Awakening of Humanity: The Dawning of a New Earth and Unitive Age* (2024). King's applications of Spiral Dynamics to theology led to extensive new paradigms by using an integral approach to long held religious worldviews. He is a frequent speaker, teacher and podcaster on numerous platforms, as well as a business leader. In 1999, the technology company he founded was named Dealer of the Year in N. America. He currently works in Evolutionary Leaders, Theology Without Walls, and other independent groups focused on trans-narrative and trans-religious outcomes. See *https://issuu.com/lightonlight/docs/awakeningofhumanity; https://www.presence.tv/; https://www.evolutionaryleaders.net/.*

Audrey E. Kitagawa. Audrey E. Kitagawa is chair of the Parliament of the World's Religions, president of the Light of Awareness International Spiritual Family, and president/founder of the International Academy for Transcultural Cooperation. A respected global leader, she served as UN Advisor on Children and Armed Conflict and currently represents United Religions Initiative at the UN. Audrey is chair emerita of the NGO Committee on Spirituality, Values and Global Concerns and was enstooled as a Queen Mother of Development in Ghana, where a school bears her African name. A frequent author on globalization, identity, and spirituality, she has published widely in academic and interfaith journals and contributed to multiple anthologies. Her honors include the Spirit of the UN Award and the "Pride of Eurasia" medal from Kazakhstan for contributions to spiritual education and culture. *See lightofawareness.org; multiculturalcooperation.net.*

Ken Kitatani. Ken Kitatani is Chief of Executive Board and Committee of i-ceed.org (International Council on Environmental Economics and Development) and Founder, Executive director of the Forum 21, both affiliated with the United Nations. Deeply engaged in spiritual advocacy at the United Nations, he serves on the executive boards of the Committee for Spirituality, Values and Global Concerns and the Committee of Religious NGOs. He also co-chairs the Advisory Board of the Center for Earth Ethics at Union Theological Seminary. A Columbia University graduate in East Asian Studies, Kitatani supports global dialogue on ethics, sustainability, and spiritual values through diplomacy, education, and partnership. He is also co-founder of the Bio-Cultural Sacred Sites circle of the Evolutionary Leaders, proactive internationally with First Peoples and foundational cultures. See *i-ceed.org; forum21.co.*

Julie Krull. Dr. Julie Krull is an Evolutionary Leader, award-winning author, dynamic speaker, and popular host of *The Dr. Julie Show: All Things Connected.* A coherence strategist for the Holomovement and founder of the nonprofit Good of the Whole, she mentors leaders and organizations in transformational change and conscious evolution. Her work focuses on global coherence, sacred activism, and cultivating a culture of wholeness. Named a "Renaissance woman for the Dawning Unitive Age," Krull is a respected visionary, spiritual guide, and co- creative mentor who supports high-impact individuals in leading breakthrough innovations rooted in wisdom, service, and planetary unity. See *goodofthewhole.org.*

Emanuel Kuntzelman. Emanuel Kuntzelman is an entrepreneur, writer, philosopher, philanthropist, and social-transformation activist. After a decade-long spiritual quest traveling the world, he began his professional career writing for *Reader's Digest* and went on to found multiple cultural exchange organizations in the U.S., U.K., and Spain and, most recently, the now burgeoning Holomovement international network. He created Greenheart International in 1985, and still serves as its chief advisor, co-founded Madrid's Fundación por el Futuro, and helped launch the Global Purpose Movement and Purpose Earth. A board member of Humanity's Team, Unity Earth, Integral Transformative Practice, and Laszlo Institute, he is also a member of the Evolutionary Leaders Circle. Kuntzelman co-edited the anthology *Purpose Rising* (2017) and has contributed extensively to spiritual and cultural publications, continuing his lifelong commitment to the Holomovement. See *holomovement.net; greenheart.org; purpose.earth.org.*

Chief Phil Lane Jr. Hereditary Chief Phil Lane Jr. (Ihanktonwan Dakota and Chickasaw) is an internationally respected leader in community and economic development. For over fifty years, he has worked with Indigenous Peoples from the Americas, Asia, and Africa. He served for sixteen years as an associate professor at the University of Lethbridge and founded the Four Worlds International Institute in 1982. Chief Lane is also Chairman of Four Directions International and Compassion Games International. He was the first indigenous recipient of the Windstar Award and received the Ally Award for his work addressing Canada's Residential School legacy. Chief Lane was enstooled as a Hereditary Chief in 1992, and currently serves on the AISES Council of Elders and hosts the Shift Network's Global Indigenous Wisdom Summits. See *fwii.net.*

Ervin László. Ervin László is a Hungarian philosopher of science, systems and integral theorist, and former concert pianist. With a PhD from the Sorbonne, he has authored around 75 books and more than 400 scientific and philosophical papers. A leading advocate of quantum consciousness and systems philosophy, he founded and directs the Club of Budapest and the Laszlo Institute of New Paradigm Research. His honors include four honorary doctorates, the Peace Prize of Japan, the Goi Award, the Assisi Mandir of Peace Prize, and Nobel Peace Prize nominations in 2004 and 2005. See *ervinlaszlo.com; thelaszloinstitute.com; clubofbudapest.com; ervinlaszlobooks.com.*

Thomas Legrand. Thomas Legrand holds a PhD in economics and serves as lead technical advisor for the UNDPconvened Conscious Food Systems Alliance, focusing on sustainable finance, climate, and forest conservation. He authored the internationally acclaimed *Politics of Being: Wisdom and Science for a New Development Paradigm* (2022). Based near Zen master Thích Nhất Hạnh's Plum Village monastery in southern France, Legrand brings contemplative insight into food systems transformation. Through his UN and academic partnerships, he integrates inner development with global ecological and social change. See *politicsofbeing.com.*

David Lorimer. David Lorimer is a writer, editor, and spiritual activist. He is programme director and global ambassador of the Scientific and Medical Network and Chair of the Galileo Commission. He has edited *Paradigm Explorer* since 1986, and founded the *Beyond the Brain* conference series. Lorimer is author or editor of over a dozen books, including *Survival? Death as Transition, Resonant Mind, The Spirit of Science, Thinking Beyond the Brain,* and *Radical Prince.* His most recent books include a collection of essays, "A Quest for Wisdom," and his collection of poetry, *Better Light a Candle.* His recognitions include the Visioneers Lifetime Achievement Award (2020) and the Aboca Human Ecology Prize (2021). He is a Creative Member of the Club of Budapest and founder of Character Education Scotland. See *davidlorimer.co.uk; scimednet.org; galileocommission.org.*

Sally Mahé. Sally Mahé is senior advisor and a founding staff member of the United Religions Initiative (URI), a global grassroots interfaith network active in over 1,000 Cooperation Circles across 108 countries. With a background in social justice and education, she holds master's degrees in education (focused on law) from Harvard, and theology and spiritual counseling from General Theological Seminary. Mahé co-authored *The Birth of a Global Community* (2003) and *A Greater Democracy Day by Day.* As director of Organizational Development and Global Programs, she has guided URI's growth and continues to consult on communications, interfaith training, and spiritual leadership. A passionate advocate for spiritual democracy, she maintains the weekly *Every Voice* blog sharing reflections from URI members around the world. Based in the San Francisco Bay Area, she lives with her children and grandchildren nearby. See *uri.org.*

Yanni Maniates. Yanni Maniates is chair of the UNITY EARTH USA board and a long-time spiritual teacher, author, and publisher. He directed New ERA and the International Religious Foundation from 1979–1985, then served as director of Paragon House Publishers in New York. Earlier in his career, he helped build a 100,000-volume theological seminary library and worked as a rare book librarian at Yale. For over 35 years, he has taught meditation, intuitive development, and Hermetic and Perennial Wisdom teachings. Manniates is the author of six books, numerous articles and courses, and meditation CDs. His work centers on guiding people into "The Embrace" — a direct experience of the Divine. He and his wife recently opened a spiritual and healing center in Williamstown, NJ. See *insideoutjourneys.com; unity.earth.*

Brian McLaren. Rev. Brian D. McLaren is an author, speaker, public theologian, and activist known for his work in reimagining Christianity for a more just and generous world. A former college English teacher and pastor, he is a senior fellow at Auburn Seminary and a leader in the Convergence Network. McLaren works across faith traditions to promote spiritual vitality, social justice, and environmental sustainability. He is the author of more than a dozen books, including *A New Kind of Christian, Do I Stay Christian?*, and *Faith After Doubt.* McLaren is widely recognized for his ability to translate complex theological ideas into accessible, transformative teachings for contemporary spiritual seekers. See *brianmclaren.net.*

A.K. Merchant. A.K. Merchant is an interfaith leader from India known for fostering spiritual harmony and cultural dialogue across religious traditions. Among many other positions, he serves as Secretary General of the Temple of Understanding India Foundation. With deep roots in Indian spiritual heritage, they serve as a guiding voice in international interfaith forums and educational initiatives. Dr. Merchant draws on a broad understanding of diverse philosophies to cultivate unity, compassion, and mutual respect. Their work emphasizes the transformative power of shared sacred values in creating cohesive, spiritually enriched communities. A. K. Merchant's contributions inspire ongoing collaboration between faiths and are rooted in a vision of global interspiritual resonance. See *shastriinstitute.org.*

Dena Merriam. Dena Merriam is the founder of the Global Peace Initiative of Women (GPIW), a spiritual and interfaith organization working for peace and ecological sustainability. In 2002, she convened a meeting of women religious and spiritual leaders at the Palais des Nations in Geneva from which emerged the GPIW. A veteran of the interfaith movement, she served as vice chair of the Millennium World Peace Summit of Religious and Spiritual Leaders at the United Nations. Merriam holds a master's degree in sacred literature from Columbia University and has organized forums alongside global climate and development gatherings, including the UN Climate Change Conferences and G20 meetings. Her work emphasizes spiritual leadership, the sacred feminine, and the evolution of consciousness. She is the author of *My Journey Through Time: A Spiritual Memoir of Life, Death and Rebirth.* See *gpiw.org.*

Oscar Miro-Quesada. Oscar Miro-Quesada Solevo is a respected Peruvian kamasqa curandero, altomisayoq adept, visonary founder of The Heart of the Healer (THOTH) and originator of Pachakuti Mesa Tradition cross-cultural shamanism. He is co-author of *Lessons in Courage: Peruvian Shamanic Wisdom for Everyday Life* and an internationally acclaimed teacher, healer, and earth-honoring ritualist. Solevo is an OAS Fellow in Ethnopsychology and UN Invited Observer to the Permanent Forum on Indigenous Issues. Since 1986, he has guided ethnospiritual apprenticeship expeditions, with emphasis on Peru and Bolivia. He is a frequent faculty member at learning centers worldwide, dedicating his life to the revitalization of aboriginal wisdom traditions as a means of restoring sacred trust between humankind and the natural world, and has appeared on CNN, Univision, A&E, Discovery Channel, and *Ancient Aliens.* See *heartofthehealer.org.*

Matt Mitler. Matt Mitler is an actor, director, therapist, and founder of Dzieci Theatre, an experimental ensemble dedicated to the work of sacred theater and service. Integrating performance with spiritual practice and care for the dying, Dzieci combines ritual, improvisation, and physical theater rooted in Grotowski-inspired methodologies. Mitler has led workshops throughout the U.S. and Europe, guiding individuals in creative and spiritual self-discovery. His work bridges artistic expression and contemplative practice, often offering theater as both transformative journey and healing balm. See *dziecitheatre.org*.

Deborah Moldow. Rev. Deborah Moldow is an ordained interfaith minister committed to assisting in the transformation of human consciousness to a culture of peace. She is founder of the Garden of Light, an online platform for the emerging global spirituality, and serves as director of the Evolutionary Leaders Circle of the Source of Synergy Foundation that brings together visionaries committed to the acceleration of conscious evolution. Moldow co-edited *Our Moment of Choice: Evolutionary Visions and Hope for the Future,* a collaborative book by forty-three Evolutionary Leaders. She is also Vision Keeper at UNITY EARTH and advocates for unity, peace, and interfaith collaboration through her work in spiritual leadership and global networks. See *evolutionaryleaders.net; gardenoflight.org.*

Mindahi Crescencio Bastida Muñoz. Mindahi Crescencio Bastida Muñoz has served as director of the Original Caretakers Initiative at the Center for Earth Ethics and co-founder of the Bio-Cultural Sacred Sites circle of the Evolutionary Leaders. He serves as general coordinator of the Otomi-Hñahñu Regional Council in Mexico, a caretaker of the philosophy and traditions of the Otomi people, and has been an Otomi Ritual Ceremony Officer since 1988. Born in Tultepec, Mexico, he holds a doctorate of rural development and is president of the Mexico Council of Sustainable Development. Bastida Muñoz is a member of the steering committee of the Indigenous Peoples' Biocultural Climate Change Assessment Initiative, and has served as a delegate to several commissions and summits on indigenous rights and the environment. He has written extensively on the relationship between the State and Indigenous Peoples, intercultural education, collective intellectual property rights and associated traditional knowledge. See *centerforearthethics.org; sacredstories.com.*

Elena Mustakova. Dr. Elena Mustakova is a Bulgarian-American psychologist, social scientist, spiritual philosopher, and educator dedicated to the evolution of individual and collective consciousness toward a peaceful planetary civilization. With four decades of consulting in diverse historical and geopolitical contexts, she integrates Bulgarian roots, Western democratic values, and Middle Eastern spiritual sensibilities to foster resilience, dialogue, psycho-spiritual integration, and community health. Her groundbreaking work in moral psychology won dissertation awards at Harvard and the Association for Moral Education. She has served as professor, author, and senior editor of *Toward a Socially Responsible Psychology for a Global Era* (Springer, 2014). Her Nautilus Award–winning book *Global Unitive Healing: Integral Skills for Personal and Collective Transformation* has been called "potent and wise medicine for our time." Most recently, she co-founded the Unitive Justice and Global Security Thought Leaders Synergy Circle, the Unitive Earth Governance Collaborative, and IntegraLight Transdisciplinary Institute in Bulgaria. See *elenamustakova.net.*

David T. Nicol. David T. Nicol, PhD, is the co-founder and executive director of the Gaiafield Project and Institute for Subtle Activism. He is also co-founder of BeThePeace, one of the world's largest global meditation events that occurs annually on the International Day of Peace (September 21). He is the author of *Subtle Activism: The Inner Dimension of Social and Planetary Transformation,* the first comprehensive study of the idea that collective focused intention can powerfully contribute to social change. He teaches on subtle activism in the Philosophy, Cosmology, and Consciousness program at the California Institute of Integral Studies, for the Shift Network, and for the Institute for Subtle Activism. A former environmental lawyer from Australia, he now lives in Mendocino with his wife Kate and dogs Jackson and Peaches. See *gaiafield.net.*

Terry Patten. The late Terry Patten (1951–2021) was a gifted spiritual teacher, author, and activist known for his integral approach to consciousness, personal transformation, and global change. Raised in an intentional peace community, he studied intensively under spiritual teacher Adi Da Ram Jas and later co-founded Tools for Exploration, a pioneering company in consciousness technology. He co-authored *Integral Life Practice* with Ken Wilber and collaborators and was the author of *A New Republic of the Heart,* which explores how inner work and social action can unite in service to the planet. Patten taught worldwide, led online communities, and mentored change-makers. His legacy includes work in conscious activism, evolutionary spirituality, and fostering integral communities. See *terrypatten.com.*

Chief Dwaine C. Perry. Chief Dwaine C. Perry of the Ramapough- Lunaape Nation is a lifelong advocate for indigenous rights and social justice. From helping to integrate a barbershop in Suffern, NY, in 1965, to founding the Ramapo Munsee Museum and the Embassy of Sovereign Indigenous Nations of the Western Hemisphere, he has led with vision and courage. A Vietnam veteran, Chief Perry earned degrees from Pace University and Southern New Hampshire University and was mentored under the honorable Conrad Lynn. He helped form an indigenous rights group instrumental to the modern restructuring of the Ramapough Nation. He has met with indigenous elders and leaders globally, established the Split Rock Sweetwater Prayer Camp in New Jersey following his journey to Standing Rock, and continues to champion human rights today. See *riverkeeper.org/.*

Jamal Rahman. Imam Jamal Rahman is a celebrated speaker on Islam, Sufi spirituality, and interfaith relations. Originally from Bangladesh, he is a graduate of the University of Oregon and the University of California, Berkeley. He has been featured in The New York Times, CBS News, the BBC, and various NPR programs. Cofounder and Muslim Sufi minister at Seattle's Interfaith Community Sanctuary and adjunct faculty at Seattle University, he is a former host of Interfaith Talk Radio and travels nationally and internationally, presenting at retreats and workshops. Since 9/11, Jamal has been collaborating with Rabbi Ted Falcon and Pastor Don Mackenzie. Affectionately known as the Interfaith Amigos, they have toured the country sharing the message of spiritual inclusivity. He teaches widely drawing upon the practices, insights, and wisdom within Sufism, Hinduism, Buddhism, and Taoism. See *jamalrahman.com.*

Rajashree Maa. Rajashree Maa (Joni Dittrich, PhD) is founder of KaliKi Reiki® and The Wisdom School in Fairfield, California. Master of four reiki lineages and a respected interspiritual teacher, she holds a degree in world religious studies from the University of Michigan, studied theology at Vanderbilt University and earned a master's degree in human development counseling, and received her PhD in psychology from the University of Memphis. After over thirty years of practice as a clinical psychologist, in 2008, following mystical encounters with Divine Mother, she midwifed a new reiki lineage into the world. Her book, *May the Loveforce Be With You – KaliKi Reiki: Healing Through Divine Mother & Yogic Wisdom* (Light on Light Press), outlines her teachings on healing and "wisening" into wholeness and unity through universal Loveforce energy, individually and collectively, through spiritual practice. See *thewisdomschool.us; kali-kireiki.com.*

Jon Eliot Ramer. Jon Eliot Ramer is an entrepreneur, civic leader, inventor, and musician dedicated to global compassion and collaboration. He is the visioneer of OneWorld.earth — "Unite Humanity, Restore Mother Earth." He co-founded ELF Technologies and launched the International Campaign for Compassionate Cities, helping to inspire over 450 campaigns worldwide. In 2012, he created the *Compassion Games: Survival of the Kindest,* now serving over 18 million people. Ramer also founded SINE (Synergized Impact Network Exchange), a global alliance amplifying social change initiatives. He serves as CTO of Four Worlds International Institute and sits on the advisory board of the Mahatma Gandhi Institute of Education for Peace and Sustainable Development (UNESCO). A longtime meditation and wisdom teacher, Ramer is also the lead guitarist and songwriter for the band Once And For All. See *oneworld.earth; compassiongames.org; sine.network.*

Leslie Reambeault. Leslie Reambeault, LCSW, is a licensed clinical social worker and ordained Interspiritual Minister practicing near Santa Fe, New Mexico (also licensed in Illinois). She founded *InsideOut Healing Happens,* offering psychotherapy, energy work, eco-spiritual mentoring, and Light Body practices. Reambeault has advanced training in Internal Family Systems (IFS), Somatic Experiencing, and Integral Somatic Practice, and works with first responders and survivors of abuse. She served as dean and co-director at One Spirit Interfaith Seminary, ordained in 2012, and supports ceremonies and life-event rituals across traditions. Reambeault lives in La Cieneguilla with her partner and their poodle, Lahli. See *lesliereambeault.com.*

Kate Sheehan Roach. Kate Sheehan Roach is an interfaith, interspiritual, and interdisciplinary writer, editor, and community builder. With roots in academic publishing, she now works with visionary authors whose work integrates spirituality, mysticism, and contemplative depth. Based in Philadelphia, Kate leads content development at Contemplative Life and co-founded Transformation365. She holds a BA with honors from Mount Holyoke College and an MA in history from the University of Connecticut. Certified by Contemplative Outreach to facilitate Centering Prayer workshops, she serves on its national service team and sits on the North America Leadership Council of the United Religions Initiative. Her work bridges scholarly and contemplative traditions, supporting writers who bring mystical and contemplative depth to their audiences. See *writingforyourlife.com; linkedin.com/in/kate-sheehan-roach-7695517.*

Brian Russo. Brian Russo is a visionary educator and systems thinker dedicated to co-creating a regenerative Earth. He is the founder of Rainbow Circle, a dynamic framework that maps knowledge, organizations, and missions into twelve interconnected domains, promoting organizational interoperability and unitive visioning. As a high school teacher of English, history, and religion, he inspires students to build a world aligned with the good of the whole. Russo contributes to multiple Synergy Circles of the Evolutionary Leaders, including Education, Wholistic Design & Biomimicry, and the Unitive Narrative. A sound healer, he offers vibrational therapy through overtone singing and crystal bowls, drawing on his rare ability to hear otoacoustic emissions. Russo lives near Boston with his wife Caileigh, enjoying nature, music, and family life. See *rainbowcircle.com; besoundnow.com.*

Sacred Feet Dharma Heirs. The Sacred Feet Dharma Heirs are the ordained spiritual successors of Swami Shraddhananda (Rev. Dr. Sonya L. Jones), who founded the interspiritual lineage known as Sacred Feet Yoga. These heirs — Chamatkara (Sandra Simon) (also Dharma Books Editor at Light on Light Press), Amrita (Jenny Williams), and Swami Prakashananda (The Right Rev. Bishop Christine Deefholts) — continue her legacy through teaching, writing, publishing, and spiritual leadership. They carry forward Shraddhananda's vision — guiding practitioners in the Sacred Feet Yoga Teachings and supporting practices that focus on kindling and facilitating the universal sacred energy within (Maha Kundalini Shakti, Tara, Windhorse, the Holy Spirit, Ruah, Ruh, etc.) which, by the grace of the divine, plumbs the depths of the soul, releases emotional or behavioral patterns which no longer serve, and helps us to "hold our seat" along bumps in the road until we are free and able to live every moment from our natural, innate state of divinity. See *jefifoundation.org/sacred-feet-yoga/; lightonlight.us.*

Sagar Swami (Bhakti Rasayana Sagar Swami Maharaj) is a bhakti yoga monk, teacher, and consultant originally from Russia and active across four continents. A sannyasi in the bhakti tradition, he has provided lectures and spiritual counsel to leaders in over twenty countries. His teaching bridges sacred scripture with contemporary insights, including learnings from Harvard Business School. Sagar Swami fosters interfaith understanding through global forums, government collaborations, and United Nations–aligned initiatives. He is the spiritual head of the Russian branch of the International Business Forum "Artha" and shares teachings worldwide through podcasts, video series, and devotional retreats that integrate spiritual wisdom with practical application. See *sagarswami.com.*

Swami Shraddhananda. Sw. Shraddhananda, also known as Rev. Dr. Sonya L. Jones, founder of Sacred Feet Yoga, entered mahasamadhi on February 16, 2021. She established Sacred Feet Yoga in 2010 as an interspiritual system. A major leader in the interspiritual experience, she was a co-founder and director of Sannyas for the Community of the Mystic Heart, host of its retreats, and editor of its book, *Mature Interspirituality: Wayne Teasdale's Nine Elements and Beyond.* She also served as Book Review Editor for *Light on Light* magazine. A dedicated teacher, writer, and spiritual guide, she inspired students worldwide through her compassionate service, deep interspiritual wisdom, and steadfast commitment to spiritual practice. She is survived by three ordained Dharma Heirs: Jenny Williams (Amrita), Sandra Simon (Chamatkara) (now Dharma Books Editor for Light on Light), and Sw. Prakashananda (Rt. Rev. Christine Deefholts), who continue her work through Sacred Feet Yoga and The Sacred Feet Publishing Imprint under the umbrella of The Jones Educational Foundation. Hundreds of former students and colleagues remember her with affection and gratitude for her joyful presence and enduring legacy. See *jefifoundation.org/sacred-feet-yoga/; lightonlight.us.*

Ralph Singh. Ralph Singh is a spiritual educator, interfaith leader, and advocate for character education rooted in spiritual values. A founding member of the Global Peace Initiative of Women and a longtime contributor to the Parliament of the World's Religions, Singh also serves as chair of the Wisdom Thinkers Network, a nonprofit dedicated to sharing interfaith wisdom through storytelling and education. Singh developed the "Schools of Character" and "Exploring Spirituality" programs for educators and authored the award-winning *Stories to Light Our Way* audio curriculum. A devotee and translator for Babaji of Gobind Sadan, he has shared interfaith and Sikh teachings at forums from the Millennium Peace Summit to the Smithsonian. Singh is based in New York and continues to foster spiritual literacy and community-building globally. See *wisdomthinkers.org.*

Susan Soleil. Susan Soleil is Director of Spirituality at ProSocial World and a long-time collaborator with the Charter for Compassion. With over thirty years in the nonprofit sector — locally, nationally, and globally — she leads the Spirituality program at ProSocial World, integrating contemplative practices, interspiritual tools, and community building to deepen collaboration and well-being. Soleil plays a key role in designing and facilitating interfaith convenings like the "Prosocial Spirituality" workshops at the Parliament of the World's Religions. She works closely with the Charter for Compassion team to promote cultural evolution through compassionate action. A heartfelt speaker and facilitator, Soleil grounds broad spiritual ideals into practical pathways for collective and individual transformation. See *prosocial.world.*

Melissa Stewart. Melissa Stewart is an educator, minister, and spiritual leader associated with One Spirit Interfaith Seminary. With extensive experience in interfaith education, she offers formation programs for spiritual directors and ministers across traditions. As a faculty member, Stewart integrates contemplative practice, pastoral care, and spiritual accompaniment into her teaching. She supports emerging ministers in developing skills for guiding others in sacred presence, compassionate listening, and community building. Her work emphasizes deep spiritual formation and empowering interspiritual leadership from a foundation of awareness and service. See *melissastewart.com.*

Daniel J. Stone. Daniel J. Stone is a visionary facilitator, consultant, and pioneer in large-scale social transformation. He co-hosted the 2024 Cathedral St. John Divine event in advance of the United Nations Summit of the Future that is elaborated in these Volumes. He has led interactive processes that engage thousands on issues of global significance, including rebuilding the World Trade Center, post- Katrina recovery in New Orleans, health care reform, and advancing the One Health movement. He designed and produced participatory sessions for the Clinton Global Initiative and the World Economic Forum in Davos, helping world leaders identify strategic priorities for collective action. Stone consults widely with organizations across sectors — health care, higher education, nonprofit, corporate, and spiritual — guiding transformative change. A follower of Avatar Meher Baba for nearly forty years, he also draws on Sufi healing practices in his work. His mission is to make real and lasting change for individuals, organizations, and society as a whole. See *danielstone.com; sdgthoughtleaderscircle.org.*

Wayne Teasdale. Br. Wayne Teasdale (1945–2004) was a Catholic monk, mystic, and leading voice in the interspiritual movement. These volumes are published on the 25th anniversary of his naming the "Interspirituality" paradigm. After ten years as a lay monk associated with St. Joseph's Abbey under Abbot Thomas Keating, he studied at Bede Griffiths's ashram in India. Teasdale coined the term Interspirituality to describe a mystical path embracing wisdom from multiple religious traditions, rather than merging doctrines. His books *The Mystic Heart* and *A Monk in the World* are considered foundational to contemporary interspiritual dialogue and practice. In 2002, he co-founded The Interspiritual Dialogue network with international colleagues (which is now also the parent of the Light on Light Press). A close associate of H. H. the Dalai Lama, Br. Teasdale was also a social justice activist and educator, promoting compassion-in-action rooted in contemplative awareness. He served on the Parliament of the World's Religions Board, was part of the Monastic Interreligious Dialogue, co-authored the Universal Declaration on Nonviolence, and taught at DePaul University and Catholic Theological Union. See *isdna.org; interspirituality.com.*

William Thiele. Rev. William Thiele, PhD, is the founding spiritual director of the School for Contemplative Living in New Orleans, Certified Compassion Cultivation Training (CCT) teacher, adjunct faculty at Loyola University, licensed professional counselor, spiritual director, retreat leader, and author. He is best known for *Monks in the World: Seeking God in a Frantic Culture* and *The Gate of Heaven Is Everywhere.* For over fifteen years, he has led small groups, workshops, classes, retreats, and an annual conference focused on contemplative living. He is also pastor at Parker United Methodist Church and collaborates with Pace Groups, Angelo clergy, and Angola State Prison program. Thiele integrates psychological insight with Christian mysticism and interspiritual wisdom. His work fosters transformation through silence, service, and soul-centered community. See *theschoolforcontemplativeliving.com/.*

David Sun Todd. David Sun Todd is a subtle activism practitioner and educator blending meditation, social engagement, and evolutionary spirituality. As a pioneer in the subtle activism field, he explores how collective intention and focused awareness can support social and planetary transformation. Todd leads contemplative gatherings, educational programs, and international dialogues that integrate inner practice with outer service. He serves on spiritual coalitions and platforms that promote compassionate action rooted in awakened consciousness. His work encourages individuals and communities to ground social change in spiritual presence and thoughtful action. See *davidsuntoddart.com.*

Kim Vanderheiden. Kim Vanderheiden is an artist, writer, and community advocate exploring the connections between justice, relationship, and spirit. As founder of Painted Tongue Studios and Braided Bridge, she works at the intersection of creativity, spirituality, and social transformation. Her visual art — spanning printmaking, painting, and book arts — often serves as contemplative practice, with pieces held in major collections including the Metropolitan Museum of Art, the Library of Congress, and the British Library. Kim is also the creator of *Justice*

Conversation, an ongoing online forum and podcast dedicated to restorative justice and nonviolence practices. Through East Bay Homebridge Connect, she supports people experiencing homelessness, while her writing has appeared in *The Conscious Lawyer* and other publications. Rooted in Catholic spirituality yet open to interfaith wisdom, Kim's work invites reconnection with ourselves, each other, and the sacred fabric of life. See *kimvanderheiden.com; justiceconversation.org.*

Andre van Zijl. Andre van Zijl is a Zimbabwean-born award-winning artist, whose work has historically reflected socio-political and global culture translated through a multi-disciplinary universal integrative lens. His art is represented in many important international museums and public and private collections, including the "South African National Gallery" and the British Museum. Van Zijl is also an art instructor, co-founder and director of All Paths Divinity School, a board member of the SoCal Parliament of World Religions, and an elder of the Mankind Project. He lives in Los Angeles with his wife Debrah and states that their two adult children, Jarryd and Sarina, "are our best artworks." See *andrevanzijl.com/about/.*

Llewellyn Vaughan-Lee. Llewellyn Vaughan-Lee, PhD, is a Sufi mystic teacher and author known for his work on spiritual ecology and the unity of spiritual traditions. A successor in the Naqshbandiyya-Mujaddidiyya Sufi lineage, he founded The Golden Sufi Center in California to share the teachings of Sufism and support spiritual awakening in the modern world. A scholar of Jungian psychology and dreamwork, he holds a PhD on Shakespeare's archetypes. He has written numerous books, including *Dreamwork within a Sufi Tradition, The Return of the Feminine and the World Soul,* and *Spiritual Ecology, Alchemy of Light,* and *Seasons of the Sacred,* emphasizing spiritual responsibility, oneness, and the anima mundi. His teachings overall integrate Sufi mysticism with ecological consciousness and feminine spirituality. See *goldensufi.org.*

Nicholas Vesey. Rev. Nicholas Vesey is minister at Aspen Chapel (Colorado) since 2014, serving an interspiritual community that draws on the world's wisdom traditions. Ordained in the Anglican / Episcopal Church, he integrates Christian theology with sacred texts from Taoism, Hinduism, Buddhism, and Islam. A committed seeker for over forty years, he is the author of *Developing Consciousness: A Roadmap of the Journey to Enlightenment* (2011) and *Living the Life-Force* (2019). Vesey hosts weekly contemplative services and podcast-style talks ("Wisdom from the Top of the World") and leads courses such as *Developing Consciousness* and *How to Be Good.* He presented at the Spiritual Paths Institute's InterSpiritual Service and at community forums discussing unitive consciousness. He lives in Aspen Valley with his wife and two children. See *nicholasvesey.com.*

Charles Vogl. Charles Vogl is an advisor, speaker, and author of several books, including the international bestseller *The Art of Community.* He holds a Master of Divinity from Yale and is a former Yale Divinity School Jesse Ball duPont Foundation scholar. Vogl works with Google in several capacities, including as a trusted thought leader for the Google School for Leaders, which develops over 20,000 Google managers. He integrates spiritual traditions with leadership and ethics, and his work is used to advise and develop leadership and programs worldwide within organizations including Airbnb, LinkedIn, Twitch, Amazon, ServiceNow, Meetup.com, Wayfair and the US Army. Vogl helps leaders build values-driven communities through timeless principles of belonging, purpose, and connection. His work bridges organizational leadership and the deeper spiritual dimensions of communal life. See *charlesvogl.com.*

Alejandra Warden. Alejandra Warden is an educator, spiritual teacher, counselor, and international speaker. Her work focuses on nurturing a relational consciousness of oneness grounded in the feminine understanding of unity. Drawing from Sufism, the Sacred Feminine, and a Catholic upbringing, her teachings naturally have an interspiritual dimension. She specializes in meditation and analysis of dreams and spiritual experiences. Author of *Remembrance: A Vision of the Sacred Feminine and the Renewal of the Earth* and *El Llamado de mi Corazon,* Warden founded Essential Oneness.org and is the director of Charis Circles for the Charis Foundation of New Monasticism and Interspirituality. See *EssentialOneness.org; charisinterspirituality.org.*

"We". We refers to the editorial team of the Light on Light Press listed on the copyright page and in the "Message from the Publisher" at the end of each Volume. For History, Commentary and Interval sections, this team employed a "journalistic approach," studying available printed and online resources along with twenty-five years of saved correspondence and attachments. The goal was a "We" voice that would communicate these sections to readers in a conversational tone.

Grand Father White Morning Owl. Grand Father White Morning Owl is a Native elder, interspiritual teacher and renowned artist honored for his contributions to the Dawn of Interspirituality Conference (2013) and active participation in the Interspiritual Dialogue Network. Rooted in indigenous wisdom and ceremonial tradition, he bridges ancestral teachings and contemporary interspiritual practice. He offers leadership in ritual, council, and sacred listening, encouraging deep cross-cultural understanding. Grand Father White Morning Owl's teachings foster unity between indigenous cosmologies and interfaith currents, helping to illuminate shared values of reciprocity, respect, and relational responsibility to the Earth and one another.

Ken Wilber. Ken Wilber, a visionary thinker of inspired genius, is the developer of an integral "theory of everything" that embraces the truths of all the world's great spiritual, scientific, and philosophical traditions. Often called the "Einstein of consciousness studies," Wilber is the most widely translated academic writer in the U.S., with twenty-five books published in over thirty languages. He is the founder of the Integral Institute, a multidisciplinary think tank addressing global issues through the Integral Approach, and co-founder of Integral Life, a platform for advancing integral awareness and practice. A preeminent scholar of the Integral stage of human development, Wilber has been a close friend of the interspiritual movement for many years, particating in programs and publications with Br. Wayne Teasdale, Kurt Johnson & Light on Light, and many others. Based in Denver, he remains an active author, teacher, and leading voice in the evolution of human consciousness. See *kenwilber.com; integrallife.com.*

Monica Willard. Monica Willard is the primary United Religions Initiative (URI) Representative to the United Nations in New York, coordinating URI's global field team at the UN and leading the NGO delegation in interfaith advocacy. She has worked with UN Department of Public Information (DPI) on annual International Day of Peace observances since 1997, co-founded the UN NGO Committee for the International Day of Peace, and served as its Co- Chair. Former President of the Committee of Religious NGOs at the UN, she organized events during World Interfaith Harmony Week in the General Assembly. Honored with the Spirit of the UN Award and Chapel of the Four Chaplains Award, Willard also supports global peacebuilding on issues like nuclear disarmament and women's empowerment. See *uri.org/monica-willard.*

David Sloan Wilson. Dr. David Sloan Wilson is SUNY Distinguished Professor of Biology and Anthropology at Binghamton University. He has made fundamental contributions to evolutionary theory in addition to its human-related applications. As president of the Evolution Institute and editor in chief of the online magazine, *This View of Life,* he is working to establish a new paradigm for economics, public policy, and public discourse that is firmly based in science, the way we are as a species, and the evolutionary processes that shape all species. His books include *This View of Life: Completing the Darwinian Revolution and Evolving the Future, Darwin's Cathedral: Evolution, Religion, and the Nature of Society,* and *Evolution for Everyone: How Darwin's Theory Can Change the Way We Think About Our Lives.* Dr. Wilson, Evolution Institute and Prosocial World have co- created numerous programs with the global interspiritual community, especially on altruism and a values-based future for our world. See *evolution-institute.org; thisviewoflife.com; prosocial.world.*

Shannon Marie Winters. Shannon Marie Winters is an ordained interfaith-interspiritual minister and co-founder of Light on Light Publications, where she also serves as Managing Editor. A leader in spiritual publishing, she was instrumental in the founding of Light on Light Press and produces *The Convergence, Conscious Business,* and *Light on Light* e-magazines. She collaborates with the International Day of Yoga Committee at the United Nations and is the author of *Joy Alchemy®*

and *The Gospel of Joy*. Shannon co- edited *Universal Principles and Action Steps,* a global compilation of visionary teachings from thought leaders and NGOs. Also a scientific communications executive, she bridges science and spirit through her editorial work and international outreach. See *lightonlight.us; issuu. com/ LightonLight.*

MESSAGE FROM THE PUBLISHER

Light on Light Press produces enhanced content books spotlighting the sacred ground upon which all religious and wisdom traditions intersect. Its foundational aim has been to stimulate and perpetuate engaged interspiritual and perennial wisdom dialogue for the purpose of assisting the dawning of a unitive consciousness that will inspire compassionate action toward a just and peaceful world.

In this express context, we are delighted to publish *Interspirituality: The Heritage* and *Interspirituality: The Future* on the 25th anniversary of Br. Wayne Teasdale's now classic book, *The Mystic Heart: Discovering a Universal Spirituality in the World's Religions*, in which he named "Interspirituality." It also commemorates the 10th anniversary of *The Coming Interspiritual Age* whose generative organization, The Interspiritual Dialogue, was founded with Br. Wayne Teasdale in 2002 by members of this editorial group, and became the charity that is now the parent of The Light on Light Press.

We deeply thank the more than 120 Featured Authors gathered in these Volumes. Their articles, excerpts, abridgements, and twenty-five years of correspondence and attachments have made the books possible. Honoring them, we expressly have not distinguished particular editors from our own Light on Light team other than our list below. It worked as a team, with a journalistic approach, aiming to curate these wonderful materials and, as the "We" voice in these

Volumes, "report *on*," and share, this last quarter century of interfaith and interspiritual expansion and impact.

In the spirit of Br. Wayne Teasdale's identification of Interspirituality as "The common heritage of humankind's spiritual wisdom; the sharing of mystical resources across traditions" and The Interspiritual Age as "the age we are now entering, where people are no longer isolated within their home tradition but are exploring other traditions, finding what is useful to their own growth," we feel privileged to present the content herein. It bears on the critical topics of our global landscape today: partnership consciousness, peace, justice, governance, economic equality, environmental health, science and the wisdom traditions, and a sustainable and regenerative future — in a phrase, "a world that works for all." May it be so.

The Editors
Rev. Shannon Marie Winters MS
Rev. Kurt Johnson PhD
Robert Atkinson PhD
Nomi Naeem MA
Chamatkara (aka Sandra Simon)
Karuna (aka Rev. Caroline Ashley)
Karen J. Gordon
Roger P. Briggs

Printed in Dunstable, United Kingdom

75627669R00281